Lee Roberson –
Always About His Father's Business

An Authorized Biography

By James H. Wigton

Copyright © 2010 by James H. Wigton

Lee Roberson – Always About His Father's Business
An Authorized Biography
by James H. Wigton

Printed in the United States of America

ISBN 9781609579883

All rights reserved solely by the author. The author guarantees all contents are original and do not infringe upon the legal rights of any other person or work. No part of this book may be reproduced in any form without the permission of the author. The views expressed in this book are not necessarily those of the publisher.

Unless otherwise indicated, Bible quotations are taken from The King James Bible.

www.xulonpress.com

To my family
Jackie
Libbie & Rey, Dan & Carrie, Julie & Brad,
Trey, Zack, Jay, Nick, Rylee & Blake

Dr. Lee Roberson

Table of Contents

Preface ix
1. An Empire of Evangelism 19
2. "Lee Was One of My Boys" 29
3. The Call 45
4. The Church of the Green Light 60
5. Always About His Father's Business 76
6. Everything Rises or Falls on Leadership! 88
7. "We Had No Days Off!" 120
8. Barnabas 137
9. The World's Largest Church 151
10. A School to Train Preachers 194
11. Crisis 214
12. World-Wide Faith Missions 244
13. The Spurgeon of His Generation 256
14. The Pastor's Touch 276
15. Chattanooga 292
16. 'Til Death Do Us Part 308
17. "Don't Limp" 331
18. I Promise 346
Timeline of the Life of Dr. Lee Roberson 355
List of Principal Sources 357
Author 361

Preface

Several years ago Don Sisk and John Reynolds approached me about the possibility of my writing a biography on the life of Dr. Lee Roberson. All three of us believed the story of Lee Roberson's life needed to be put in print. For many years Sisk was the executive director of Baptist International Missions, Inc., a world-wide missions enterprise which Roberson helped start and which is based outside Roberson's home city of Chattanooga, Tennessee. Reynolds, pastor of Volusia County Baptist Church in Orange City, Florida, is a graduate of Roberson's Tennessee Temple University and an experienced writer and editor. A pastor for more than 30 years, I had been trained in journalism years ago and worked on newspapers during high school and college. I had authored numerous Christian magazine articles, but never a book. As a pastor, I had known and admired Roberson for years. All three of my children are graduates of Tennessee Temple. When Sisk and Reynolds approached me, I did not hesitate. I embraced this opportunity.

All three of us feared Dr. Roberson would squelch the idea. We knew him to be a humble and modest man who did not like to draw attention to himself. He was then already in his 90s. But to my pleasant surprise, Dr. Roberson approved the project. When I approached him, I assured him that his life story would be an inspiration to young preachers and to the spreading of the gospel worldwide. Speaking of the proposed biography, he said to me, "No one has ever done anything like that." He gave me the go-ahead and started listing ways he could help me. He immediately started assisting me by giving me a pictorial book about Highland Park Baptist Church, published years ago by the *Chattanooga News Free-Press*. Over the next couple of years he continued to give me other books of his – mostly of his published sermons. On my second visit to interview him for this book, I initially received the impression that he had changed his mind about doing the biography. When I sought clarification, Dr. Roberson said my project was okay with him – that he just found it difficult to talk about himself. He proceeded to grant me hours of interviews over several sessions.

So, this is very much an "authorized" biography. I am writing not as a critic but as an admirer and friend who had the full cooperation and support in this enterprise of Dr. Roberson, Dr. J.R. Faulkner, and many other people associated with Roberson's ministry. It was legendary how short and brief Lee Roberson kept visits in his office through the years – usually no more than 10 or 15 minutes. However, for this biography, he sat down with me on four different occasions – each time for one hour and 15 minutes. On each occasion I was the one who drew the interview to a close. He was in his 90s. I did not want to wear him out mentally or physically, or wear out my welcome. I just sensed that an hour and a quarter was a long enough period of time for one interview. Dr. Roberson's longtime associate and right-hand man, the late Dr. J.R. Faulkner gave me ample time also. I interviewed Dr. Faulkner for a total of approximately 13 hours over multiple sessions. He was eager for this book to be published, and I am sorry that he did not live long enough to see it happen.

Although Dr. Roberson's memory slowed before his death at age 97, when I met with him for these interviews he was still very alert and very much in control of what he said. His memory was sharp – especially in regard to names and events associated with his younger years. In our interviews, I am convinced that he knew what he was saying and that despite his age he deliberately chose to say what he said. He talked about what he wanted to talk about and answered what he wanted to answer. He was very much in control and skirted an occasional issue which he chose not to address. Nevertheless, anyone is capable of misspeaking – especially at age 90. To avoid inaccurate recollections of memory, I would often ask him the same question on different occasions. His answers were remarkably consistent. For example, on no less than three occasions

Dr. Roberson clearly named the same three preachers as the ones who most inspired and impacted him when he was young – R.G. Lee, George W. Truett, and J. Frank Norris.

There may have been a few questions I was either too intimidated to ask or felt inappropriate to ask, but I had enough of a journalist in me to ask him *almost* anything. Naturally I treated him with the utmost respect. I was a little surprised that many of the men associated with Dr. Roberson carried such love and respect for him that I could not get them to talk about *anything* which could be perceived as remotely casting him in any way less than a 100 % favorable light. For example, I have ample evidence that during the period of time in the mid-1950s when Highland Park Baptist Church left the Southern Baptist Convention, Dr. Roberson had some kind of a short-lived nervous breakdown. Thereafter, he experienced a remarkable and rapid recovery, and the church hardly knew about it. But there is such an awe of him that I could not get several men to talk about it – men who surely knew about it. Some would not admit it even happened. In my mind, such an experience does not show an embarrassing or negative side of Dr. Roberson. First, it shows he was human. But more importantly, it shows his extraordinary perseverance and God's transforming power in his recovering so quickly and going on for such remarkable achievements as his life showed for the Lord. Students of Charles H. Spurgeon's life will remember a similar event in his life – when the seating stands where people sat to hear him preach at the Surrey Gardens Music Hall in London, England, collapsed, and seven people were killed. Spurgeon, like Roberson, was so affected emotionally that he was unable to preach for about two weeks. Then God miraculously brought him through the personal crisis.

I found remarkable the loyalty, admiration, and love for Roberson by the preachers who were trained under him at Tennessee Temple. This included a cross-section of men who did not all remain in Roberson's separatist, independent, fundamental Baptist movement. Some became Southern Baptists, as Roberson had been for many of his early years. Others worked in broader evangelical ministries, or nondenominational ministries. But each of the men to whom I spoke retained a decidedly loyal admiration of, love for, and devotion to Dr. Lee Roberson.

When the door opened for me to write this biography, I had to wonder why the Lord chose me for this project. I am not a graduate of Tennessee Temple. The names, places and events associated with Temple – common knowledge to so many graduates – were not common to me. I had to learn them. I had to research and ask questions to learn various aspects of Dr. Roberson's life and ministry, which were common knowledge to others. But perhaps being somewhat of an "outsider" gave me a valuable perspective. I might not have been as apt to be intimidated by the Lee Roberson mystique, nor perhaps am I as prone to get caught up in "hero worship" of the man. Personally, I had nothing but admiration, love, and respect for Dr. Roberson. But there was just enough independence and journalistic background in me to ask some probing questions. I am not afraid to show the human side of Dr. Roberson. The Presbyterian preacher, Dr. Ben Haden, who – like me – had a background in journalism before God called him to preach, and who – like me – had roots going back to the Mansfield, Ohio, area, asked me if this biography was going to be a "glory piece." I told him that was not my intention, but I should add this perspective. I have had the opportunity to get to know personally many of the great Baptist preachers and missionaries of the past generation. All are human. On occasion I have been a little disappointed the closer I got to some great men. Such was certainly *not* the case with Dr. Lee Roberson. The closer I got to him, and the more I listened to him and watched him – the more impressed I became with the man. This was an unusually remarkable man of God. I am reminded of the famous quote D.L. Moody once attributed to Henry Varley, "The world has yet to see what God will do with a man who is fully and wholly consecrated to the Holy Spirit." In Lee Roberson, I believe we saw such a man. Roberson was not perfect, and many of us would have done some things differently. But he was a very unusual and remarkable man – truly sold out to what he believed God wanted of his life.

Lee Roberson was also a maverick. He served cooperatively as a Southern Baptist until he was 46 years old. Then he became an icon of the independent, fundamental Baptist movement. Some of my independent Baptist friends may disagree with the portrayal of Roberson's relationship with Southern Baptists, largely described in Chapter 11, and his position on the "King James only" issue, largely described in Chapter 13. I was surprised to learn that Roberson never spoke against Southern Baptists and he cooperated on a limited basis with conservative Southern Baptists his entire life. I was also surprised to learn that while he used the King James Version of the Bible most of his ministry, he never took the "King James only" stand of many of his followers. As his biographer, my goal was to reflect his life accurately. I have served as pastor of both independent Baptist and Southern Baptist churches. I brought no agenda to this book other than to reflect the uniqueness of Dr. Lee Roberson.

There is no way to tell the story of Lee Roberson's life without the unique stories and anecdotes that surrounded his ministry. I tried to avoid a chronological emphasis on numbers displaying the extraordinary growth of his ministry, which I felt could be statistically boring. Everything Dr. Roberson attempted to do would result in growth – church membership and attendance, college enrollment, finances, etc. This book makes that clear, without endless detail. Some of the numbers one commonly hears were somewhat apocryphal. For example, for many years I had heard that Tennessee Temple University peaked at around 5,000 students. Dr. J.R. Faulkner, who was in a position to know and who was totally loyal to Dr. Roberson and his ministry, assured me that the peak was 4,100 – and that number included all of Tennessee Temple schools, not just the college. A man intimately acquainted with Roberson's ministry told me that the bus ministry peaked at 3,000 riders under the leadership of Clarence Sexton. However, Sexton – also loyal and supportive to Roberson – told me himself that his high average was just over 2,000. Now, on special evangelistic days it was higher, but I tried to maintain accuracy. The numbers of Dr. Roberson's ministry were impressive enough in reality. They do not need exaggeration.

Also, I did not try to list all the key participants in Dr. Roberson's ministry for the church, the college, and the school. No large ministry can succeed without an army of faithful, dependable, and dedicated workers at all levels. Dr. Roberson was well served by an unusual number of dedicated and gifted personnel. My first fear in trying to make sure everyone was included in the book was that it would simply be boring for the average reader. Secondly, I was sure I would miss some people who deserved mention. Thirdly, it would have required an impossible research effort, especially regarding people who are no longer alive. Mentioning as many people as possible might have been meaningful to those directly involved with Roberson's ministry, but overall I did not think it would serve the biography well. However, to give an accurate picture of the ministry it was important to tell the smaller stories of a good number of those who worked under or were trained by Dr. Roberson. Naturally, I was most able to use those whom I had the opportunity to meet or already knew personally.

I want to thank the dozens of preachers and friends of Dr. Roberson and Tennessee Temple who granted me interviews and gave me material for the book. For those whom I did not have the opportunity to interview, and for the many who are not mentioned in the book, please forgive me. Many are overlooked. Among those I was able to interview, I want to give a special "thanks." Besides the time I spent with Dr. Roberson and Dr. Faulkner, some of these interviews were invaluable. Giving me remarkable insight into Dr. Roberson's early years was his only sister, Darlene Munafo. During the nine-year period I served as senior pastor of Temple Heights Baptist Church in Tampa, Florida, my wife and I drove across Tampa Bay to St. Petersburg, where Mrs. Munafo lived. She gave us a delightful interview. Providing extraordinary insight into Dr. Roberson's early years at Highland Park were Jean and Elgin Smith, missionary Garland Cofield (Jean's brother), attorney Glenn Copeland, and the late pastor Bob Kelley. I thoroughly enjoyed interviewing Presbyterian Dr. Ben Haden, who gave me an outsider's view from another great preacher – and a non-Baptist – in Chattanooga. Others who were especially helpful included: Ron Bishop, Ed Carter, Wendell Evans, E.C. Haskell Jr., the late Max Helton, Bill Long, Bill Mattheiss, Jerry Mattheiss, Dorothy McCormick, Orman Norwood, Nat Phillips, Randy Ray, Jerry Reece, Cliff Robinson, Clarence Sexton, Gloria Shadowens, Glenn Swygart, Tom Wallace, and, Walter Wendelken. And a double-thanks to Sheila Wharram. Sheila is Dr. Orman Norwood's secretary at the

International Board of Jewish Missions in Chattanooga. Especially close to the Roberson family, Sheila was perhaps the best friend of Dr. Roberson's wife, Caroline. Sheila was invaluable in giving me insight, details, and accuracy for this biography. Clarence Sexton provided me with the "Timeline" of Dr. Roberson's life, listed at the back of the book. David Bouler and Roger Stiles were very helpful in ensuring that I had an overnight room at Tennessee Temple on my visits to Chattanooga. And, of course, John Reynolds was a big help, not only in getting me started but in guiding me to many of the right sources.

Besides Lee Roberson and J.R. Faulkner, many of the men in this book deservedly carried the titles of "Dr." and/or "Rev." I used the titles occasionally but did not see the point of telling the story of a man's life in a book brimming with the constant repetition of such titles. I even frequently dropped the title from Dr. Roberson's name. While many of us have never heard him called anything but "Dr." Roberson, the tedious repetition of such a title in print would be inordinately superfluous.

I was fascinated by the intense loyalty of his friends to Dr. Roberson. There seemed to be an aversion to commenting on anything which could cast Dr. Roberson in anything but a positive light. This fierce loyalty was widespread. It was especially obvious in people like Dr. J.R. Faulkner and secretary Dorothy McCormick, both of whom worked closely with Dr. Roberson. I admired their loyalty.

Probably my favorite interview was with E.C. Haskell Jr., who gave me amazing insight from his 20 years of working with Dr. Roberson at Tennessee Temple. The men who worked with Dr. Roberson admired him and thought very highly of him. Nevertheless, among those who adored him, some of them – men like Haskell, Bill Long, and Walter Wendelken – were willing to share stories which showed the human side of Lee Roberson. For example, Haskell tells of episodes where Dr. Roberson came back to apologize to people. Wendelken shares private insight from Dr. Roberson on how his upbringing had affected him in social interactions.

Thanks also to Kevin Woodruff, Tennessee Temple librarian, and John Reynolds, for helping to assemble the pictures in this biography. Before his death, J.R. Faulkner had offered me access to a drawer full of pictures and photographs from the Lee Roberson years at Highland Park. Kevin Woodruff took charge of the pictures and helped get them into this book. Kevin also gave me access to other research materials.

I also certainly want to thank my wife of more than 35 years – Jackie. A graduate of Ohio State University, a school teacher, and an inveterate reader of books, her advice and input were invaluable to me. She was the first editor and proof-reader to look over the manuscript for this biography. Thanks are also in order for two churches I served as pastor – Temple Heights Baptist Church in Tampa, and Delaney Street Baptist Church in Orlando, which graciously permitted me the time in my busy schedule to complete this biography.

From my sophomore year in high school until my senior year at Ohio State, when I came to Christ and was called to preach, my goal had been to be a newspaper reporter and editor. I received a Bachelor of Arts in Journalism from Ohio State University, where I was editor of the campus newspaper, *The Ohio State Daily Lantern*. I worked on newspapers all through high school and college before going off to seminary at age 24. Partly because of my journalistic training, I made extensive use of quotes in this biography. Also, unlike many biographers, I had the opportunity to interview the subject of the biography (Dr. Roberson), as well as many people from his life. Most of the quotes came from audio-taped interviews. Other quotes came from sources included in the *List of Principal Sources* at the back of the book. To avoid distracting the reader with a plethora of footnotes, I took the liberty of categorizing the footnotes in that list. Otherwise, the book would have been awash with footnotes, as I used extensive quotes. My journalistic training also motivated me to report facts about Dr. Roberson's life and leave much of the analysis to the reader. In many ways Lee Roberson was a mystery – an enigma, but I believe a true portrait of his life is presented in this book. Also, I took the liberty of occasionally using the first person. It seemed logical, as I am telling the story of a man's life – a man whom I knew personally and with whom I had personal interaction. I liked the similar style used by James Bradley in telling his story in the book, *Flags of Our Fathers*. I think it is an effective style in looking back historically at events where I was present and also at events where I was not present – but events where many of my interviewees were present and later told to me.

Through the years Dr. Roberson preached for me as a guest speaker at the churches I served as pastor in Michigan, Indiana, and Florida. After Dr. Roberson went to heaven, I accepted the call to Delaney Street Baptist Church in Orlando, Florida. Upon arrival, I was pleased to learn that Dr. Roberson had also preached at Delaney Street in years past.

James H. Wigton, Ph.D.
Orlando, Florida
pastorwigton@gmail.com

CHAPTER 1

An Empire of Evangelism

The atmosphere in the Sunday worship services of Highland Park Baptist Church in Chattanooga, Tennessee, was never the same after Lee Roberson came to town. Church members and visitors quickly found the climate of the church services electric with anticipation and excitement. From the time he became pastor of the church, Lee Roberson ushered in a calculated blend of American revivalism, southern hospitality, and dignified Sunday worship – always with an evangelistic fervor. And nobody, it seemed, wanted to miss church at Highland Park!

Church members changed their vacation plans and church families scheduled holiday activities so as not to miss a church service at Highland Park. Jean (nee Cofield) Smith was a teenager when Lee Roberson arrived as the new pastor. A few short years later her husband, Elgin, joined the church. "It was exciting," said Jean Smith. "You didn't ever want to miss a thing. You would change your vacation – to stay there. You knew something was going to happen that was good. You didn't want to miss anything. It was exciting. Things were happening." Jean remembered re-scheduling vacations and "almost anything – even Thanksgiving Day," to be present at Highland Park Baptist Church. "I would get so aggravated at him [Roberson]," she said with a laugh. "Thanksgiving Day – *that* you ought to be spending with your family. He would plan something big – to get the church filled up on Thanksgiving morning. We wanted to stay home with our family – but we didn't want to miss. We would take off and go – burn the turkey, or whatever, then come back home. You just didn't want to miss. It was great. We have one daughter, and we are so glad she was brought up in that church!"

Even from the beginning of Roberson's ministry in Chattanooga in 1942, he carried an awe-inspiring presence as a leader, as Highland Park Baptist Church grew in membership and attendance by leaps and bounds. Roberson, then 33, was handsome and commanding in stature. Jean Smith remembered Roberson's early years. "He was such a leader, but you loved him," she said. "You were afraid of him, but you loved him. Things were happening." Elgin Smith added, "People were scared of Dr. Roberson. He was a powerhouse. Souls were being saved by the hundreds. You just never saw so many people being saved. We had 25 to 30 every Sunday." Years later neither Jean nor Elgin recalled a Sunday in Roberson's 40-year pastorate at Highland Park when someone did not publicly come to Christ when the gospel invitation was given at the end of the church service. "He probably would have quit – if no one came forward," Jean said with a laugh.

It was not long after his arrival in Chattanooga before Roberson founded Tennessee Temple College (later University), and it seemed like there were people everywhere – on Sundays at Highland Park Baptist Church and on campus during weekday classes at Tennessee Temple. Not only was the campus filled with students and their families, but church members and Temple students were scattered throughout the city. All over Chattanooga people knew about Highland Park Baptist Church and Tennessee Temple University, as they saw the impact of the ministry throughout the city. Highland Park and Tennessee Temple people were readily recognized for their conservative and traditional standards of dress and conduct and for their aggressive commitment to evangelistic witness and soul winning.

Years later Baptist evangelist Ron Comfort said that Highland Park Baptist Church was the most exciting place in America to preach at during the 1970s. Joe Shadowens attended Tennessee Temple as a student and later became an evangelist serving out of Highland Park. His wife, Gloria, later became Dr. Roberson's secretary. "When we came," Gloria said, "My husband said, 'There's something about the feeling here.' It was electric. What's going to happen? Always something would happen." Sheila Wharram arrived from England in the 1970s. She was later to serve at the International Board of Jewish Missions and became a close friend to the Robersons. "I had never seen anything like it," she said. "It reminded me of the Billy Graham crusade in London. It was this way every week!"

Soon after Roberson started Tennessee Temple University it quickly became the largest Bible college in the world. Ben Haden, Chattanooga's renowned Presbyterian TV preacher, marveled at how Baptist parents and pastors, literally from all over the world, chose to send their sons and daughters to sit under Dr. Lee Roberson at Tennessee Temple. Haden pointed out that it was clear such people trusted Lee Roberson. Baptist evangelist Ed Carter agreed. "There was an excitement there," said Carter. "Students were excited. It was amazing. People looked at Dr. Roberson as the grandfather of those students. They trusted him with their children."

And the college quickly became as crowded as the church! A new ministerial student at Tennessee Temple would arrive for his first mid-week church service on a Wednesday evening and would have no choice but to hunt for a place to sit in the balcony of the 3,500-seat Chauncey-Goode church auditorium. "You had to go early for everything," said Ron Bishop, the college basketball coach. "If the ballgame was at 7:30 – if you didn't show up by 7:00, you weren't going to get in the gym. The same was true for church."

Tom Wallace, who was later to become a prominent Baptist preacher, arrived as a student in 1952. "I looked at the main auditorium," he said. "It was the largest thing I had ever seen. I told my wife, 'Let's go in at the last minute. They've got plenty of seats. I don't want to get there early.' When we got there, we had to sit in the aisle. They had put up chairs. There wasn't a seat left. So, we walked down the aisle and joined. They put us right to work!"

Highland Park Baptist Church under Lee Roberson was the forerunner of what was to become the mega-church movement in America. In the aftermath of World War II, the American soldiers who had led the Allies in defeating two of history's greatest military powers – Germany and Japan, returned home to marry and begin raising their families. The ensuing "baby boomer" population explosion of more than 70-million people between 1946 and 1962 spawned growing cities and suburbs throughout America and mushrooming growth in many churches. The result was the establishment of the nation's first mega churches which promoted a deliberate focus on church growth. No church movement grew faster than the evangelical and fundamentalist – predominantly Baptist – churches of the South. And among those, none grew faster nor larger in the 20 years following World War II than did the Highland Park Baptist Church of Chattanooga, Tennessee, under the leadership of its dynamic pastor.

Highland Park Baptist Church was a mid-sized Southern Baptist church – with a membership of about 1,000 and a weekly Sunday morning attendance of about 400 – when Roberson arrived as its new pastor in December of 1942. It was not long before the church became a bee-hive of activity with a fervent atmosphere and a zealous commitment to evangelistic growth. For 10 years, from 1946 to 1955, Highland Park Baptist Church was the national leader of the entire Southern Baptist Convention in annual baptisms – no small feat. By the 1970s Highland Park Baptist Church was listed as the largest church in the world by the church growth experts. The church's college, Tennessee Temple University was founded in 1946 under the leadership of Roberson. At its height Tennessee Temple was matriculating approximately 2,500 students annually from all 50 states and several foreign countries – primarily to train young men and women for the ministry at home and abroad.

Roberson was to serve as pastor for 40 years and six months – during which at least one person "came forward," by walking the church aisle during the evangelistic invitation in every service – Sunday morning, Sunday evening, and Wednesday evening, except for one Sunday evening service, in all those years – a remarkable achievement! More than 60,000 persons were baptized at Highland Park Baptist Church during Roberson's 40-year pastorate – enough people to populate a small city. The church's midweek prayer meeting, attended weekly by about 10 people when Roberson arrived, became the largest Wednesday night midweek service in the nation before he retired – with some 3,500 persons attending each Wednesday! By 1978, four years before Roberson's retirement from the pastorate, Highland Park Baptist Church had an average Sunday school attendance of 9,400, and the church saw 3,400 people baptized that year alone. Tennessee Temple Schools' enrollment reached 4,100, in the early 1980s. "That would include the whole thing – the college, the high school, the elementary school, and the Bible institute," said J.R. Faulkner, Roberson's associate for more than a half-century. By the time Lee Roberson retired in 1982 church membership had surpassed 60,000.

Historically, statistics for world-wide church growth, membership, and attendance have sometimes been difficult to compile and verify. Nevertheless, in 1973 when Highland Park Baptist Church membership reached 37,489, the *Chattanooga News-Free Press* published a book about the church, designating Highland Park Baptist Church "The World's Largest Church." For a number of years Elmer Towns, author and church growth expert, published an annual list of the largest Sunday schools in America. Always high on the list, Highland Park became No. 1 in the early 1970s. In his book, *The Ten Largest Sunday Schools*, Towns called Highland Park Baptist Church "an empire of evangelism."

With the growth of Highland Park Baptist Church, Lee Roberson's influence expanded – especially among Baptists. During his early years as a Southern Baptist some preachers were predicting that he would become president of the Southern Baptist Convention. Later he was to become second to none in prominence among independent Baptist preachers in America in his generation. His influence expanded with the worldwide development of such ministries as Southwide Baptist Fellowship, informally headquartered at Highland Park Baptist Church, the growing worldwide outreach of Tennessee Temple University, and the global impact of Baptist International Missions, Inc., also based near Highland Park Baptist Church. In 2001, J.R. Faulkner claimed that the historic number of Tennessee Temple graduates was over 12,000 – with full-time Christian workers serving in different ministries (pastors, assistant pastors, missionaries, evangelists, teachers, etc.) numbering in the hundreds. "There would be no way to know [how many]," concluded Faulkner.

Roberson rose to the top as a leader among Baptists. He championed the theme, "Everything rises or falls on leadership," as he challenged Baptist preachers across America to take charge of their pulpits and lead their churches. To a generation of Baptists the name Dr. Lee Roberson became synonymous with leadership. Jim Vineyard, a well-known independent Baptist pastor and author in Oklahoma City, claimed that no preacher in the world knew more about Baptist churches in America than did Lee Roberson.

Through the years Roberson authored a number of books, primarily compilations of his sermons. The publisher of one of his books wrote of Lee Roberson, "This fast-moving world has always taken time to slow down and salute a man that knows who he is, knows what he is doing and knows where he is going. Dr. Roberson is such a man, he is a leader. Thousands of preachers and Christian workers and businessmen quote this author's famous saying, 'Everything rises or falls on leadership.'"

Roberson was unashamedly an old-fashioned fundamentalist. He was a dynamic pastor of one of the world's largest churches, founder of an eminently successful Christian college, and devoted Mondays and Tuesdays of nearly every week of the year to preaching throughout America in churches and church conferences. Wherever and whenever he preached he emphasized a literal interpretation of the Bible, the spiritual new birth, the work of the Holy Spirit in the hearts and lives of believers, and a strong emphasis upon evangelism – both personal and church-wide. Lee Roberson was a traditional, southern revivalist with a keen eye on the literal Second Coming of Christ.

Roberson's strong leadership was tempered by a devotion to Christ which reflected the love of God for his people. "He loved us – especially Jean," Elgin Smith recalled. Roberson started encouraging Jean Smith to sing in church as a soloist while she was still a teenager. "We've always loved him," Elgin said years later.

And how Highland Park Baptist Church grew! "We couldn't build fast enough," said Elgin Smith. "We would have to build or expand to add room for 200 more people – and before you were done, there would be 500! But he didn't want to go to two services. He loved a big crowd! He wanted everybody together."

Within a year of Roberson's arrival as pastor in 1942, seating on Sundays at Highland Park Baptist Church was over-crowded. Excitement also over-flowed as souls were saved and lives were changed for the cause of Christ. A new temporary tabernacle quickly went up and soon was filled. Highland Park soon became a pioneer in Sunday school bus ministry. The church focused on personal evangelism through soul winning and weekly Sunday school growth campaigns. The people caught the vision of what Roberson was trying to accomplish with the church. They fully supported their new pastor, and miraculous growth ensued.

Over the course of four decades the church growth never seemed to stop. Some people associated with Roberson's ministry considered the years of 1975 to 1980 to be the peak of his ministry. The Temple student body had grown to 4,000 students. The atmosphere was one of excitement and enthusiasm. "We were training preachers, missionaries, and evangelists," said Ron Bishop, a staff member. "We had a broad spectrum – preparing people for business, law, and medicine. It was fun, exciting. We loved going to chapel. At 4,000, we couldn't fit everyone into Chauncey-Goode (then the main auditorium) with the church people. So, Sunday morning and evening we started having student services in the gym. They assigned students and rotated (attending the main auditorium or the gymnasium). I preached down there numerous times. It was exciting! Preaching in chapel may have been my favorite place in all the world to preach!"

"It was so captivating," said Tom Wallace. "I came out of a rough south Philadelphia neighborhood. I got saved. I quit smoking. I would still drink beer a little. I went to Temple. No one drank or cussed. What a difference! I got caught up in it. I was captivated. I would go home – I couldn't wait to go visit my folks in Philadelphia. We would get there, and within a half-day we were ready to come back. We just couldn't cope. My dad was an alcoholic and a smoker. My parents went to church only Sunday mornings. We'd go back Sunday evening and Wednesday. They didn't understand and would get so aggravated at us. We were uncomfortable and miserable and wanted to get back to Temple – like it was supposed to be. It was kind of a 'millennium' down there!"

"It was shocking to me," said Glenn Swygart, later a long-time instructor at Tennessee Temple. "I came from a non-fundamentalist background – raised Methodist in Lima, Ohio. I had been saved nine months. It was like dying and going to heaven. It was spiritual, friendly, godly living."

Ed Johnson, a student in the 1960s and later a successful Baptist pastor in Minneapolis, described his time at Tennessee Temple as the "glory years." He said, "They were fantastic – hard to describe. The spirit on campus was like electricity. It was incredible when you stepped on campus. People would get to Chauncey-Goode an hour before services. We would – row 5, middle section!"

Randy Ray, later a successful pastor in Nashville, Tennessee, and in Tallahassee, Florida, attended Tennessee Temple from 1973 to 1975. "I think I was at Temple during its absolute peak," he said. "The atmosphere was genuinely electrifying."

It was obvious God's hand was upon Lee Roberson. And Roberson possessed a strong sense of authority. He appeared to be fearless in his own pulpit and as he traveled to preach. In Roberson's book, *The Key to...Victorious Living*, he tells the story of one of his revival meetings in those early years where he preached in a large Southern Baptist church. The series of services concluded on a Sunday morning when he preached to a packed house of 1,500 people. New converts flooded the aisle and crowded around the altar and choir loft as people prayed to receive Christ as their Savior – from boys and girls to middle-aged men 55 and 65 years old. In the midst of the evangelistic invitation, the dignified, robed choir director of the church walked in and told Roberson it was time for him to start the doxology. As it became clear to Roberson that the choir had been waiting outside the main auditorium through the entire song service, sermon, and invitation, Roberson was stunned. So, Roberson informed the choir director that the choir loft was filled with enquirers and seekers from the altar call and that there was no room for the choir now. Roberson continued to urge people to come forward to receive Christ. "We care not for that," the choir director told Roberson. "They've got to move. This church runs everything a certain way, and I do not intend to see a change. I care not who you are." The choir director, who had missed the entire week of revival meetings, did not even know who Roberson was, and Roberson had been at the church all week as the guest evangelist!

Roberson later apologized to the pastor for his response to the choir director. As Roberson sized up the situation, he told the choir director with the long flowing robe, "Sir, go back in there and take off your night gown and come out here and help us win souls." The choir director left and never came back. The choir left with him. Roberson, afraid that he had caused trouble for the church's pastor, sought out the pastor and said, "I want to apologize. I did something I shouldn't have done. I insulted your choir director and your organist. I said a thing I should not have said. I never said that before. I don't intend to ever say it again. I want to apologize to you." The pastor responded, "Just a minute, Brother Roberson. Don't apologize. Let's praise God from whom all blessings flow. I have been trying to get rid of that fellow for years. He's gone now. It is all over!"

Lee Roberson was a visionary who believed in a God-inspired vision and purpose for a man of God who was led by the Holy Spirit. In his book, *Fire-Works Don't Last*, he challenged Christians and preachers, "Get the vision. Keep it before you continually! Get a vision of what you think God wants you to do. If God changes that vision, then enlarge it and move on out. If God says, 'This is as far as I want you to go,' then take it that far and stop. But do what God says." This philosophy was the key to his success at Highland Park Baptist Church. Roberson said, "That has been the secret of what we have done here through the years. I have to pray much about this. I have to pray much about this church, about Tennessee Temple University, about Camp Joy and everything we are doing. I do not like to move unless I feel so led of the Lord. If God says, 'Move out and do more,' then I want to do that. But we have to have a vision."

During Lee Roberson's 40-year ministry at Highland Park Baptist Church, the church not only built multiple buildings and started Tennessee Temple University, but it also opened Temple Baptist Seminary, Tennessee Temple Academy, Camp Joy, Union Gospel Mission, Zion College, World Wide Faith Missions, the church newspaper, *The Evangelist*, and WDYN-FM radio station –

plus more than 70 separate area Sunday chapels, a number of which became full-time, independent churches.

Ed Johnson said of Roberson, "I really believe in the 20th century he has probably done as much or more for the cause of Christ than just about any other preacher you can point to in our fundamental, independent Baptist groups. Even Dr. [Jack] Hyles would tell you that Lee Roberson had a great influence and great impact on his life. I think history will show that he has prepared as many preachers for the gospel ministry as any other preacher you or I could point to – and that would include Jack Hyles."

When Lee Roberson died at age 97, Baptist icon Jerry Falwell released a public statement which said, "Dr. Roberson was one of the finest Christian men I have ever known. He was one of my mentors and role models... As our nation has accelerated toward politically-correct systems that promote religious and cultural diversity, this old war horse of the faith never wavered in his bold proclamation that the crucified Christ is the only way to heaven and the only way to discover true spiritual peace."

Lee Roberson was devoted to a literal interpretation and proclamation of the Bible as the Word of God. No verse of Scripture better summed up his life than I Corinthians 15:58, *"Therefore, my beloved brethren, be ye stedfast, unmoveable, always abounding in the work of the Lord, forasmuch as ye know that your labour is not in vain in the Lord."*

CHAPTER 2

"Lee Was One of My Boys"

In 1909, eight years before America's entry into World War I, the nation's population stood at just over 90-million. Indiana rivaled Michigan as the leader in the blossoming automobile industry. In 1909 American auto production was 123,990 passenger cars, led by 17,771 Fords. Indiana was home to the Dusenberg, the Marmon and the Stutz. The U.S. death toll in horse-related accidents surpassed motor vehicle deaths by 3,850. That year President William Howard Taft was the first U.S. president to ride in the inaugural parade in an automobile – a White Steamer. Ladies' skirts were growing shorter to accommodate stepping into and out of the automobile. A loaf of bread cost 4 cents, and a first-class postage stamp was 2 cents. The electric toaster was invented in 1909. For the first time, senior citizens, at age 70, drew retirement pensions, and the federal income tax was enacted. Commander Robert E. Peary reached the North Pole. Yale College won the NCAA football championship, and in Louisville, Kentucky, a three-year-old horse named *Wintergreen* won the Kentucky Derby. In northwest Indiana the town of Crown Point became host to Indiana's first ever automobile race – two years before the inaugural Indianapolis 500. This was life in America in 1909.

And in 1909 a few miles north of Louisville, across the Ohio River on a little farm amidst the hills and the hollows outside the town of English in southern Indiana, the first child of Charles and

Dora Roberson, a son, was born in a small farmhouse. English, a small town of 500 people, served as the county seat of Crawford County. It was located where two small rivers – Bird Dog Creek and Brownstown Creek – come together to form the Blue River. The town was laid out in 1839 and incorporated in 1884. At the time of the Civil War the town of English, Indiana, consisted of a grocery, a log school house and "a cluster of log cabins." In 1884 the railroad came through.

Lee Roberson was born on November 24, 1909, in a humble boarded farmhouse on a 50-acre property with a barn – all of which his father had purchased for $500. The new baby's given name was Laverne Edward Roberson, but he never used Laverne. And hardly anyone knew his middle name until it was printed in his funeral service bulletin 97 years later. All his life he simply went by Lee Roberson. He signed everything Lee Roberson. His son, John, told the funeral audience on May 3, 2007, that even he would receive a birthday card from his dad not signed "Dad" – but signed, "Lee Roberson."

Lee Roberson's father, Charles, was one of 13 children – he had 11 brothers and one sister – who grew up on a farm in southern Indiana just a few miles from where Lee was born. Their farmhouse had a big, long, old-fashioned kitchen with a large fireplace right in the middle. There was no other heating or air-conditioning. The bedrooms were cold in the winter and hot in the summer. There was a cistern just outside the back door, where they drew their water. Charles' father – Lee's grandfather – was a dignified gentleman with a heavy white beard. As a young man, he had fought for the North in the Civil War. He fought in the famous Battle of Lookout Mountain near Chattanooga, where Lee was to serve as a pastor for 40 years.

Most of Charles Roberson's siblings lived to be elderly. One brother drowned in a reservoir in Montana. One died of typhoid as a child, and one died at 64. The others lived long lives. The youngest was Irvin. Like the rest of the family, Irvin had little interest in church as a youth. In his sermon, *My Favorite Teacher*, Lee Roberson told the story years later of how his Uncle Irvin came to Christ. "A few years ago," he said, "he was alone in a hotel room. He put a Bible down before him and began to read. He faced his life, the failures of life, [and] the uselessness of life. He spent the entire night in prayer and waiting before God. He stated that it was one of the worst nights that he had ever spent. Yet out of that night came the greatest victory. He won the battle. He accepted Christ as his Savior, and so the life was changed and transformed."

The Charles Roberson family was poor. When Lee was two, the Roberson family moved to Louisville, where he attended Henry Clay Elementary School on the west side. When Lee was nine, his family moved to a nine-acre farm, with a four-room house, outside the city of Louisville near the rural town of Fern Creek. It was a poor farm, purchased inexpensively by his father. Lee learned from his father how to plow a field with a team of horses. His father built chicken houses, handling as many as 2,000 chickens at one time. As a boy, Lee operated house-to-house routes in Louisville to sell chickens, which he had killed, cleaned, and prepared. Some hens were kept for eggs, which were also sold on the route, but most of the chickens were sold at broiler stage. The routes were run regularly on Saturday mornings, when people expected them. Sales were not difficult. Lee also milked four cows morning and night, which kept his family plentiful with milk, cream and butter. He always remembered how relatives would come on Sunday afternoon for a family dinner on the farm.

Lee Roberson's mother never finished elementary school, and his father only went through the eighth grade. For years his mother made his clothes – out of flower sacks. Dr. Roberson once told his preacher boys at Tennessee Temple that he had never worn an undershirt growing up. All his life he was a little intimidated by wealthy people. He had grown up so poor that well-to-do people made him feel uncomfortable. Otherwise, he looked at his life as being rather normal. Charles Roberson said years later, "Lee was a good boy – always did what he was told." When Lee was a boy, the Robersons rarely attended church. Lee remembered one time in a church when someone called his dad a hypocrite – apparently for attending church while living a rather worldly lifestyle. Charles Roberson angrily stalked out of the church. "I'm no hypocrite!" he said. "I do cuss, but I don't lie about it!"

During those days while Lee was a boy in Louisville, word came that his grandmother was seriously ill. The family went quickly to her home in southern Indiana, where she soon died. Upon their return to Louisville after the funeral, Lee became ill with typhoid fever. A relative who had attended the funeral also died. When a number of family members who had attended the funeral became ill with typhoid, a search into the cause led to the water well at the family home. The well was cleaned out, and a dead rodent was found in the bottom – the cause of the typhoid.

Lee Roberson had one sister and no brothers. He was 13 when his sister, Darlene, was born while they lived in Fern Creek, Kentucky, near Louisville. Many years later, Darlene told me, "So I must have been a surprise to the family because my mother said she had thought she would not have any more children. Here I came along! My brother didn't seem too happy – I was told that!" Lee and Darlene lived with their parents on a small farm – with much of the food coming from the chickens, eggs, and garden.

At age 14, young Lee Roberson was invited to Sunday school at a country church called Cedar Creek Baptist Church on Bardstown Road outside Louisville. He was invited by a young man – not much older than Lee – named Claude Martin. Lee told Claude that if he did not like Sunday school, then he wanted to be taken home afterwards – and not stay for the morning worship service. After his first Sunday school class there, Lee said he did not like it and that he wanted Claude, who did the driving, to take him home. So, he did. But when he dropped Lee off, Claude asked if he could pick him up next week for Sunday school. Lee gave his approval.

Along with about 12 to 15 other boys on that first Sunday, Lee sat in a Sunday school class, taught by Mrs. Daisy Hawes, at Cedar Creek Baptist Church. The boys sat on folding chairs. On Lee's first Sunday in the class, Mrs. Hawes opened her Bible and asked the boys, "Before I teach the lesson for today, I would like to ask, how many of you boys are saved?" Most hands went up. Young Lee thought to himself, what a strange thing to ask. Mrs. Hawes then explained the personal need of salvation, making clear such verses as John 3:16 and John 5:24 and the need personally to accept Christ into one's heart as Savior. The entire procedure made Lee angry. He thought to himself, "Never again! I don't want that stuff." When he walked out, that was when he initially asked to go home. When Claude returned the second week to pick him up for Sunday school, Lee told him that he was finished with Sunday school. But Claude persisted with arguments as to why he should go, and Lee gave in. Lee said later, "I couldn't get rid of him, so I went with him."

The second week Mrs. Hawes followed the same procedure. Again, many of the boys raised their hands to acknowledge that they were saved, but Lee could not do so. Again, she presented the gospel. Again, he left after Sunday school and went home. But he could not get the truth of what she had said out of his mind. "It rang in my heart," he explained later. "I was lost, condemned, hell-bound. I could be saved by receiving Jesus Christ." The following week he continued to ponder this truth, until on his knees by his bedside in his country house the following Wednesday, he prayed, "Lord Jesus, I now receive you as my savior." The assurance of his salvation immediately filled his heart with "the peace of God, that passeth all understanding." Lee Roberson said years later that he never had a doubt about his personal salvation after that day.

The next Sunday Claude showed up with his Model-T Ford to pick Lee up for Sunday school for the third consecutive week. Lee bounded eagerly out to the car – dressed in his Sunday best, a suit someone had given him, a shirt made by his mother out of an Obelisk flour sack, and a tie that had been handed down to him. In the classroom, Mrs. Hawes said once again, "How many of you boys are saved?" Lee Roberson quickly raised his hand. The teacher looked at him and smiled. And as she always did, she again presented the wonderful message of salvation.

After Sunday school that morning Lee stayed for the church service – something he was hardly ever to miss again over the next 83 years of his life. That same day his parents came to church for the service. The pastor of Cedar Creek Baptist Church, Rev. J. N. Binford, preached the sermon and gave a gospel invitation. Lee Roberson walked down the aisle to the front of the church to confess publicly his faith in Christ. In that hour both of his parents also came forward and were saved. (Darlene was just a baby.) Roberson said later, "We hadn't planned it, but it was a wonderful night." All three were then baptized in that church later on the same day. Charles Roberson was a devout church member the rest of his life.

For many years Daisy Hawes kept a long list of boys' names in the back of her Bible – boys whom she had led to a saving relationship with Jesus Christ. They did not all become famous preachers, but she was proud to say, "Lee was one of my boys!" Daisy Hawes died in 1976.

Pastor Binford had a lasting impact on Lee Roberson. Binford had previously served as pastor of the large Emmanuel Baptist Church on the edge of Louisville. But he had sensed God's leading to take the smaller, rural Cedar Creek Baptist Church. Binford was a devoted man, a good pastor – a loving man whom people loved. Young Lee Roberson studied Binford. Roberson said later that he gained many of his biblical convictions from Binford. Binford preached the Word of God – "straight down the line," Roberson said. He was a "settled" man who never varied to show favoritism to anyone. "I learned a whole lot from him," Roberson said. "I noticed how he did it. He didn't get upset, over-bearing. But he said, 'This is it; this is how we do it – this is how we run the church…' I'd watch him – all the way through." Young Lee noted Binford's zeal and compassion. Cedar Creek was not a large church, but it was aggressive in evangelism, active, and Bible-centered. The pastor believed in organization and in being faithful to Christ. The gospel singing was plain and vigorous.

It was Binford who first put Lee Roberson to work for the Lord. During a Sunday evening Baptist Young Peoples' Union meeting, the small crowd started singing the gospel song, *Standing on the Promises*. With no leader and no pianist, the singing was erratic and half-hearted. Blessed with a strong and good voice, young Lee picked up the songbook and began singing robustly. The young people fell in line behind his leadership, and the singing immediately improved. When Binford heard about it, he asked Lee to lead the singing at Cedar Creek Baptist Church in the church service that very night. Lee led the music at Cedar Creek for months after that. In later years Roberson gave Binford credit for starting him off right – during some of his formative years at ages 14 to 17. The country church, on the edge of Louisville, was packed and jammed with people all the time. It was here, Roberson said, that he got his "Three-to-Thrive" idea – a principle he made famous years later as he urged church goers to be faithful to attend three services weekly – Sunday morning, Sunday evening, and Wednesday evening, in order to thrive spiritually. "I got it from him. He had as many people Wednesday evening as he had Sunday morning," Roberson said. Late in life Roberson credited much of his own style of ministry to Binford.

Tall and broad-shouldered, Lee played football and learned to golf in high school. The first high school he attended was a public boys' high school called Louisville Male High School. To reach the high school, he would walk one mile from Fern Creek to catch the inter-urban car (electric passenger railroad), then transfer to a city street car and again transfer to another car on Brook Street. He thought about a career in music – or maybe becoming a writer. He graduated early from the large Louisville Male High School – with a two-year commercial degree at age 14. Lee had studied business, typing, and accounting under Sam Tinsley, a well-known principal. Since no jobs were open for a 14-year-old bookkeeper, Lee enrolled at Fern Creek High School and received another high school degree four years later before he went off to college. Meanwhile, he got a job as a choir director. Darlene fondly recalled, "He had a beautiful voice – a beautiful voice!" And Lee Roberson never forgot that at Louisville Male High School he was given a New Testament – a testament issued by the Y.M.C.A., given to him by a teacher, Mr. Elliott. He also remembered Mr. Carnegie at Fern Creek High School – a man who weighed more than 300 pounds. A strong disciplinarian, Mr. Carnegie read the Bible daily to the students in school.

Young Lee Roberson wanted the best for his sister. As he grew older, Lee became more of a father figure to his sister. He would call Darlene by the nickname, "Sis." Darlene remembered, "And I looked up to him – oh, how I looked up to him!" But by then he was gone most of the time – off to college. "My mother used to tell me how smart he was," Darlene recalled. "My brother was so smart he had to skip a grade. They skipped the seventh grade and put him in the eighth grade." That was at the Fern Creek School. Darlene always seemed to live in Lee's shadow academically, never quite measuring up to her parents' expectations. "When Lee would come home," she said, "I'd have to show him my report cards. If I had a D, I'd hear a sermon, 'There's just no point in this, Sis' – he always called her 'Sis' – 'There's just no reason you can't do this!'"

When Lee would come home from college Darlene would be on her best behavior and try to do everything just right – to please her older brother. He taught her to drive a car when she was 14 – an old Chevrolet. He would teach her how to shift gears and then take her out on country roads and let her drive. His sister was thrilled! "He was a lover of cars," she said. "He always had a brand new car. One time he had a convertible. Boy, did I ever think we were in style when we were riding in that! He took my mother and me up to Cincinnati, Ohio, to the Conservatory of Music – because he was going to go there for awhile, and he wanted to look into it. I was always bragging about my brother. 'My brother will be home, and he's going to do this and do that.'"

Lee Roberson had an extraordinary voice and was advised to take voice lessons. "My dad was mystified," Roberson recalled. "He couldn't carry a tune and knew nothing at all about singing. He asked me, 'What in the world are voice lessons?'" Years later Roberson told me that he was tempted to pursue a career in music. "I loved it. I studied voice a long time. I sang on the radio in Nashville hundreds of times. It was a big station back in those days. But I got away from it. I couldn't keep up the schedule – mixing the two things (preaching and music). So, I gave it up." Later he thoroughly enjoyed being in charge of music for four years in one church.

In elementary school, Darlene learned to play the piano by ear. The family knew nothing about having lessons, but Lee saw to it that his sister got piano lessons. Like her brother, she could sing. He saw to it that she got voice lessons – Lee paid for the lessons. Their parents knew nothing about such lessons and would not have paid for them. In no time she was singing on radio. A contralto, she won singing awards all over Louisville. "He wanted me to be an opera singer – he really did! He loved good music," she said. Lee always had the radio on in the car – turned to music. "He brought me home a dog and left it with me. My brother loved dogs." Lee and

Darlene named the dog *Lawrence Tippett*, after the famous opera singer! After high school Darlene attended a business college in Lakeland, Florida. But the music stayed with her for her entire life. She married and spent her life as Darlene Munafo in St. Petersburg, Florida, where her husband taught music in the public schools. They had two sons and a number of grandchildren and great-grandchildren through the years. Both sons were graduates of the University of South Florida in Tampa – one a professional photographer, the other a certified public accountant. Darlene was always active in church – singing both in the choir and solo – and playing the piano. When she visited her brother, she would sing solo, or duets with her brother, at Highland Park Baptist Church, and then she would sing on his radio broadcast.

In later years after Dr. Roberson resigned as pastor of Highland Park Baptist Church, Jerry Matthias, then the church's music director, had an office next to Roberson's. Roberson was then pastor emeritus at Highland Park. Matthias told me that Lee Roberson knew music! Jerry said, "He would get up in the pulpit and call a song – 'Let's do it in C today. Or the key of G. Or A-flat.' He knows the difference even to this day! (Dr. Roberson was then in his 90s.) He listens to music. He knows music done well." Roberson's music training gave him tremendous breathing control. He later told his preacher boys in college that at one time he could exhale for 4 minutes and 20 seconds!

Lee's mother never could accept his call to preach and did not approve of his going into the ministry. She gloried in his musical ability and hoped he would seek a professional career in music. She wanted him to be an opera singer. Church members in the early years in Chattanooga remember hearing Dr. Roberson occasionally tell from the pulpit how his mother did not want him to be a preacher – that she wanted him to go into music. But God had spoken to his heart, and he refused. Years later his mother came to Highland Park Baptist Church for one service. He introduced her publicly in the church service. She sat right down front to the left – the only time she ever heard him preach. His parents were later divorced, and his father, who remarried, came with his wife to visit and hear Lee preach many times.

One of the heart-breaks of Lee Roberson's life was that his parents were divorced after he left home. J.R. Faulkner, Roberson's partner and associate for 40 years at Highland Park Baptist Church, never heard Lee Roberson mention the divorce. Gloria Shadowens was his secretary for 25 years later in his life. She never heard him mention his parents' divorce and only heard him mention his mother once. "He never spoke of that, nor does she," family friend Sheila Wharram said of Lee and Caroline Roberson. Roberson was always a very private man. And as a man of God, he simply did not believe in divorce. When his family was touched by divorce, as many families are, he never would say a thing.

Lee would confide later in life that he had a rough childhood, and that his mother had a rough life. He believed that this upbringing kept him from being as free as he wanted to be at social gatherings. Associates who worked with him never felt he was one to whom you could get real close. Unlike many preachers who frequently reference their families in sermons, Dr. Roberson rarely spoke of his family. Late in life Dr. Roberson told me that he had met his maternal grandmother only once when she was up in years. He described her as being the same way as his mother.

Lee's mother only went to school through the fourth grade. Her parents were divorced. She was raised by an aunt. She was waiting on tables in a boarding house by the time she was 13. She married Lee's father when she was 16. After they were divorced, she moved to Florida where she died at a relatively young age. Lee and his family attended the funeral in the Tampa area. Lee described his mother as a very temperamental woman who was inclined to cry a lot. He did not believe the divorce was his father's fault. His mother would get emotional, "out-of-control about things," he said. But Lee's dad never complained. Charles Roberson never seemed to get upset at all. A quiet man, he would never speak a harsh word. "I never heard him say a harsh word in my life," Lee said. "He lived and died that way."

More than once, as Darlene was growing up, Lee's mother left their father. Each time Charles would go after them, and bring wife and daughter home. Her father reassured Darlene that he would come and find her – no matter where her mother took her. It was a tremendous time of difficulty for young Lee. His sister told me, "I remember him coming to the door pounding on the door, one night. 'Mom, Mom, come on, let me in!' It was an embarrassment for him. It hurt him very much. He was older, and he guarded me. I chose to get married too young, too." Both children believed that given a choice, their father would not have divorced.

Lee Roberson always admired his father and spoke well of him. In later years, Lee was to describe his father as one of the finest Christian men he knew. His dad signed his name "C. E. Roberson." His dad was a man of broad stature – a stately man, tall, but not quite as big physically as his son was to become. Young Lee looked very much like his father. A friendly man, C. E. Roberson had little formal education, but he worked hard and knew how to handle people. For a number of years he farmed, raised chickens (for eggs), and worked on a streetcar. But when Lee was in elementary school, his dad did not yet know Christ and did not attend church. He was a motorman on a street-car in Louisville. When the street-car workers went on strike, Charles Roberson joined them. "He tried to make as much trouble for the company as he could," Lee recalled. "Many nights we would lie behind the sign-boards on Broadway and fire slingshots at the cars going by. We tried to break the windows out of the streetcars, and we succeeded! But later my dad was so ashamed of his actions. It embarrassed him for anyone to mention it." During the strike, Charles Roberson boarded a street-car and got into a fight with the conductor. He spent a night in jail before Lee's mother bailed him out.

Charles Roberson did have a sense of humor and a penchant for pithy sayings. In her 80s, Darlene Munafo told me that their father had sayings that she still remembered. "I never get out in a line of traffic but what I don't remember, 'Now, listen, just don't get anxious. Just wait. It'll let up.' And it does!" Their dad had a saying for everything, it seemed. And he was quite a gardener. For many years, he and his second wife had a big back-yard garden – with corn, okra, tomatoes. They would not buy canned goods and were very health conscious in most areas of diet. "Dad ate eggs and bacon every morning of his life," Darlene said. "My brother still does it. My brother still eats his eggs and bacon and hash-browns, and Dad did the same thing. Now can you beat that? Now we all are *not* supposed to eat bacon and eggs!" Her dad lived to 94. Her brother lived to 97.

Primarily through the years Charles Roberson worked with his hands as a carpenter, and he became a builder of houses in the Louisville area. He built scores of houses – primarily two-story houses – employing a number of men. He bought two or three run-down farms near Louisville and would build new houses on them. As a youth, Lee Roberson was quite proud of his father's rough and hard working hands. At age 94, Charles Roberson put a roof on a house. Lee later described his father as a man of ability but not many words. He said, "He didn't talk too much – very quiet. Never joked. I never heard him one time in my life tell a joke. He was friendly but didn't joke or fool around. He worked awfully hard." Lee Roberson learned from his father how to work. At age 17, Lee spent the summer working in the wheat fields of Kansas for $4.00 per day for ten hours of work.

A genteel man, Charles Roberson became a staunch Christian and a man of strong convictions. Dr. Roberson once told the childhood story in the pulpit of the time when he accidentally kept a pocket-knife he had been permitted to play with while visiting relatives. When he pulled the knife out at home, his father demanded to know where he got it and insisted that he return it. Lee walked a mile in the dark to return it – "scared to death." He apologized and never forgot the lesson.

When Lee Roberson's father died at age 94, Lee was still pastor of Highland Park Baptist Church. Dr. Roberson traveled up to Louisville and preached the funeral service. A number of church members from Highland Park made the trip, too. In his 90s, Lee Roberson's eyes filled with tears as he spoke to me about his father. He reached for a Kleenex.

Late in life Dr. Lee Roberson told me that the call of God to preach the gospel "hit me pretty solidly around [age] 18. That's when I first began thinking about it." He remembered the day when a guest preacher meticulously groomed in a frock-tailed coat – something never seen in the country church before – caught the attention of the young people at Cedar Creek Baptist Church outside Louisville with the words, "I believe God is calling someone to preach the gospel." At the conclusion of the sermon, the guest preacher gave the invitation by saying, "If you feel that God is calling you into a full-time ministry, will you come forward?" Roberson said later, "I felt that he had spoken to me. I left my seat and walked to the front. I said to my pastor [Binford], 'I believe God wants me to preach.' I did not know all it meant, and I was scared half to death. But I believed He had called me." Roberson said that he never doubted the call to preach or lost interest in it – from that day on.

Pastor Binford directed Lee to stand in front of the church facing the congregation of Cedar Creek, as the pastor publicly asked if any other young men felt the same calling of God. Eight other boys joined Lee Roberson at the front of the church. But Lee was the only one who ever preached. None of the others followed through on this commitment. Some came to great bitterness in life. One ended up in the penitentiary. One committed suicide just after passing his 30th birthday. But on that day the members of the church came by to shake hands, encourage and congratulate the nine young men. Lee's parents came by. Friends came. Then the assistant Sunday school superintendent, a deacon named W.A. Luckie, came. He took Lee Roberson's hand and whispered in his ear, "Young man, if God has called you, then don't you dare do anything else. Be submissive to His will. When I was your age, I was called to preach, but I turned away from it. I made a bargain with God. I thought it would be all right to use my life to make money and to send others into the fields of service. I have since discovered that I was wrong. I have never been happy since the day that I refused to answer His call. I should have given my obedience to the Lord myself." These were words Lee Roberson would never forget – and words to which he would forever be true. Because he already had a two-year diploma from a business school, Lee's mother had lined up a job for him at the office of L & M Railway. But the call to preach revolutionized his life. He never looked back.

Within weeks Lee Roberson was licensed to preach by his church. His father understood his call to preach. His mother did not understand. His mother considered it a waste of time – a waste of his life. But his father liked it and was very much in favor of it. In his

90s, Dr. Lee Roberson told me, "He helped me all he could. I think of it often." Cedar Creek Baptist Church gave Lee a vote of approval to study for the ministry, and Lee Roberson went away to college in 1928. He hitch-hiked the main highway 150 miles to reach the now defunct Bethel College, then a small Southern Baptist school in Russellville, Kentucky – just west of Bowling Green, Kentucky, and north of Nashville, Tennessee. He didn't have a dime. He was wearing a home-made shirt. His parents were poor, and he was poor.

Young Lee Roberson went to the office of the college president, Dr. O.W. Yates. "I told him, 'I'm here, I'm going to be a preacher, and I have no money at all – not a dime.' He said, 'Well, we'll work it out of you.' I cut grass all over Russellville. He helped me. I washed dishes in the dining hall." Years later Lee Roberson looked back on Dr. Yates as a very fine man. "He knew we didn't have anything, and he made it so I could keep on going to school." Lee worked all the way through college and seminary. At Russellville he cut grass and mowed lawns. He washed dishes in the dining hall for 25 cents per hour – applied to his school bill. It was an old-fashioned country school. For six months of the year, he did all the dishes every morning, noon, and evening! "I had no money," he told me. "Not a penny from my parents." He majored in history, as he prepared for the ministry. By the time he left Bethel College he was the choir director in his church. He studied voice, sang in the Glee Club, and sang solos in various churches. His mother and his sister would bring his laundry down to him – his sister did the driving.

After transferring to the University of Louisville, in 1931 Lee completed his degree, with a major in history. He continued to work in the city – in an office, while he attended Virginia Avenue Baptist Church. Virginia Avenue, a split off of Parkland Baptist Church, was led by the pastor, L. W. Benedict. Benedict invited Lee to work for the church where he took his first full-time church position as an assistant pastor. His salary was $40 per month during the Depression, as he continued classes at both the University of Louisville and Southern Baptist Theological Seminary in Louisville. His responsibilities included being director of the 36-seat choir, which he expected to be filled, and director of visitation, and teaching a Sunday school class.

When Benedict led his church to establish a radio station – WLAP (We Love All People) – Roberson ministered on the air with him for two years. Benedict persuaded an unsaved businessman named Dinwiddie to purchase the radio station for the church. Later, when Benedict learned that Dinwiddie was facing serious financial difficulties during the Depression, Benedict gave the radio station back to Dinwiddie. During Roberson's years at Virginia Avenue Baptist Church, the radio control room was behind the choir loft, and the two radio towers stood on top of the church building. During those college days, Roberson was also a soloist with the university choir and sang over radio in Louisville. Radio was forever to be a part of his life and ministry.

Benedict was a pioneer in aggressive outreach visitation, and he planted a seed in Lee Roberson that would guide his ministry for decades to come. Benedict sent Roberson out to visit the Sunday school's entire Junior Department – both teachers and pupils. Roberson said later, "I won souls and brought them down the aisles on Sunday. After the juniors came other departments. I made hundreds of calls! It was good for me, taking away some of my timidity and giving me a heartfelt concern for souls. I learned the importance of going to homes and presenting the gospel. As a consequence, we reached many people in the west end of Louisville." Lee lived at the Benedict home for one summer. He said later that Benedict taught him everything he knew. Lee was very impressed when Benedict told him that they were going to read the Bible through aloud. Each morning at 5:00, they began reading. "I would read a chapter," Roberson said, "and he would read a chapter. The rule was that we make no comments. The first day we read Genesis and Matthew. The next day Exodus and Mark, and during the summer we read on. There were times when I was half asleep, but the experience never left me. This is God's Book, and it should be read with profound respect, mingled with love and awe." It was also at Virginia Avenue that Roberson learned from Benedict to give an invitation at the close of every church service. "I saw Brother Benedict do it," he said later. "When I became a pastor I did the same thing."

After graduating from the University of Louisville, Lee Roberson enrolled at Southern Baptist Theological Seminary in Louisville, where he studied Greek for three years under the renowned A. T. Robertson. He always remembered the venerable professor's tease, "Young man, it's a good thing your name is Roberson and not Robertson!" He also studied under Dr. John R. Samprey, Dr. Kyle Yates, and Dr. W.O. Carver. Lee lived on campus at Southern seminary and spent part of his time going across town to the University of Louisville. Still poor, he said, "I did everything under the sun to get money. I would take any job I could find." He joined Walnut Street Baptist Church in Louisville, where he came under the influence of the pastor, Finley F. Gibson. Roberson said later he learned much about visiting homes from Gibson, who was at Walnut Street for more than 25 years. Gibson visited homes daily. "He told me that his average call was about seven minutes," Roberson said. "He never wasted words. He was kindly, but direct." Gibson saw tremendous church growth at Walnut Street.

It was also at Walnut Street Baptist Church that Lee Roberson heard the renowned evangelist Mordecai Hamm a number of times. Young Lee Roberson was impressed with Hamm's teacher style of preaching. He said later, "Big tall fellow – never raised his voice. Bald. He preached to 2,000 to 3,000 with no P.A. [public address system]. Everyone could hear him. I don't know how he did it." He heard Hamm frequently. Hamm preached pretty lengthy messages.

But it was Finley F. Gibson who had the most influence on the young preacher. A short man of slight build, Gibson was well-known in his day as he preached weekly to crowds of 2,500 to 3,000 people. Like clock-work, Gibson preached 29 minutes and said a prayer on the 30th minute. This was an influence which would stay with Dr. Lee Roberson his entire life – punctually preaching 25 to 30 minutes. "I watched him," Roberson said of Gibson. "That's where I got the time idea of mine, which kept me from going over length – a certain time limit." Many years later Lee Roberson remembered with admiration Pastor Gibson as "an unusual man. Only man on the platform. No one else there. Choir directly behind him. He had a way of doing it, and they respected him. He was positive, dynamic. And they listened!"

CHAPTER 3

The Call

For most of the second half of the 20th century Dr. Lee Roberson was preaching in many of the largest independent Baptist church conferences in America. Around 1990 one prominent Baptist pastor told me that no preacher in America knew more about Baptist churches in America than did Lee Roberson. While the great Highland Park Baptist Church of Chattanooga, Tennessee, certainly became – at one time – the largest church in America, Lee Roberson also had the experience of serving smaller churches as pastor.

While a student at age 19, Lee was offered the position of pastor at a church in Jeffersontown, Kentucky. He did not accept the call to become pastor – but it was there that he preached his first sermon, on the "Parable of the Sower," from the Gospel of Mark 4:1-12. He always remembered, "I typed my initial message on green typing paper, double-spaced. I stayed close to my manuscript, except for the moment when I lifted my hand from the paper and a gust of wind from a little window at the side of the pulpit blew all the sheets of my sermons to the floor. A bit humiliated, I bent over and picked up the sheets, arranged the pages and resumed my sermon. The message was exceedingly short, much to the relief of both preacher and audience."

Lee Roberson was called to his first pastorate in 1931 at Prescott Memorial Baptist Church, in what was then the small town of Germantown, Tennessee, just outside Memphis and near the

University of Memphis. Then just 21 years old, Roberson was to serve at Prescott Memorial for 12 months. The little Germantown church requested his ordination from his home church in Louisville. His pastor there, Rev. L.W. Benedict, arranged for his ordination to the gospel ministry in that same year of 1931. Lee was examined by about 15 ministers, including professors from Southern Baptist Theological Seminary in Louisville, plus other pastors of the city. Roberson recalled later that the examination was not difficult, except for the questioning of his first pastor, Rev. J.N. Binford from Cedar Creek Baptist Church. "Brother Binford had never been to college or seminary, but he knew the Bible," Roberson said later. "He threw the questions at me hard and fast." The questioning was done in the afternoon, with the ordination to follow that evening at Virginia Avenue Baptist Church in Louisville. Binford preached the ordination sermon. "I remember the ordination prayer, but especially I recall the laying on of hands," Roberson said. "This touched my heart. I had been called to a small church, and I felt that God would use me in that place. I had a strange burden upon my heart after the ordination. There was no lightness, no flippancy. Instead, I felt I had assumed a load. I had a responsibility, one that I could never escape."

Prescott Memorial Baptist Church had been organized in 1865. The old church building had been constructed before the Civil War. The ceiling was high, and the windows were tall, from floor to ceiling. There was just one room, the main sanctuary. At Roberson's first service in the Germantown church there were 32 people present. He both led the music and preached the sermon. The church had one deacon. From the start of his ministry, there was evangelistic growth – as the church attendance increased from 32 to 132. The homes in Germantown were large, old and mostly unpainted. The church building itself was a small but beautiful building made of brick – basically a one-room auditorium with nothing else. It is still there to this day. During Roberson's year there, the church expanded by adding a Sunday school wing to the back of the church building. To build it, Roberson himself carried every brick from the railroad station at Germantown up a hill to the church and built the addition with his own hands. Later it was painted white.

The small church suffered financial pressure and had a difficult time paying its young pastor. The church set his salary at just $50 per month but still owed some unpaid salary to the previous pastor. Roberson rented a room in the attic of a large rooming house on Snowden Circle in Memphis. He ate his meals at a hamburger stand – hamburgers cost a nickel each in 1931. The only thing he owned was an old Chrysler automobile his father had bought him for $110. It barely ran.

It was at Germantown that Lee Roberson learned to trust God to meet his financial needs. Through the years he often told the story of how a one-dollar bill kept appearing each morning under the door of his room in Memphis. A dollar each day was not an insignificant amount of money in the early 1930s. One night he carefully set a trap to detect who was giving him the one-dollar bill – slid under the door each night in an envelope. He discovered a widow lady who wanted to help meet his financial needs. She insisted that he not identify her to anyone, or she would quit donating the money. He quickly agreed to keep their secret! It was a faith-story of God meeting his needs – a story he loved to tell through the years.

Roberson always remembered his first baptismal service at Prescott Memorial, a church service where he baptized 27 people. He said he had no difficulty in baptizing anyone except for one tall lady. Baptizing by immersion, his intent was always to dip the baptismal candidate completely under the water. But after three tries, he said, "I still did not get all of the tall lady under. But, I had done my best. She was saved – that was the best thing."

While Lee Roberson was serving as pastor in Germantown, J.R. Black of Temple Baptist Church in Memphis invited him to lunch. Black's church was growing, and he asked Lee to join his staff as an assistant pastor – directing the choir and assisting in other areas of congregational leadership and visitation. Black offered the young preacher $75 per month in salary. Roberson accepted. He said later, "As soon as he finished his glowing offer I made my acceptance. I didn't pray. I didn't wait. It looked good to me – I accepted." The Germantown church would not hear of his leaving. So, he just up and left – and wrote a letter back informing them that he would not return. He started the next Sunday at Temple Baptist in Memphis.

More than 30 years after Lee Roberson left Prescott Memorial Baptist Church outside Memphis, the church took a decidedly liberal theological turn. To its credit, in 1968 it became the first Southern Baptist church in the Mid-South to integrate when it voted to accept into membership an African-American student from the nearby University of Memphis. However, when the church embraced theological liberalism, the local Southern Baptist association voted the church out of the association. Prescott Memorial established theologically liberal affiliations and began advertising itself in modern times in a way completely contrary to the conservative, biblical views to which preachers like Roberson always adhered. The church embraced social activism, accepted homosexual members, and called a woman as pastor – all steps which Roberson and other conservative Baptists considered unbiblical. Dr. Lee Roberson was not proud of the later history of Prescott Memorial. In later years most of his references to his Germantown ministry omitted the name of the church or informally referred to the church as Germantown Baptist Church – not to be confused with the large, doctrinally sound and biblically conservative SBC church later bearing the same name.

Serving under J.R. Black in Memphis after he left Germantown, Roberson enjoyed the 55-voice choir, worked successfully at church visitation and brought in new church members on a regular basis through soul winning. But almost immediately after going to Temple Baptist, Roberson felt he had made a complete mistake. He said later, "I made a big mistake! I stepped out of the will of God." Roberson told Pastor Black that he had made a mistake and wanted to resign. The pastor insisted that he stay, claiming that his abrupt leaving would embarrass the pastor and hurt the progress of the church. Roberson agreed to stay for an indefinite period. He enjoyed the ministry and the people there and saw people come to Christ, but he could not escape the feeling in his heart that he was out of the will of God. "I had looked at the bigness of the job, the increase in salary, and foolishly accepted the position," he said. "At once I knew I was out of the will of God." He tried to resign after one month, and then again after two months, but the people urged him to stay. After the third month, he again tried to resign, but the pastor persuaded him to stay another month. Roberson said, "I worked another month in misery." After another 30 days, Roberson packed his suitcase and drove to Nashville. He sent a telegram by wire back to Dr. Black, which read, "As of last night I have resigned. God bless you. L.E. Roberson." Black never answered the wire. Roberson had resigned – with no place to go.

It was during his years in Germantown and Memphis that Lee Roberson, as a young pastor, came under the influence of Dr. R.G. Lee, the great Southern Baptist pastor of Bellevue Baptist Church in Memphis. Lee Roberson studied hard at his chosen profession. He studied preachers. "I studied all of them," he told me. He would read all the books about preaching or by preachers which he could get his hands on. He loved biographies. He was greatly influenced by the biography of Charles Spurgeon. But R.G. Lee was the first of three men who had great personal influence on Lee Roberson – along with Dr. J. Frank Norris of First Baptist Church of Fort Worth, Texas (and later Temple Baptist Church of Detroit), and Dr. George W. Truett of First Baptist Church of Dallas, Texas.

Roberson studied all three legendary preachers carefully – especially Lee and Truett. He knew all three men personally. "I went to Lee over and over again," Roberson said. "I was with Truett on different occasions. I would be preaching in the same meeting. Never went to his church. But I studied him quite carefully." Roberson noticed how carefully Truett selected men to assist him. Roberson said, "He was a great, great preacher – tremendous preacher. Amazing man. Big fellow. Beautiful voice. Very dignified. His ministry centered on the preaching entirely. The men would report to him what they were doing." Roberson sat at Truett's side a number of times at banquets and church meetings. He heard him preach many times and stayed on one occasion at the home of Truett's daughter and her husband in Tuscaloosa, Alabama. J. Frank Norris was a fundamentalist and a fighter. Roberson got to know Norris personally – a friendly, amiable man. He described him as being very gracious and kind in private. "In the pulpit – a fighting giant. Tried to tear everything up. Privately, not that way at all. Very quiet. Very gracious. A real gentleman. When he got in the pulpit, something different altogether. A fighter. He loved to fight. Oh, brother!" Roberson told me with a smile. Roberson felt that Truett's style was one which he could emulate more than Lee's and one with which he felt more comfortable. But his favorite preacher was R.G. Lee. "I studied Lee a whole lot," Roberson said. "I was with him. I pastored near him in Memphis for years. I got to know him quite well. I had him over here [to Chattanooga] quite often to speak. A real gentleman. A real scholar. He studied. He worked at it. He worked at preaching. Studied hard. Memorized everything. Had a great memory. I had a little church on the edge of town. He had a big one, of course. He had just been there a short time. I'd go to see him and talk to him. I had him out to speak at my church. He came out to our country church on the edge of Memphis and preached like he was preaching to 10,000 people. I had him quite a few times." Roberson described R.G. Lee as "an old-fashioned, southern gentleman – a real gentleman." He was a strong and great preacher, who knew the Word of God and had a great memory. Roberson recalled that in those days R.G. Lee was very popular and was talked about everywhere.

After Roberson left J.R. Black and Temple Baptist Church in Memphis, he had no place to go to continue in the ministry. He stayed with friends, Rev. and Mrs. R. Lofton, at Springfield, Tennessee, about 20 miles north of Nashville. After a few months, he was invited to preach at a small country church at Greenbrier, about seven miles from Springfield. In 1932 at age 22, Roberson was called to the pastorate of First Baptist Church of Greenbrier. "This time I waited on God," he said. "I prayed earnestly. The Lord directed me to take the church." The church was pretty much in a "run-down" condition. The roof leaked, and the steeple was leaning precariously. First Baptist

Greenbrier had no baptistry, so Roberson baptized in a creek or in the baptistries of other nearby churches. Greenbrier was not a large church, but again, there was growth as the church increased from 125 to 350 in his three years. His salary was $75 per month, and he lived in a little room at the back of the church for three years. There were no conveniences – no bathroom, no telephone, and no cooking facilities. It was an eight-by-twelve foot room, heated by a small old-fashioned iron stove called a monkey stove. He had a small radio. He had to carry water in a bucket up a hill from a neighbor's well some 100 feet from the church. The only bathroom was an old outhouse about 75 feet behind the church building. He would often have his meals at the homes of his church members. Otherwise, he would eat at the old General Store at Greenbrier or the hamburger stands in Springfield. At the invitation of a church family named Mr. and Mrs. Los Pinson, he ate breakfast at their home daily for about one year. He insisted on paying them a small sum for breakfast.

Lee Roberson had an extraordinary voice and took voice lessons during college and while he was serving his early, small pastorates in Tennessee. At one time, Roberson was recommended to, and accepted by, a well-known teacher in Louisville named Mr. Shearer. "He was a German and gave emphasis to breath control," said Roberson. "On my first lesson my exhalation was 31 seconds. In a few months I exceeded four minutes." Later he studied with William Layne Vick in Memphis, and then with John Sample, the noted music teacher out of Chicago who trained John Scott Thomas. Lee paid $9.00 per lesson during the Depression in those days. He lived on 60 cents per day. Lee also studied trumpet. At one time young Lee Roberson was the featured soloist on a radio station WSM-FM in Nashville, Tennessee. He also sang on WHAS-AM in Louisville, and during his Memphis days he sang on radio station WMC.

To supplement his income as a pastor at Greenbrier, Roberson sang every week on radio station WSM in Nashville and WSIX in Springfield, Tennessee. "I liked it," he said. "I got to thinking that I might be able to do something like this." Already he had studied singing in Memphis and studied under Sample, who wanted Roberson to give himself over to music and attend the renowned Juilliard School of music and arts in New York City. Roberson was offered a scholarship at the Cincinnati Conservatory and studied there for awhile with John Hoffman. Roberson was also offered a rare contract to be trained for singing by John Sample.

In his 20s young Lee Roberson got more aggressively involved in training for preaching. Late in his life he told me that he was tempted to pursue a career in music. "I loved it," he said. "I studied voice a long time. I sang on the radio in Nashville hundreds of times. It was a big station back in those days. But I got away from it. I couldn't keep up the schedule – mixing the two things [preaching and music]. So, I gave it up." Roberson could not help but note the emptiness of the words to songs, such as *Invictus*, which he sang dozens of times. He said later that he would rather sing *Jesus Is All the World to Me*! Later in his 20s he thoroughly enjoyed being in charge of music for four years in one church.

While he was at Greenbrier, a musician named DeLuca with the Nashville Conservatory guaranteed Roberson five lessons per week, plus a job singing in Nashville. Lee was ready to sign until he realized that his music teacher would control his schedule. He said later, "I told him then that I was pastor of a little country church and preached on Sunday morning, Sunday night and Wednesday night – that I led singing in all of the services and sang all the solos. He said, 'Well, give it up. Turn your back on that. You do what I say, and I will guarantee you big money – thousands a year, maybe $150,000 a year [in the 1930s!]. Just sign the paper.' Then, all of a sudden, I realized that God had called me to preach – called me to a ministry." Lee Roberson refused. He said later, "I can still see that hot-headed Italian as he took the paper, looked at it, and said, 'You mean you won't take what I'm offering you? Remember, you are only the second man I have ever given that offer.' I said, 'I'm sorry, but I can't sign it.' I walked out, got in my old Chevrolet and drove up Church Street, right in the center of Nashville, the happiest man in the world – happy because I had said 'yes' to the Lord and to His will."

As the Greenbrier church grew, the members added a Sunday school building to it. But the church was small, and there were not many phone calls. The church had just three deacons. "We had one or two deacons' meetings in the three years that I served there," Roberson said later. So, Roberson spent much of his time studying the Bible. Through his study of the Bible during his time at Greenbrier he became convinced of the truth of the Second Coming of Christ and the pre-millennial position in eschatology. He was unfamiliar with books and scholarly writings on the Second Coming. But he took his Bible and began marking in the New Testament every verse which referred to the Second Coming of Christ. He marked them "SC" for "Second Coming." Then he went through the entire Old Testament doing the same thing. It made enough of an impact on him that he mentioned frequently throughout his life that this doctrinal discovery occurred at Greenbrier. In some respects, it transformed his ministry. The first Sunday following his initial study, he preached on the subject, *"I Will Come Again."* No less than 13 people responded to the invitation, accepting Christ as Savior. He always continued to preach the truth of the Second Coming. In one sermon he said, "This church believes the whole Bible. We believe every word has been fulfilled or will be fulfilled. The Bible teaches that Jesus is coming again. It tells us that He is coming in personal and bodily form. Since He is not here now in this form, we therefore, do look for His coming. We believe that Christ is coming and will receive His own."

During his three years at Greenbrier, Lee Roberson also assisted the nearby Barren Plains Baptist Church near Springfield, Tennessee. With his help, the church went from having a preacher speak once a month to having a full-time pastor with services every Sunday. And it was in 1934 that Lee Roberson visited the Moody Church in Chicago and heard the famous H.A. Ironside preach.

It was also during his years as a pastor in Tennessee when Lee Roberson's famous wedding story occurred. He loved to tell the story in great detail and eventually published it in his book, *Diamonds in the Rough*. He was asked to be the best man at the wedding of his friend, Elbert Gallagher, in Louisville. The wedding was to be at the Virginia Avenue Baptist Church with Rev. L.W. Benedict presiding. Roberson drove from Greenbrier to the Friday night wedding. Gallagher was one hour late for his own wedding. The preacher and people were nervous, as no one knew what was causing the delay. During the wait, Benedict asked Roberson to sing a song to keep the anxious crowd occupied. Roberson walked out on the church platform and arbitrarily chose to start singing, *In the Garden*, which begins with the words, "I come to the garden alone." As he sang those initial words to the song, the crowd exploded in laughter. The red-faced Roberson retreated to the pastor's study and lamented his choice of songs.

By 1935 Roberson accepted the position of Evangelist for the Birmingham Baptist Association of the Southern Baptist Convention in Alabama. He was elected to the position by the association, and he moved to Birmingham. There was no salary. He lived on love offerings from his regular revival meetings. Over a two-year period he conducted 55 revivals in churches and tents – and saw many people come to faith in Christ. In those days, revival meetings often lasted 10 days, or even two or three weeks – something rarely seen years later. A revival as short as one-week was almost unheard of in that era. Roberson often preached nightly in different churches for as many as 11 or 12 consecutive weeks. He had remarkable weeks of revival meetings as an evangelist – sometimes with 200, 300 or 400 public salvation decisions in one series of meetings. His evangelism efforts were greatly blessed by the Lord.

A handsome-looking young man, Roberson preached revival meetings during those days at the Ensley Baptist Church in Birmingham, where he met the lovely Caroline Allen. He said later that the first time he saw her he knew that she was the one he was to marry. The day the two met, Caroline went home and told her mother that she had just met the man she was going to marry. Caroline Allen became Lee Roberson's wife and life partner on October 9, 1937, at the Ensley Baptist Church. She was to become widely known as "Mrs. Roberson." Caroline was born in Birmingham on November 1, 1915. She received Christ as her savior at age nine after hearing the famous Dr. George W. Truett preach the gospel. Caroline attended Ensley Baptist Church until marrying Lee Roberson. The Ensley Baptist Church had been started as a new church mission through the Birmingham Baptist Association in 1898. It had a strong history of sending and supporting missionaries. The church once seated 1,500 people but faced changing demographics and dwindled in membership in the 21st century until it retained only 32 members. After 105 years of service, it closed its doors on October 2, 2006, in a joint service which transferred ownership of the property to Abyssinia Missionary Baptist Church, a predominantly African-American church in Ensley that needed to expand.

On October 7, 1937, Roberson closed a successful revival meeting at First Baptist Church of Appalachicola, Florida. On Friday, October 8, he then drove his new red, convertible Buick Roadster to Montgomery for the wedding. He was 28 years old. "I had waited for the right girl," he said later. He had the car washed, polished and ready to go. But on Saturday morning, the day of the wedding, as he drove to Birmingham, in the suburb of Homewood, a truck pulled in front of him, and his car was wrecked. The Drennen Buick Company hauled the car away and loaned Roberson an old Chevrolet. He arrived at the Ensley Baptist Church in time for the wedding.

Due to his late arrival from the revival meetings he was preaching in Florida, Roberson had not participated in the wedding rehearsal. Upon arrival, he received instructions from the pastors and was ready to go. The crowd was already assembled when he arrived. Two pastors officiated – Dr. C.R. Miller, Caroline's pastor, and Dr. E. Floyd Olive, Lee's pastor. The best man was R. Lofton Hudson. "The various people came in and then the bride – she was beautiful!" Roberson said. Roberson was wearing a dark blue double-breasted suit and a dark blue tie. He said later that the wedding seemed to take an unreasonably long time – as far as he was concerned!

With the Lofton Hudsons following, the newly-weds drove the old Chevrolet to Decatur, Alabama, where they had their wedding dinner at a little restaurant called the "Why Not Café." The meals were 75 cents each – the whole wedding dinner for four people totaled $3.00. On Sunday, October 10, the newly-wed Robersons worshiped in the morning service at the First Baptist Church of Huntsville, Alabama. For the evening service they attended the First Baptist Church of Chattanooga, Tennessee. The pastor, Dr. John Huff, preached from I Corinthians, chapter nine, on, *"So Fight I."* At the time, it never occurred to Lee and Caroline Roberson that they would one day return to Chattanooga.

One month after the wedding, on the first Sunday of November, Lee Roberson became pastor of the First Baptist Church of Fairfield, Alabama. The newly-weds took up residence at 4700 Carnegie Avenue, just a few yards from the church. Three years later during this pastorate their first daughter, LeeAnne, was born. The Fairfield church had been experiencing some difficulties before Roberson arrived, but under his leadership it showed extraordinary growth – with church attendance increasing from 115 to 852 over five years. The church surpassed 1,000 on special occasions. All of this growth occurred without a bus ministry – a ministry which would later become a famous part of Roberson's outreach. Roberson had as many as 15 to 20 deacons at the Fairfield church – good men whom he described as aggressively evangelistic and spiritually minded. During his five-year ministry at Fairfield, as time permitted, Roberson preached more than 50 revivals and evangelistic meetings away from the Fairfield church, in Alabama and nearby states – many of them around the Birmingham area. He was typically away from the church preaching one Sunday per month. During the Fairfield pastorate in 1939 Roberson was asked to become State Evangelist for the Southern Baptist state convention in Alabama, but he declined as he did not feel this was God's will for him at that time.

At Fairfield, Lee Roberson set in motion many of the ministry concepts which later were to blossom at Highland Park Baptist Church in Chattanooga. He emphasized three big services per week – "Three to Thrive!" He gave a three-fold gospel invitation at the end of every service – for salvation, membership, or rededication. People responded at almost every service, and new converts were being baptized constantly. New people were coming to the church all the time. He said later, "We must have had Wednesday nights when nobody responded – but I can't recall [any]." First Baptist of Fairfield was a small town church on the way to Birmingham. It had a beautiful building – a big, old-fashioned church building, and wonderful people – upper middle class. During Roberson's years there, the church built a large attractive stone building next door for Sunday school. His approach was much the same as was to become famous later at Highland Park but at Fairfield with a small town atmosphere.

Roberson also faced a bit of a church battle in Fairfield. His predecessor, whom he described as a dear, gracious and loving man, had not emphasized standards of Christian discipline and conduct. As Roberson began to emphasize standards from the pulpit, such as no card playing – not an uncommon fundamental yardstick in those days, he ran into a beehive of opposition. Accusations were made. Letters were flying around amongst church members. But he did not compromise what he believed was right, and the church continued to grow.

Roberson remembered the day in Fairfield when one of his own Sunday school teachers got saved. The lady, Mrs. Jack Stone, had been teaching the young ladies' Sunday school class for years. She had lived an outwardly exemplary life. A university graduate and a high school teacher, she was a civic leader and president of the local PTA. She knocked on the Robersons' door one day at 5:00 AM. When Roberson answered the door, she fell into the living room, and confessed, "I have never been saved. I want Christ as my Savior." Lee Roberson's preaching had revealed to her that she had never truly opened her heart to Christ. Caroline quickly joined them, and Mrs. Stone accepted Christ as her savior that morning.

Fairfield was on the edge of Birmingham. People were driving and walking to First Baptist Church. After five years of Lee Roberson's pastorate, the church had grown from a small church to a large church. Sunday morning attendance was averaging more than 850, and for three consecutive years First Baptist Church of Fairfield had baptized more converts than any other Southern Baptist church in the state of Alabama. Great things were happening. The crowds were coming. A beautiful building was paid for, and everything seemed to be going forward. Lee Roberson had no desire to leave First Baptist Church of Fairfield, Alabama. After all, his wife was from Birmingham.

On an autumn Sunday morning in 1942, Roberson stood to preach at First Baptist Church of Fairfield and noticed four or five men who were visiting. After the service they introduced themselves to Roberson. They were from the pulpit committee of Highland Park Baptist Church in Chattanooga, Tennessee. They were looking for a new pastor for their church. Already they had endeavored to call Dr. John C. Cowell of First Baptist Church of Decatur, Alabama, to be their pastor. Dr. Cowell had preached one Sunday at Highland Park and was well received by the church. But after a lengthy discussion with the committee, Dr. Cowell had declined their invitation to present himself as a candidate for the position. Arnold Chambers, chairman of the Highland Park pulpit committee, pressed Cowell for an alternate recommendation. At first Cowell declined to give a name, and then he said that if he ever had to leave his church there was one man whom he would recommend to his deacons to replace himself. "Who?" Chambers asked. "Lee Roberson of Fairfield, Alabama," said Cowell. Chambers had never heard the name of Lee Roberson before, but he wrote it down on the back of an envelope, shoved it in his pocket, and waited a month until the committee had enough time to get over the disappointment of losing out on Cowell as a possible pastoral candidate.

A month later Chambers and another Highland Park deacon discreetly visited First Baptist Church of Fairfield unannounced to hear Lee Roberson preach. Years later Chambers told writer Ray Staszewski of *Realife* magazine, "Upon seeing him in the pulpit, I got a strong impression, 'Don't look any further, this is My man.' I never put a whole lot of credence – now I could be absolutely wrong – about the Lord speaking to people. I think He impresses you – He can! But the impression I got when I saw him [Roberson] in the pulpit was – it had to be from the Lord because the impression was – almost verbal, 'That's My man.' Not 'your man,' but 'My man.' He didn't say 'your man – you found you a pastor.' No, it wasn't that. He said, 'Don't look any further.' Of course, subsequent events certainly proved it. He was destined to be pastor of the Highland Park Baptist Church. God put him up there, but He used human instrumentality. There was a need at that time of a pastor, a real pastor and evangelist, and a church that was ready. There was a group of us who had been praying to the Lord, saying, 'Lord, we've got a nucleus here, and if you send the right man, I believe we can have a great soul-winning work here.' And we prayed about it."

When all the committee members visited the Fairfield church in the fall of 1942, they told Roberson they were looking for a new pastor and invited him to preach at Highland Park. He agreed only to preach for them for one Sunday but told them he was not interested in leaving Fairfield. Roberson preached at Highland Park Baptist Church in Chattanooga on a rather cool fall Sunday on September 27, 1942, to a small crowd in attendance. The previous pastor had left because of dissension in the church, which was now divided and very much in need of a pastor to lead them. These were difficult times at Highland Park. The ministry at Fairfield was booming, and Highland Park was not nearly as large as First Baptist of Fairfield. "I got in my car and started back home to Fairfield," Roberson said later. "'That ends that,' I said. I was not the least concerned. But I did tell the Lord, 'Lord, I want Your will to be done.' The Lord spoke back to me, 'I want you to go to Chattanooga.'"

Aware of the dissension in the church, the pulpit committee had spent much time in prayer. The weekly committee meetings began in the upstairs Phillips Friendship Classroom with every deacon on his knees praying. "We didn't mention anybody, didn't even talk about a pastor, didn't mention a pastor, because we had to get right," said Chambers. "Nobody would come to the church with us fighting. And we did get together. A lot of people went around and begged one another's pardon and got right with the Lord and made it easy for someone else to come."

Highland Park extended a call to Roberson. He prayed much about being their new pastor. To be certain of God's calling, Roberson waited and prayed. The Highland Park committee sent Dr. T.W. Callaway, pastor of St. Elmo Baptist Church in Chattanooga, to visit Roberson and encourage him to consider accepting the call to Highland Park. Roberson was not yet convinced. He spent several days praying and waiting on God for clear direction. "I answered them that I would come," he said. "God gave me a direction for my life and ministry." Roberson announced that his first service at Highland Park would be the Wednesday midweek service on November 18, 1942.

It was very difficult for the Robersons to leave Fairfield, but they were convinced it was the Lord's will. On Wednesday, November 18, Lee Roberson, with his wife and daughter, drove to Chattanooga. They stopped on Main Street at the Farmer's Market for some hamburgers for supper. Then they went on to the midweek church service at Highland Park Baptist Church.

CHAPTER 4

The Church of the Green Light

The city of Chattanooga possesses a deep southern charm, extraordinary mountain surroundings, a railroad crossroads, and a vital Civil War history. After the Western and Atlantic Railroad made it a southern hub by routing the railroad's end at Chattanooga, the city became a battleground in 1863 for control of the south's railroads during the Civil War. Today a national military park and national cemetery stand as testament to the Battle of Chickamauga. Lookout Mountain, from which you can see four states on a clear day, has joined the Chattanooga Choo-Choo terminal station, Ruby Falls, Rock City, and the Tennessee Aquarium in making Chattanooga a popular tourist destination.

Along with this extraordinary heritage, Chattanooga also is a city with an unusual nationwide spiritual impact through its churches in the last half of the 20th century. Certainly the leadership of Dr. Lee Roberson at Highland Park Baptist Church and Tennessee Temple University helped to put Chattanooga on the map – in the minds of many devout Christians, especially among independent Baptists. But besides Roberson, the city of Chattanooga was also served by one of America's renowned Southern Baptist pastors, Dr. J. Harold Smith, who spent nearly a decade at Woodland Park Baptist Church. And one of the nation's leading Presbyterian ministers, Dr. Ben Haden, served First Presbyterian Church for 31 years and became famous for his nationwide television ministry, *Changed Lives*.

In 1942 Chattanooga joined all of America in praying for its soldiers then serving in World War II. The U.S. population stood at 135-million. A first-class postage stamp cost 3 cents. That year a horse named *Shut Out* won the Kentucky Derby, and for the first time Ohio State was crowned college football's national champion. A movie named *Casablanca* premiered in theatres across the land. Bing Crosby released *White Christmas*, which went on to become the all-time top-selling song from a film. Also, in 1942 RCA Victor sprayed gold over Glenn Miller's million-copy seller, *Chattanooga Choo-Choo*, creating the first ever "gold record."

And in 1942 change was coming to the city of Chattanooga. The city would never be the same. In November of that year Rev. Lee Roberson, at age 32, came to Chattanooga, Tennessee. He accepted the call to become the new pastor of Highland Park Baptist Church, succeeding Rev. Carl A. DeVane, who had been at the church for four years. Roberson was the 19th pastor in Highland Park's history. At his first church service as the new pastor on Wednesday night, November 18, Roberson immediately moved the Wednesday midweek prayer meeting from a church basement room into the main sanctuary. Arnold Chambers, the chairman of the pulpit committee which brought Roberson to Highland Park, recalled that first midweek service years later. "I just sat back and luxuriated," he said. "I said, 'Thank you, Lord. This is the greatest man for our church that we could get.' I had to pinch myself." Roberson turned 33 a week later on November 24. By December 13, 1942, Roberson had begun a radio program at the church. It was then called, "Call to Consecration," but later the name was changed to "Gospel Dynamite" – still running to this day.

In 1942 the Highland Park area, just east of the center of Chattanooga where the Tennessee River snakes through town, was a fashionable area. The church was easily visible at the corner of Bailey Avenue, a main thoroughfare, and Orchard Knob Avenue. Leading church members wanted to call a pastor who would lead the church to evangelistic growth. Some of the men of the church, including a young man named Arnold Chambers, had been stirred spiritually through the evangelistic services of Mordecai Hamm, the same evangelist whose preaching brought Billy Graham to Christ.

The chairman of the Board of Deacons was Bob Shedd, a businessman of strong, biblical convictions. When the deacons heard about Lee Roberson in Fairfield, Alabama, they sent a delegation to check him out. All that they saw and heard was good. They were impressed that this was the man they needed to call. So, they invited him to Chattanooga.

Lee Roberson arrived in Chattanooga with a philosophy of ministry he had established at Fairfield. He was determined to make Highland Park Baptist Church a hub of evangelistic activity that would reach into the tri-state metropolitan area. The theme, "The Church of the Green Light," was soon adopted from the Gospel of Mark 16:15, *"Go ye into all the world and preach the gospel to every creature."* A large banner above the choir loft announced the church's primary mission. The church stationery was adorned by a printed traffic signal with a green light and the word *GO*. A church sign with a replica of a traffic light – with the green "Go" signal lighted – actually hung at the church corner of Bailey and Orchard Knob avenues, until the city made the church take it down due to the possibility of confusing motorists.

"As a little boy," recalled Bob Kelley, one of Roberson's preacher boys, "I never forgot – as long as I live – the 'Church of the Green Light.' There was a great big old green, yellow, red light – a sign in the form of a traffic light, right on the corner. Never has there been a church so well named. Green, with the letters 'GO' emphasized. That was his life!" Roberson declared that evangelism at home and abroad was the single most important reason for the church's existence. Roberson began emphasizing three big services per week, "Three to Thrive" – which he had learned from his first pastor, J. N. Binford at Cedar Creek Baptist Church in Louisville – Sunday morning, Sunday evening, and Wednesday evening services. He set out to reach all classes of people – rich and poor. The whole city was his target – a mission he never relinquished. In the latter part of his 40-year ministry at Highland Park, the area surrounding the church deteriorated economically. The demographics changed significantly. Many of the Highland Park church members had moved out to the suburbs. But one of the reasons Dr. Roberson would not consider moving the church was his desire to reach the entire city.

After Lee Roberson's arrival in 1942, Highland Park Baptist Church was never to be the same. All the ministries of Highland Park began to reflect single-minded allegiance to the Great Commission. Old church records show that years before Roberson's arrival the church once voted to invite its own deacons to attend the Sunday evening services. Under Lee Roberson, deacons were expected to support the ministry faithfully – Sunday morning, Sunday night, and Wednesday night. Roberson began to emphasize three aspects of ministry which would characterize Highland Park through the years – a strong visitation program, Wednesday night prayer meeting, and a strong Sunday school. He increased the already strong missions program – by giving through both "faith" mission boards and the Southern Baptist Cooperative Program. One observer told how the young pastor "loved the Lord and loved lost souls." Each afternoon Roberson would take men from the church with him and call on non-members and absentees. It wasn't long before the place began to get very busy. The baptismal waters were used every service. It was not uncommon to see 20 to 25 adults walk down the church aisle responding to the gospel invitation at the end of a church service.

Besides his evangelistic emphasis, Roberson boldly preached separation from worldliness – defined in those days as going to movies, dancing, smoking, drinking, etc. He preached the inerrancy of the Bible and the pre-millennial return of Jesus Christ. He emphasized faithfulness to the program of the local church and established standards of personal conduct for all church workers and officers.

Garland Cofield, who was to serve for many years as a missionary to the North American Indians of Canada, was a boy in the church with his family when Roberson arrived. (Garland's sister was Jean Smith.) Cofield remembered Roberson's predecessor, Rev. Carl DeVane, as a stately, dignified preacher. The atmosphere changed with Roberson, who emphasized music and preaching. Cofield remembered that some people, including two or three key members, left the church – with all the changes. But most people stayed, and those who stayed grew spiritually. Cofield said, "My mother, who was a very spiritual person, got her first real burden for the lost people when he [Roberson] came. She and my dad were at every service. My dad was laid back – never missed a service

– giving his tithe. Mother sang in the choir. The church got too small for the crowds. He built the Tabernacle on a vacant lot and put in a sawdust floor. It wasn't long until that was filled up. He brought in great Bible teachers, evangelists, and great singers. He brought in the best there were." Garland went off to the Navy and then came back. One Sunday morning he went forward to dedicate his life to missionary service, and then Garland enrolled in Roberson's new college, Tennessee Temple.

The growth of Highland Park Baptist Church began almost immediately after Roberson's arrival. And the atmosphere was exciting. One soldier serving in World War II heard from his young wife back in Chattanooga – she could not wait for him to get home and see this preacher. When the soldier did get home – from all he heard, he could not wait to get to church. When Lee Roberson had first come to the church, the total active church membership was about 800 with a regular Sunday attendance of 400 – comfortably filling the original building, later named Phillips Chapel, which had seating for about 450. Every church service had an evangelistic emphasis and a three-fold gospel invitation – for salvation, membership, or rededication. "I did a lot of preaching, advertising, emphasizing from the pulpit – be here!" Roberson recalled. "Three to thrive – Sunday morning, evening, and Wednesday prayer meeting. Make every service a big service – with choir, specials – nothing relaxed! Some churches now let down during the week, with an informal gathering. I tried to make Wednesday evening just as big as Sunday morning." The choir rehearsed Wednesday after the service – and then sang in all three services each week.

Lee Roberson said he actually had no idea from the beginning how large the Highland Park ministry would grow. But at Highland Park he found a people who were open to his leadership and had a desire to go forward for the Lord. Compared to his previous smaller pastorates, he saw a dignified church membership awaiting him in Chattanooga – including many wealthy people, "old-fashioned aristocrats," he said later. "They were the old line of 'First Baptist' people – dignified; wear a coat and tie to every service." But they were ready to do something. They were ready to reach the masses.

From the beginning, Lee Roberson began establishing mission churches, later known as chapels, in the region. When he arrived, Highland Park was sponsoring one such mission chapel, Central Avenue Baptist Mission, located in the old "flat iron" building at the corner of Central Avenue and Cemetery Street near Main Street. In the years to come there would be dozens of mission churches. In the early years Roberson would preach at the mission church services himself, always returning to Highland Park in time for Sunday school. In those early years the mission chapels were encouraged to become autonomous Southern Baptist churches. But later, after differences with the Southern Baptist Convention, the mission churches were tied permanently to Highland Park, as ministries of the mega-church. After just two years at Highland Park, Roberson had established five such chapels – giving the total Highland Park ministry 1,100 new members and a Sunday school enrollment of 1,700. By 1946 Highland Park was leading the entire Southern Baptist Convention in baptisms. In 1954 Highland Park baptized 1,251 believers, and the church evangelism reached 967 more people who were baptized in other churches.

Growth for Highland Park Baptist Church came so quickly that the brick church building could not hold the crowd. The old telephone company lot across from the church was purchased, the building torn down, and a temporary tabernacle was quickly established. At first, it was a tent, but a fire forced the church to build a temporary wooden frame tabernacle. The people took to it. "When I built that first Tabernacle across the street – that was revolutionary," Roberson told me. "It charged the atmosphere. We used that for four or five years – right across from the old auditorium. That brought in a lot of people." The people coming in were more middle class than the fashionable Highland Park membership. But the membership embraced the growth and never seemed to object to what was going on. They were used to doing things a certain way, but gradually they saw what Roberson was trying to do, and they embraced it. Unlike some churches which go through a difficult transition, the membership caused him no significant trouble and stayed with him all the way through.

Bob Kelley, later a graduate of Tennessee Temple and an outstanding Baptist preacher, grew up in Chattanooga. During his childhood, he was not a professing Christian. Later he vividly remembered Roberson's early years at Highland Park. "In those days," Kelley recalled, "all the young people around Chattanooga, Oak Grove, [and] Ridgedale were somehow touched by Highland Park Baptist Church. There were witnesses everywhere. An evangelistic atmosphere or climate permeated everywhere from Highland Park Baptist Church. Buses were running. I remember bicycling up Orchard Knob. A Tennessee Temple College student yelled, 'Hey, boy, are you saved?' I just pedaled faster. It was that way everywhere – almost a blanket of evangelism and soul winning that covered that area. There were important people all over Chattanooga – influential people – who got saved and joined Highland Park."

During his junior high school years, Bob Kelley was invited by a friend to visit Highland Park Baptist Church. Bob sat in the balcony – in 1952 or 1953. Years later, he remembered his impression of Dr. Roberson. "He's like Moses," he thought. "Highland Park touched all areas – because of Camp Joy," he recalled. "My friends were getting saved at Camp Joy. It was common knowledge among the boys of Chattanooga that if you go to Highland Park, you are going to get saved. If you go to [the church's] Camp Joy, you are going to get saved. So, I made up my mind I wasn't going to go. I knew I would get saved." He was invited a second time to the church by a friend. "A boy put his arm around me in the balcony and witnessed to me," he said. "It was Jerry Reece – a Tennessee Temple student then. I wouldn't get saved. But Jerry wrote me a nice letter – witnessed to me. My mother kept it and gave it to me after I got saved at Highland Park." Jerry Reece went on to become a great missionary, serving primarily in the Spanish-speaking Caribbean. Bob Kelley got saved at age 19, following the continual witnessing of his future brother-in-law, Tommy Tillman, later a missionary himself.

After Roberson's arrival in 1942, it was not long before he started a Bible college – later to become the renowned Tennessee Temple University. Starting a school was a shock to the people of Highland Park, but they accepted it. Another shock came when Roberson began running Sunday school buses into the poor areas of town. But again, the people of Highland Park Baptist Church embraced his evangelistic efforts. "They responded very beautifully," Roberson said. "They accepted all of it. They never objected. Many of them left quite a bit of money to the church when they died. They would remember the church in their wills. We received thousands of dollars. The Phillips family, the May family, the Stanley family – wealthy families, dignified people – they may have been a little shocked, I guess, when the bus crowd starting coming in big numbers." E. Cecil Phillips, the son of a previous pastor, Dr. J.B. Phillips, was a deacon when Roberson arrived. The younger Phillips was a prominent realtor in Chattanooga and president of the Chattanooga Federal Bank. Phillips always called Roberson, "Brother Preacher." Phillips was very fiscally cautious but would support necessary expenditures as the ministry expanded. Arnold Chambers, the pulpit committee chairman when Roberson arrived, was also a deacon and later became the head of Chattanooga Federal.

As the church grew and expanded to multiple buildings, one new main auditorium after another replaced the previous building – beginning with the Tabernacle in 1943. Through the years it became difficult to refer to one building as "Highland Park Baptist Church." Years later Roberson honored the founding families by naming the original church building Phillips Chapel and the second main auditorium (after the Tabernacle) as Chauncey-Goode auditorium. Originally named the Orchard Knob Baptist Church, the church had begun in 1890 holding services at the Orchard Knob schoolhouse in the semi-rural suburban area of Highland Park outside what was then the small river town of Chattanooga, where the downtown and all residential communities were packed closely together along the riverfront. When more space was needed, the church moved in 1891 to the corner of Beech Street and Duncan Avenue and adopted the name Beech Street Baptist Church. The lot was purchased for $800 in February of 1891. The church was founded by Dr. James M. Chauncey, a Chattanooga businessman and lay preacher, who was an aggressive church planter. In September of 1891 the church joined the Southern Baptist Convention by seeking admission to the Ocoee Baptist Association, followed by a pledge of $10 for missions. Later the church held services at Eastside Junior High School on Main

Street, and in 1903 the church moved to the permanent property at the corner of Orchard Knob and Union avenues, where the church name was changed to Highland Park Baptist Church. The members dug a basement, put a roof on it, and were holding services there when Evangelist J.B. Phillips arrived as pastor in 1921, the same year in which Chattanooga hosted the national annual meeting of the Southern Baptist Convention. Phillips was instrumental in building the church which later became known as Phillips Chapel, completed in 1922. Phillips was strong both as an evangelist and as a Bible teacher. He held both evangelistic services and Bible conferences at the church, which grew in membership from 455 to 1,325 under his leadership. Phillips brought great men in to speak, including the famous evangelist Billy Sunday and William Pettingill, one of the renowned Baptist preachers in those days. Members of the Phillips family still in the church when Roberson arrived included the son and daughter-in-law of the previous pastor. Two pastors served between Phillips and Roberson, who arrived in 1942. Roberson remembered a family by the name of May as aristocratic, wealthy people with a beautiful home. They pitched in and helped Roberson and served in the church, including as deacons. They responded favorably to Roberson's leadership. Roberson said, "It was a change for them. I could see that. I said to them that I wanted to reach more people." He emphasized soul winning and personal witness.

The key to changing the atmosphere from an upscale, fashionable church to an evangelistic church reaching the masses was the construction of the temporary, wooden Tabernacle. The overflowing church crowd met first in a tent for several weeks while the frame Tabernacle was built. The Tabernacle seated 1,100 persons and was 50 feet in width and 135 feet in length, with sawdust covered floors. It was built of rough timbers. The roof was made from the tent, which had also been used a few months before in a revival meeting. The Tabernacle was cold in the winter months, as pot-bellied coal stoves were used to heat it, and in the summer it was unbearably hot. It covered one-and-a-half lots at the corner of Union and Orchard Knob avenues, across the street from the original Phillips church building and where the Tennessee Temple University cafeteria later was to stand.

Roberson spent only a couple of years in the original "Phillips" building before the Tabernacle went up. The Tabernacle was used from 1943 to 1947. "My older brother was saved in the old wooden tabernacle – with the saw-dust floor and stoves," Bob Kelley said. "My dad was saved there, too." Church attendance had doubled in 1943, and by Roberson's third year at Highland Park attendance surpassed 1,000. Arnold Chambers said years later, "Some of our greatest years were experienced in that humble site. When I go back and think of the height of the thing [the Highland Park ministry], I go back to that tent. The Lord blessed us." Roberson constantly emphasized to the church membership that the Tabernacle, with the tent top, was temporary. He was amazed at how successful it was. He realized it was an unseemly affair. The canvas was baggy. The poles were leaning. The ground was soggy and wet much of the time. He was criticized by some for using it.

On May 17, 1945, plans for a new church auditorium were announced. Land was purchased and the former pastorium next to the church was torn down. During the four-to-five-year period in the Tabernacle, the large main church auditorium, known today as Chauncey-Goode, was constructed at a cost of $175,000. Originally built to seat 2,500 people, it was soon expanded to seat 3,500 people. The new steel-framed building was built to last for many years. It was completed in 1947. The Tabernacle came down. The key wealthy leadership of Highland Park stayed with Roberson.

As the ministry expanded immensely, Roberson worked to tie the older, established church members in with the growing new crowd. "I tried to keep changing and adding men to my board of deacons, making it bigger – good men, strong men. They liked that. It was much a matter of holding the people by their loyalty," Roberson said. The new auditorium was named Chauncey-Goode – after Rev. J.M. Chauncey, the founder of the church, and his son-in-law. Chauncey's daughter married Charles Goode, a wealthy businessman in Chattanooga. He owned a furniture manufacturing company downtown. He was a wealthy, generous donor to the Highland Park ministry. Chauncey's daughter, Mrs. Charles Goode, was still in the church under Roberson for years. J.R. Faulkner remembered her as being "dressed like the old antebellum lady of the South, with her plume hat. We have a set of white china that she bought in Paris as a gift for her wedding. She ran a business on Main Street downtown and became quite wealthy. She lived in a big home."

Roberson gave three gospel invitations each week – at the end of each service. He began baptizing three times per week. He said, "Keep the main thing right before their eyes, so they could see it. Some of the old timers were a little shocked by it. But they stayed. They never did leave." He stayed with the traditional type of song service, sermon, and invitation. "They had been doing that for years. I did not try to drive them away – as many do."

And oh, how the crowd followed Lee Roberson's leadership. Early in his ministry at Highland Park he began a Sunday evening radio broadcast called, "The Back Home Hour," over Chattanooga's WAPO radio station. Begun on January 31, 1943, the broadcast was received enthusiastically. It was a 30-minute broadcast using a choir, trio and quartet, and then closing with a brief Bible message. The church's Sunday evening service started at 7:30 and would end at 9:00 – sometimes 9:15 or 9:30. At 10:05 PM Roberson would go on the radio live with the "Back Home Hour," broadcasting from the pulpit of the main auditorium. He wanted to keep the church crowd there after the 7:30 PM service and have a full choir for the radio broadcast. So, during the 9:00 to 10:00 PM hour each Sunday he would have an informal "happy hour" with a missionary speaker or a Christian testimony – for the full hour! Some 200 people would stay through the end of the "Back Home Hour" – broadcast live until 10:45 PM every Sunday!

One of the regular soloists was Jean (nee Cofield) Smith. She was a member of Highland Park at age 12, along with her family, when Roberson arrived. He encouraged her to sing, and for years she became one of his favorite singers. Years later she remembered that after the evening service there was about a half-hour to get ready for the broadcast. Besides those who remained at church following Highland Park's evening service, visitors who had heard about the broadcast would come from other churches all over town after their various Sunday evening services. The 450-seat Highland Park Baptist Church was packed out at 10:00 PM. The broadcast would open with a quartet or sextet, then a solo, the sermon, and announcements.

In 1944 a college student named Blair Truett handled the radio monitor for the Sunday night "Back Home Hour" broadcast at the basement door of the original Phillips building. One Sunday night during the broadcast he fell asleep, and his family went home without him. When they realized he had not come home, they called Roberson at the parsonage next door to the church. The pastor went to the church building and found the young man asleep at 3:00 AM. "I heard someone snoring," Roberson said.

The radio broadcast was a success. Roberson would receive letters from listeners in all of the southern states, some northern states and Canada, plus correspondence from U.S. sailors aboard ships in the Caribbean Sea – the sailors were receiving the bouncing radio signal at night. The "Back Home Hour" radio broadcast was very popular until the onset of television. The program was discontinued on December 6, 1959, and then later revived in a different format on WDYN-FM, Sunday evenings from 9:30 to 10:30.

Nat Phillips, later a long-time teacher at Tennessee Temple, was a teen in Chattanooga when Roberson arrived. Two years after Roberson came to Chattanooga, Nat received Christ as his Savior at Highland Park. He remembered tent revivals, Bible conferences, missions conferences, and the late Sunday night "Back Home Hour" broadcasts. "I would come," he said. "It was hero-worship for me. He was not like any pastor I had known." One veteran missionary said years later about attending Highland Park in those days, "You knew you had been to church!"

J.R. Faulkner, who was to become legendary as Roberson's right-hand man over four decades, joined the pastoral staff in 1949. By then, Jean Cofield had married Elgin Smith. Elgin joined Highland Park Baptist Church on October 9, the same Sunday that Faulkner joined. J.R., who led the choir, said, "I would take a Sunday afternoon nap from 1:00 to 2:00. Undress and go to bed. Still do it. Back here [to church] at 5:30 – all day. We had training union at 6:00. Choir. I would coordinate specials. I would fill out the format [evening order of service] and have it ready for 'Doctor' when he hit the platform."

Almost from the beginning of his ministry in Chattanooga, Highland Park Baptist Church mushroomed in size under the leadership of Lee Roberson. Beginning in 1946 the church led the entire nationwide Southern Baptist Convention in baptisms annually for a decade. At Highland Park Roberson was the first Southern Baptist pastor worldwide to baptize more than 1,000 persons in one year. On his 10th anniversary as pastor in 1952, Highland Park's membership was more than 10,000, with an average Sunday school attendance of 3,730. The enrollment of Tennessee Temple schools, after just six years of operation, was more than 600 students, and Highland Park had planted more than 35 mission chapels all over Chattanooga. There was a strong evangelistic emphasis at Highland Park. The sermons were short, but the gospel invitation was long. As long as Roberson could encourage someone to come forward, the invitation continued. The Sunday service was usually over at 12:10 or 12:15 PM. The regular church service would be punctual, but the invitation would depend on how many people came forward to be saved or baptized. Sometimes as many as 30 or 40 people were baptized at the conclusion of one Sunday morning service.

There were constant evangelistic emphases. Eddie Martin, one of the biggest names in Southern Baptist evangelism in those days, held a tent revival with a huge tent at Highland Park. Roberson's large tent gave Martin a vision for what could be done with tent revivals across the South. Martin invited young Garland Cofield to travel with him as a singer – which he did for four years. Later Roberson introduced Garland to the famous evangelist, Hyman Appelman. Garland traveled with him for a year as a song director and advance man. Garland remembered Appelman: "He preached with his whole body. What a preacher!"

Besides Faulkner, others who helped with the choir and leading the congregational singing at Highland Park included Vic Werner in the early years, later assisted by Garland Cofield, and then followed by Danielle Brown.

From the beginning of his ministry at Highland Park, Roberson emphasized Sunday school for church growth. He brought in the renowned Sunday school expert, Dr. Louis Entzminger, for a Sunday school enlargement campaign. Entzminger, who died in 1958, had worked for many years in Fort Worth, Texas, with the famous J. Frank Norris, one of Lee Roberson's mentors. Entzminger's six-point Sunday school record system was used extensively in Southern Baptist Sunday schools. Roberson believed that the early growth of Highland Park came 90 per cent through the evangelistic outreach of the Sunday school.

Church bus ministries were almost unheard of when Lee Roberson started busing children and some adults to Sunday school in 1949. Later Highland Park became a national leader in bus ministry, which became widely used in the 1960s and 70s. Nationwide records of early bus ministry beginnings are sketchy. During World War II, the Akron (Ohio) Baptist Temple, under the leadership of Dallas Billington, bused people to church due to the war's gas shortage. But some church scholars believe Lee Roberson's was the first regular evangelistic, weekly, Sunday school bus ministry in America.

M. J. Parker had been an alcoholic before coming to Christ. A white-haired man, he was in his 50s when Dr. Roberson baptized him and his wife. After a challenge from his Sunday school teacher at Highland Park, he was sitting in the church's New Year's Eve "Watch-night" service at the end of 1948 when he responded to the public invitation to dedicate himself to serving Christ in the new year. Thereafter, Parker, whose full-time job was with the National Linen Company, started picking up children for Sunday school and bringing them in his car. When Parker walked into a sporting goods store to buy a baseball, he told the clerk he wanted to give it to a young boy to encourage him to come to Sunday school. Upon learning the purpose, the clerk gave him a second baseball for free. Parker found two boys on the street corner that week and took them to Sunday school on the promise of a free baseball. "I began by asking two boys to ride with me to church one Sunday morning in my old beat-up car," he said. "The next Sunday the two boys brought their brothers with them." After filling up his car, Parker asked a neighbor, C.L. Thomas, to help by using his car. After filling two cars with kids, he then filled up the church bus. Dr. Roberson told him that if he could get 30 children to ride the bus, then he would buy him another bus. And then another – until finally 12 buses were bringing kids to Sunday school in a little over one year. By April of 1948 they had begun renting buses from the Hamilton County public school system. Later buses were purchased outright. M.J. Parker was a great personal soul-winner. In one year alone he personally led 287 people to Christ and brought them down the church aisle to make a public profession of faith in Christ.

Roberson was an enthusiastic leader and promoter. When J.R. Faulkner joined the staff in 1949, Dr. Roberson was having Sunday school contests between classes to build attendance. "He was an amazing man – to put one class against another," Faulkner recalled years later. "We had more fun – for years!" Faulkner recalled three ladies' classes named the Friendship, Temple, and Grace classes. Each had a dynamic lay leader. The men's class met in the chapel – the original sanctuary. "I taught that for nine years in the early days," Faulkner said. There were constant contests. For example, a "football contest" – themed with competing teams (classes) – would be held for the entire Sunday school in the fall.

As Highland Park Baptist Church began to grow, the brick church at the corner of Orchard Knob and Union was over-flowing. The first additional building purchased was the Hamilton Apartment house next door. It cost $42,500 in 1944, plus about $8,000 for remodeling. It was paid for within one year.

The college was started in 1946 – immediately after the end of World War II. Tennessee Temple College seemed to get a jump start from the patriotic enthusiasm of young men who were thankful to be delivered home from the war and who wanted to serve God. The seminary was added in 1953.

Roberson was always looking to do something big, to have a crowd, and to provide for people. Thanksgiving was a big weekend at the college. There was a big Thanksgiving Day service and a weekend basketball tournament. He wanted to have something for the students – many of whom did not have enough money to go home for the holiday. They stayed on campus. Over the years they were joined by students from foreign countries who could not go home over the holiday weekend due to the distance.

Jerry Mattheiss, who was later to serve in music ministry at Highland Park, was a child in Panama City, Florida, in those days.

Jerry's pastor, Hugh Pyle, returned from a visit to Chattanooga and started to pattern his ministry after Lee Roberson's. "He had never seen anything like it," recalled Jerry. "As soon as Tennessee Temple opened in 1946, he started pushing it. Dr. Roberson was ringing a bell! People would come from miles to hear Dr. Lee Roberson preach!"

Attorney Glenn Copeland grew up in the church. He said that in the early years at Highland Park the church members knew that Roberson was a godly man, and that the Lord was leading him. "I don't think we realized then what a great man he was – as we do today," Copeland said years later.

CHAPTER 5

Always About His Father's Business

Ben Haden was well-known for his nationwide evangelical TV broadcast, *Changed Lives*. He served for 31 years as pastor of First Presbyterian Church in Chattanooga. Haden and Lee Roberson were friends, but not close friends. As preachers in different denominations and different movements within the evangelical world, they were cordial acquaintances who treated each other with respect. Years later Haden spoke of Lee Roberson with admiration, "His was a life of accomplishment. He was simply always about his Father's business. Whew – charging!" He concluded with laughter.

E.C. Haskell, Jr., worked closely with Dr. Roberson. Haskell's father, a dentist, was chairman of the Board of Deacons at Highland Park Baptist Church for 30 years and was perhaps as close a friend to Roberson as anyone outside Roberson's own family. E.C. Jr., who was at one time a pastor and later a missionary with the Association of Baptists for World Evangelization, spent 20 years on the staff of Tennessee Temple University. He saw first-hand Roberson's unusual single focus in life of always being about his Father's business. As dean at Temple in the 1970s, Haskell set up a display for a three-day promotion of the college at a local shopping mall. The mayor proclaimed "Tennessee Temple Week" in Chattanooga. Haskell invited Dr. Roberson out to the mall to see the promotion for the college. Haskell vividly recalled Roberson's incredible response, "Well, I've never been to a mall before. What do they do at a mall?" Haskell explained to Roberson about the stores, the shopping, the enclosed area, etc. – what it was like to shop at a mall in the 1970s. Roberson said, "Is that right? I've never been to a mall. Will it be hard for me to find my way around?"

Lee Roberson was a man focused singularly on the work of the Lord. He denied himself many of the pleasures of life common to nearly everyone else. When I interviewed Dr. Roberson extensively in his early 90s, his mind was clear, and his memory was sharp – especially regarding earlier years. I was not surprised that he clearly described to me that he had personally experienced a "death to self" spiritual crisis during his younger years. But I was surprised that he said this occurred in his life after he moved to Highland Park Baptist Church in Chattanooga. So, I pressed him on the matter. He consistently insisted that this personal spiritual crisis of death to self occurred after he moved to Highland Park.

"I came to understand the fullness of the Spirit after I'd been preaching a number of years," Roberson told me. "I never got it before. Then I began to see what it meant. Emptiness of self. Dying to self. I began dealing with it quite a bit. I got a hold of that somewhere. Dying to self. Reckoning self to be dead. Death to self. 'I die daily.' That's what [the Apostle] Paul said. That's what I need." He felt that by human nature we are all tempted to be emotionally high for awhile, and then discouraged or depressed. He liked the idea of being the same all the time – everyday the same even keel. "Reckon self to be dead. I still do it. I still do it now. I'm dead to self. So if someone criticizes me at the end of my message, I deserve it. I go on my way. Getting self out of the way is the important thing," he said. In his early years of ministry, Lee Roberson took as his guiding "life's verse" from Scripture, Philippians 1:21 – *"For to me to live is Christ, and to die is gain."* (He later changed his life verse to Romans 8:28 after the death of baby Joy.) Roberson often invited L.E. Maxwell to speak at Tennessee Temple. Maxwell was the author of a book on the New Testament subject of death to self, entitled *Born Crucified*.

In the preface to his book, *Be Filled With the Spirit*, Roberson wrote, "I well remember the time when I first laid hold upon the words, 'Be filled with the Spirit.' A new day came in my ministry, for which I continually thank God." In his sermon, *The Key to the Overcoming Life*, Roberson said regarding the fullness of the Holy Spirit, "All I know is emptiness and willingness. You've got to be empty of self and willing for God to fill and empower you. That's all I know. You've got to be empty of your desires for the things of this world, empty of your own longings and ambitions, and ready and willing for God to take you, fill you, empower you. Anyone, whether young or old, can be filled with the Spirit of God, if he is empty and willing."

The late John R. Rice, an independent Baptist evangelist who founded *The Sword of the Lord* magazine and publishing house, used to joke that Lee Roberson had so much of God's power on his life that he could almost get up in the pulpit and quote, *Mary Had A Little Lamb*, and a revival would break out.

Roberson developed a focus that controlled his ministry. "I kept my mind and ministry settled – winning people to Christ, getting people to grow in grace," he said. "Stay out of controversy in the pulpit – stay out of it and stay on the main line. I think that helped me a lot. I tried to avoid personalities and stay on the main line: preaching the gospel, emphasis on winning people to Christ, emphasis on developing the spiritual life, dying to self, the fullness of the Spirit, the second coming – kept on the positive side, kept negatives away from the people." Veteran missionary Garland Cofield said of Roberson, "I can say this without any reservation. He is the most focused person I have ever known. That man is focused on what he figured was his job and his work. Nothing ever side-tracked him – he was focused." Clarence Sexton, who served on the church pastoral staff under Roberson and later became a highly successful pastor himself, said, "He knew what had to be done – just do it. There's the water – jump in. You read the Bible, pray, go to church, preach, sing, and build. He was always looking for ideas, imaginative things, stories – he studied people. He would use anything he saw that he thought would help. He was criticized for traveling and neglecting his church, but he used all his travels to build up the church." (Certainly his many travels multiplied the church through the continuing recruitment of college students.)

Such a single focus on ministry commanded a respect of those in his ministry. "He had a very loyal following," said Bill Mattheiss, who served under Roberson at the church and college. "There was no question on his commitment to Christ and that he was filled with the Holy Spirit. We were very conscious of the fact he had a higher walk in life. He did not dabble in anything – any worldly business or scheme, or civic organization. People respected him." Roberson's singular focus could make him sometimes appear very direct in his dealings with people. As one missionary put it, "He puts on no airs. What you see is what you get." Normally, he had a reputation for displaying a heart of compassion and sympathy in dealing with people. One prominent preacher, who worked closely with Roberson, said, "But he was very direct and could be – and Dr. R.G. Lee could be like that, too – almost rude. But he had a soft heart. You could tell he was saying what he said in love." He could appear to be abrupt and a bit gruff – because he was always about his Father's business.

E.C. Haskell, Jr., said, "When I think of Dr. Roberson, I think of a guy who was about as one-dimensional as anybody I've ever known. I mean this guy knew next to nothing about what was going on around him or in the world. He didn't know doodly-squat about what was going on [in daily society]. But in the ministry and in Scripture and prayer – that was his life. And evangelism was his life." David Bouler, a successor of Roberson as pastor of Highland Park Baptist Church, called him "the most focused man I've been around in my life."

In his sermon, *Man's Mightiest Thought*, Dr. Roberson told how he took time alone to review his focus in the midst of his 40-year Chattanooga ministry. "I took some time away from this pulpit to re-think my approach, and to re-evaluate that which we are doing in this place," he said. "I was carefully re-thinking my work and the work of this church." Among the conclusions he came to was "dissatisfaction with my own spiritual progress." So, at the completion of this prayerful time of study, he wrote out two conclusions: "*First*, that I re-emphasize the matter of soul winning and evangelism. There is nothing so important in this world as the winning of a soul to Christ. *Secondly*, that I do all in my power to help Christians to live victoriously. This is one of the great needs of this day! We have so many defeated Christians – so many weak Christians! We need victorious Christians to show forth Christ."

In the preface to his book, *Preaching to America*, published in 1999 by *Sword of the Lord Publishers*, he wrote, "I have had two purposes in my entire ministry of 71 years. My first purpose has been to win souls. Without Christ, men are lost and hell-bound. I have wanted to tell them that the only way of salvation is trusting in the Lord Jesus Christ as their Saviour...The second purpose of my ministry has been to help Christians grow in grace and become mature, worthwhile servants of our Lord."

Randy Ray, one of Roberson's preacher boys who became a very successful pastor in Nashville and later in Tallahassee, asked Roberson one day over lunch in Nashville, what drove him – or motivated him – to succeed. As Ray recalled, Roberson said to him, "First, I always have to be excited about what I'm doing. I keep that in my mind. If I don't like it, I leave it. Even if it's a program at church, I leave it in the middle. I just get out. Second, there has to be a little something that causes you to want to be the best at something. He said that's something that's important to me. Now here's the difference between me and Jack [Hyles] – 'I remember him saying this' (said Ray) – I *want* to be the best at something. Jack *has* to be. He *has* to be the best. He *has* to be the biggest, and he *has* to be the best. I don't *have* to be – but I really *want* to be." Jack Hyles and Lee Roberson frequently preached for each other through the years. And at one time it was Hyles' church, First Baptist of Hammond, Indiana, which surpassed Highland Park Baptist Church as the world's largest church. Ray recalled that the famous Baptist Bible Fellowship preacher, A.V. Henderson, used to say that great men accomplish great things because they are partly driven by a certain amount of ego – the spiritual key being to keep ego balanced with humility. Roberson, like Hyles, came from a poor, under-privileged background which served to motivate him to use his extraordinary gifts. Ed Johnson, a Temple graduate and pastor of a Minneapolis church for many years, was impressed with Roberson's spirituality, humility, and determination. "He wanted to build a ministry that would impact the United States of America for Jesus Christ," said Johnson.

Lee Roberson said that he did not set out to build an empire. While pastors of large churches are sometimes criticized for a preoccupation with numbers, Roberson was motivated by a concern for people. He would admit to being concerned about numbers. "One is a number," he often said. "One soul is a number, and I am interested in reaching as many souls for Jesus as possible." Always his focus was upon fulfilling God's will. In his sermon, *Inspection Day for Highland Park Baptist Church*, he said, "When Christ walks into our midst – He is here now – may He find us, first, preaching the whole counsel of God; second, working in the power of the Holy Spirit; and third, focusing on the main task." Ron Bishop, who served under Roberson at Temple, said, "You never got tired of hearing Dr. Roberson preach, because you knew behind that preaching was a man who lived a life of integrity and consistency."

Jack Hyles, who for many years held a five-day annual Pastors' School drawing thousands of preachers from around America, once heard Lee Roberson say, "I am always looking for ways to motivate Lee Roberson." A light went on in Hyles' thinking, and Hyles publicly taught that principle for years – to focus mentally on what motivates you from within. Jim Vineyard, a preacher who worked for both men, said of Roberson's ability to motivate, "Dr. Roberson could do something to men – as no one else in this generation. He could get them to do something for God. He was able to motivate, and he was able to keep other people motivated. He could have been a success at anything he did." Dorothy McCormick, Roberson's secretary, said, "He would touch someone – like a spark. You can't explain it."

Lee Roberson was different. "It takes a crank to turn a wheel," said one well-known preacher, a close friend who deeply admired Roberson. "Founders – they're different. It's almost like they come from some other planet. They make demands that make the ordinary person tired. But they never demand more than they do themselves. I had never seen that before in anybody until I saw him." African-American evangelist Ed Carter, who was trained at Tennessee Temple and based his ministry in Chattanooga, said of Roberson, "He was a genius – one of the most you'll ever meet. He practiced what he preached – to the glory of God. He was one of the most

Spirit-filled men I've ever met. The first time I saw him, I trembled. I thought, 'This is a man of God—a genuine man of God.' He does all to the glory of the Lord. Humble. Dynamic. Strong conviction. A man of compassion." Many preachers expressed the opinion that if Roberson had not chosen the ministry he certainly could have been a success in the business world.

"He was absolutely filled with the Spirit of God," Baptist pastor Bob Kelley told me. "He sought that fullness all the time. He preached on it. You could see it in his life. He never let anything become a rival to the work of Jesus Christ. He insisted always that the work of Jesus Christ would come first. He would not let anything hinder it. He made up his mind – what would be his focus, his ministry."

Lee Roberson was determined and not intimidated by anyone. He told publicly of the evangelistic outreach mailing list he developed in Chattanooga – to every unsaved or un-churched person or family he could find. He would send a ministry letter regularly to those on the list. Once you were on that mailing list, he would not let you off until you either came to Christ, moved away, or died. People would call, complain, and insist that their names be taken off the mailing list. He would tell them, "I can't do it." He insisted they either had to get saved or move away. Nothing would deter him from his focused determination.

People were impressed with his faithfulness. Family friend Sheila Wharram said, "He is so faithful. That's what he taught me – one thing I got from his ministry. In this day and age you don't see that – faithfulness." From the early years at Highland Park, he was very consistent – never late for his daily radio broadcast at the church. Even snow could not keep him away, as he made the drive from his Missionary Ridge home.

"He conducted himself in such a way that demanded respect," said Walter Wendelken, who served on the Highland Park staff under Roberson for many years. "The way he carried himself magnified the Lord in every way. I think some people were possibly actually intimidated by that demeanor, position and character that he carried with him. He wanted people to recognize that he was a man of God. He protected that image in every way that he could."

Missionary Garland Cofield expressed the view of many people that Roberson's standards and expectations for others were never higher than what he demanded of himself. Cofield said, "He must have made some real hard and fast rules about himself – his conduct and deportment. The way he acted in public. He always carried himself well." And always there was that unseen presence of God in his life. "Some ethos about him – his presence," said Cofield. "I think he could walk into a barber shop, and all of a sudden that place would become different – just his presence." E.C. Haskell Jr. added, "He had a way of taking over a room when he walked in. He just captivated the room – his presence. And he wouldn't have to say anything."

Wendelken felt that the intense loyalty displayed toward Roberson by many of the people in his ministry was due to the example of Roberson's own life. "We had a very small salary," he said. "But we were willing to do it because he had a small salary. My wife worked in the church office and would see the checks. He lived what he preached. Every man has his faults and weaknesses, but you overlook all those. He was dedicated, a servant – trying to serve the Lord."

Lee Roberson tried to avoid being subject to the hero worship that sometimes surrounds a prominent leader. "He had a way of doing that," said Wendelken. "It was even hard to give him a compliment. He would wave it off. He had a hard time accepting a compliment. His background made it difficult." He did not like the attention of seeing himself honored. Jim Vineyard, who worked for both Jerry Falwell and Jack Hyles, was impressed with Roberson's humility. The success of others, such as Falwell and Hyles, did not bother Roberson. "He enjoys their success," said Vineyard. Roberson did not feel competitive with others succeeding in the ministry. And Roberson, always in demand as a guest preacher all over America, would not cancel a small church on his schedule in order to speak at a big church – where both the crowd and financial honorarium would be larger. Evangelist Ron Comfort said, "He made you feel like you were the most important person in the world and that your ministry was more important than his." When Comfort decided to start Ambassador Baptist College, he received little encouragement from most existing Christian colleges – except Tennessee Temple. Lee Roberson spent hours with him – giving him advice, ideas, and direction, and answering his questions. He wanted Comfort to succeed.

In the pulpit, Roberson expressed humility. In a sermon entitled, *Prayer*, he said, "I confess that I am not as good a Christian as I should be and as I want to be. I am guilty of sins of omission and commission. I am guilty of a wavering faith. My faith is seldom disturbed by disappointment, but my faith is often disturbed by people. I am guilty of putting my trust in man, and hence turn away from a simple faith in the Lord God. This is a confession of my own heart."

When the Bill Rice Ranch, a Christian campground, was remodeled, a room was designated in Lee Roberson's name – with a plaque honoring him. When Roberson preached for Pastor Bob Kelley at Franklin Road Baptist Church in Murfreesboro, Tennessee – not far from the ranch, Kelley wanted to take Roberson to show him the remodeled room and the plaque. "No, Bob, I don't want to see it," Kelley remembered Dr. Roberson saying. "He would not go," said Kelley. "He's gracious, humble. Mrs. Roberson said, 'I want to see it.' She went. Any other preacher would have wanted to see it. He didn't. When a church gave him gifts, he wouldn't say much. He wanted things given not to him but to Camp Joy or some other project. He was 'dead to self.' It didn't matter who said something – positive or critical. He was just dead to it."

Lee Roberson never appeared to want any favors or honors or recognition. When the Tennessee Temple basketball games were packed out with fans, security chief Bill Long would set parking cones out to reserve a parking space for Dr. Roberson. Caroline Roberson liked that, but Dr. Roberson did not much go for that. "When he walked into the gym, we would follow him in and watch him through out the game," said Long. "I'd have an officer there. When they would go to leave, he would follow them out to their car. He never asked for anything like that. He had a humble, sweet spirit." Long said he never sensed a threat to Dr. Roberson's safety. Only when Jerry Falwell visited did Long bring out extra security but never encountered a problem.

Lee Roberson believed in and practiced "death to self" and surrendering oneself to the power of the Holy Spirit. "Whatever you have heard from him in the pulpit," said his secretary, Gloria Shadowens, "he is like that day after day. He is always gracious and a blessing – even in the face of unkindness. 'Die to self' – he lives that. We know he's human. I'm not saying he doesn't have a fault. We just don't know what it is. [She laughed.] He's a Christian gentleman. He really is." Roberson did not want to talk about himself. He would often change the subject by asking about you and your life.

In a sermon he preached in Chattanooga, *The Great Question and the Great Answer*, Roberson pointed to three different crisis hours of spiritual decision in his own life. "The first was years ago in Louisville, Kentucky, when I heard a message on the Scripture, *Christ liveth in me*, from Galatians 2:20," he said. "The contemplation of that theme did something for me. I have never forgotten it. The second great hour of my life came in a city a few hundred miles from here. I was in the midst of a revival meeting. God had to bring me down and almost put me on the shelf so that He could teach me the lesson of the fullness of the Holy Spirit. The third great hour was when I caught hold of the truth of 'dying to self.' I read the little books by a Scottish author, *When Did You Die?*, and *How to Die Daily*. The simple thoughts of these books pointed me to a great and important teaching. I had to come and say with [the Apostle] Paul, 'I die daily.'"

But even reckoning himself dead to self, Lee Roberson was human. He wore a ring on his finger and hated for the ring to get turned around. If he was upset by criticism or aggravated by criticism, he would turn the ring around on purpose, which would thereupon arrest his attention, taking his focus off of the cause of the aggravation. Dorothy McCormick recalled his words on at least one occasion when someone called to criticize the church. "When you criticize my church, you're criticizing me. I'm Highland Park," she recalled Roberson saying at the time.

Generally, said J.R. Faulkner, criticism rolled off Lee Roberson like water off a duck's back. "He said you never answer your critics," said Faulkner. "You never saw a word in *The Evangelist* answering any kind of criticism." (*The Evangelist* was Highland Park's monthly publication.) In his sermon, *The Episode of the Fifth Rib*, Roberson said that he prayed every morning for his critics. "I pray for them sincerely, for God to speak to them and make them right," he said. "I want my heart right toward those who are opposed to that for which I stand. Jesus said, 'Love your enemies…pray for them which despitefully use you…" (Matthew 5:44)

"When he talked about dying to self, it was a fact," said Bob Kelley, "I've never heard Dr. Roberson say one unkind or gossipy statement about anyone, and I've talked with him a lot – a whole lot. I've never heard him criticize any person living, or make an unkind statement – never. He just wouldn't do it. He would not let any outside sources put pressure on him." Jerry Mattheiss, who knew Roberson for more than 50 years and whose office was immediately next to Roberson's in later years, said, "I've never heard him say one negative word about anyone."

Dorothy McCormick, who worked closely with Roberson as his secretary, was always impressed with the respect he showed to every individual – no matter their station in life. Bob Kelley said, "Dr. Roberson was not a respecter of persons. Everyone was on the same level with Dr. Roberson. If a man stunk at the mission, he would put his arm around him and win him to Christ. He just never showed favoritism. He was the champion of the underdog." If a mentally challenged man came forward to the altar multiple times after church services, Dr. Roberson treated each time as if it were the first – always showing tenderness and respect. Dorothy McCormick said, "He loved people – didn't matter if you had money or not, rich or poor, black or white."

And Lee Roberson never lost faith in people. In one of his sermons, he told of the early days in Chattanooga when he overheard two men – both of whom he knew personally – criticizing him and mocking the supposed size of the crowds in the Tabernacle. Roberson had always thought that one of the two men in particular was a good friend. Other episodes of criticism and betrayal by others occurred through the years. Roberson, like many a preacher, was tempted to become cynical toward people and distrustful of them. But he deliberately rejected such a temptation and maintained faith and trust in people all the days of his life.

Probably no other preacher friend was closer to Roberson through the years than was Texas pastor Clyde Box. Box affectionately called Roberson "the most unusual man I've ever known." Box quoted Shakespeare's Antony referring to Brutus in *Julius Caesar* regarding Lee Roberson:

> *His life was gentle, and the elements*
> *So mixed in him that nature might stand up*
> *And say to all the world "This was a man."*

"He was what he seemed to be – simple and spiritual," said Box. "There was no pretense. He was what he seemed to be."

Roberson's life was committed to one purpose – to serve the living God. His main focus in life was to die to self in order to serve the Lord in the power of the Holy Spirit. Even his physical appearance and personal habits reflected that single devotion. Always he dressed the same, maintained the same hairstyle, and followed the same weekly and daily schedules. He wanted nothing to distract him from his focus of being always about his Father's business.

CHAPTER 6

Everything Rises or Falls on Leadership!

Lee Roberson knew where he was going, and he knew what he wanted to accomplish. Under his leadership, Highland Park Baptist Church and Tennessee Temple schools experienced astounding growth. Roberson was a firm believer in the importance of leadership in any enterprise – especially in a successful ministry. He became widely known for his oft-quoted insistence, "Everything rises or falls on leadership!" Roberson and J.R. Faulkner taught regular leadership classes to the preacher boys in the college. Late in life, Dr. Roberson told me that he believed leadership was the key to success in any walk of life anywhere in the world – be it the church, the mission field, the business world, or whatever. For example, he believed the missionary should use the national people he leads to the Lord to make the mission grow. But, he said, it still all comes back to the missionary himself and his own leadership. Roberson kept stressing to me that a leader must be "right" – which I understood him to mean right in his approach, right in his actual leadership, and especially right with the Lord and right in his walk with God.

Dr. Wendell Evans spent 11 years on the faculty of Tennessee Temple University, the last five years as dean, and served later as president of Hyles-Anderson College in Crown Point, Indiana. Evans believed Roberson had a God-given gift of leadership, as opposed to a humanly developed ability to lead. Even Roberson's physical presence projected that of a leader. Dark-haired, he stood 6-foot tall, weighed about 200 pounds, and had a strong, authoritative voice and presence. Partly due to his long life, in later years as a national leader, he had a full head of graying hair which eventually turned predominantly white. Evans saw him as what one would expect the presence of Moses to be – when Roberson would come into a room. "He had great leadership ability," said Evans. "He was a tremendous motivator – especially one-to-one in his office. He could give you a five-minute 'pep talk' that was unbelievable. He was a true encourager!"

Roberson believed that proper leadership could make anything go forward. A church program or a school must be promoted. Leadership is the key to making a Sunday school function properly and increase numerically. Roberson's sister, Darlene Munafo, told me with a laugh, "You never said, 'I can't,' in front of my brother. That word was absolutely a no-no. You never say, 'I can't.'" Darlene had learned this principle vividly from Lee when she was a teenager. "Here, Sis, do you want to drive a car?" he once asked her. Oh, no, she did not want to drive a car! "But if you drive *one*, you can drive them all," he told her. So, she let him teach her how to drive a car. She said the lesson was clear: "Don't say you can't. That was the way. I never forgot that. I always could drive other people's cars – my dad's, if needed. My brother taught me not to say, 'I can't.' And I never went to visit up there [to Chattanooga] but what he would put me on the spot. He would call me up and ask me to sing – when I didn't even know that I was going to do it!"

Presbyterian minister Ben Haden said of Roberson, "He's a builder. There are only a handful of people that I've ever heard of who are anything like him. You just choose the acreage somewhere and turn him loose. And he'd have – success. I don't care where it is or how tough it was. He'd figure out a way to do it. He's ingenious."

From his early Chattanooga days in the old Phillips chapel Roberson was viewed as a preacher who could be very dogmatic, full of energy – a great leader, with vision, who could stir the people up. He was predictable. On public issues, you would expect him to take a stand. On church issues, he was direct. From the beginning, he would challenge the church members to come out on Thursday for the church's outreach visitation program. "How many are coming? Stand up!" he would challenge at a Wednesday evening prayer service. People would feel "ashamed" if they didn't come out for church visitation. Lee Roberson was not a man to whom you could say "no."

To Roberson, leadership meant keeping things simple, not complex – so that people could grasp and gain an understanding of what he was doing and what they needed to do. This also made his ministry "copy-able" by his many students. And he believed that what he was doing could be done anywhere in America or in the world. He did not believe there were geographic or demographic areas where it was "too hard" to succeed in evangelistic ministry. He encouraged soul winning and church building everywhere. He kept things alive, exciting, and positive with the encouragement to reach more people, send out more missionaries, and train more preachers. There was nothing dull or dead about his approach.

In leading a local church Roberson gave his people simple principles which they could grasp. In 1971, he told the *Chattanooga News-Free Press*, "I meet with new members and stress five things. First, it takes 'three to thrive.' To grow as a Christian, attend the services of the church Sunday morning, Sunday evening, and Wednesday evening. Be in the right place. Second, Bible reading – read the Bible through. Third, pray. Be faithful to pray with the family at a 'family altar.' Fourth, witnessing. You can't be selfish and have a burden for people who don't know Christ. And fifth, giving. When God's people tithe, assemble themselves together, pray, witness, He is going to bless them."

Roberson had a confident style of leadership wherever he went and in whatever he was doing. Tom Wallace, a graduate of Tennessee Temple and a veteran Baptist pastor, remembered the time when Roberson was preaching at a special service in Wallace's area early in Tom's ministry. Wallace, a Philadelphia native, was then serving a church in Elkton, Maryland. Wallace and his wife went to hear Roberson, their mentor and hero. Although he rarely went out to eat after evening services, after that service, Roberson said, "Tom, are you busy? I'm hungry." The Wallaces were honored to take Roberson out to a restaurant. "But nothing was open," Wallace said. "We wanted to get a T-bone for him. But we ended up at a little hamburger joint. 'No, that's all right,' he says to us. So, we ordered hamburgers. The girl comes out to serve it – in real tight pants, smacking her [chewing] gum, and brings his hamburger wrapped in a napkin. We were humiliated. But Dr. Roberson takes over. 'Girl, can you put that on a plate?' In just a few minutes he had her saying, 'Yes, sir!' He just took over. Leadership." From early in his ministry Roberson was the type of pastor to make an evangelistic visit at a home – trying to bring the family to faith in Christ and into the church. Once invited into the home, if the television set was running, Roberson would walk over and turn it off and ask if the family would give him their attention for about five to 10 minutes. He would get right to the point. He had such an authoritative confidence that rarely would anyone object.

Lee Roberson believed that a church should be led by the pastor. Just a couple of weeks after he became pastor of Highland Park in 1942, the new Rev. Roberson noticed a group of men meeting in one of the church offices as the Wednesday evening midweek prayer service was about to begin in the main sanctuary. Arnold Chambers remembered the day. "Who is that in the office?" Roberson asked. The finance committee was having a meeting, he was told. "We don't have meetings in there while the church service is going on," he replied. "Go in there and tell them they have to break up and come in here." A few moments later Roberson was told that the men had said, "In a little while. We have some business to attend to." Roberson immediately responded, "You go back in there and tell them that if they're not out of there in 30 seconds, I'll come in and adjourn it for them." Chambers recalled, "Boy, they came out of there tough, but they came out. They learned. And he was right. They were not offended by it. We had always had such meetings during the prayer service."

Chambers remembered another event which clearly showed Roberson's leadership early in his Highland Park pastorate. In a Sunday morning church service Roberson announced plans for a Sunday afternoon evangelistic neighborhood census to be held that very day. He was going to send out teams to do a church census of the community surrounding Highland Park Baptist Church. "Now, I want a raising of hands of all those who will agree to meet here at 2:00 this afternoon and go out and help us with the census," Roberson said from the pulpit. "We will have everything all arranged for you." Only a scattering of hands were raised. Roberson then said, "I want to tell you folks something. If there aren't 150 people – that's what we need – here this afternoon at 2, I am going to take the varnish off those benches tonight." The people showed up that afternoon. "Of course, I was rejoicing," said Chambers. "It was wonderful. I think everybody was luxuriating in the fact that we not only had a pastor, but we had a leader. We had somebody who was going to take us somewhere."

The members of Highland Park Baptist Church clearly followed the leadership of their pastor. In fact, Roberson became something of a father figure to many church members and Tennessee Temple students. In Roberson's day his influence and stature among fundamental Baptists in the South was unparalleled. In 1990 Jerry Falwell dedicated the book, *The Fundamentalist Phenomenon*, to Lee Roberson. For his 1984 doctoral dissertation at Trinity Evangelical Divinity School in Deerfield, Illinois, J.R. Faulkner's son, James Randall Faulkner, talked with Roberson about leadership. "My personal desire is to please God as I seek to do His will," said Roberson. "As I read the Bible and pray, He gives me an impression as to what I am to do. I continue to pray until I am sure that He is leading me, and then I secure the prayers and backing of our leaders before we tackle a project or make a final decision." Roberson humbly added, "But I never dreamed God would give us all this."

In his sermon, *Building A Great Church*, Roberson said, "Leadership is the key. Everything rises and falls on leadership. The pastor is to be a leader. Normally, the church will do no more than the pastor wishes or does. The pastor who wants his work to go forward must give himself to his task. For more than 55 years I have been declaring, 'Everything rises or falls on leadership.' Original? I don't know. It has been a part of my thinking for a long time. And it is true! Leadership is the key to success and victory. Failure comes when leadership fails." In his sermon, *The Dynamic of Leadership*,

Roberson said, "Did you ever see a car, ship, plane, or bus in motion without a driver or pilot? It is not possible, is it?"

As a leader, Roberson usually had the last word. After graduation from Tennessee Temple and ordination, missionary candidate Jerry Reece along with his wife, Gail, came up for approval before the Board of Directors of Baptist International Missions, Inc., in Chattanooga. Years later, as Reece sat beside me aboard an American Airlines flight returning from a missions conference in Santo Domingo, Dominican Republic, he told me what happened at that BIMI meeting. After Jerry and his wife were excused from the meeting, they were asked to wait outside while the board considered their case. They were not supposed to be able to hear the deliberations, but by chance they could hear from outside the room. There seemed to be a caution by some board members which caused discussion about requiring the Reeces to await further training before being officially commissioned as BIMI missionaries. After a period of talk, Roberson's authoritative baritone voice could be heard – clipped, confident, and conclusive: "Okay, they'll do just fine. Let's move on." Reece remembered with a laugh, the case was closed and decided with Roberson's words. They were approved for missionary commissioning. Needless to say, the Reeces went on to a career of more than 40 years as successful BIMI missionaries. Jerry Reece became a prominent mission field director for BIMI.

In the 1970s missionary Roy Seals was a student at Tennessee Temple. His father was serving on the mission field in Mexico when Roy's grandfather died in the United States. Roy's father could not get out of Mexico in time for the funeral, so from Mexico he called his son, Roy, and asked him to leave campus to represent the family at the memorial service. The only problem was the expense for Roy to attend the funeral. Roy's father had enough money in his BIMI account to cover the expenses, but it would take time to access it. When Dr. Roberson learned of the situation, he made one phone call: "Give Roy Seals the money. He'll pay it back [from the account] next week." Roy attended the funeral.

On one occasion when a new funeral director came to Chattanooga, he was immediately informed that a preacher named Lee Roberson would have more funerals than anyone else in town

– because of the size of his ministry, both in church members and radio audience. J.R. Faulkner remembered the director. "His name was Gene," Faulkner said. "He was told, when you work with Dr. Roberson, you do what he says. He takes charge." At Gene's very first funeral in Chattanooga, a car pulled up. A preacher named Lee Roberson leaned out the car window and called to the new funeral director – waving his arm vigorously, "Direct like this. We've got to get this thing going!" Roberson was in charge everywhere he went.

For a number of years the *"Through the Bible"* radio broadcast of the acclaimed evangelical radio Bible teacher, J. Vernon McGee, was carried daily on Highland Park Baptist Church's WDYN-FM station. When McGee made a statement inconsistent with Roberson's independent, fundamental Baptist beliefs, a radio listener called in to complain and draw it to Roberson's attention. Roberson wrote McGee for a clarification. He received no response. He wrote McGee a second time. Again, no response. Thereupon Roberson did not hesitate to cancel J. Vernon McGee's popular program on WDYN radio and replace it with a daily Bible study taught live by Tennessee Temple's own Dr. Fred Afman. After initial complaints over the loss of McGee's broadcast, radio listeners accepted Afman's broadcast, which became a successful program for many years to come.

Lee Roberson believed that a leader must focus on detail. He viewed the public worship services as important. Certainly the preaching and the music were important. But he also gave specific attention to the church bulletin, the announcements, the gospel invitation, and every part of the church worship service.

However, Roberson's leadership was not a hands-on, micromanaging leadership. On the contrary, he knew how to put other people to work. He knew how to delegate authority, and it seemed that he could sense potential in others. Often he would delegate to J.R. Faulkner, his top associate, and Faulkner would delegate to others. "Dr. Roberson had complete control of all the activities of the school," said staff associate Walter Wendelken. "He was right on top of all of it. Even Dr. Faulkner didn't make many decisions except with the approval of Dr. Roberson. We worked closely together." Tom Wallace remembered a staff meeting during his college days. "M.J. Parker ran the buses," Wallace recalled. "[Roberson said],

'Parker, how many buses are we running?' I was flabbergasted. I thought Doc knew everything. But he had completely turned that over to Parker and let him function and operate." It was the same with Camp Joy – totally under the control of Tom Buffington; and the same with the Union Gospel Mission, run by Roy Richardson in those days. Roberson would provide the overall leadership and raise the funds for each ministry. He wanted to know everything that was going on. For example, while running the college required the disciplinary action of occasionally expelling students, no student was to be expelled unless Roberson knew about it in advance. He would hire trustworthy personnel and let them function freely. "But nobody ever challenged him," Wallace concluded. Sometimes, Wendelken felt, "Dr. Roberson was afraid to delegate too much for fear it would take them too long to do it. He was a great motivator. He knew how to motivate, to get people busy and keep them busy in the work of the church. He delegated responsibility – but not too much authority. He controlled everything."

Ron Bishop, Tennessee Temple's athletic director and head basketball coach, appreciated the fact that Dr. Roberson would delegate Bishop's area of responsibility to Bishop and then not bother him. "He took himself out of the way and let me do my work," said Bishop. "He watched it. As long as it was going well, I never heard from him. He took his hands off. He gave me a job. He delegated to me. He was an excellent person to work for, because he didn't try to micro-manage. If we had a ballplayer get in trouble, he would call me to see how we could handle that situation. But he never interfered with the coaching responsibilities. He was loyal. If you were loyal to him, he was loyal to you."

Part of Roberson's philosophy of leadership meant always looking forward. He was a great one for promoting a special emphasis in the church, and then when it was over, looking forward to something new – especially if the promotion was unsuccessful. For a special Sunday in the 1950s Roberson brought evangelist Lester Roloff to Highland Park Baptist Church for a week-long revival series of services for the church and college people. Roloff, a friend of Roberson's, was very popular nationally in independent Baptist circles. Roberson really pushed the Roloff meetings. "I never knew him to put such an emphasis," said Wallace. Workers were trained and ready for a great evangelistic response to the altar calls. "But if flopped," said Wallace. "It just didn't go. Everybody loved the guy [Roloff], but the meeting just wasn't what Dr. Roberson said it would be." At the next Saturday staff meeting, Roberson said, "Well, I believe we took a beating last week. But we're not going to take it sitting down. Here's what we're going to do Sunday." Wallace recalled, "That was all he said about it – and away we went. We were excited about next Sunday immediately, and forgot all about it. The next time we had Roloff, it clicked – and ever after that."

Roberson was always looking forward. Once a special date or church emphasis arrived, he then moved on to the next promotion. For example, for Mother's Day, there would be a big promotion leading up to the special Mother's Day service. The mothers would be recognized, and then the focus would immediately shift to the preaching of the Word of God, and then to the next Sunday's program. Bob Kelley remembered when Roberson returned from a trip to the Holy Land. Kelley recalled that Roberson announced, "Well, I enjoyed my trip. Everything I saw over there was old. We need something new. Let's build something!" Kelley added, "I can't remember when there wasn't some construction going on – or houses being built."

Not everyone completely agrees with the concept that everything rises or falls on leadership. In every walk of life, including the ministry, there are people who struggle or fail in one place and then succeed marvelously in another place. Environment, opportunity, location, and the willingness of people to follow all play roles. One famous Baptist preacher claimed "followship" was almost as important as leadership. For example, years ago the esteemed Grace Brethren pastor, Jim Custer, struggled with a dwindling church in Dallas Center, Iowa. He moved to a new pastorate in Worthington, Ohio, outside Columbus, and watched his new church grow quickly to become the largest Grace Brethren church in America (later relocated to suburban Westerville). Custer himself said that the difference between the two churches' growth was in the people. One group of people wanted to follow its pastor and grow. The other group of people did not want to follow leadership and was no different in its approach than the mainline denominational church across the street from them. There are many such stories to tell. But to Lee Roberson, it was full speed ahead. A leader can do anything! Roberson's sister pointed out, "My brother had a hard time accepting people with their faults. I know that – because he was always so positive and could accomplish anything he wanted to accomplish."

Jean Smith remembered Dr. Roberson as a very strong leader right from the beginning of his ministry at Highland Park. "Strong, but not a dictator," she said. "But he was strong, and he led us in the right way. He let people do their jobs. He knew how to delegate. He was led by the Lord – in everything he did. Sometimes a little harsh. We didn't always agree, maybe. But it worked. His leadership worked." Her husband, Elgin Smith, served as a deacon, trustee, and executive committee member for 30 years. Elgin said, "Dr. Roberson in a way sometimes was harsh – but people loved him. You can get away with that if the people love you – and they did." Jean observed, "I've often said if he told me to go jump off the bridge, I probably would have. We just loved him that much and had that much confidence in him." While the lay leadership of Highland Park Baptist Church clearly followed Roberson's leadership, Elgin Smith did not view them as "yes-men." His view was, "Everyone assumed Dr. Roberson was a man of God. God had led him there. Things were happening. Souls were being saved. Money was no problem. Everything was going well."

Randy Ray, one of Roberson's loyal preacher boys, remembered seeing the tough side of Dr. Roberson. As a new graduate student at Tennessee Temple, Randy listened in church as Roberson said from the pulpit, "I want everybody to look this way. I've seen two or three ushers or deacons going to get their car. The service is not over. I know who they are. We're not finished with God's work here. Ladies, they're going to get the car for you, so you can be the first at the restaurant. If they ever do this again – [and he smacked the pulpit], they're through! Finished! Now, be dismissed." But Ray was quick to point out, "That was one side of him. His other side was as tender and tearful as anyone you'll ever meet. His presence was just phenomenal – like Moses. The first time I encountered him on campus – behind a building – the sense of his presence was intimidating. As time went on, I learned to love that presence." Ray viewed Roberson as the greatest leader he has ever known.

Glenn Swygart, a long-time teacher at Tennessee Temple, saw Roberson's leadership as well organized and fast moving. "Some faculty members didn't understand him," Swygart said. "They looked at him as more of a dictator. Being from the school, I understood. Some coming in didn't. He would say things that sounded rough sometimes – particularly if some problem came up. But most of us who knew him knew he was doing it basically just to correct the problem. I never really objected to anything like that. But some did among those who came in. Those that went to school here understood." Roberson could be abrupt. When a faculty member brought a pet squirrel to the faculty meeting, Dr. Roberson was not happy about it. He immediately declared that they could not have such a thing in a faculty meeting! Swygart said you never wanted to be caught doing anything wrong. Swygart added, "The joke was that if he performed your wedding, you could never get a divorce! If Dr. Roberson did it, it was permanent!"

Roberson established the doctrinal statement of Tennessee Temple University. When an instructor was hired, he or she had to sign a confession of faith – agreeing to the doctrine of the college. "We all believed the same," Roberson said. "So, we had no problem there." But with as many people as there were involved in Roberson's ministry – faculty, deacons, finance officers, plus as many as 500 people employed at the ministry's height – there were bound to be personnel problems from time to time. "When you have people, you have problems," Roberson said. "I called them in and talked with people when I had to straighten it out. I dismissed some who did not behave. I did it quietly. Nothing said [publicly]. I never tried to make a big thing out of it. That kept us from having public discussion. We had none at all – none at all. I don't make a show of it or anything. I never say a word in the pulpit – never did in all my 40 years. I never brought anything [of this nature] to the pulpit." On the rare occasions when a ministry employee had to be dismissed, Roberson would turn it over to the Board of Deacons to investigate and to handle the dismissal. He did not like negatives and confrontation. "He was never a one-on-one type person," said Bill Long. Long, who had great admiration for Roberson, was a police chief in West Virginia when he quit his job and joined Roberson in Chattanooga. Long served as head of security for the ministry and taught at the college. "I would go in to talk with him about a problem with somebody," said Long. "Then instead of calling them in and dealing with it across his desk, the next chapel service he'd preach a little short 'sermonette' on that particular point – the idea being that anyone who violates this will be in trouble, etc. He wasn't much on eyeball-to-eyeball correcting problems personally."

Some ministry problems, which did not reflect on, or embarrass, one individual, were handled publicly. One year a Sunday school class raised the money and bought a new piano. The class's students kept the piano locked up, except when one of them came in to practice. Dr. Roberson publicly put a halt to the practice. He declared that all of the church's equipment was for the Lord's work and was to be available to all. He stressed the unity of being one church.

If a staff member's employment relationship was severed, the employee was usually finished immediately. On occasion, a college teacher would approach Roberson in late winter or early spring and inform him that he would not be renewing his teaching contract, but that after the semester ended he was going to move to teach at another college for the following school year. Roberson's response typically would be to wish him well and instruct him to clean out his desk, as the termination would be effective immediately. Of course, as time went on, teachers who were planning to leave the school learned to wait until the last minute to tell Dr. Roberson about it. But Roberson's thinking was clear. When one college professor told Roberson that he was leaving at the end of the summer term – because he had a doctor's degree, a family to support, and simply was not making enough money, Roberson simply made that his last day at Tennessee Temple. One professor recalled Roberson's thinking, "We don't want anyone around here who is negative and has criticism for the school." J.R. Faulkner said, "He didn't want anyone hanging around to finish out a contract once they talk about going somewhere else. 'You go now.' That's always been true with him. The thing back of that is that person's going to stay around here and talk to people all about why he's going to leave, giving his reasons for why he's leaving. It keeps putting 'a buzz in someone else's bonnet,' and they'll be the same way. And so it just results in trouble."

However, Roberson did handle some leadership matters – especially in the college – in public. Some even viewed him as having a temper in his younger years. Students remember occasions in chapel when Dr. Roberson would ask visitors to leave. He would put a sentry at each exit door, turn off the radio broadcast, with no one moving in or out. "You better hang on," said one Roberson admirer. "He had something to say. Someone had done something wrong. Or something he wanted to emphasize. At one time he had quite a temper. That booming voice – he got his point across." When the Christian Charismatic movement – emphasizing the idea of supernatural miracles and personal spiritual gifts of the Spirit – became popular, it split churches, colleges, and even denominations. A group of Tennessee Temple students started meeting privately seeking the supposed Charismatic gifts of the Spirit, such as "speaking in tongues." One of the students, an outstanding young preacher, brought a doctrinally Charismatic message in the college chapel service which resulted in an altar full of students seeking to follow this movement. Tom Wallace was there and remembered Dr. Roberson's response. He came into chapel and announced that he knew what was going on. "We have a problem," Roberson said. "I know who you are. I have your names on this piece of paper here. Now, I want to ask everyone who is innocent to stand. If you're involved in this, don't you dare stand up. I know who you are. You keep your seat. I'll call your name [if I have to]." Wallace wondered if he really did know the names of the students involved in this. Whereupon, Roberson said, "Now, everyone look around. Those seated are not like us. They're doing something we're not for. I want you to 'mark' them. If any of you are approached by them [about the Charismatic teaching], I want you to come straight to me. They're on their way out. Now, if you don't like it, *you're* out!" Wallace recalled, "He nipped it in the bud. Most of them left the school. It split other schools in half. He handled it."

Some matters handled in public were purely tactical, in order to have a desired effect on others. Nat Phillips, a long-time Tennessee

Temple teacher, remembered the day Roberson stood in the pulpit at chapel and pointed toward the back to a row of boys. He singled out a young man in a red shirt and said, "See me after chapel." The young man, newly enrolled in the college, was a Baptist pastor from nearby Dalton, Georgia. When he met with Roberson, he protested, "Dr. Roberson, we weren't doing anything." Roberson said, "I know you weren't. But we couldn't get everyone to quiet down. That red shirt stuck out. I thought if I did that, I could get everyone to quiet down." It worked. The young pastor, of course, did not face any discipline.

Stories of Dr. Roberson's public admonitions are legendary. Baptist evangelist Ed Carter remembered the day at the Union Gospel Mission's old building in downtown Chattanooga when Roberson was preaching. Incredibly, a man sitting in the rescue mission chapel congregation lit a cigarette, began smoking, and started to blow smoke rings during the chapel service. Roberson, in the pulpit preaching, caught sight of it out of the corner of his eye. Hardly straying from his sermon, Roberson roared, "Put that cigarette out!" Carter recalled the mission man's reaction: "He swallowed it. The next thing you saw he was running down the hallway to get a glass of water!" On another occasion, two Tennessee Temple students, a boy and a girl, were discovered alone together in a vehicle at a park – a violation of the college's strict rules. Roberson called them by name in chapel, commanded them to stand up, directed that they pack their bags, and announced that they were expelled from the college as of that minute. "You know we don't tolerate that sort of a lifestyle here at Tennessee Temple," Roberson said publicly. Carter said, "That day I saw grown men crumble and wilt in their seats. It was like Acts, Chapter 5 [God's judgment of Annanias and Sapphira]. Fear fell upon all of them. That's what happened that day." If a student fell asleep in chapel, he could count on being singled out and corrected in public. Bob Kelley remembered seeing Roberson red-faced, with his neck red, when he was angry – in the pulpit, but not in private. "One night he got up and let go," Kelley recalled. Dancing was considered taboo in many fundamental church circles in those days and certainly to Roberson. "Someone had been seen at a dance – a leader in the church," Kelley remembered. Did he call their name? "No," said Kelley. Then he added, "Someone once put a glass of beer at his table. He knocked it off – maybe at an airport – for what it would look like."

When Ed Carter was first invited to speak in the college chapel, someone warned him privately not to go over his time limit. Carter was told, "If you hear Dr. Roberson jingling the change in his pocket, you had better wind down [your sermon], or he'll wind you down." Carter said, "I made sure I stayed within the time. I had seen him come up behind speakers, pray – 'Father, thank you for the service. Bless us now in Jesus' name. Amen!' – and close! I didn't want that." Temple professor David Winget remembered speaking in chapel as a student. When the length of his sermon went way too long, Roberson tugged on his coat from behind. "Time's up!" said Roberson. Winget never forgot it.

Roberson had a forceful spirit but generally controlled his temper. "It's never bluster," J.R. Falkner told me. "Never any blustering out – none of that with him. He would sit quietly at a meeting – executive staff, Sunday school, whatever – and finally say, 'All right, I think we've said enough. I think we understand. Let's draw it to a close. This is what we're going to do.' He would explain the plan of action, and then say, 'Let's have prayer.' He had everything firmly under control. I'm not bragging, Brother Wigton, when I say this. He never had a staff that would give him any trouble."

But Roberson could also be direct. In his sermon, *Toying With Trifles*, he told the story himself of a visit he made to a hospital room in Chattanooga. The patient, a young lady, was recovering from a serious automobile accident in which a family member had been killed. Roberson was asked to pay her a visit in the hospital. "I introduced myself," Roberson said, "but she apparently did not hear, for her eyes were focused on the TV set on the wall, turned on full blast. I told her that I would like to pray with her. I asked that the volume on the TV set be turned down. She said, 'No, this is one of my favorite programs. You can pray, but I am going to watch my program.' I became a little stern and told her to turn it off at once. She did, and I prayed."

As Roberson's leadership influence spread across the nation, he traveled more and more. He would speak frequently at other churches, always talking about Tennessee Temple and handing out inquiry cards for potential college students to sign up. When he first moved to Highland Park Baptist Church he continued to leave town to preach some revivals at other churches which involved Sunday absences from Chattanooga. But it was not long before he decided to focus his primary attention almost completely on the Highland Park ministry.

Ed Johnson, the pastor of First Baptist Church of Rosemount in Minnesota, learned from Roberson that a preacher may do more for God's glory by staying in one place than by moving around to different churches. "You build a reputation, a testimony," said Johnson. "You can impact an area, a city, a state. He said this to me the first time he came to my place in 1972. I had gotten there in 1967 with 20 people. Now we had 200. He was leaving for the airport on Tuesday night. He said, 'Brother Ed, you've been here five years. God has blessed you. Now, if you'll stay 10 years, you'll accomplish more – likewise, 15. If you don't get where I'm going with this, I'll take your degree back." Ed Johnson stayed at that church for decades.

During those days it became common for many independent Baptist churches to host Sunday through Tuesday or Sunday through Wednesday special church services or conferences with guest speakers. Well-known pastors of large, successful churches – men like Lee Roberson, Jack Hyles, Tom Malone, Harold Sightler, Jack Hudson, Curtis Hutson, et al – would not miss their own church services on Sunday but would come in for the conference as guest speakers and preach on Monday and Tuesday. Oftentimes an evangelist like John R. Rice or Dolphus Price would preach on Sunday, and then join with the guest pastor as both preached on Monday and Tuesday in morning and evening meetings. Rice, editor of *The Sword of the Lord* magazine, would also often host *Sword* conferences at various churches. Roberson was in great demand for such church services and used these opportunities not only to preach the Word of God to the people present, but also to promote Tennessee Temple University – where the young people from these churches would receive a thoroughly biblical training consistent with what these host pastors believed. Occasionally such services were held later in the week – almost never in conflict with a regular Wednesday or Sunday service back at the guest speaker's home church.

In 2002 J.R. Faulkner remembered those previous days: "Dr. Roberson was a great promoter. He knew how to go. He would go out on Monday-Tuesday, Thursday-Friday, and hit these churches. That just kept building. As we got more graduates out there [as pastors], they liked for him to come [to their churches]. And he's still going. He loves to get with his boys. That's why he goes – every week of the year. Doctor stressed [such promotion] from day one. Leadership in the classes. Responsibility. They personally had to go and then promote it among their people to visit. And write these letters. Every class was urged to write letters and cards and follow-up and visitation in the hospitals. Of course, he was setting the pace. He did it himself."

As Roberson traveled, he was always promoting his college. Nothing seemed to stop him. As he traveled to preach in church conferences out-of-town on Mondays and Tuesdays, he would constantly seek to recruit new students. He would collect names and addresses of potential students, and upon his return he would send the prospective students a Tennessee Temple college catalogue.

Always as he traveled he carried an accordion type attaché case – filled with books. He would read five or six books per week. He traveled the world tirelessly preaching the gospel at home and abroad. In 1971 Roberson arrived late on a Tuesday night at Chattanooga's Lovell Field, now called Chattanooga Metropolitan Airport, from a preaching mission in the Philippine Islands. Also arriving at the airport was Frank Rosser, one of the great Baptist International Missions missionaries to come out of Tennessee Temple under Roberson. Rosser had just returned from a mission trip to England. They flew into Chattanooga together from New York City. With the jet lag, both men were "walking dead – zombies," asleep on their feet, said Rosser. Roberson was too tired even to drive home from the airport. He said to Rosser, "Frank, how are you getting home?" By taxi, Rosser answered. Roberson replied, "Here, drive my car. Take me to my house. Take the car on home. I'll be in chapel in the morning. Give it to me there."

As he traveled, Roberson confidently dispensed advice to the many preachers who looked up to him. Baptist pastor Jim Vineyard built a large church in Oklahoma City, after working as an assistant pastor for three celebrated Baptist preachers – John Rawlings, Jerry Falwell, and Jack Hyles. In the early 1990s, Vineyard told me that he believed no pastor in America knew as much about Baptist churches as did Lee Roberson. On Roberson's first visit to preach for Vineyard in Oklahoma City, Roberson looked over Vineyard's ministry at Windsor Hills Baptist Church and advised Vineyard, "Brother Vineyard, you have a good reputation for starting these junior churches [children's services conducted separately at the same time as the regular church worship service]. That's not the way to do it. The kids need to be in here with you. They need to hear their pastor. They need to hear you preach to them. That's the way to do it." Children's church services have become increasingly popular throughout America, and Vineyard himself had authored books on children's church services. Nevertheless, at the time, Vineyard immediately followed Roberson's advice and changed his procedure. "We do it exactly like he told us – ever since," said Vineyard. "We put the juniors [children] in the balcony." Before I accepted the call to become the pastor of Temple Heights Baptist Church in Tampa, Florida, the church had removed the traditional pulpit chairs and pulpit from the platform – with a small speaking podium and a more contemporary look, like many churches do now-a-days. Roberson was a guest speaker during the interim period between pastors. With a wave of the hand from the platform, he proclaimed to the church, "Get those chairs back up here!" When I arrived as the new pastor a few months later, the pulpit chairs were back on the platform – but there was still no pulpit, only the small speaker's stand. The church had quickly done exactly what Dr. Roberson said to do – and no more!

A key inspiration of Roberson's leadership was the example he set. After working for Roberson, Dr. Wendell Evans continued to serve as president of Hyles-Anderson College during the years that his late wife, Marlene, faced cancer, and then through her death, and through significant health difficulties of his own. Evans simply kept working. Evans said to me regarding Roberson: "How could I retire as long as he's alive? Where could I go to hide from Dr. Roberson? You never have the nerve to tell [him] you didn't have time to do something. How could you face a man like that, if you retired? He's such a motivator – his life, the fact he just keeps going." Cliff Robinson, one of Roberson's key staff members for many years, said, "You had to be on your toes. You just *had* to do your job. If he gave you something to do – he expected you to do it. All of us close to him realized that – so we did our best to do exactly what he wanted done. Especially Dr. Faulkner! And Dr. Roberson was at it all the time – up early and stay up late at night."

When noted pastor and Christian radio broadcaster Warren Wiersbe spoke at a Highland Park Baptist Church conference, in the midst of a busy conference day he was surprised when Roberson got into a car to go visiting and witnessing. "Where are you going?" Wiersbe asked. Roberson told him he could accomplish six or seven calls that day before the evening church service. Wiersbe immediately purposed in his heart to be a more diligent soul winner. John Maxwell, the prolific evangelical author on the topic of leadership, heard Roberson proclaim in a conference, "Everything rises or falls on leadership!" Maxwell went home that day and purposed to be a leader like Lee Roberson. The late Bill Bright, the famed founder of Campus Crusade for Christ, was sitting one day as a young man in the balcony at a church conference in California when he was inspired by the speaker – Lee Roberson – to sit down and write out his visionary plan for Campus Crusade.

To Roberson, principles of leadership began with personal purity – a right relationship with God for the leader. Roberson always urged his preacher boys to confess their sins and strive personally for clean living. "The one thing that impressed me most about Dr. Roberson was his holy life," said Bob Kelley. It was Roberson's view that a leader must lead not only with words but with his life – setting an example and avoiding personal hypocrisy. "Get involved," Kelley remembered Roberson saying. "Lead with your life. Do something for God!"

As a leader, Roberson would come up with what appeared to be a "spur of the moment" idea and give an assignment to someone. Sometimes he would announce an idea spontaneously from the pulpit, and J.R. Faulkner would grab a pen and paper and be writing it down as Roberson spoke. Fred Afman, a long-time Tennessee Temple Bible teacher, was on his way to teach his seminary class on a cold February day when Dr. Roberson met him on the walk and said, "Fred, I want you to take a radio program." How long of a broadcast is it? "A half-hour." How often do you want me to teach it? "Every day." Okay. In one short walk on campus a half-hour daily radio broadcast was added to Afman's already busy full-time teaching load. "I may have blinked, but I said, 'Yes, sir, I'll do it,'" recalled Afman. Marlene Evans, the late wife of Dr. Wendell Evans, was quite active in the church and college during their years in Chattanooga. During those years Highland Park Baptist Church had a special Sunday evening "forum" for one hour preceding the evening church service. The forum, a time of public training and teaching in the main auditorium, would often include a film, a missionary, or a special guest speaker. Once when the evening forum guest speaker cancelled out on short notice, as Roberson was making the Sunday morning announcements the same day from the pulpit, he declared, "We're going to have a great patriotic program tonight. Mrs. Evans, you'll be in charge of it." For Marlene Evans, who was sitting at the piano, that Sunday morning public announcement was the first she was informed about the program she was to lead that very night. But she worked all day and had the patriotic service ready for that evening! Such a charge was not only challenging, but it was also rewarding, as it showed the confidence that Dr. Roberson had in an individual like Marlene.

Sometimes a person had to scramble to learn and keep up with what Dr. Roberson wanted. Walter Wendelken served for many years as Roberson's assistant pastor for church outreach visitation. When Roberson first became acquainted with Wendelken, he liked what he saw in Walter. So, Roberson took Walter with him to make a pastoral home visit – calling upon four ladies. Roberson put him right to work – Wendelken was to do the talking, as Roberson listened, during the home visit. Years later, Walter, who was awe-struck at the time by Dr. Roberson, told me, "I don't know how to this day I got in or got out [of that home]. I am blank. But I started working the visitation program." Dave Winget, a long-time teacher at Tennessee

Temple, learned always to be prepared to speak in chapel. It was not uncommon for Dr. Roberson to say, "Dave, I want you to speak in chapel tomorrow." Winget said, "You couldn't say, 'I'm not ready.'" During college chapel Roberson once announced from the pulpit in the main auditorium, which had lots of huge windows with no shades: "Dr. Faulkner, tomorrow morning we are going to show a film. I want all those windows blacked out." Faulkner had a team at work that day cutting and taping tin-foil to the windows to make the auditorium as dark as possible for the next day's film. In such incidents, Roberson was showing tremendous confidence in the capabilities of the people upon whom he called. They responded.

In turn, Roberson never forgot his own indebtedness to such faithfulness. When Bill Long unwittingly violated the rules by taking up a love offering for a missionary in his college class, he was corrected in a staff meeting. But Dr. Roberson quickly defended Bill's intentions and dismissed the issue. In his doctoral dissertation at Tennessee Temple, Dr. Faulkner's son, J.R., Jr., who grew up in the church and attended the college there, expressed a remarkable analysis of Roberson's leadership. J.R., Jr., recognized a "fierce loyalty" to Roberson by the people in his ministry at Highland Park – "earned by his love for them and work on their behalf. True leadership is achieved by giving oneself in selfless service to others. This is never done without paying a price. There was never any doubt as to who was in charge at Highland Park. Some called him authoritarian, but church members believed that his authority was earned through sacrificial service to the Lord and the church." Such sacrifice motivated teachers – many of them ordained preachers – to work for a college that could not afford to pay much in salary. But those working at Tennessee Temple caught the vision. "He wanted to win souls, build this church, and God enabled him to do it," said Temple's Nat Phillips. "The school – Dr. Roberson started this thing with something in mind. And even though they couldn't pay much, you just couldn't teach at Tennessee Temple without giving your best and your all!"

One year while Roberson was on a rare vacation, the ministry executive committee dismissed from employment security chief Bill Long and his wife in a financial move to cut back on staff payroll. Part of the Longs' compensation package included dormitory housing and meals, as they served as dorm parents. After the executive committee meeting, two key leaders privately expressed their appreciation to Long for his measured response to his own firing in the meeting and told him not do anything until he met with Dr. Roberson. They accurately figured the firings would not stand, once Roberson became aware of what had transpired in his absence. Sure enough, when Roberson returned from vacation, he called Bill Long into his office and said, "Bill, you just keep going right on like you've been doing. I'll just take care of everything." Three or four weeks later, Long remembered walking down the hallway past Dr. Roberson's office. "He came out and put his arm around my shoulder," Long said. "'Bill,' he said, 'I wonder if you would do me a favor.' I said, 'Sure, anything you say.' 'Would you write a letter to the executive committee and apologize to them for not moving out of the dorm when they ordered you to do that?'" The Longs' jobs were secure. To save face for the committee, all Long was asked to do was to apologize. Dr. Roberson had arranged it all. Of course, Long complied.

Roberson would show loyalty and support to his staff. Whenever E.C. Haskell, Jr., would get upset with action the college board had taken, he would find a sympathetic ear in Dr. Roberson, who would often say, "You're right. Let's take that to the board. You present it, and I'll support you."

As a leader, Roberson never wanted to give the image of being weak or needy or having a problem. He was always top-side in his attitude. To him, leadership meant never expressing his own anger, his own hurts, or his own problems. He never wanted to appear weak or want people to feel sorry for him. He felt that a leader should not talk about his own problems or even illnesses. He was very hard in the pulpit on whiners or the idea of being a whiner or complainer. He felt that a leader should project an image of satisfaction, confidence, and selflessness. A leader should not talk about self or be preoccupied with self – just simply try to please God. And a leader should never be negative in public – always positive.

"He always knew where he was going," said Cliff Robinson. "He was a great motivator. He knew how to motivate, how to get people busy and keep them busy in the work of the Lord. He just kept on pushing evangelism. Thousands were added to the church. One Sunday we had over 10,000 on a special day – that included the chapels. We were running 6,000 in the hey-day in Chauncey-Goode. It was amazing."

Roberson taught generations of preachers a confident style of leadership. J.R. Faulkner was co-teacher of the campus leadership class with Dr. Roberson – a class the preacher boys affectionately called "Robersonology." A key principle taught in leadership was always to exhibit a positive attitude. Roberson insisted on a style of public leadership that was always positive – never negative. "Negatives in public – he was death on that," said Bob Kelley. "He would say, 'Don't be negative! Don't be negative! We don't need that. Young men, always be positive. Be steady.'" Faulkner explained, "You speak like a professional. This is the way it is, man. See, a positive attitude will get a lot of things done – even if what you're trying to do is a delicate matter. If leadership stays positive, it gives confidence to the support and those with whom you're working. So, I deal quite strongly on that positive [attitude]."

The college class on pastoral leadership, taught by Roberson and Faulkner, was influenced by a successful downtown businessman in Chattanooga – a man who was a trustee at the college. The unnamed businessman gave Faulkner a subscription to a monthly business magazine. Each month a biographical sketch of a rags-to-riches success story challenged the reader. "I would look forward to reading it," said Faulkner. "What made each man a success? I would draw material from it – make it part of my notes. That's how I built my syllabus for those boys. That was really a sugar-stick for me – to get that magazine." Roberson was not afraid to learn from secular success stories from everyday life – lessons which could be applied in church ministry. In the Gospel of Luke 16:8, Jesus speaks of the children of this world sometimes being wiser than the children of light in matters of everyday life. When Roberson first moved to Chattanooga, a well-known businessman named Engle owned the minor league baseball team, the Chattanooga Lookouts. He constantly filled Engle Stadium, named after him, through various promotions. Faulkner remembered Roberson saying, "Now, that man knows how to get things done!"

When Randy Ray graduated from Tennessee Temple in the 1970s, Dr. Roberson told him, "Now, Randy, you're big, and you're loud." He slapped his desk and said, "Now, use it! People will listen to you and respond to you when you walk in the room because of your size." Randy later told me, "I never forgot that." My son, Dan Wigton, graduated from Tennessee Temple in 1999. During Dan's years on campus, Dr. Roberson was still active as chancellor of the school he founded. Traveling and speaking, he still maintained an office on campus. Upon graduation, Dan had his first ministry position awaiting him as a youth pastor in Tampa, Florida. The young preacher went in to seek Dr. Roberson's advice. Dan met with Roberson briefly in his office. Dr. Roberson challenged him to act confident in his youth work. He insisted that 22-year-old Dan was to act like he had been doing youth work for 50 years. Dr. Roberson prayed with him. As Dan exited toward the doorway of his office, Dr. Roberson called after him, "Now, remember – 50 years, 50 years!" Dan not only succeeded as a youth pastor, but by age 29 he had become senior pastor of a fairly large church, Lima Baptist Temple in Lima, Ohio.

Lee Roberson always expressed an authoritative confidence. Clarence Sexton, a Tennessee Temple graduate who served on Roberson's pastoral staff, later established a Baptist school named Crown College near Knoxville, Tennessee. As Crown expanded, Sexton planned to add a seminary for ministerial students. He sought Roberson's advice on the idea of naming the seminary, "King Seminary," to go alongside Crown College. Roberson was vigorous in his disapproval. No, he insisted, after all of the advertising for the name "Crown College," the name "Crown" should be carried over to the seminary. Why would you change it then, Roberson asked? Sexton named the new seminary, Crown Seminary.

Such confident insistence earned Roberson the accusation by some of his being a "dictator." Bob Kelley believed that some of the charges of being a dictator stemmed from jealousy on the part of the critics. Ron Bishop, a former employee and strong supporter of Roberson, said, "I heard that word [dictator] so many times it was sickening. I did not think he was a dictator. He was a strong leader." People followed Lee Roberson. But as one Highland Park deacon later said, "It's easy to follow somebody who's not making mistakes." And Roberson was not over-bearing. If he brought a project to the deacons, and there was a negative reaction, he would back off. When he moved forward, it was because he had good reason and the backing of the men. Bill Mattheiss, a long-time deacon, said, "He did not intimidate. When he spoke, you felt like this was what God was leading him in his life. People like to follow when something is happening. There are results. People's lives are being changed. They're going off in the world as missionaries. When things are happening, people don't grumble. We never felt we were being railroaded – 'if you don't do it my way.'" Roberson commanded leadership. When a Sunday school director came in late for a meeting – a businessman who had just come from work, Dr. Roberson would say, "Hi, you need to be here on time." On occasion, Roberson would approach trusted staff members like E.C. Haskell, Jr., and ask for a frank assessment regarding a church or college matter. "I'm asking you this because I feel like you will tell me the truth and not just what you think I want to hear," Haskell recalled hearing from Roberson. "I've got a few men here who tell me just what they think I want to hear – and I don't need them."

The Board of Deacons at Highland Park Baptist Church grew in numbers along with the church – running 65, then 70, then 80, and finally close to 100 deacons – during Lee Roberson's years. In his 90s, Roberson told me that he always had a large board of deacons on purpose. I asked him, why? He said, "Safety, safety." He explained that with a small deacon board, a very few men can begin to control everything the church does. For example, he said, two or three men can dominate a seven-member deacon board. He did not like the idea of a small group of men deciding everything for everyone else in the church. He felt that a larger group would reflect the will of a greater number of the congregation. Plus, with a larger group, the pastor's influence usually carries greater weight. The majority are likely to follow the view of the leader. He added to the size of the group regularly with "deacons-in-training," younger men who would train with the deacons for 12 months. During that time they would meet with the deacons and learn the responsibilities of the deacons. After the 12 months, they would be ordained as deacons with the laying on of hands.

Lee Roberson would send preachers and missionaries out of his independent Baptist college – with no insurance, no retirement plan, and often no funds. Just go. When Sexton started a college, Roberson told him to forget about the cost of the buildings – just put the students in tents, if need be. In other words, Sexton said, "There's the water – jump in! He knew what had to be done – just do it! You read your Bible, pray, go to church, preach, sing, and build."

But Roberson's approach to ministry was not simply based on energy and action. When Bill Long moved from West Virginia to Chattanooga, he found a church and college there which were "the most highly organized I've ever been around. His staff was right in line with carrying out his wishes." Such leadership instilled in the Tennessee Temple family a sense of accountability to what Dr. Roberson said was the right way. "If we drove to West Virginia and started back [to Chattanooga] on a Sunday," said Long, "we *had* to stop some place for church on the way home. One time we had two sick babies. We stopped. She [Mrs. Long] stayed in the nursery with them. We had that drilled into us as Sunday morning, Sunday evening, and Wednesday evening. Accountability! We knew what was expected. We knew what would happen if we didn't fulfill it or carry it out. We did our best to please him."

Roberson was strict and ran a tight ship in such areas as the personal grooming standards he expected of his college students, or permissible music – even in the 1960s and 70s. He did not give in to modern fads. There were no mustaches or beards at Tennessee Temple – unless the individual had worn one for five years before coming to Temple. Security chief Long remembered when Tennessee Temple hosted a national Christian athletic tournament. Long would not admit the pep band for one Christian college because he considered it too jazzy and worldly for Temple's conservative standards. The guest college president protested. When Dr. Roberson arrived, Long told him what he had done and why. Dr. Roberson said, okay. Long never heard another word about it.

Not everyone who followed Roberson's leadership completely agreed with his strict standards of Christian conduct – yet many such people loved him, trusted his walk with God, and followed him regardless. Elgin Smith said, "There were times we didn't agree. We always loved him and always believed in what he was doing. We never supported his trying to force on his constituents his preference in dress, hair, mustache, and so forth. But he was determined. We loved him. We just didn't always agree with him, but we still loved him." Attorney Glenn Copeland saw Roberson's leadership as one of respect, with a loving following. People had confidence he would not lead them astray. They believed he was following God, and they felt that if God was leading him, then whatever he proposed would be successful.

Not one to second-guess himself, Roberson would take risks. In a public church service, Roberson was spontaneous, and people responded to his leadership. He might turn to the church organist in the middle of a song and raise the music by one key. He sought perfection, and he pretty well got what he wanted. In college chapel he would call on a student or faculty member impromptu to sing a song. Orman Norwood learned to carry a song-sheet in his pocket all the time. If Dr. Roberson would call on him without warning, Norwood would hand his song-sheet to the pianist on his way to the platform. Roberson would sometimes spontaneously call on certain individuals to sing his favorite songs.

Roberson felt that key elements to leadership included faithfulness, steadfastness, honesty, and integrity on the part of the leader. Dorothy McCormick, Roberson's longtime secretary, saw it this way: "He was just so respected. The deacons respected him. There was never a split in the church. There was something about him – when he came on the platform. It wasn't that people looked at him as a 'god' or something. When he went to the basketball games, when he walked in, they would all stand up and clap for him. The people loved him. They didn't have to do that. They wanted him there." Such standing applause would occur no matter what point the basketball game was at – when the Robersons walked in. "It was always kind of embarrassing to him," said E.C. Haskell, Jr. "People from other schools [visiting teams] couldn't understand it. 'You guys don't worship him, do you?' No. Respect! It was not anything he expected or demanded."

Haskell saw another side of Roberson which commanded respect. Lee Roberson did not always understand modern cultural matters of the world, nor did he always understand the impact of his own words. But if he made a mistake, he was willing to correct it. People loved that side of him. Haskell remembered when Tennessee Temple music faculty member Joy Martin was leading one of the ministry's choirs in a special Gilbert & Sullivan production. Just prior to a college faculty meeting, a woman church member telephoned Dr. Roberson to complain about the church presenting this musical drama, which the caller termed a "Broadway" production, which had starred Linda Ronstadt. Over the phone Dr. Roberson pleaded that he had no knowledge of it. He walked into the faculty meeting and "chewed out" the staff, Haskell said. "Who approved this? Why are we doing a Broadway production?" he demanded. The first performance was scheduled for that very night. "You could hear a pin drop," Haskell recalled. "For 10 minutes he was upset. I followed him to his office. I said, 'Doc, I got to talk to you.'"

Haskell explained to Dr. Roberson that his words may have been well intended, but that they were demoralizing to the faculty – as if he did not trust their decision-making process. Roberson said, "Well, we're not for Broadway productions." Haskell said, "We're not doing a 'Broadway production.'" He explained to Dr. Roberson that almost no plays or musicals exist which were *not* performed on Broadway. "If it doesn't make it on Broadway," Haskell explained, "it usually does not make it into print. 'Broadway' is a street – not a theater. Everything that we've ever done here has probably been done on Broadway." Haskell later explained, "Now, he had a great respect for Danielle Brown, Dr. Fred Brown's wife. He thought she 'walked on water' – almost. I said, 'Do you know the cantata Mrs. Brown performed with her choir year after year – that's being done on Broadway right now.' He said, 'You're kidding!' I said, 'Dr. Roberson, it's not a matter of a big theater called 'Broadway' – and everything they do is wrong. We can question whether we want to do musicals or plays, but if we're going to do them, we must realize we cannot bring in anything that hasn't been done on Broadway."

Haskell then suggested to Dr. Roberson that his words had really embarrassed the faculty. "There are six faculty members that are performing in this tonight," Haskell told him. Then Roberson said, "Well, if there's nothing wrong with it, they shouldn't feel embarrassed about it." Haskell replied, "But, Doc, you don't have any idea how heavy your words are." Roberson said, "What do you mean?" Haskell told him, "You have the ability – in a sense – of 'life and death' with your words, as far as the faculty is concerned. If you come in, and you're unhappy – and you chew them out, that's heavy to them." Roberson couldn't see it. "He just felt," said Haskell, "I've had my say, and if it's okay, then they ought to do it." Haskell then told him, "I want you to talk to Joy Martin, because I know Joy's probably distraught." Roberson said, "Well, bring her in here." Haskell recalled, "So, I said, 'I'll be right back.' I went up to Joy's office. I said, 'Joy, you're going to go talk to Dr. Roberson.' She said, 'No, I'm not.' I said, 'Yes, you are.' She said, 'If I do, I'll just go in there and just cry.' I said, 'Well, then, you need to do that. He needs to see that, because he doesn't realize how heavy his words were.' She said, 'I'm not going to go.' I said, 'Joy, it would be embarrassing, but if I have to, I'm going to carry you down there.' So, she went. I took her down there. I knocked on the door, closed the door and left. She did end up crying. Dr. Roberson told Mrs. Martin, 'I have full confidence in you. He's [E.C.] given me a little explanation about what you're doing, and I'm sure what you are doing will be all right, and I'll be there tonight.' He loved it. The next day in chapel, 'How many were there? Only going to be performed two more times. Now, I want every student, every faculty member to be there.'" Such a gesture on Roberson's part increased the respect of the faculty for him and his leadership.

Haskell recalled another time Dr. Roberson apologized. Roberson walked into college chapel one day and misunderstood a skit the students were performing to promote an evangelistic outreach. He thought he was interrupting horse-play on the platform. He clapped his hands and said, "Chapel's over! Go to your classes!" The president of the student body later explained to Roberson that he had witnessed a creative announcement for "Round-Up Sunday," a Sunday school evangelistic emphasis. Roberson, who loved and fully supported Round-Up Sunday, got up in chapel the next day and apologized before the student body. "I was wrong," he said. "I made a quick judgment." His confession served to endear him to the students.

J.R. Faulkner saw in Roberson certain characteristics which put him "head and shoulders" above other preachers as a leader. When Roberson was in his 90s and Faulkner in his late 80s, Dr. Faulkner said to me about Roberson, "He was a man of his word – great character, great integrity. He lived what he preached. He gave by example what he was asking the congregation to do from the pulpit – to this very day he is continuing it in his retirement years. He would not forsake his pulpit." Walter Wendelken said, "The key was his own conviction and dedication to the Lord. He was not interested in money. He was very frugal. He expected the same from others. The salaries of the church and school were not exorbitant – just the minimum. He himself lived that way. That's why so many others were willing."

Whatever it is about someone that causes them to be a leader, Lee Roberson had it. Veteran missionary Jerry Reece saw several things that make people follow a leader: "He had a certain charisma that gives confidence. He chose the right path. You were motivated to follow. You saw those kinds of leadership qualities in Dr. Roberson. There never seemed to be a doubt as to what he wanted to do. And the people gladly followed his leadership – the way he set up leadership in the church, where men were in on decisions and the important things presented to the people. The church seemed to be running very smoothly, especially in those days when we were growing so rapidly."

During Reece's student days at Tennessee Temple, he had been a class officer. But he did not consider himself a prominent student, and he did not see Dr. Roberson very often. After 15 years of serving on the mission field in Central America, Jerry Reece and his wife, Gail, returned to Chattanooga, where Jerry was scheduled to speak to a missions group on the Tennessee Temple campus. When he saw Dr. Roberson on campus, Jerry was stunned when Roberson called him by name, saying, "Hello, Jerry, how are you doing?" Reece said, "I could not believe it – after all the hundreds of students, 15 years later!" Roberson never forgot a name or where you were from. "He was an unusual individual," said Jerry Mattheiss. "Nobody else like him."

At times Lee Roberson almost seemed to possess a sense of divine intuition. Roberson baptized Bob Kelley at Highland Park when Kelley was 19 years old. As Kelley was changing into his street clothes after the baptism, he overheard Dr. Roberson say to an associate, "Tommy, I think that boy will preach." That statement stayed with Kelley as if it were prophetic. He said he never forgot it. The surprising thing was that at the time Kelley was baptized Dr. Roberson did not know him personally. "He could sense when someone would preach, when someone would fail, or could not be trusted," said Kelley. "He knew whom to avoid." Bob Kelley was to become one of the leading independent Baptist preachers in America, serving 43 years as a pastor of churches in West Virginia, Tennessee, and South Carolina. A well-known pastor in Florida had a similar story. As a young man, this individual was in the army – singing with an ensemble in a Baptist church where Roberson was the guest preacher. He overheard Roberson say to someone, "I believe that boy will be a preacher." He was soon called to preach and served the same large Baptist church for 35 years.

Roberson's confident authority stayed with him all his life. In later years he conducted a funeral service at a funeral home where he had ministered countless times through the years. The grandson of the funeral home's founder was now operating the funeral home. The funeral service did not start on time. The casket bearing the body of the deceased was brought in late. Everything was running late. And the young funeral director was not wearing a suit coat. Time was valuable to Lee Roberson, and doing things right was important. Dr. Roberson corrected the young funeral director right then and there. "Your grandfather would never have run it like this. He was always on time!" said Roberson.

However, when Roberson was not the one in charge, he could graciously adjust. During Roberson's early years in Chattanooga, a young Garland Cofield traveled with him to a revival meeting in a small, rural Southern Baptist church. Dr. Roberson sat on the front row, awaiting his turn to preach. Cofield was seated in the back of the sanctuary. "Everyone was shouting and praising God," said Cofield. "When they introduced him, they were going about things – doing things that never would have happened at Highland Park. I was in that service – people shouting up in the choir. Hands up – going up and down the aisle. When they introduced him, he said, 'I don't have a clue as to where I am, but I'm having a great time.' He could roll with the punches. It was so different from his normal service at Highland Park."

CHAPTER 7

"We Had No Days Off!"

Lee Roberson's work ethic, professionalism, consistency, and commitment to the Lord were legendary throughout the Highland Park Baptist Church and Tennessee Temple University family and much of the independent Baptist movement. He lived his life by schedule. His wife, Caroline, once said that when Lee was out of town she knew exactly what he was doing by looking at her watch. J.R. Faulkner told me, "His schedule was so rigid you could set your clock by it. He could leave out of here after his radio broadcast on Monday morning or after chapel, depending on his flight. He liked never to miss chapel and always hoped his plane would leave later. He was away for meetings Monday and Tuesday, and Wednesday morning he was right back on the radio." Those who knew him called Roberson the most disciplined man they ever knew.

People who worked closely with Roberson and knew his schedule recognized him as a man of routine. He sought deliberately to develop certain habits and hold to them. He would rise daily at 6:00 AM. On rare occasions, if he were ill, he might turn the alarm off and sleep a bit. Otherwise, he was up at 6:00 every day. Roberson and his wife would individually have their personal devotions with the Lord – in Scripture and prayer – until 6:15. Breakfast with his wife was at 6:30 – he ate the same thing for breakfast every day, and then the couple would have a devotional time of daily worship together. Neighbors would see Dr. Roberson step out on the front porch of his house and pick up the daily newspaper at exactly the same time each day – you could set your clock by it! When Roberson was traveling, he kept a similar schedule. He would leave the motel for breakfast at 6:30 AM.

On the many days when he was home, Roberson would read the morning newspaper, watch the TV news, and then go to his study to prepare for the morning radio broadcast. Lunch was at 12:00 noon, and dinner at 5:30 PM. Every morning Roberson would come to his church office by 8:00. His live radio program was broadcast from his pulpit in the church's main auditorium from 8:30 to 9:00. From 9 AM to 10:00 he was in his office. College chapel was at 10:00 AM Mondays, Wednesdays, and Fridays. After chapel he would counsel with students until 12:00 noon. After traveling most Mondays and Tuesdays, he was back in town every Wednesday for lunch with his wife. For many years she would join him and they would dine in the school cafeteria with the students. Because of his traveling and short nights, often he would go home for a nap between 1:00 and 2:00 PM. He had the ability to relax and fall completely asleep for 20 minutes or so, and then get up and go back to work. After lunch he would return to the office and sign his letters of correspondence – already typed by his secretary, and then make pastoral visits – primarily to the hospitals – until 4:00 or 5:00 PM. Thursday afternoons he would visit the nursing homes. That was his pattern "every day of the world that he's in town," said J.R. Faulkner.

Traveling on Mondays and Tuesdays, Roberson would keep the same schedule as much as possible – beginning with his search for breakfast each day at 6:30 AM. He would pretty much accept invitations to preach wherever he was invited. "People would request my coming. I encouraged it. I liked to be home Wednesday through Sunday," he said. He would be back in the office on Wednesday – always making all the hospital calls himself Wednesday through Friday. "I would get my sermon, and on Sunday preach," he said. By Friday he would go to all the college activities – all the recitals, the ballgames, etc., attending everything that he could.

"The dedication of that man – I tell you," said Faulkner. "I was so awed by the price he would pay to set a right example before these students. Traveling all night long and then coming right on in here at 8:00, 8:30, without a wink of sleep. Maybe wash his face and shave; get a bite of breakfast; come right to the radio broadcast; go through that – 10:00 be in chapel for an hour with the kids. Then right into his office. Read his mail and take it home with him – 12:15 home, grab a bite of lunch, sleep an hour – maybe; dictate another hour or so; by 3:00 he'd be down here getting his hospital list. He'd be visiting those sick in the hospital." Walter Wendelken felt the same way as Faulkner. He said, "I could not physically possibly keep up with his schedule. He could be in an airport at 2:00 or 3:00 in the morning – study and read the Bible, waiting on an airplane. I suppose he napped. He never mentioned it."

During his first year at Highland Park, Roberson invited the famous gospel musician, Homer Rodeheaver, to lead the music during a revival. Rodeheaver, who carried a big trombone, was then elderly. He had worked for years with the renowned evangelist Billy Sunday. In his sermon, *The Hourglass Sermon*, Roberson told about the day Rodeheaver took the 33-year-old Lee Roberson aside. He recounted Rodeheaver's words, "Young man, I'm afraid you are going to go too far. Some of your members have come to me about the way you work and preach. They think you're too enthusiastic. I recommend that you take it easy, that you not work and preach quite as fast. Relax a little more. Take a little more time in what you're doing." When Rodeheaver finished, Roberson responded, "Mr. Rodeheaver, you take care of the music, and I'll take care of the preaching." Rodeheaver then graciously apologized, approvingly comparing Roberson's work pace with the legendary Billy Sunday's.

While Roberson traveled for many years by airplane, in the early years at Chattanooga he often drove by car to speak in church meetings. Garland Cofield, later a missionary, and other young men of the church would often ride with Roberson to sing at his meetings. "We traveled around with him," recalled Cofield. "He'd go out sometimes two or three times per week at night. We would sing and start off the service, then ride back to Chattanooga with him." Cofield remembered that Roberson was always on the go – "He would eat a meal quickly – before you got through your salad!" Because the team would often return to Chattanooga as late as 1:00 or 2:00 AM, most of the boys would fall asleep in the car while Roberson drove. But Garland would stay awake and pepper Roberson with questions. Roberson would keep talking and driving. As they drove, in order to protect his throat and voice from any draft, Roberson would never lower the car window. "How do you stay awake?" Garland would ask. "Well, I lift up my left foot and just hold it," was Roberson's answer. Years later when a young man fell asleep in the Bible institute, Roberson publicly gave him the same advice – raise your left foot off the floor and hold it up in the air in order to stay awake!

Jerry Reece, a very successful missionary with Baptist International Missions, Inc., remembered his freshman year at Tennessee Temple hearing Dr. Roberson say in chapel, "Now, young men, if you really spend more than five hours in bed, you're lazy. You shouldn't get used to sleeping too long." Reece said, "He had the ability to get along on a small amount of sleep. That was amazing to me. He was going like a house afire. I need a little more sleep than he does. I tried it for about two weeks. He would fly all night and come to chapel. We knew, and that was impressive to us. Once in awhile you catch him nodding – not much."

During his pastorate in Fairfield, Alabama, and in his early years at Highland Park, Roberson frequently traveled away from his own pulpit to hold revival meetings. He would sometimes be away preaching at other churches, even on Sundays – with someone else filling his own pulpit. With the tremendous growth of the Highland Park ministry, Roberson began to have second thoughts about being away so much of the time. Then, when he was holding a 10-day revival meeting in Waycross, Georgia, he received a long-distance phone message that his chairman of the deacons, Bob Shedd, had just died. The funeral service was arranged for Sunday afternoon. Roberson loved Shedd and deeply appreciated his support at Highland Park Baptist Church. Shedd was the deacon chairman when the church called Roberson as pastor. It was Shedd who first gave Roberson a tour of the Highland Park facilities. Roberson went to considerable trouble to arrange a private flight home to conduct the funeral and then return to the revival at Waycross. On the flight, as he pondered and prayed, he decided to give up extended revival meetings. He began immediately to cancel such engagements. He was confident that this was the Lord's leading in his life. Thereafter, he began confining his travels primarily to two-day meetings on Mondays and Tuesdays each week. He would accept all such meetings with the understanding that he would cancel, if the needs of his pastorate in Chattanooga demanded so, but he found that to be rarely necessary. For many years as he traveled, Roberson would fly out of Chattanooga to Atlanta on the same schedule every Monday morning. From Atlanta it was on to Tampa or New York City or Chicago or wherever.

Roberson told me that he did most of his sermon studying at night – some in the mornings, but mostly at night after hours. He kept a dictaphone at home and would dictate sermons. His secretary would type them out later. In the early years – before the days of dictation taping – he would dictate directly to his secretary. In the later years he would leave her a dictation tape by the time he went to the Wednesday 10 AM college chapel service.

Lee Roberson had a strong physical constitution. E.C. Haskell, Jr., who worked directly under Roberson at Tennessee Temple, said, "I don't think that anything he eats bothers him. He doesn't lay awake at night. He had a hard time understanding anyone with an illness. I used to tell him he was a V-8 engine and doesn't understand others who have a V-6 or V-4. 'We're going to get there, but not as fast as you. Everyone can't operate the same as you do. It doesn't mean they're weak. It's the way they're built.' That helped him."

Haskell once traveled with Dr. Roberson to a revival meeting in Peoria, Illinois, where E.C. led the singing and, of course, Roberson preached. That night a 16-inch snowstorm kept them from flying out after the service. "He was really distraught that he couldn't get out the next morning," Haskell remembered. "So, I told him, 'I have to go to Indianapolis. I'll take you. You can catch a plane there.' He said, 'Let's leave tonight. I'll pay for the gas and the food.' We drove. I literally had to watch the fence-posts [to stay on the road – because of the snow]. I got him to the airport in the morning. He caught his plane. We must have stopped two or three times for hamburgers. He'd say, 'I think we need another hamburger.' He was funny!"

Roberson's work ethic rubbed off on those around him. "We had no days off," said J.R. Faulkner. "I didn't have a day off except the afternoon on Saturday after lunch." Jerry Reece said, "I can remember as a student seeing Dr. Faulkner take a handful of vitamins and swallow them at once. I thought – how in the world does he do that?" Those who worked for Roberson knew his pattern, and they had to be dedicated in order to keep up with him. His secretary, Dorothy McCormick, said, "He got what he wanted because you wanted to do it." She would work Saturdays and Sundays for him. She would type his correspondence letters on Sunday, so he could leave town on Monday to go preach in other cities. "You did it because you loved your work, and you respected him," she said. I asked Dorothy if she was paid extra for such weekend work. "No, sir!" she said. Dorothy wasn't the only one who worked like that. Many people would not put in that kind of schedule, but some did for him. Louzelle Ware, McCormick's predecessor, put in the extra hours for years. "She probably spoiled him," Dorothy said. "But you did it voluntarily. Sometimes he needed it. He didn't have to ask. He knew you'd do it." Did she feel taken advantage of? "Not at all," she said. In Roberson's later years, his secretary, Gloria Shadowens, followed suit. "I always did whatever he needed done," she told me. "I just knew to do it – whatever he needed done."

This relentlessly expectant atmosphere generated even more pressure on the pastoral staff. Working for him, in one word, was "intense," said Clarence Sexton. "He expected you to have someone saved, down the aisle and baptized every service. He employed people to make it happen." Roberson used to say that he had a 40-hour job for anyone who could consistently win souls to Christ and get them down the church aisle to make a public profession of faith on Sunday. Oftentimes Roberson would come up with new ideas – maybe a full orchestra for the next Sunday, or, a band playing with Dr. John R. Rice visiting on the coming Sunday. "That was the cue – you do it!" said Sexton. "All the time!" A whiner or complainer did not work for Lee Roberson.

Although there was a college administrative staff meeting every Saturday morning, the church pastoral staff did not have regular staff meetings, nor did the secretarial staff. For many years, the church pastoral staff consisted of just three assistants working with Dr. Roberson – J.R. Faulkner, Cliff Robinson, and Walter Wendelken. Faulkner was Roberson's top associate. The church music was among his many duties. Cliff Robinson handled the college. Wendelken was in charge of visitation – pastoral calls, evangelistic soul winning, shut-ins, homebound, hospital, nursing homes, etc. Roberson would take the lead in organizing the Thursday night evangelistic visitation.

"The pastoral staff – we were meeting constantly," Faulkner told me years later. "You don't have a staff meeting. We never had but three men helping Dr. Roberson – Walter Wendelken, Cliff Robinson, and me. We ran the place. Now-a-days there are 25 people. We had 4,000 in school, Sunday school meeting everywhere, three church services in the main auditorium, Phillips Chapel and the gymnasium. Choir. Ushers. Baptizing. It's a different day now. Preachers get tired and take a week off. 'I gotta go rest.' Rest?! But with Dr. Roberson, we never heard of resting! I sleep at night. We live in a different day."

"You don't have a staff meeting with Lee Roberson," said Sexton. "You wait for his prompting. You already knew what he wanted – you just go do it." But Roberson did want reports each week from the pastoral staff. Sexton recalled the day when Dr. Roberson kept getting requests that staff meetings be held. One staff member, whose first name was Ed, pointed out to him that "everyone across the country" holds church pastoral staff meetings. "All right, all right," Roberson said. He agreed to hold a staff meeting that Thursday at 8:30 AM as soon as he finished the radio broadcast. Sexton was there. "I remember," he said. "We're all sitting around the balcony. Dr. Roberson spoke up, 'All right, Ed, you wanted to have a staff meeting. What do you want to talk about?' That was the last staff meeting."

Still, Roberson was always available for his staff. To communicate with Dr. Roberson, a staff member would first send a note to Roberson's office, which was right next door to J.R. Faulkner's office. "I would see him at least once a week," said Wendelken. "When I needed to see him, he was available. I kept close contact with him over visitation. Whenever I felt his presence was important, he would always go. He would come in on Wednesday mornings sometimes without any sleep at all and go right on all day – maybe to a funeral. We ministered to our members and friends [of the church]."

Roberson was always there with his staff for the Thursday evening supper for all workers before the big evening church visitation outreach. After the supper, prior to visitation, the Sunday school leaders would meet with Roberson for about 15 minutes. He also would meet with the college faculty Thursdays at 10:00 AM, and he met with the finance committee once a month before a Wednesday evening church service. Likewise, he met Saturday mornings with the administrative staffs of the schools.

In Lee Roberson's pastorates, the leader of the church was very much the pastor. "The whole system's built on the premise the pastor should be the overseer of the whole thing," said Faulkner. "Some people didn't like that." Yet Roberson valued his deacons and met with them monthly. When a man was nominated for deacon, Roberson would bring him into his office, review his qualifications and tell him what was expected of a deacon. He would approve the men chosen by the selection committee, and then the committee would report to the church. "We had at one time 60 or 70 deacons," said Roberson. "Good men, solid men. Never miss a service. All were tithers. Strong. Helped the work to go on." Roberson would usually float new ideas — "about buildings, about what we should do," he said – publicly to the church, and then meet with the deacons to discuss and decide. It was Roberson's goal to make known to all the people what the church was going to do – and to keep nothing hidden from the church.

Deacons' meetings were short, concise, and brief. Attorney Glenn Copeland, a longtime deacon, said, "He'd tell you what his thoughts were, and everybody would approve it and go right on. There were not any knock-down, drag-out meetings." I asked Copeland if the deacons were "yes-men." His response: "I don't think so. We respected him. We knew he was very intelligent. A man of God. Our leader. We didn't question that. Normally his ideas succeeded. They went through. He had a vision." Bill Mattheiss agreed: "We realized he was God's man." The deacon board of 65 to 70 men – and later almost 100 – included mostly middle class laymen, but also a number of professional men – several bankers, several real estate men, several attorneys, and many businessmen. Roberson enjoyed widespread support. For a time, there was one deacon who seemed to oppose everything. But Roberson loved him, too. In the meetings Roberson would say with a smile, "Someone has got to oppose it."

Dr. E.C. Haskell Sr., a dentist, was the chairman of the deacon board for 30 years. Haskell was the type of dentist who would open his dental office from 8:00 to 9:00 PM on a Saturday to put a temporary crown on the tooth of a suffering missionary who had just arrived home from the mission field. Dr. Roberson once told E.C. Haskell Jr. that his father, E.C. Sr., was Roberson's best friend. Dr. Haskell was viewed as a fine man, but not the leader of the church. Roberson was the leader. One deacon said kindly, it was a "one-man church."

Coach Ron Bishop, whose basketball teams won national championships at Tennessee Temple, had a unique position in that he was highly visible on the sports pages and TV sports news of Chattanooga. His success gave Temple a lot of publicity and influenced the public image of the college. Roberson had confidence in Bishop. "He would call me," said Bishop. "He would mentor me and coach me – to make sure the impact on the city was what he wanted. We respected each other. I knew what would please him and what would bring him displeasure." Bishop, also a preacher and pastor, later founded SCORE International, a sports evangelistic ministry. On one occasion when Bishop preached at a church conference with Roberson, the two stayed in motel rooms next to one another. "For the first time in my life I stayed in a motel room and never turned the TV on," said Bishop. "I had so much respect for him – I didn't want him to think I watched TV all the time. I feared I'd be watching a ballgame, and he'd be there reading and studying his Bible."

Bishop's goal was always to please Roberson, with whom he had a great working relationship. But Bishop knew what it was to see Roberson upset with staff members who missed church services or missed chapel. "I've seen him get very agitated," Bishop said. "He raises his voice. He turns red in the face, and if you're in his office, he'll stand up. You know the interview's over. If you worked for him, you knew."

Bill Mattheiss, who handled finances in the college, saw a great sense of respect – even fear – among those who worked for Dr. Roberson. Yet he himself considered it easy to work for Roberson. Mattheiss said, "For example, on one occasion I made the payroll decision to pay the students, and we ran over several thousand dollars. He called me in and said, 'What is this about?' I explained. He said, 'You made the decision, and I will stand behind you.'"

Mattheiss recalled that Roberson always wanted to know where his employees stood spiritually, as well as being very interested in them and how they were doing with their jobs. The ministry's large staff was remarkably free of widespread disobedience or independence, scandal or moral corruption. "You just didn't see it here," said Mattheiss. Roberson maintained high expectations in hiring. For years, said Mattheiss, Roberson would not hire a divorcee. There were no second marriages among the ministry staff. Nor would he hire people he considered flamboyant or flashy.

Those who worked for Roberson had tremendous confidence in his integrity. "He was a man of impeccable integrity," said Bishop. "This man was a man of great character and integrity. He was faithful. When he said something, it was credible. He was loyal. If you worked for Dr. Roberson and you did what you were supposed to do, he would be loyal to you. This is a man of credibility. Whatever he says, I can believe."

Those who worked for him tried to keep up with him. Roberson had a reputation for saying he would rather wear out than rust out. He would say that he was going to keep going as long as he could. Time proved him right.

Lee Roberson had a life-long habit of going to the office daily – even on Thanksgiving Day or Christmas Day. In later years he would return home from his Highland Park Baptist Church office at noon on Christmas, with a comment such as, "Honey, I'm back from the office. There's nobody down there. I just don't understand that." He always went in on Saturdays, too. The first interview he granted me for this biography was on a Saturday morning in his office at Highland Park Baptist Church. He was the only one there. He was the one who let me in the door on a rainy, chilly Saturday morning. On a holiday, he would want to stay out of the way of the family preparing food in the morning, so he would go to the office. He was the type of man who wanted everything on time. So, he was home by 12:00 noon for the holiday meal. If the meal was not ready, he would come out to the kitchen and stand and wait. He was a man of habit, a man of schedule.

Although Roberson could be rigid, those who worked directly for him considered Roberson kind, considerate, and very caring for them personally. Strong in the pulpit, Roberson had a pleasant sense of humor one-to-one. But he did not put up with any foolishness. No one kidded with him much, although Cliff Robinson was one who did joke with him occasionally. "He gave you lots of leeway," Dorothy McCormick said. "You just knew you needed to have the work done. He would never say to you, 'Do this.'"

Roberson turned to his staff constantly for assistance and details. For example, Dorothy explained, Roberson would ask her, "'Who's my attorney?' I'd say, Glenn Copeland. 'Get him on the phone.' He'd always talk to him. 'Who's my man?' 'Who's this?' I learned more phone numbers and names." Roberson would call Copeland for advice on legal issues or public laws. He did not have time for little nit-picky things. Roberson gave Dorothy freedom in hiring the student scholarship girls who assisted her in the office. "He left that up to me," she said. E.C. Haskell Jr. said Roberson was a "lion" in the pulpit but a "lamb" in his office. "It was amazing," said E.C., "so I felt if I ever wanted anything, I'm going into his office. He was great to deal with!"

Roberson used a dictaphone in preparing his sermon outlines for typing, as well as for his correspondence letters. In his early years, prior to electronic dictation, he would dictate directly to his secretary, but in later years he seldom gave dictation directly to a secretary. Much of his dictation he did at home. For example, his secretary would type Wednesday afternoon his sermon outline for what he was going to preach Wednesday night. There was always a certain amount of pressure from his fast-paced style and busy schedule. On Saturday mornings during his pastorate when Roberson came in for the staff meeting for the schools he would bring in one or two old-fashioned dictation belts for his secretary. The dictation might include a letter to a missionary in some far off African or Asian location, with a geographiuc name which was difficult to pronounce. His secretary would hear Roberson's voice on the dictation tape, "Whew! What a name!"

Roberson always used a black, felt-tipped pen to sign his name, write notes, or edit his sermons. He wrote in large handwriting. "Everything was big with him," said Dorothy. "He used a felt pen – black, the kind with a little white ring around the top. He would get his pocket-knife out and whittle the white plastic ring off every one. He didn't like it when they made new, fine-point felt pens. He liked the old-fashioned felt pen. You could write big and black!"

Consistent with his precise character, Lee Roberson never liked anything to be messy – the office, the desk, or the desk drawers. He wanted everything business-like. He wanted everything done properly, in order, and with proper authority. When someone came on campus without authorization to sell eggs to the students, he was upset and ordered the eggs out. He did not like clutter. He would occasionally get angry with those working for him. But as one of his staff said, the anger would never last. "He never belittled you, or was critical, or cut you down in front of others," said Dorothy McCormick.

As he was always professional and proper, there were no personal gifts from Lee Roberson to his female secretaries. Mrs. Roberson might bring them a gift from a trip – perhaps a Bible from the Holy Land. Mrs. Roberson would see to it that the secretaries received Christmas gifts. She handled all such matters. Dr. Roberson was always careful and respectful about his relationships with people and about even any potential appearance in such relationships. There was never a hint of impropriety in his life.

To work directly for Dr. Roberson was considered an honor. "I felt so proud to be his secretary," said Dorothy McCormick. Ron Bishop said, "I would have rather died when I was a coach at Tennessee Temple than to do anything that would bring reproach on his name, as well as the name of Tennessee Temple, Highland Park – not to mention the name of the Lord. I greatly respected him to the point of fear."

When Gloria Shadowens' husband enrolled as a ministerial student, she began working in the campus offices. She was Ron Bishop's secretary for one year in the dean of students' office. One Saturday evening later in Roberson's ministry he called her at home. "I need some letters typed," she recalled him saying on the phone. "Can you come in and do them for me on Monday?" On Monday she completed his letters, and then returned to her office. He called again on Tuesday and asked for more help. The procedure was repeated both Thursday and Friday, whereupon Roberson said, "When are you moving your stuff over here?" She was hired. "It floored me," she said. "Assuming I was going to be his secretary had not entered my mind. 'Well, go get your stuff!'" She was thrilled. She said it was an honor to be his secretary then for more than a quarter of a century. Gloria knew that Roberson's previous secretary, Dorothy McCormick, seemed always to be afraid of him – despite her love and admiration for him. "I thought I would be afraid, too," Gloria said. "I feared I might fail. I thought maybe he would be hard. But he was totally easy to work for. He was very talkative sometimes. I loved that. He would come out and sit down and start talking about school days, earlier days – the early days at Tennessee Temple. I loved that."

Bill Mattheiss said he never knew anyone who did not enjoy their position working in Dr. Roberson's ministry – despite limited salaries. "I can't remember ever seeing dissatisfaction," he said. "That speaks volumes – to keep our staff happy."

No matter how busy Lee Roberson was, he gave people the impression that he had time for everyone. While it might take weeks to receive an appointment with a pastor of another large ministry, Roberson made himself available almost anytime. A visit in his office would not last long – even for a faculty member, usually 10 to 15 minutes. "He'll graciously have you outside before you know what has happened," said Jerry Mattheiss. "But what he has said to you in the 10 to 15 minutes will speak volumes!" Nevertheless, he always had time for anyone who came in. Skillfully, he would listen for a few minutes, give his advice, pray with you, and before you knew it, you were out the door. He would drop to one knee, he would put his hand on your shoulder – if you were a man, and he would pray.

Students would come in with a reverential fear but would be greeted by a warm handshake which would completely disarm them. If you sent him a card or letter, you would get a thank-you note in return.

To travel with Dr. Roberson was a privilege a few staff members enjoyed and to which they looked forward. Many of the Tennessee Temple graduates, pastors and missionaries, would look forward to preaching with him at a conference or hosting him as a guest preacher. But they found him to be a very private man. "I don't think you'd ever meet a more private man," said Clarence Sexton. Cliff Robinson remembered traveling as Roberson had books out in the car and was working on sermons, while Cliff did the driving. Roberson was a man of few words. "I don't know that he ever said anything about a ballgame that happened yesterday," said Faulkner. "With you and me here – just talking, 'Hey, did you see that game yesterday?' I don't recall that ever happening in the 40 years that we were working so closely together." Even Roberson's wife, to whom he was very close and totally devoted, said he could drive down the road for miles and not say a word. Walter Wendelken, said, "I never saw any preacher so free of mannerisms, quirks, or expressions. He knew what to say and how to say it in a few words. He was very good at that. He was always emphasizing that he wanted people to work and live for the Lord."

Roberson never socialized much – even with his key staff members – and never seemed to have real close friends, other than his wife. Wendelken recalled being at Roberson's home only on rare occasions – such as a supper for bus workers. Wendelken could remember only one occasion when Roberson took the senior staff and their wives out to eat together – it was to a Mexican restaurant. "Dr. Roberson had everyone at arm's length," said Wendelken. "Dr. Haskell – I suppose – was as close to him as any church member. But Dr. Haskell could never get 'on the inside.' He [Haskell] mentioned that to me. Dr. Roberson didn't want people to say he had favorites, that he liked anyone above someone else." When Roberson would ride in a car alone with Wendelken going to a funeral, Wendelken recalled, "He would do most of the talking – about the church, the work, his goals – things like that. He never disclosed intimate information – as far as I know. He never did to anyone – problems, disappointments, successes were never spoken of." Roberson's sister, Darlene Munafo, said, "He was the type of man – he would never tell you his problems. If he had a problem at all – he's not going to tell you. He's not like that. He's a very inward person. He may feel something, but you're not going to know it." Roberson was not one to do personal favors or give gifts to the staff. But always, Wendelken said, there was an intense loyalty to him because of his own intense life of serving God.

"I attended very few social gatherings," Roberson told me. "I didn't go. They had them, but I didn't go. They knew I wouldn't go – meetings of different types in homes. I rarely went to any of them." According to Faulkner, "He put in appearances. He just went in and shook hands and was gone. He never stood around. He was no man for idling his time away. Never. After church, only if he hadn't had supper, he would stop [at a restaurant] with his wife. Never with preachers." With a laugh, Faulkner added, "I went many times in lieu of the fact he wouldn't. I remember taking the man who was head of the New England fellowship of pastors out." Tom Wallace said of Roberson, "He was real blunt. He would speak real short, and that was it. You couldn't drag him into a long conversation about anything." On the phone, Dr. Roberson would never talk long — strictly business. "If I wanted to know what was going on," said Wendell Evans, "I would talk with Mrs. Roberson!" The only way to engage Lee Roberson in conversation was to talk about ideas and ask him questions, according to Evans. Roberson would not talk about people.

As a rule, Lee Roberson would not go out to eat with preachers after an evening church service. Most preachers make it a habit to do that very thing. But early in Roberson's ministry, when he invited preachers to his house for refreshments after an evening service, two well-known preachers got into an argument over biblical prophecy. It disturbed Roberson so much that he said, "I'll never do that again."

Roberson generally made an exception for Clyde Box and his wife, Betty, who would often join Lee and Caroline Roberson for fellowship at home or at a restaurant – even after an evening church service. Box, who served for many years as the pastor of Brook Hollow Baptist Church in the Dallas suburb of DeSoto, Texas, became a frequent guest speaker at Highland Park and a recurrent social guest of Roberson. For one reason, Box was always upbeat in attitude and spirit and made Roberson laugh. For another, Box did not talk about people. God knit their hearts together during a 1976 trip to the Holy Land. They enjoyed eating together. Clyde and Betty Box often ate chicken in the college dining hall with the Robersons. "He ate chicken with a fork," Box said with a laugh. "I couldn't. I ate it like you're supposed to eat it!"

J.R. Faulkner once traveled with Roberson on a missions trip to the islands of the Caribbean Sea. Roberson preached, while J.R. led the singing. They visited St. Thomas, Antigua, and other places, preaching for missionaries such as Ray Thompson of BIMI. "In Puerto Rico we spent a night together in the same room," said Faulkner with a laugh. "We slept in the same bed together. I liked to roll out – I was so afraid I would touch him. I couldn't sleep. That was where we didn't have water to take a bath. It was primitive. They had to boil our water – issue enough to wash your face. If you wanted a bath, you would go to the ocean."

Looking back over his career, Roberson told me he tried to treat all staff and deacons the same way – on an even basis. For example, he deliberately did not socialize with his deacons outside the meetings – "like some pastors who will go with their deacons on trips," such as vacations, he said. "I was afraid of that," he said. "I just treated them all fairly and squarely – and met with them every time they met. I didn't have any close association with any one of them above another. They were all the same way." I asked him why. "You get criticized, if you do that," he said, "and I felt I would. Like some pastors take trips with their deacons and family. They'll be gone for 10 days. I did none of that. I didn't want them to feel that I played one above another. I tried to teat them all the same way."

Lee Roberson was loyal to his staff and lay leaders. Shortly before Roberson retired from the pastorate of Highland Park Baptist Church, a staff member warned him that some of the church leaders might not be loyal to Roberson's desires in selecting a successor. "Dr. Roberson rebuked me," the staff member told me. "[He said], 'These men have been loyal to me for 40 years. I'm going to be loyal to them.'"

Lee Roberson never changed very much, even as he became a world-famous preacher. To the day he died, his phone number was still in the phone book. And as long as he served as pastor of the church, until nearly age 75, he himself visited all church members in the hospitals and the nursing homes.

CHAPTER 8

Barnabas

Ben Haden, the nationally renowned evangelical TV preacher, served as the pastor of First Presbyterian Church in Chattanooga for 31 years during the same time when Lee Roberson was pastor of Highland Park Baptist Church. Haden was not particularly close to Roberson and his ministry, but he knew Roberson and watched the extraordinary Highland Park ministry from a close distance. Haden saw in Roberson's long-time associate, J.R. Faulkner, "a real Barnabas" – a comparison to the Apostle Paul's faithful associate, co-worker and co-traveler on Paul's missionary journeys in the New Testament book of Acts. "Dr. Faulkner was as wonderful a team player as I have ever seen," Haden said. "I would wonder – in private, I would love to know how much credit he is to his [Roberson's] ministry. I'd give anything if I would have had that man – and I've had some good ones. But I've never had a man like Dr. Faulkner. He takes the back seat. He's gracious." Black evangelist Ed Carter, a Tennessee Temple University graduate, saw the ministry relationship of Faulkner and Roberson like that of Aaron and Moses in the Bible.

Just as Roberson's endeavors were becoming celebrated across the world, Faulkner's loyalty and work ethic were emerging as legendary in Baptist circles. With a laugh, Orman Norwood, director of the International Board of Jewish Missions in Chattanooga, remembered the day when someone asked Dr. Roberson what he would do if J.R. Faulkner were to leave him. Roberson reportedly said, "I'd hire five other men and go right on!" Faulkner, said Norwood, was the man behind the throne – a man who was totally devoted to Lee Roberson. The secret of the two men's combined achievement proved to be how much work Faulkner accomplished on behalf of Roberson. Referring to the extraordinary ministry of Highland Park Baptist Church and Tennessee Temple University, Norwood concluded: "I've never known a 'second man' like J.R. If you have conflict and competition, you won't have what you have here."

J.R. Faulkner deliberately saw himself as the No. 2 man in the Highland Park ministry – not the No. 1 man. That position belonged to Dr. Lee Roberson. Faulkner saw his own position as a support role to make everything function and come out the way that Lee Roberson wanted it. Bill Long, the former West Virginia police chief who became director of security at Tennessee Temple, told me, "We always spoke here of Dr. Roberson as probably one of the top 10 leaders in the world in Christian ministries – one out of the top 10. Dr. Faulkner, we always said, was the top #1 out of 10 of 'second-place' men [assistants]. He was a leader in his field unquestioned." Long added, "Sitting at the pulpit, Dr. Roberson could just move his hand, or nod his head, and it would give a whole message to Dr. Faulkner on what to do now – without saying a word, because he was so aware of what he wanted and expected. He knew more about him than anybody. He was a great man – probably responsible for Dr. Roberson's success." Ben Haden said, "I think the public at large would look at it as a one-man show. I think it is at least a two-man show, with Brother Faulkner."

J.R. Faulkner joined Lee Roberson in Chattanooga in 1946 just after Tennessee Temple College was started. Faulkner was recommended to Roberson by the school's new vice president, Dr. John Herrmann. Faulkner joined Roberson straight out of Bob Jones College, where Faulkner graduated in 1946. Hiring J.R. Faulkner was a decision Lee Roberson never regretted. Late in life Roberson told me, "Dr. Faulkner was a live-wire. He stayed that way all through over 40 years. He was a promoter – a pusher, a pusher. He loved it. He loved to promote things. It's good to have someone like that. You can't do it all yourself. You do it by yourself, and you'll wear yourself out. He was a big help to me – a great help!"

In 1946 Faulkner was already in the Chattanooga area, serving as pastor of Eastlake Baptist Church in Rossville, Georgia. A multi-gifted man, Faulkner had driven his 1935 Model A Ford from the Bob Jones College campus, then in Cleveland, Tennessee, to the Rossville church for a month-long revival. Faulkner conducted the music and the chalk board artistry for the revival services. In October of 1944 the Eastlake church asked him to come regularly on a part-time basis for the Wednesday and Sunday services for $25 per week. As assistant pastor, he was to direct the music. "I had not even thought of pastoring or preaching," Faulkner recalled. When the pastor at Eastlake resigned on a Sunday morning in February of 1945, he turned publicly to Faulkner – with no prior warning – and announced that J.R. would be preaching in the evening service. Faulkner's response was, "I'm not a preacher! You can't do that!" The church responded with, "We love you! We want to vote on you!" Dr. Herrmann, who had been J.R.'s psychology professor at Bob Jones, encouraged him to take the church. In due time, Faulkner accepted a nearly unanimous call to become the pastor of Eastlake Baptist Church. By 1949 when Faulkner went full-time with Dr. Roberson, the Rossville church had grown under his leadership from 100 to 350 in Sunday school and was supporting such independent Baptist "faith" missionaries as Roy Ackerle, along with the Southern Baptist Cooperative Program.

James Rufus Faulkner, Jr., was called "Jay" as a child and "J.R." his entire adult life. He had grown up in humble circumstances during the depression years in Charlotte, North Carolina. He was seven when his mother died. For the rest of his life J.R. remembered the rainy day in 1922 when his mother was buried in a hillside cemetery at Charlotte. Jay had seven brothers and one half-sister. At age 16, J.R. was on his own. To make ends meet, he worked in a grocery and ran a 19-mile newspaper route on a home-made bicycle. He served as an usher (using flashlights) in a theater, worked as a shipping clerk, and with a friend started the Alexander School of Dancing. "I was tap-dancing," Faulkner recalled. "I finished a four-year program in tap-dancing. In my late teen years I was dancing and singing in a quartet. I did a soft-shoe with a black face. I was the top tenor – I could slip into a falsetto, with four-part harmony. We would sing, *Bicycle Built for Two, Sweet Adeline*. We sang a medley at the graduation of a nursery school – a priest stood and called for *My Wild Irish Rose*. I had a lot of fun tap-dancing."

By age 23, J.R. was serving as sales manager for United Artists when the famous evangelist Mordecai Hamm came to town in 1937. In a revival that touched the entire Charlotte area and was to impact the world, J.R. Faulkner was saved – as were Billy Graham and T.W. Wilson. Thirteen people from Faulkner's advertising office came to Christ – they had all been invited by two co-worker Christian young ladies. "I went on a Sunday night because I had promised the girls," J.R. said. "I heard the gospel and got under conviction." Shortly thereafter the newly converted Faulkner was invited to visit Bob Jones College, a fundamental Christian college in Cleveland, Tennessee. "I lit up a cigarette on the Bob Jones campus," Faulkner said years later. "My friend almost knocked it out of my hand. 'J.R., you can't do that here!' I went off campus and smoked a cigarette. They worked on me." Meanwhile, back in Charlotte, Faulkner began attending a new Bible institute – started as a result of the successful Mordecai Hamm revival. He attended evening classes for three years, as he continued working in Charlotte.

During those years J.R. became a life-long friend of Billy Graham, Cliff Barrows, Grady Wilson, and T.W. Wilson. "Mrs. Wilson [the two boys' mother] took me under her wings," said J.R. "She was so excited about my conversion!" J.R. was in the same young adult church group with Billy Graham and the Wilsons. By the fall of 1941, J.R. was leading music in Sunday school and worship services at the same church and in revival meetings with the Wilsons throughout Charlotte. J.R. was their song-leader before Cliff Barrows and before they hooked up with Billy Graham. Grady Wilson mentions J.R. in his autobiography, *Count It All Joy*. Faulkner said, "He gave me one of the red Scofield Billy Graham Bibles. Grady filled the whole front page with comments. He took me on my first street meeting. His daddy took me on my first jail service."

It wasn't long before J.R. decided to enroll at Bob Jones College (now University). There he also met friends of a lifetime – Roy

Ackerle, later a great Baptist missionary, and Fred Afman, who taught some six decades at both Bob Jones and Tennessee Temple. At college, it seemed fitting that the tall Afman was the center on the basketball team, and the enthusiastic and energetic J.R. was a cheerleader! Faulkner's major at Bob Jones was Bible, with a minor in music, and he nearly had enough credits for a master's degree in art as well.

For four years at Bob Jones, J.R. worked closely with Dr. Bob Jones, Jr., on the stage in the college's Shakespeare dramas. J.R. was to become a life-long friend of Dr. Bob Jr., president of the college and son of the founder. "Bob Jr. taught me to appreciate great music – taught me the arts," said Faulkner. "We did fun things, which endeared me to him. He put me in his first play." J.R. always retained a deep loyalty to Bob Jones University, which later moved its campus to Greenville, South Carolina, and to Dr. Bob Jr. in particular. "That dear man instilled in me some things – love for good music, appreciation for the finer things in life, etiquette at a table," said Faulkner. "I was just unlearned and untaught – not rough. I didn't run with that kind." Faulkner was a life-time member of the BJU Alumni Association because of his deep appreciation for what the institution had instilled in him. He encouraged a similar loyalty to Tennessee Temple on the part of his students. And always he sought Dr. Bob Jr. for advice and counsel. "He was an unusual man. I made a lot of mistakes because technically I was learning as I went along," J.R. said. "I made my share of mistakes. But he would understand. We'd talk." When Dr. Bob Jr. lay on his death bed, suffering from liver cancer, at age 86 in the fall of 1997, J.R. called him to express his love over the phone. At the funeral of Dr. Bob Jones Jr., J.R. Faulkner was publicly recognized for a personal friendship which covered decades.

In addition to his theatrical involvement during his student days at Bob Jones College, J.R. was president of Pi Gamma Delta and sang in the Glee Club. He was a regular in vespers, the Sunday afternoon worship service. It was at vespers where J.R. first met Lee Roberson. Roberson had been invited to Cleveland, Tennessee, to speak at the Sunday afternoon vespers services at Bob Jones College. Thereafter, Faulkner began to visit Highland Park Baptist

Church in Chattanooga for Sunday evening services – sometimes to do chalkboard ministry or sing, while his wife accompanied him on the piano. They would stay for Roberson's "Back Home Hour" radio broadcast at 10:00 PM and then drive the 30 miles home to Cleveland.

When Roberson started Tennessee Temple College, he himself was to be the president, and Herrmann the vice president. Herrmann and his wife, who had two master's degrees in music, were impressed with the abilities of both J.R. and his wife, who also had a master's degree in music. Herrmann believed J.R. could lead the music and teach Bible in the college – initially in the daytime only, as he continued with his Rossville church evenings and weekends. Herrmann also believed J.R.'s wife, Madelyne, could teach music in the college. With the confidence of the Herrmanns, the Faulkners began serving on a part-time basis at Tennessee Temple – a service which was to stretch over the next seven decades. In the beginning, J.R. taught art (including chalkboard), Christian doctrine, church history, Baptist history, church leadership, song-leading and conducting, and music synopsis.

After Dr. Herrmann recommended Faulkner to Lee Roberson, J.R. initially split his time between Tennessee Temple and the Rossville church from Temple's beginning in September of 1946 until 1949, when J.R. went full-time with Roberson. Faulkner finally resigned the Rossville church in October of 1949. "The hardest thing I had to do," J.R. said, "because we were going great guns." The church was growing. In the summer of 1948 a tent revival lasted 10 weeks. Later J.R. brought in Cliff Barrows and Grady Wilson for revivals. Ray Hoskins, a Rossville city commissioner, was saved and joined the church. Hoskins, a military veteran of the South Pacific in World II, was planning to go to a VFW dance and party when T.W. Wilson showed up at the commissioner's home and led him to the Lord. Later J.R. baptized him, performed his marriage, and eventually buried him. J.R. loved the ministry in Rossville. "It was hard for me to leave there," he said. Finally, J.R. took a $90 per month pay cut, drove his 1942 Pontiac to Chattanooga, and joined Lee Roberson full-time at Highland Park Baptist Church and Tennessee Temple schools.

It was at Tennessee Temple that Faulkner assumed a role unparalleled in Baptist circles in the position of an assistant pastor – "the second man" – as he led the singing, coordinated the services, directed the choir, and helped manage the college. Many preachers called him "the best No. 2 man in the country." Temple students heard Faulkner say many times, "God's called me to be the second man. I am in God's will serving under Dr. Roberson." And Temple students always remembered J.R. Faulkner speaking about Lee Roberson with admiration and respect. J.R. exemplified and taught a selfless philosophy of loyalty and faithfulness when you are not the "top dog."

When Faulkner was in his late 80s, he described his philosophy to me: "We don't promote it, but Dr. Roberson was 'king of the roost' here. Someone else might be president [of the college]. I was president for 15 years. It didn't bother me. We knew who was No. 1 here. It didn't bother me at all. I was still an associate pastor and vice-president even though I was president and co-pastor of the church. I just kept doing what I was doing – what needs to be done, what you're called upon to do, what you're qualified to do. Get with it, and just do it. I teach the [college] boys here, you can't go into an organization with an agenda – unless they hire you for that." Faulkner's attitude toward the captain (Roberson) was simple: "I go in to push you and to carry out your plans for this organization. And I try as soon as I can – as I did with Dr. Roberson – to have a clear mental picture of what was expected of me. And that was No. 1 priority right there. And then I did as many things apart from that as I was capable of doing – to let him know that I am whole-heartedly with the program. So, I made myself available for everything – like all the advertising, the newspaper, the bulletin. I designed the bulletin front every Sunday for 40 years. But that to me was gung-ho. I tried to tell the preacher boys you make yourself valuable to your pastor or – if you're working at a school – to the president of the school. Make yourself available for other things. If you can push him up the ladder, that empties a rung for you. I told Dr. Roberson yesterday in a letter, 'I am no fool. I recognize the blessings that came to me and to my family through your spirit of kindness and generosity that you have bestowed upon me through all these years that we've been here. Everything that we've enjoyed' – and I named four or five things that happened to us – 'was due to your kindness and your interest and love for us.'"

Faulkner served at Roberson's side for 60 years. I asked Dr. Faulkner if he had ever "stood up" to Dr. Roberson. His answer was extraordinary in its enlightenment. It revealed Faulkner's heart and character. "There was no need for it," he said. "I didn't come with an agenda. My agenda is to satisfy you. As long as I can agree with you doctrinally, and there's nothing to challenge you with the way you interpret the Word of God, the mechanics as to how you do it is your business – between you and God. There's nothing spiritually involved in what you're doing that you want me to help you. I have no place to argue with you. It's just – give it my best to have to carry it out. There were few, if any, times I had with that man [Roberson] anything I could question that would be contrary to my understanding of the word of God. Mechanics? Yes, there have been a few times where I would say, 'Ouch! I wouldn't have done it that way, Doctor' – the way I feel inside," he said with a laugh. "But that's preference – for the most part. Sometimes it would have some reason to it." I asked Dr. Faulkner, "When you felt that way, did you express that to him?" He responded quickly, "Oh, no! No – not once it's done. No. When the play is called, that's it. It's what I've taught these preacher boys, too. When that quarterback called that play, you've got one thing to do. Execute it, or get out of the game. It's as simple as that. And I've played by that rule all these years, and I've had no problem with it." On at least one occasion when Roberson took a certain task away from Faulkner's responsibilities and gave it to someone else, Faulkner did not like it at the time. But he did not question it. With staunch humility and loyalty, he assumed Dr. Roberson had a reason, and Faulkner continued in trust and respect.

The commitment of loyalty to the boss, and respect for chain-of-command, was germane to Faulkner's philosophy of service. "It's so hard to get this across to kids," Faulkner said, "and it makes life so easy for yourself – to be wholeheartedly in the operation. For example, a music leader is not to go into a church, to a pastor, and try to sell him on a bill of goods on what his music should be. You're a musician. Find out clearly what that pastor wants, and then you take your abilities and adjust them to the requirements of the job – as he wants it – to support his pulpit ministry, to set the atmosphere for the preaching in that church, and to create a worshipful spirit of music. If he wants a moderation between the two – the contemporary and the traditional – fine. You've got all the gifts for that. Totally traditional? Whatever."

Co-workers recognized that Lee Roberson and J.R. Faulkner worked together very closely with a relationship of mutual respect. Walter Wendelken, who served on the church staff with them both, said of Faulkner, "He wouldn't give you advice or permission for even a simple thing. He was as loyal as he could be." Bill Long said, "He was the man who saw to it that it was done the way Dr. Roberson wanted to do it." Long, as security chief, knew everything was set to go on Sundays when Faulkner arrived a half-hour early to check everything. J.R. would dip his hand in the baptistry – to make sure the water was warm enough, check the auditorium sound system, the lighting, everything – to be sure it was ready for Dr. Roberson.

Faulkner was the type of assistant to intercept phone calls or interruptions, and other minor problems – anything that could distract from Roberson's time and focus on the spiritual work of the ministry. Roberson saw in J.R. Faulkner a great ability to solve problems. But J.R. told me with a chuckle, "I had a greater ability to forget those things [problems]. Put them under the rug. I cannot recall one day that I was in a state of wrath in the 56 years I've been here – or allowed inner feelings. If I was upset with something, God gave me an ability to live with it and pray it down. I never let it stay with me. And I tried to get this into the hearts and minds of others."

J.R. Faulkner learned always to be ready to preach. He never knew when he might be called upon to fill in for someone at the last moment. Lee Roberson would not hesitate to cancel an out-of-town speaking engagement to stay home for an unexpected funeral. His first priority always was his pastorate. In such cases, he would send J.R. on the road in his place to fulfill the out-of-town engagement. "I stayed ready," Faulkner said. To this day, he told me, he kept four sermons in his briefcase at all times – outlines on how to run a Sunday school, how to build a church, youth ministry, and music ministry. In his late 80s in is office, he showed me the outlines tucked in his briefcase – ready to go. "I'm ready," he said. Similarly, Faulkner would keep a funeral sermon ready – always ready to help a Chattanooga funeral home, if there were a need for a preacher on short notice. He said, "I teach these preacher boys you're like a spare tire. You need to be ready for a funeral. I've had 15 minutes to get to a funeral home to conduct a funeral." Faulkner had a standing relationship with Chattanooga funeral homes that if for any reason any minister failed to show up for a funeral, if he could, J.R. would come. "Give me a ring. If I'm at my desk, I'll be dressed right, and I'll be there, and I'll conduct the funeral," he said. "And it happened several times, especially at Chattanooga Funeral Home. I kept my funeral message right there in the corner. I'd ask a couple key questions, and I was ready to go."

For many years Dr. Lee Roberson held the position himself of President of Tennessee Temple University. Faulkner, his right-hand man in both church and school, always affectionately and respectfully referred to Roberson as "Doctor." Faulkner never forgot the day Roberson came to him and said, "Come on, let's go. I'm going to surprise you today." A Board of Trustees meeting was scheduled for the college. "I said, 'What's that?'" Faulkner recalled. "He said, 'I'm going to make you president of the school.' I said, 'Doctor, what are you going to do?' It was a thunderbolt! He said, 'I'm going to be chancellor.' I said, 'What does he [the chancellor] do?' He said, 'I don't know.' That's just the way he talked. He said, 'I'm going to tell the men today I want them to elect you as President.' Well, what am I going to do? 'Just keep on doing what you're doing.' The next thing I knew I had a correspondence from the DeMoss people. We had a $5-million gift [for the college] in my name." J.R. became the president.

Faulkner was equally honored on the day when Dr. Roberson decided to name him co-pastor of Highland Park Baptist Church. Ben Haden insisted that being "co-pastor" with Lee Roberson was an oxymoron. Haden, a great admirer of Faulkner, said with a laugh, "Being co-pastor with Lee Roberson is like pretending to be a coevangelist with Billy Graham." Nevertheless, Roberson insisted on the promotion for Faulkner. He asked the deacons to match his identical salary and benefits for Faulkner. J.R. was astounded.

Did J.R. Faulkner ever consider leaving Highland Park or moving on to another ministry? "I'm glad you asked me," Faulkner told me. "I hadn't been here six months when one of the deacons approached me. He had come from a Baptist church, and they were without a pastor – they had a great pastor. This fellow, a deacon, came to me. 'Brother Faulkner, I'm going to recommend you to that church.' I said, 'You're what?' 'I'm going to recommend you to that church. Boy, you could take that and do a great job.' I said, 'Listen, I am not for sale. I am right where God put me.'" Faulkner also told me about another church that offered him a new automobile and parsonage. "I don't believe in that," he said. At a time when Faulkner was making $7,500 a year, a Christian businessman offered him $15,000 to come to Philadelphia and be the corporate chaplain for his business. Again, I asked, did you come close to leaving? "No, never," he responded. "I never had the slightest desire to go anywhere as far as the ministry's concerned." Evangelist Ed Carter said Faulkner belongs in the Guinness Book of Records as the assistant pastor to serve one pastor for the most consecutive years – from 1949 to 1983.

Faulkner possessed a remarkable sense of joy and peace in choosing to spend his life ministering under the shadow of Lee Roberson. Still, J.R. Faulkner became a leader in his own right – revered and respected in Baptist circles all across America. Faulkner was to become senior pastor of Highland Park Baptist Church in 1983 when Roberson stepped down. Faulkner was regularly a national officer in such ministries as Southwide Baptist Fellowship and Baptist International Missions, Inc. He was the moderator of Southwide's annual meeting on three different occasions.

Bill Mattheiss worked directly under J.R. Faulkner for 24 years. "I worked 24 years with him with never a disagreement," said Mattheiss. "We worked through problems, of course. He was a prince of a man. I have great respect for him. Under pressure he could get quick and short – if he needed something done right now. It was easy for me to work for him. He was a prince of a fellow.

He knew people, and he knew what God wanted him to do. And he knew how to motivate and lead."

Years after the retirements of both Roberson and Faulkner, Tom Wallace told me about the day Tennessee Temple University ran out of money. The Board of Trustees had a serious discussion to consider how to close the university. Wallace, a graduate and prominent pastor, was on the board. The mood was somber. The decision appeared inevitable. J.R. Faulkner, still on the board, stood to his feet and addressed the meeting: "Gentlemen, we are at the same place where Dr. Roberson and I have been at no less than a dozen times through the years. God has never let us down. God always has provided." His words caused a complete turnaround in the meeting. The school stayed open, and Tennessee Temple is open to this day.

J.R. Faulkner and his wife, Madelyne, raised five sons in Chattanooga in a large, four-bedroom, four-and-a-half bath house. When I interviewed Faulkner during his late 80s, he and his wife had 17 grandchildren, 10 great-grandchildren – and one on the way! Through the years J.R. Faulkner kept up with the demanding pace that Lee Roberson set. He worked seven days per week, taking only two weeks vacation – one Sunday and two Wednesdays off. "I'd try to get home on Friday, so I could come to the office on Saturday and get my wits together before Sunday," he said. "That was it! No other time." On a weekly basis, after the Saturday morning radio broadcast and the college administrative staff meeting, the staff had lunch together – and then Saturday afternoon was free. J.R. might have to be back for a school ballgame or a college recital in the evening. But he spent Saturday afternoons with his boys. Every Sunday all five boys sat down front in church, right in front of the church platform – "where we could see them" – every service. J.R. gave his sons tithing envelopes. Every Saturday evening the Faulkners made out their tithe – and divided it up. Today all five boys are serving God in the ministry.

Vacations were always built around the boys, usually camping trips to such places as the Cumberland Mountains in the Appalachians or the apple orchards of Ohio – once for 10 days near Washington, D.C., where they visited the United States Congress. Faulkner did not travel away from his boys much until they were married. After that, he and his wife traveled quite often, primarily missions trips – to South America or Europe, or wherever Tennessee Temple graduates or Highland Park missionaries were serving, or to the Holy Land. One vacation was taken in the Caribbean islands with Dr. and Mrs. Roberson. Faulkner recalled, "But he [Roberson] thought of that as a missions trip. That was when he was speaking at all our missionaries [our graduates] in different places, and I was leading the singing."

In an interview in 1987, Dr. Roberson said of J.R. Faulkner that he was "at his best as a preacher of the gospel, a song leader, a platform man, a coordinator of work, a promoter par excellence, a teacher, an artist, and a counselor." Faulkner, he said, "earned the reputation of being one of the foremost 'second men' in Fundamentalism." Faulkner himself likened his place to that of Aaron, who assisted Moses, in Exodus 4:16, *"And he shall be thy spokesman unto the people...and thou shalt be to him instead of God."*

J.R. Faulkner spent his life working for Lee Roberson. "I was honored – deeply honored," he said. "I always held him in the highest regard. I had great respect for him. I love the man. Did you know there's never been a cross word between us? He has never called me into his office to reprimand me or to ask why I did so-and-so. He was gracious enough that if there was something that he didn't quite agree with, it's just amazing how he could get it across to a person like me working at his side without offense. He'd say, 'Brother Faulkner, don't you think maybe so-and-so and so-and-so?' And he would talk to me like I'd talk to him. Now, you're my employee. I don't go to you and tell you how we're gonna do so-and-so. I might say, 'Brother Roberson, I'm sure you've thought of this many times, but I just had a thought about...' I leave him open to where he doesn't have to tell me yes or no – on the first hearing. You always put a suggestion in the form of a question. You don't put a superior in a spot where he's got to take a chance of offending you in some way or in any way that would question something he's already done or committed himself to or committed the organization to doing. It's my job – once a play is called, to carry it out to the best of my ability, and not to ask him why. You never dare get in a position where you want to say or come near to saying that 'I told you so.' But there's never been a cross word between us. There's never been a note written in a way of a correction or that type of thing. I tried to avoid that happening."

Years ago a guest chapel speaker at Tennessee Temple University mentioned in his sermon that most pastors do not have a pastor themselves – someone to whom to go for counsel. As the preacher continued his sermon, Dr. Roberson scribbled a hand-written note and handed it over to J.R. Faulkner. It read, "You're my pastor." Faulkner, remembering how awed he had been when he first came to Highland Park, was speechless. "Oh, boy!" he told me years later. "It can really get to you."

CHAPTER 9

The World's Largest Church

The growth of Highland Park Baptist Church was explosive under the pastoral leadership of Lee Roberson. And as the church spawned various world-wide ministries, Roberson's first priority was always the local church itself. "The church is my baby," he once said. By the 1960s and 70s Highland Park Baptist Church had become the model church in America for the independent, fundamental Baptist movement. Attending church at Highland Park was exciting. It seemed there was never a dull moment. Lee Roberson was certainly captivating as a preacher, and the music was inspirational. But more than that, things were happening! Roberson called Highland Park the "Church of the Green Light" – everything was on the go! In every service people were walking the aisle to profess publicly their faith in Christ. People were being baptized as a public confession of their faith in Christ at the end of every service. And Roberson was constantly promoting church growth through special programs, Sunday school growth competitions, guest speakers, etc. The leading preachers in America's Baptist circles were guests in the Highland Park pulpit on a regular basis.

In a news feature story published on August 29, 1971, *Chattanooga News-Free Press* reporter Helen McDonald Exum described a typical Sunday morning at Highland Park Baptist Church in those days. "Everywhere there were people – downstairs, upstairs, in the aisles hunting for a seat," she wrote. "There were children from four years old and up. There were women of every age, and more men than most people have ever seen at one time in a church."

Lee Roberson loved a big crowd. Highland Park Baptist Church had multiple Sunday morning church services as space required when the crowd overflowed and a building program was under way. In those days his idea of multiple services was not repeating the same service, with the same speaker and same sermon, at different hours – as many churches do today. He held simultaneous services in different buildings with different preachers. But normally Roberson wanted everyone together at the same time in one church service. Even when he retired in 1983 after building the new auditorium, the initial proposal was to include expansion for a balcony to bring the seating capacity to 10,000. It was not Lee Roberson's intent eventually to hold multiple Sunday morning services. Late in life Roberson told me that his favorite part of the ministry was the public church worship service. The Sunday morning worship service was a little more "polished" than the others. The orchestra was very good. Sunday evening was less formal. Wednesday night was also a big service. Dr. Roberson would preach on Wednesday just like he did on Sunday morning and evening. Every service was a big service – with different "flavors."

Under Roberson's leadership, Highland Park quickly became a pioneer in church bus ministry and in weekly Sunday school growth campaigns. Roberson operated constant promotions and strategies to motivate more people to come to church and to bring more visitors under the preaching of the gospel. Each autumn a 10-Sunday attendance campaign would kick off on Labor Day weekend. The Sunday before Labor Day, for most churches, is the lowest attended church service of the entire year. But Roberson annually opened the college the first week of September and pushed Labor Day Sunday as "Round-Up Sunday" – bringing in special guests, such as Miss South Carolina, who gave her personal testimony of faith in Christ one year. Each year Roberson's "Round-Up Sunday" held one of the largest crowds of the year. On the first Sunday of September in 1982, one year before Roberson retired from the Highland Park pastorate, the attendance was 14,563! A similar campaign was promoted each spring – using motivational ideas simply to get people to come to church. One year Highland Park Baptist Church celebrated "Mayors' Day" and invited the mayors of not only Chattanooga – but all the surrounding cities, towns, and villages. The mayors, always glad to receive favorable attention in front of a large crowd and to receive the implied blessing of Dr. Lee Roberson, were glad to come. The mayors were honored on the platform during the Sunday morning service. One or two were to speak briefly – sharing thoughts about their personal faith, and all were properly recognized. Afterward a luncheon was provided for the mayors and their families.

The influence of Highland Park Baptist Church was such that not just mayors but even presidential candidates and governors were glad to come. In 1980 Tennessee Temple University hosted a rally for presidential candidate Ronald Reagan. Roberson prayed with him privately before the program. Through the years various U.S. senators, congressmen, and three or four Tennessee governors spoke at the church – on "Governors' Sunday." The governor of Tennessee flew in on a National Guard plane. Georgia Governor Lester Maddox spoke there. J.R. Faulkner described Maddox's mother as a devoted, born-again Christian, who had visited Highland Park Baptist Church unannounced. She sat in the balcony. When Dr. Roberson learned she was there, he had her stand and recognized her publicly. On another occasion, Tennessee's U.S. Senator and later Ambassador Bill Brock was a guest. It was not uncommon to have other civic leaders there, such as the Chattanooga police chief. On Roberson's 30th anniversary as pastor, Tennessee Gov. Winfield Dunn came to the church and presented him with a state certificate of meritorious service.

In Highland Park's Sunday school the focus was on the constant teaching of the Bible – the Word of God. Highland Park Baptist Church did not subscribe to Sunday school quarterlies or curriculum. Cliff Robinson wrote all the Sunday school lessons, which he would review with the teachers in meetings every Wednesday night in Phillips Chapel before the midweek service. More than 350 Sunday school teachers and officers from as many as 109 classes and departments – there were four junior departments – would attend the weekly Sunday school staff meeting. Most of the teachers used Cliff Robinson's lessons – outlines of nearly all the books of the

Bible, written over 28 years. "We covered every book in the Bible – except First and Second Chronicles and First and Second Kings," Cliff said. Lee Roberson always taught a Sunday school class. For years he led the Fellowship Bible Class downstairs, then the Men's Bible Class in the old auditorium. Roberson told me privately that he liked to teach the older ladies, as they rarely complained about anything and seemed very much to appreciate him!

Promotional contests nourished church growth. "Doctor was having contests," J.R. Faulkner said in reflecting back. "He was an amazing man – to put one class against another." A typical Sunday school campaign would last one month – occasionally six weeks. A theme would be chosen and promoted in Sunday school staff meetings on Wednesday nights before the midweek service. Roberson insisted that the teachers and officers be there. Kenton Hixson was the Sunday school superintendent at Highland Park for many years. But always the key promoters were Roberson and Faulkner. The goal was to get the people excited. For example, in 1964 when Republican Sen. Barry Goldwater of Arizona was challenging incumbent Democratic President Lyndon B. Johnson for the White House, the Sunday school theme was "Gold Rush '64." A banner with five wagon trains representing five Sunday school divisions was mounted on a map stretching on the wall from Chattanooga to San Francisco. Faulkner would hang the banner every Wednesday night for the Sunday school teachers' meeting. J.R. wrote letters to the mayors and chambers of commerce along the route. The Sunday school campaign tracked across the map on the wall. "I had actual letters from mayors 'welcoming' us to their city," Faulkner recalled. The mayor of Sacramento sent a key to his city. The winning team, or Sunday school division, received a pot filled with gold nuggets (chocolate candy wrapped in gold foil). Another Sunday school campaign involved the theme of sending a rocket to the moon. There were five rockets. J.R. Faulkner gave away Mars candy bars.

The ministry's security chief, Bill Long, was a former police chief in West Virginia who was first invited to Highland Park on "Policemen's Sunday." At the time Roberson put up a big banner on Bailey Avenue promoting the Christian testimony of Police Chief Bill Long. Another featured speaker was a policeman from

New York City who gave his personal testimony of faith in Christ. Colonel Harlan Sanders of Kentucky Fried Chicken fame gave his personal testimony on a special day – the dining room was packed after church as chicken was served family style. Mrs. M.J. Parker was head of the campus dining hall. The college students voted for their favorite chicken between the colonel's chicken and Ma Parker's chicken. The colonel lost. (Roberson, who was raised throughout childhood in Louisville, was once named an honorary "Kentucky Colonel.")

Roberson loved big cakes, so Faulkner would make them for special occasions. And Roberson loved fireworks. The "Church of the Green Light" was for the church that was always on the go. Faulkner put up a simulated traffic light on the corner – "just exactly like a street light," Faulkner said. "The city made us take it down. We used to let that light change from red to green. People interpreted it as a stop-and-go. We had to take it down. We tried to just leave the green light on, but even that was thought to be dangerous, so the light had to go out, and eventually the sign came down."

It came as little surprise that Roberson's unconventional promotional approach to Sunday school growth was criticized. In his sermon, *Fireworks Don't Last*, Roberson told about an unnamed pastor of a Baptist church who stood in his own pulpit on a Sunday morning and said of Roberson's ministry at Highland Park, "He's running a three-ring circus. I want to prophesy to you that it will soon be gone. A thing like that can never last." Roberson pointed out that in the same year that he himself baptized 555 persons, the critical pastor baptized only five and soon lost his pastorate.

One unnamed friend of Roberson told *The Chattanooga News-Free Press*, "He's a promoter. If he were in business for himself, he would be a millionaire. He has all the drive, imagination – a different sales promotion or contest every week." And even some Highland Park Baptist Church insiders felt there were too many promotions. One veteran college teacher, always loyal to Dr. Roberson, told me, "Too many! Faulkner did that. Everything you could think of – biggest banana split in the world. A piece of Russian candy. Everything!" One secretary, also very loyal to Roberson, told me the ministry heard the criticism all the time that Highland Park was "a three-ring circus." Faulkner told me of the 13th anniversary service held at the city auditorium. The special cake was set on fire and burned up! "I guess in some ways I felt like we went overboard on promotions," confided E.C. Haskell Jr., also very loyal to Roberson. "He [Roberson] knew how to promote meetings – and so forth. Maybe in Sunday school he over-promoted. It got to where promotions were not unusual. Almost every Sunday there were promotions."

Nevertheless, Roberson and Faulkner were committed to promotion. A promotional leader was assigned for each month of the year. Faulkner attributed the success of promotion to hard work. He also said, "We have promotion in our Sunday school, but that doesn't keep people. You can get people through promotion, but keep them through a strong Bible teaching program." Every Sunday was a special day for Roberson. "We had an attendance goal for every Sunday in Sunday school – every Sunday of the world," said Faulkner. "We would lay out plans for the whole year – special Sunday for 52 Sundays. It started shortly after I came here. He had me doing it. He would say, 'Now fix up our calendar for the year.'"

Roberson loved the big cakes Faulkner would make for the special days – monster cakes. The heaviest weighed 1,450 pounds. It was paraded down the main church aisle. "We made it downtown in a bakery shop," said Faulkner. "Dumb us! We didn't measure to see how wide the door was. We couldn't get it out of the bakery. We had to get the glass company to come take the window out and piano movers to come move the cake and bring it to the church!" Faulkner recalled with a laugh that when the U.S. space program sent the first rocket up from Cape Canaveral – astronaut Alan Shepard Jr. becoming the first American in space in 1961, Roberson wanted a cake with a rocket on it to celebrate the event which coincided with the anniversary of Highland Park Baptist Church's radio ministry. At a certain point a button was to be pushed igniting a pressure tank which lifted the rocket up right in the main church auditorium. When the valve opened, it blew the top off the rocket – hitting the ceiling of the sanctuary, sending smoke everywhere, and dusting both Dr. Roberson and the mayor of the city – both dressed in dark suits. And when America was involved in the Korean War, Faulkner put together a cake with a battle scene with planes and guns discharging flames from lighter fluid. With four spotlights shining and the choir singing, the top of the cake opened and out of a bird cage flew a white dove of peace – trained by a church member. The crowd loved it!

And, oh, how the church grew! In 1971 Highland Park Baptist Church was called "the largest church in the world." For six of the seven years from 1969 to 1975 *Christian Life* magazine ranked Highland Park Baptist Church's Sunday school second or third largest in America. No one disputed that Highland Park had the largest midweek prayer service in the world, averaging more than 3,000 each Wednesday night. The Sunday bus ministry was bringing in around 1,400 people weekly. J.R. Faulkner was speaking to 1,200 to 1,300 people in the main auditorium Sunday school class alone – a class that averaged giving $1,100 per month over a 140-month period in special offerings to Camp Joy. In 1973 the Sunday school consisted of 109 classes in the main church alone, staffed by 470 volunteer workers. The church's World Wide Faith Missions program was helping to support no less than 532 missionaries around the world. The Sunday school was running 45 bus routes weekly. The ministry publication, *The Evangelist*, had a circulation of 67,000. The daily radio broadcast, *Gospel Dynamite*, was on the air daily Monday through Saturday. The church services were broadcast live over WDYN-FM radio Sunday morning and evening, as well as Wednesday evening. Tennessee Temple schools had an enrollment of 4,548 – 3,598 in the university; 359 in high school, and 591 in elementary. The church services were interpreted for the deaf – all services. The total membership of Highland Park Baptist Church was 57,325. Sunday evening training union had 5,342 people in attendance – 3,051 in the main church and 2,291 in the area chapels. It was called the largest training union in the world. The church baptized 1,505 people in 1971 alone. There were 3,014 new members added to the church in one year, and in one year there were 2,008 public professions of faith for salvation – 1,316 in the main church and 692 in the chapels. The average number of public professions of faith per week at Highland Park Baptist Church in the main church alone was just over 25 persons.

As the crowd grew, it became difficult to find a seat or for a family to find enough space to sit together. Roberson was focused on reaching people with the gospel. He had no patience with critics or complainers. In his sermon, *Missionaries Won't Strike*, he said, "We have had some to complain about Highland Park, that we do not have room to find places during the services, and hence, they want to quit. They are not willing to be separated from their families for a few minutes. They do not like things that may go a little bit against their personal desires. Yes, the devil wants you to 'strike' for more pleasant surroundings."

In 1981 the Sunday school *average* attendance for Highland Park Baptist Church was 8,969 – including 4,793 in the main church and 4,176 in the 70 chapels operated in a 70-mile radius of the church. These were phenomenal numbers in those days for a church which was a pre-cursor to the modern day mega-churches. The pastors of the chapels included mostly Tennessee Temple preacher boys, plus at least seven faculty members. Chapel numbers were always included in the overall Highland Park numbers, but a Chattanooga newspaper at the time published a photo of the over-flowing main church auditorium and found it refreshing that Roberson did not brag on the numbers. It was so crowded during the 1970s that the college students would rotate every third Sunday in attending the church service in the main auditorium – spending the other Sundays in the gymnasium where they listened to rotating preachers, such as Ron Bishop or Cliff Robinson. In 1981 the church dedicated a new 5,000-plus seat main auditorium on Bailey Avenue. When Lee Roberson concluded his 40½-year ministry at Highland Park in 1983, he had baptized more than 63,000 persons.

"Highland Park was built on confrontational evangelism – face-to-face, all the time," said Bob Kelley. "Door-to-door visitation was the method. Dr. Roberson would bring in visitation specialists [e.g., Joe Shadowens] – to spend the day door-to-door taking a census. This was how he got prospects for Thursday evening visitation." The church kept careful records of the census of the Chattanooga area. The office which handled visitation, soul winning and evangelism was in the basement of Phillips Chapel. Walter Wendelken was in charge. The church diligently listed every un-churched or unsaved family by name and street address, creating an extensive mailing list. Thousands of families received regular letters from Dr. Roberson and invitations to church evangelistic events. Roberson would joke publicly that once you got on that church mailing list there was no way off until you moved away or died.

And there was no end to Lee Roberson's efforts at evangelism. In 1950 he organized Highland Park Baptist Church's Union Gospel Mission. A rescue mission which never closes any time of the week, it was established in downtown Chattanooga to provide hot meals, groceries, clothing, and a bed for the destitute, transient and homeless of the city. Totally operated and supported by Highland Park Baptist Church, the rescue mission held nightly gospel services and reached thousands of people annually. On February 21, 1973, a second rescue mission was opened in Dalton, Georgia, about 25 miles south of Chattanooga. The rescue mission in Chattanooga, located at 5th and Market streets, touched the lives of 25,824 people in 1981 alone – resulting in 491 professions of faith, 180 baptisms, and 231 rededication commitments to the Lord. Some 37,000 meals were served that year alone – with 2,029 pairs of shoes and 35,266 articles of clothing provided for people in need. During the 30 year-period of 1950 to 1980 the rescue mission alone saw 21,213 salvation decisions and 4,098 baptisms. For many years the mission was directed by Willis Riley, and then later by Dwight Deal. The mission was open 24 hours per day, 365 days and nights per year.

Under Roberson's leadership it became the practice at Highland Park Baptist Church to hold an annual mid-winter revival in January, a *Sword of the Lord* conference in March, a Bible conference in April, a summer Bible and missionary conference in July, and the big annual missions conference in November. Three times a year Roberson held a special, week-long conference – missions conference, revival week, and Bible conference. Some years there were two revival meetings, one in the late summer and another in mid-winter. Cottage prayer meetings, where church members met to pray in various homes, were held in connection with the revivals. Faulkner stated the goal, "I believe that as a collective force, the prayer meetings can call on God to rend the heavens, to send revival and to shake the city of Chattanooga." The annual Bible conferences began in 1946. Church members and college students alike looked forward to the annual week-long Bible conference as a spiritually refreshing week. "What a refreshing week!" E.C. Haskell Jr. recalled. "You could just 'bathe' in it for a week."

For the special meetings Roberson brought many of the greatest preachers in America in to speak at Highland Park Baptist Church and Tennessee Temple University. He wanted guest preachers who were conservative, not leaning liberal theologically, with biblical values and respect for the Word of God. Guest speakers included a veritable "Who's Who" among independent Baptists, Southern Baptists, and other Bible-centered evangelicals – Hyman Appelman, William Ward Ayre, Joe Boyd, R.R. Brown, J.B. Buffington, W.A. Criswell, E.J. Daniels, M.R. DeHaan Sr., Theodore Epp, Herschel Ford, R.A. Forest, Charles E. Fuller, Jacob Gartenhaus, Joe Henry Hankins, Walter Hughes of Canada, Curtis Hutson, Jack Hyles, Maze Jackson, J. Don Jennings, Torrey Johnson, Bob Jones Sr., Charles "Tremendous" Jones, B.R. Lakin, R.G. LeTourneau, R.G. Lee, Tom Malone, L.E. Maxwell, Jack McArthur, J. Vernon McGee, James McGinley of Scotland, Ian Paisley of Ireland, William Pettingill, Hugh Pyle, John Rawlings, Ernest I. "Pappy" Reveal, Bill Rice, John R. Rice, Lester Roloff, Harold Sightler, J. Harold Smith, Oswald J. Smith, Paul Smith, Charles Stanley, Lehman Strauss, Howard Sugden, Beauchamp Vick, Warren Wiersbe, Walter Wilson, Jack Wyrtzen, et al, plus musicians like Rudy Atwood, Curt Davis, the Gordon Sears family, Homer Rodeheaver, Al Smith, and, Charles Weigle, et al.

One man in particular for whom Roberson had great respect was Oswald J. Smith because of Smith's emphasis on worldwide missions. He also had great respect for the Southern Baptist preacher, W.A. Criswell, the legendary pastor of First Baptist Church of Dallas. Often when these guest preachers came, there was a touch of promotion. For example, on one occasion as the church service was already starting, young Orman Norwood was at the airport picking up the guest speaker – the renowned Dr. Charles E. Fuller. Norwood quickly brought Fuller to the church, and as Fuller walked into the church service, which was already under way, Roberson had the pianist alerted to play, *Heavenly Sunshine*, Fuller's signature song from his nationally famous radio ministry. Roberson loved to tell the story of the great radio preacher M.R. DeHaan visiting Highland Park. After the altar call as the church service was completed, a muffled voice came from the back of the Chauncey-Goode auditorium pews. Roberson enquired only to find the famous M.R. DeHaan down on his knees underneath the balcony, below the clock, on the floor between two pews, leading an individual soul to Christ.

The crowds packed out the week-long annual missions conferences, which brought in 75 to 100 foreign and home missionaries. The annual missions conferences began in 1949. For the missions conference the church auditorium would be decorated with placards, flags of foreign nations, and mementos from the mission fields. To create interest and enthusiasm, Roberson would turn the whole campus into a "mission field." There would be grass huts, mud huts, and mission field scenes all over campus. One year an African village with thatched-roof cottages was built on campus to represent the Congo. African music would be floating in the air. International flags were everywhere. Missionaries would be dressed in their native costume. Missionary booths were everywhere, with missionaries handing out free curios from their various countries. Every building on campus was decorated to represent a different nation. The missionaries would be there all week – spending time talking to the college students to inspire and challenge them to the call of missions. In the main church services missionaries would give brief testimonies and show slides and pictures from their fields of service. "The mission conferences were overwhelming," recalled Bob Kelley. "So many students were called to be missionaries during those times!"

A morning worship service at Highland Park Baptist Church followed a traditional pattern. Usually four men were on the platform – Roberson, Faulkner, Cliff Robinson, and a rotating deacon to lead in prayer. The service would follow the traditional pattern of music, announcements, offering, and special music, before concluding with the sermon, and the gospel invitation, and then baptism. Roberson would direct the whole service – from opening prayer to closing prayer. The service would take on his personal tone. He wanted everything done "decently and in order" (I Corinthians 12:40). Services started on time. He was punctual. Everybody was to be in their place on time. He popularized a home-made Sunday school chorus about being in Sunday school "at 9:30 sharp!" The schedule was always the same. His punctuality was partly due to broadcasting the services live on radio – where you needed to start and finish on time – and partly due to his training under his college pastor, Finley F. Gibson. Roberson's church services started exactly on the minute – not 30 seconds late. As a rule, Dr. Roberson would preach approximately 25 minutes.

Roberson's wit and friendliness was evident throughout each church service. Newspaper reporter Helen McDonald Exum described the welcoming of visitors during a Sunday morning service: "Then he began to recognize several visitors. 'We have a group here from Chickasaw, Georgia, who are going on a mission to Illinois, under Brother Moses. Now, it would take a Moses to lead as big a group of young people as this one! And tell your minister that I heard him recently on that coffee break program he has on TV. Very good.' Then he read the name of a couple from Washington. 'We're so glad to have you. Tell the President hello, and then here are the Barney Faulkners from Charlotte. Isn't it wonderful to have them?'"

Even the announcements in any church service on Sunday or Wednesday received careful attention from Roberson. "I am a great believer in strong, clear announcements," he said. "Emphasis must be given to the worthwhile!"

For the church services Faulkner would pick the music. "If I needed four songs for an evening service," Faulkner said, "I would pick eight." The theme and development of the service would then dictate to Faulkner which four songs to use. "I would find out from his message which way he's going. It was very difficult from his sermon titles. I would try to get as close to it as possible. Then I'd choose my song service from those on the sheet." Faulkner would lay the sheet with the order of service at Roberson's chair on the platform. At times Roberson would strike a line through one of the songs. For example, Roberson never liked to use *Victory in Jesus* – too up-beat, or bouncy, for his tastes. But he would approve other songs which seemed just as bouncy to Faulkner. Roberson favored traditional hymns. "If I'd ask," said Faulkner, "he'd lean over and say, '*Amazing Grace* – sing *Amazing Grace*'." Roberson was a gifted singer who was trained in opera. Bob Kelley said Roberson's favorite song was, *Does Jesus Care?* Faulkner said, "Often I'd say, 'Come on, Brother Roberson, sing a verse.' He'd step up and sing, and I'd lead the congregation." Sometimes in the middle of a service, without warning Roberson would turn to the pianist and announce a song he wanted the church to sing right then. Roberson appreciated great music, using a magnificent organ, two pianos, an orchestra, soloists, and choir in every service. Roberson liked enthusiastic singing, with Faulkner's style of interpreting the music with the waving of his arms. "Pull it out of the audience," Faulkner said, "so you sing thought instead of every word. It's the hardest thing in the world to teach, as far as trying to get people to learn to do it." Lee Roberson liked the way Faulkner did it. Another thing Roberson liked was that Faulkner would always caution the soloists against taking too much time to talk in introducing their song or giving "testimony," when they stood to sing. He wanted them to leave the speaking to the preacher.

Honoring Charles Weigle at Tennessee Temple
(from left, J.R. Faulkner, Weigle, M.R. DeHaan Sr., Roberson)

Charles Weigle on campus with J.R. Faulkner & Dr. Roberson.

A young Lee Roberson sitting at a banquet.

Robersons at a banquet with John R. Rice (left) and Bob Jones Sr.

One of many ground-breakings at Highland Park & TennesseeTemple.

The Roberson Family

Caroline Roberson in an earlier year.

Roberson daughters LeeAnne Nichols & June Ormsheier.

A cheerful Dr. Roberson with missionary Roy Ackerle (left) and Bob Jones Jr.

Honoring Dr. & Mrs. Roberson.

The Tennessee Temple University braintrust in later years.

With Cliff Robinson (left) and J.R. Faulkner.

Dr. Lee Roberson   Dr. J. R. Faulkner

From the college yearbook in one of the early years.

A happy Lee Roberson in the pulpit in an early year.

Having fun in the college chapel.

Classic glimpses of Dr. Lee Roberson preaching in a later year.

Dr. J.R. Faulkner • Dr. Lee Roberson • Dr. Bob Jones, Sr. • Dr. John R. Rice

Highland Park Baptist Church Bible Conference, April, 1953

An early Bible conference at Tennessee Temple.

With Buddy Nichols (left) and David Bouler in a later year.

In the pulpit with Curtis Hutson in background.

Dr. Lee Roberson in the pulpit late in life.

Dr. Lee Roberson

Dr. Roberson with the author.

Music was vital to the ministry of Highland Park and very inspirational. Always traditional and led by Faulkner, the music was uplifting – never boring. "People sang lustily and from the heart," wrote reporter Helen McDonald Exum. "Our services were greatly blessed with a warm, vibrant spirit," said Faulkner. "The music was always well received – just good, old-fashioned songs." Faulkner became celebrated for the chorus, *Behold He Comes,* which he led more than 1,200 times in Sunday services, Wednesday services, missions conferences, and Bible conferences. And of course, the large choir was majestic – under leadership of people such as Victor Werner and Danielle Brown.

Trained in music, Roberson's tastes were always conservative and traditional. He attended college recitals. Privately he would question everything and seek the opinion of other musicians. He would tell the singers – the church soloists – that if they would sing about the Cross, the Second Coming, and the Blood of Christ, they would never have to worry about the message or standard of their music. When two Tennessee Temple students tried something new in chapel one day – transitioning their song with a diminished chord, bringing in a seventh chord, Roberson got right up in front of the student body and said, "No, no. Always finish out your chords. Don't leave it hanging, young men." They never did that again! One time a college student wanted to play, *Born Free.* Roberson would not permit it. The ministry's musical cantatas were of the old-fashioned kind. There was music but no drama. "It's different now," Faulkner said late in life. "That's all right. I have no argument with that. If we'd have thought of it, we probably would have done it [drama]." And of course, every Highland Park Baptist Church service had the traditional hymn of invitation at the end. Roberson might change an invitation song after one verse – always flexible to the leading of the Holy Spirit. J.R. Faulkner was always ready.

Musicians learned always to be ready – to be called upon to sing. They never knew when Dr. Roberson might call upon them without warning to sing in any church service. The regular singers knew always to have a song prepared. If called upon, they would hand the sheet music to the pianist on their way to the platform.

Normally, Roberson himself would give the gospel invitation at the end of the service. "I can't recall any Wednesday service someone didn't come forward in all the 40 years," said Roberson. "There must have been one or two, but I can't recall when they were. We had a response every Sunday service and every Wednesday night. Some were for rededication. I made no difference on that. I just keep a record on that part of the service – the invitation. I can't recall anytime when no one came forward. I can't recall any invitation here or in the old building." Church old-timers remember one service in Chauncey-Goode, the longtime main auditorum, when no one came forward at the gospel invitation – for the first and only time in 25 to 30 years. Dr. Roberson announced from the pulpit that this had better not happen again. And it didn't.

Evangelist Joe Shadowens recalled another service in Chauncey-Goode on a Sunday night. "I was in the service," he said, "when over 1,100 people came forward. We filled up the choir, four or five rows of front pews, and then spilled over to the Herrmann Building across the street. My wife and I were counselors. We worked with them until about 2:00 in the morning. He baptized every morning that week. I counted on purpose. On Wednesday night he baptized 85. We had revival. J. Harold Smith was the preacher. That was the biggest meeting I've been in." Smith preached his famous sermon on *God's Three Deadlines*. Cliff Robinson remembered, "The auditorium was filled. The invitation was amazing. The aisles were filled. The altar was filled. There was nowhere to go." Many of the people who came forward came for salvation. The scheduled four-day revival series of meetings was extended for three weeks!

A typical Sunday morning church service invitation at Highland Park Baptist Church was described in the *Chattanooga News-Free Press* report: "People came forward – a little boy about six, brought by his Sunday school teacher; a teenager; an older man; many others...The service was closed with a personal word (from Roberson) to each one who came up. 'Glenn, do you believe Jesus Christ died to save you from your sins? God bless you, son. So glad to see you. And we have a couple who are transferring their church membership from Virginia – aristocrats. It's so good to have you here. We want to pray for the Jeffers family, who have taught here at Temple and now leave for work in the West. Father, bless this family, bless this brother in the teaching ministry. Keep him in the center of Thy will, and don't let him stray. In Jesus' name, amen.'"

Each person who responded to the gospel invitation was counseled by an altar worker. The name, address, and the individual's spiritual decision or commitment were all recorded on a card, which was later given to Roberson. After the invitation Faulkner would lead a hymn while Roberson readied himself for baptism. Roberson always performed the baptizing himself. He would have one ministry attendant waiting behind the platform with his waders, and another man holding his baptismal coat. He would pull fishing waders over his trousers and change into the second-hand suit coat which was going to get wet. It took him 90 seconds to leave the main auditorium platform, change clothes, and re-appear in the baptistry ready to baptize. Altogether three or four men would be behind the scene to assist him in preparing for baptism.

Roberson did not like for people to leave the church services early – during the gospel invitation and following baptism. "Nobody leave! Nobody leave!" he would command from the pulpit. The invitation was not a little matter at Highland Park Baptist Church. Roberson made it a big thing – constantly emphasized its importance. At the end of the service he did not like for church members to leave before baptism. Because so many were baptized on a regular basis, some people wanted to slip out early. When Roberson first came to Highland Park, he threatened to call the names of those leaving early – although he never did that. However, on one occasion when it was time for the invitation, Roberson stood on a front pew, praying out loud, "God, I'm praying with my eyes open, so I can see anyone sneeking out." People who were there still laugh at the memory. In his sermon, *Witnessing*, Roberson said, "The most exciting time in our church is when we give the invitation Sunday morning, Sunday evening and Wednesday evening. But through the years we have always had a few people who will leave during the invitation when the song is going on and converts are coming down the aisles. They will deliberately pick up their belongings and walk out...They are so unconcerned they would not care if 75 or 100 people walked the aisles in a service and professed their faith in Christ. They are more concerned about getting out and going home, sitting down at a lunch table or entering into some activity for a Sunday afternoon."

Newspaper reporter Helen McDonald Exum described the close of the Sunday morning church service she visited in 1971. "With a special greeting and a special prayer for the 15 or 16 people who came forward either on profession of faith, rededication, or transfer of church letters, Lee Roberson had the benediction."

Roberson's "Three-to-Thrive" emphasis meant that a church member should be in church weekly for Sunday morning, Sunday evening, and Wednesday evening services in order to thrive spiritually. Roberson put great emphasis upon the Wednesday midweek prayer meeting. He wanted a crowd. Faithfulness by all ministry workers was encouraged. He believed that a Christian needed the midweek service as a "bridge" between Sundays. On Wednesday nights most of the 93-voice church choir sang, and Roberson preached a full sermon. The church was usually packed out. Each church he served as pastor saw a tremendous increase in the Wednesday night midweek service attendance. Roberson began his Highland Park ministry on a Wednesday night in 1942 and ended it on a Wednesday night in 1983. He called the Wednesday night prayer service "the sweetest service of the week." Before Roberson arrived in Chattanooga, the Wednesday night attendance at Highland Park was so small that the service was held in one of the Sunday school rooms in the church basement. "I was determined that this would be a service of power – a time to call our people to a deeper dedication to God," he said later.

Roberson's Wednesday night prayer meeting format began with a song service, with at least two special numbers (solo, duet, etc.). Emphasis was given to prayer. Prayer lists were made up in advance – the sick, the hospitalized, and the bereaved. Publicly 15 minutes were committed to the prayer list every Wednesday. Roberson would call upon three or four church leaders to come to the platform and lead in prayer for the many prayer requests for the hospitalized, the sick, missionaries, etc. – all printed on prayer sheets. The men led in prayer from the platform, so that they could be heard in such a large crowd. Next would come a challenge for Thursday night visitation. Hands were raised and tickets distributed for the Thursday evening supper, which preceded visitation. Then came announcements and a weekly offering for missions. Following was the sermon and the gospel invitation. "Here at Highland Park, we press upon our people three great hours – 'Three to Thrive' – Sunday morning, Sunday evening, Wednesday evening," said Roberson. "We feel that three hours are few enough to build worthwhile, witnessing Christians. In every service, singing is important. We believe in enthusiastic singing of the old-fashioned hymns and gospel songs! Prayer is important. The preaching of the Word is primary. Plain, clear, Holy Spirit endowed messages must be preached! The invitation must be plainly and meaningfully given. We invite people to come to the Savior. We invite people to unite with our church by transfer of membership, and we invite Christians to come for the rededication of their lives – for the renewal of their vows to God."

Hundreds of church members would come out for church visitation every Thursday night at 6:00. The church would provide a supper for 50 cents a person – later 75 cents. This pattern was followed the entire 40 years Roberson was at Highland Park. For many years 600 outreach visits were being made weekly by the members of the church. All the church and college staff and workers were to be there. Every Wednesday during the midweek service Roberson would challenge the church regarding the importance of visitation. "I would ask all who would go visiting with us on Thursday evening at 6:00 to stand," he said. "An usher would hand a card to each one standing. The card would read, 'I will be present for the visitation program Thursday evening at 6:00.' By giving out the cards, we knew how many would be present and how many to prepare for."

Roberson placed a great emphasis on visitation. He said that 80 percent of the thousands of people who responded to the public invitation at the end of the Highland Park Baptist Church services had already been reached and counseled by personal workers through church visitation. Roberson set the example in visiting – making as many as 10 calls daily when he was in town. He said publicly, "A home-going pastor makes church-going people." In 1969 the church set a goal of contacting all of the homes of the 322,000 population of greater Chattanooga with the gospel. In addition to visiting, thousands of phone calls, cards, and letters were sent out each month to the unsaved and un-churched of the area.

The visitation director was Walter Wendelken, but Thursday nights Dr. Roberson took charge. Later Roberson would always ask Wendelken what results he had ready for Sunday. Wendelken was an electrician in Indiana when he was saved at the age of 23. A quiet man, he talked with Roberson 10 years later about his future. "The Lord spoke very clearly to my wife and me," Wendelken recalled. "I've had very few experiences like that – 'Yes, that's what I want you to do. I want you to come here to school.' We went back, put our home up for sale and gave notice at work." He came to Tennessee Temple College as a student in 1951 and stayed to work for Roberson for the next 35 years. Wendelken never considered leaving. It was Wendelken's job to make sure there were always new people who had prayed to receive Christ as Savior and were prepared to come forward publicly at the invitation on Sunday, and that there were others ready to be baptized or new members ready to unite with the church by a letter of referral from their previous church. When the gospel invitation was given, a number of "personal workers," or altar counselors, would come forward to the front row of the church. The flow of people walking the aisle would be an encouragement for new Christians, visitors or seekers to find it more comfortable to join in the walk to the front of the sanctuary. Over an 11-year period from 1962 to 1973 the church registered 58,856 visitors from all 50 states and 71 foreign nations, truly earning the title "the South's most visited church."

Roberson used the Sunday school to build the church. The Sunday school was thoroughly organized, and the church visitation program was promoted through the Sunday school. Some 350 people would show up for the teachers' and officers' meeting every Wednesday before prayer meeting – usually about 75 per cent of all Sunday school workers. The meeting was held in the chapel next to the church auditorium. A report for each class and department was given, and goals were assigned to challenge the class workers to reach more people for Christ. The attendance of the church sponsored chapels was announced, as well as promotion plans and upcoming special meetings. Near the close of the meeting Pastor Roberson would enthusiastically seek to fire up each teacher – "challenging them to faithfulness and putting their best efforts to secure capacity attendance in the class for the next Sunday," according to one college teacher. Cliff Robinson would teach the Sunday school lesson to the teachers with suggested methods for presenting the same lesson to their classes on the next Sunday morning. Cliff felt that, "If the Word of God is applied to the heart of the teacher with fire and enthusiasm, he in turn can become a better teacher on Sunday morning." Also aiding in Sunday school preparation, Cliff Robinson prepared an outline for the Sunday school lessons that was published weekly in the church newspaper, *The Evangelist*. This outline went out to all members and helped them prepare the Sunday school lesson. Each week Robinson distributed to the teachers a three-to-five page outline of comprehensive Bible commentary on the week's lesson.

The Sunday school never operated independent of the church and Roberson's leadership. At one time the main Sunday school had 109 classes, including four junior departments. Mrs. Roberson directed a nursery with literally hundreds of babies. Much of the church visitation was organized through the Sunday school classes, as each class had a representative in charge of visitation for that class. Sunday school teachers were required to pledge themselves to faithful attendance at teachers' and officers' meetings, prayer meetings, and Sunday services. Also, a teacher was required to live a consistent life of Christian conduct. The church annually asked teachers to re-affirm such a pledge as they were installed for a new year of service.

Every Thursday some 300 people would show up for the church-wide visitation. Roberson expected his deacons to be there – as they were to show leadership in the areas of visitation, Sunday school, and tithing. A census was taken of the areas surrounding the church. Hundreds of names and addresses were collected of people who did not belong to any other church in the city. "We did not call on those who were active members of another church in the city," recalled Wendelken. The church workers caught the vision of what Lee Roberson was trying to do. Thousands were faithful to all the church services, and many would visit homes regularly on behalf of the church – some spending as many as 20 hours per week visiting on behalf of the church. Not everyone reached for Christ through the ministry of the church actually attended Highland Park Baptist Church. I asked J.R. Faulkner if Highland Park's evangelism helped fill other churches in the city. "Mercy, yes!" he answered.

Highland Park Baptist Church became the leader among church bus ministries in America – later surpassed by First Baptist Church of Hammond, Indiana, which ran buses all over Greater Chicago under the leadership of its well-known pastor, Jack Hyles. M.J. Parker was in charge of busing at Highland Park for years. Well-dressed and sharp looking, Parker was a highly motivated man who had come to Christ later in life. "It was Dr. Lee Roberson who first led me to Christ and later paved the way for me to serve the Lord in the best way I could," Parker said. With little formal education, Parker had the charisma of a salesman. He also had a dedicated focus for the cause of Christ and knew the Word of God. He motivated children to come to Sunday school by use of constant giveaway promotions in the bus ministry. If they rode the bus to Sunday school, the kids, many of whom were from poorer neighborhoods, would receive a hamburger, a sucker or small gift. "We had buses going everywhere," said Elgin Smith. By the late 1940s the church was running 48 or 49 buses, plus vans – with the city map divided up by Sunday school bus routes. Highland Park Baptist Church's buses never stopped running through-out the day on Sundays – bringing in 1,400 riders weekly to the various Sunday school and church services. The buses ran in the morning on Sunday to bring people to Sunday school and church. They ran in the afternoon to bring kids out of the lower-income projects for children's church services, and they ran in the evening to bring people back to the Sunday night service. The church maintained a garage and several automotive mechanics to keep the bus ministry operating smoothly. The ever-present Roberson met each Saturday morning with the bus workers. Each bus had a driver and a "pastor." The bus pastor's responsibility was evangelism, absentee follow-up, visitation, and spiritual counsel for the bus riders.

The bus ministry grew to the point where decorum and control of the children in the church service was a challenge. For awhile the "bus kids" were seated in the balcony, and then finally they attended their own separate children's church service, or junior church. Traditionally, Dr. Roberson wanted the children in the nursery until age four and then in the main church service, preferably sitting together as a family. He did not believe in a separate junior church for the children. But as the bus ministry expanded, he did start the separate children's church service. Dr. Roberson wanted to reach people of all ages – but he did not want disturbances in the church services which would distract people and interfere with the preaching of the Word of God. During the years when Clarence Sexton was in charge of the bus ministry, the buses were averaging more than 2,000 people per Sunday – with a promotional high-day attendance of over 10,000. Clarence Sexton was later joined by his brother, Tom Sexton, on Roberson's pastoral staff – both were to become successful Baptist pastors. Clarence, who had ridden a Sunday school bus to Highland Park as a boy, would preach vigorously on soul winning and patterned himself after Dr. Roberson. Tom was more laid back. Both men were great soul winners.

The old traditional Baptist Training Union, with 5,000 people in attendance, was held every Sunday evening at 6:30 PM, for one hour preceding the 7:30 Sunday evening service. It became the largest such training union in the world. Each Sunday evening you could set your watch by the fact that at 6:28 PM Dr. Roberson would come in the right-side door at the front of the auditorium. He would walk over to the second row and sit with his wife for the opening assembly of the Training Union hour. After a 15-minute opening, the training union was divided into groups at 6:45 PM. The largest group was the Sunday Evening Forum, directed in the main auditorium by Roberson. He would introduce guest speakers, evangelistic or missionary films or slide presentations, visiting missionaries, or special musicians, etc., for the programs.

The church radio ministry was begun by Roberson his first month at Highland Park on December 13, 1942. The name of the daily broadcast soon became *Gospel Dynamite*, with a Bible theme verse of Romans 1:16, *"For I am not ashamed of the gospel of Christ: for it is the power of God unto salvation to every one that believeth; to the Jew first, and also to the Greek."* The program was broadcast at 8:30 AM, Monday through Saturday each week, and was to become the longest running live radio broadcast in America. The daily broadcast, Monday through Saturday, initially lasted 30 minutes and was later lengthened to one hour. The format included an introduction with the Scripture verse of Romans 1:16, and a few words of welcome. During the first 15 minutes there were three or four songs, plus announcements about the ministry of the church. Roberson's presentation of a short Bible message typically lasted five to 10 minutes in length. His talk was called, "A Word from the President." Roberson, of course, was president of the college, which operated its own radio station in later years. Roberson believed that long sermons on radio were not ideal for promoting the church, but later when the church opened its own radio station, all services were also broadcast live on radio. But from the beginning Roberson's focus was on his short, five-to-ten minute daily radio message broadcast each morning. If Roberson were in town, he would speak himself.

The broadcast was carried daily on WDYN-FM and WRIP-AM radio. Gospel songs were used daily Monday through Saturday on the broadcast, with a special prayer time at 8:45 AM. At the beginning of the broadcast, listeners were invited to call the station with prayer requests. Scores of telephone calls came in each morning to the three telephones, which were staffed by secretaries. J.R. Faulkner would read the prayer requests over the air. Sometimes there were more than 75 such prayer requests. Cliff Robinson would then lead in prayer over radio. Following the prayer Roberson would have musicians sing the song, *He Careth for You*. After the prayer time, Roberson's Bible message was presented, closing at 8:58 AM. He would then challenge the audience with some closing words, urge the people to write into the broadcast, and sign off. Every Thursday the broadcast was dedicated to shut-ins (homebound). Jean Smith was designated the special singer for the shut-in broadcast.

Roberson would line up musicians from the church and college to sing on his radio broadcast. Orman Norwood remembered the morning he was scheduled to sing but inadvertently forgot about it and failed to show up. Norwood was sitting at Wally's Restaurant in Chattanooga, eating breakfast and listening to Roberson's *Gospel Dynamite* radio broadcast. Suddenly, he heard Roberson's voice live on the radio saying to his on-air associate, Cliff Robinson, "Cliff, where's Orman? Wasn't he supposed to sing? Orman, where are you?" As Orman heard those words over the air, he said later it was like God speaking to him! He hurried to meet Roberson to apologize for missing the broadcast. He never missed again!

With the growth of the college, radio station WDYN-FM, 89.7 on the radio dial, was launched by Highland Park Baptist Church on a full-time basis in 1968 – including pastoral staff members preaching daily, plus college and church music groups, and a daily "prayer time" for listeners. Each day the station would air continuously from early morning until late at night – music, sermons, and programs. WDYN began as a 10-watt radio station with an antenna on a flag pole on Missionary Ridge in Chattanooga. Within a few years it was a 100,000-watt station with a 200-foot tower on Signal Mountain reaching the tri-state area with 18 hours of Christian and educational programming. You could sometimes hear it as far away as Atlanta. Later the station went to 24-hour broadcasting around the clock. Included in the broadcasting on WDYN radio were Highland Park's Sunday morning and evening church services, as well as the Wednesday evening service, and the Radio Bible Class during the Sunday school hour.

Highland Park Baptist Church broadcast its services on TV for a short period of time. However, Roberson told me years later, "I didn't like it – something about it put a strain on the service. I would avoid some things I didn't want the public to hear. I didn't care for the TV thing at all. It never appealed to me. We had it for awhile. I didn't really get a gain from it – from a church [growth] standpoint. I didn't want to be on it. When it went off, I was glad to get out of it." The expensive cost of TV ministry was also a concern. Nevertheless, Roberson one time told Walter Wendelken he was sorry he gave up the television broadcast, as it has certainly become the dominant communications medium of the modern era.

Roberson also started a printing ministry right away when he moved to Highland Park. The ministry's publication, *The Evangelist*, began under a different name about one year after Roberson arrived at Highland Park. The first issue came out on January 19, 1944. Roberson chose the name, *The Evangelist*, after a similar paper published by the famed 19th century evangelist, Charles G. Finney.

Roberson's paper was originally a weekly publication. He would include one published sermon from Highland Park's pulpit and announcements about the church, the chapels, and the missionary work. The paper's circulation peaked at 75,000 copies – sent to all 50 states and some 76 countries. "You talk about work," said Faulkner. "That was another thing crammed into our week. We went to bi-monthly when the postal rate went up. And we had 70,000 copies going out. Oh, brother, you talk about work!" The magazine was sent all over the world to anyone associated with the church and school – students, parents, missionaries, preachers, etc. Faulkner would also write an article for the weekly advertisements in both the morning and evening Chattanooga newspapers. He would change the borders on the ads and put in the titles weekly. Roberson emphasized advertising. He liked pictures in the church ads.

All Highland Park Baptist Church services were interpreted for the deaf – with as many as 119 hearing impaired people enrolled in two special Sunday school classes. A special revival was held annually for the deaf, with some well-known evangelist brought in. Interpreters for the deaf were on hand at all regular services of the church. It seemed the ministries of the church were endless.

The always growing youth department used Word of Life Bible clubs and other related ministries to reach teenagers. A weekly radio broadcast to reach teens was aired each Saturday over WDYN-FM. The teenagers of Highland Park were even involved in the visitation program of the church – with 60 or more teens showing up weekly. After visiting, the teens would go to a home for fun and fellowship. Roberson's philosophy was, "Work first; socialize second."

Dr. Roberson was the moderator for all church business meetings. Church business matters were never handled on a Sunday. Sundays were for preaching the Word of God and giving a gospel invitation. "It was the same every week, every week – avoid everything else," Roberson told me. At first at Highland Park he held a church business meeting monthly. Later it was quarterly. Finally, he said, he liked the idea of holding it after prayer meeting quarterly. On Wednesday nights he would occasionally bring up some business matters but never allow people to respond – no discussion from the platform – never. The annual church business meeting was an overwhelming experience for the individual church member. A number of pages were handed out listing the massive church budget and the extraordinary list of church officers to be elected – from deacons to ushers. Leadership positions were elected annually. Leaders and Sunday school teachers were required to sign a four-point standard of loyalty, which included declarations of: a) Personal salvation; b) Separated living; c) Faithfulness to all church services; and, d) Loyal support for the church programs and leadership. Church members were urged to tithe to the local church. They were given an annual opportunity to sign a pledge.

The ministry finances ran smoothly, managed by such men as Ray Marler. A full financial report was given to the church annually. Other reports, such as a building project, were also given to the church. Bankers such as Arnold Chambers helped with fund raising. Roberson was always very cautious with finances. He wanted the deacons to handle business matters by following procedure and looking after details. He did not want to get the church into debt. Highland Park was always solvent – able to pay its bills and pay off its debts. One reason there were never any financial problems was because there were always so many people, which resulted in ample contributions. If Roberson held a dinner to promote a financial project, the dinner would be free. Everyone, it seemed, wanted to come. A thousand people would show up. "We just had plenty of money," said Elgin Smith. "There were a lot of people!"

Trained in accounting as far back as high school, Roberson was astute financially. He always had a finance committee functioning, and he would follow its recommendations. He constantly challenged the church on faith. If a financial undertaking appeared difficult, he would challenge the church to prayer and give sacrificially. "Dr. Roberson was never wasteful," said J.R. Faulkner. "In a building program, we always had times of raising money to finish a job – that kind of thing. He told our deacons, 'I am not to get my [pay] check until every missionary is paid.' That was a rule that he gave to the finance committee over there. He felt responsible for getting those checks out to the missionaries."

Lee Roberson believed in two biblical offices for the local church – pastor and deacon. While Highland Park had very few doctors and lawyers as church members, the board of deacons included some prominent professional men. Elgin Smith was a governor on the Tennessee Board of Realtors. Gene Hatfield, a certified public accountant and a lawyer, was the Chattanooga city auditor for years. At one time the mayor of Chattanooga was a deacon at Highland Park. Glenn Copeland, also a deacon, was an attorney. "Generally, we followed his recommendations," Copeland said of Roberson. "He was our leader." Faulkner said, "He never had deacon trouble. Doctor was such a strong personality that people respected him. And he was so wise in his deliberation and in his decisions and in his leadership. He was never driving for something unreasonable – something that was out of reach." Roberson spoke highly of his deacons. In his sermon, *Some Deacons Excel*, he said, "I pause to pay tribute to the deacons of our church. In all of the years that I was pastor, I had only the finest fellowship with our deacons. Our men have been progressive, spiritually minded and largely faithful."

The finances were handled by the finance committee. The deacons, who were required to tithe, received a report. Roberson did not handle the finances directly himself. "He did not know who gave what," said Copeland. "He didn't want to know. It was to be in confidence. He didn't want anyone else to know." Ministry purchases were generally made on a cash basis. "Very little did we go in debt," Copeland said. "If we couldn't pay for it, we didn't do it." Roberson always knew there were certain people he could call who would financially help college students in need. It was common knowledge that places like the McKee Bakery would give students jobs. But Roberson was not one to push extensively for such projects as scholarship funds and development funds. He believed the Lord would raise the money as needed, and that financial growth would come with membership growth. If the church borrowed for a building project, the goal was to pay it off with the completion of the construction. Roberson said he believed that 75 per cent of the Highland Park members were faithfully tithing – which, if accurate, was incredible!

The church offerings were handled carefully and publicly. The ushers would take the offering in the college student church service in Phillips Chapel, walk through the basement up to the main

Chauncey-Goode auditorium, receive the main offering there – and carry it all down and put it on the communion table at the front of the main church service. After the main service, the ushers would take the entire morning offering to the office safe. On one occasion, someone was caught stealing from the Phillips Chapel offering. Dr. Roberson was asked if they could not take the Phillips offering directly to the safe. Bill Long, security chief, remembered his answer was a vigorous "no!" Roberson said, "We're not going to have people wondering where their offering went." Long, a great admirer and supporter of Roberson, said, "I didn't always agree. But you either figured he was right or it didn't matter."

Highland Park's years under Lee Roberson were not in the computer age. J.R. Faulkner showed me boxes of Highland Park Baptist Church records going back decades – Sunday school programs, issues of *The Evangelist*, ordination records, etc. Few churches ordained more young preachers than did Highland Park – obviously because of the prolific training of Tennessee Temple.

Statistically, it should be pointed out that the church membership rolls of Highland Park Baptist Church were seldom, if ever, purged. Membership figures included everyone who made a public profession of faith and was baptized through the ministry of the church – including at the Union Gospel Mission, Camp Joy, the bus ministry, and the 47 branch chapels – whether or not the people realized it. In addition, most Tennessee Temple University students would join Highland Park. Consequently, many of those listed as members of the church were not actually living year-round in Chattanooga. Highland Park Baptist Church's membership was listed in 1952 at 10,000, in 1967 at 25,000, in 1975 at 40,000, and in 1982 at 57,000. On this basis, *Christian Life* magazine listed Highland Park as the fifth largest church *in the world* as late as 1983, the year Lee Roberson retired from the pastorate. Roberson and Faulkner felt that the inclusion of the chapels in Highland Park's total attendance was perfectly legitimate, because the church maintained the chapels financially and supplied the preachers. As individual chapels were successful as local churches, they would break away as independent churches and were no longer counted.

The main auditorium, known later as Chauncey-Goode, was packed out by the 1960s. The building was expanded laterally, a U-shaped balcony stretched around the auditorium, and air conditioning was installed. As Chauncey-Goode over-flowed, multiple church services were held in different buildings. Finally, it was decided to build a huge, new auditorium on the property running from Bailey to Union avenues and along Beech Street. Arnold Chambers was chairman of the building committee. The new building was built in 1982 at a cost of more than $4-million. Reflecting over his years at Highland Park, in 1983, Chambers said, "There are just two things I want to be remembered about me. First, I was chairman of the committee that located Dr. Roberson and brought him up here, and second, I was chairman of that building committee. Forget all the rest of it. Those are the only two that I'm really interested in."

CHAPTER 10

A School to Train Preachers

A young man named David Copeland was saved in a tent revival in 1942 in Chattanooga, Tennessee – the same year Lee Roberson became pastor of Highland Park Baptist Church. At the time, David was married and the father of a young family – including a son, future attorney Glenn Copeland. Glenn, who was later baptized by Roberson, was a child attending Highland Park Baptist Church along with his family when Roberson arrived as their new pastor. Then eight years old, Glenn said years later, "I raised my little hand to vote him in." Within a few short years, Glenn's young father, David, was called to preach under Roberson's ministry, but David Copeland only had a seventh grade education. Roberson advised David to enroll in Bible schools in New Orleans and Chicago, including Moody Bible Institute, in order to prepare for his calling to the ministry. But none of the schools would accept David because of his limited education. Finally, Roberson said to David Copeland, "You're not the only one. Servicemen are returning [from World War II]. Why don't we just start our own school?"

Under Roberson's direction Highland Park Baptist Church organized Tennessee Temple College on July 3, 1946. Roberson, always the promoter, called it "America's newest college." David Copeland was the first student. Roberson wanted to train preachers to staff the chapels he was starting all around the Chattanooga area. But more than that, he had a vision to send out preachers and missionaries to all parts of the world proclaiming the gospel of Jesus Christ. The previous year Roberson had been inspired by the biography of H.C. Morrison, the renowned Methodist preacher who started Asbury College. As Roberson read the book, he had written on one page in the margin, "A school to train preachers. Call Arnold." The reference was to banker Arnold Chambers, a leading deacon at Highland Park.

Initially, Temple was begun to do just that – it was training preachers and missionaries.

Lee Roberson said later that he had no desire to build a school – he simply wanted to train men to serve the Lord. He cited the need for preachers to speak at the growing chapel ministry as a primary reason for starting the school. "We began Tennessee Temple to send out the message of the Word of God," he said.

Originally planned as a two-year college and Bible school, Tennessee Temple quickly expanded to a four-year college, with an evening Bible school and a graduate seminary. University status was achieved years later in 1979. From the beginning, Roberson adopted a theme for Tennessee Temple to be "distinctively Christian." The initial announcement of the formation of the new college was made in the *Chattanooga Times* on July 11, 1946. The college was scheduled to open on September 16.

At the time when Roberson started the college, Highland Park Baptist Church's membership had increased during his three years as pastor from 1,200 to 3,100. Highland Park had already led the then 26,000-member churches of the Southern Baptist Convention in baptisms for two years, 1944 and 1945. The new college was to be financed not by the church, nor by the SBC, but by a separate board of trustees. At that time no one could foresee the impact of this new college. By the early part of the 21st century, Tennessee Temple University had more than 12,000 graduates. J.R. Faulkner said there would be no way to tell how many were serving in ministries around the world – most of them in ministry as pastors, evangelists, missionaries, Christian school and college administrators and teachers, etc.

In 1946 the church vote to start the college was unanimous. It was taken during a summer tent revival meeting with Evangelist

Paul Roberts. There was little discussion, as the people already fully trusted their pastor of three years and endorsed Roberson's plan. The night the vote was taken, a young missionary named Verna Pullen, home on a brief furlough from Africa, gave the first $1,000 for the new college. The gift – a fair amount of money in those days – was from her late father's inheritance. Dr. Roberson walked the hallway of the church offices the next day waving the check and rejoicing in the faithfulness of God. Years later, a girls' dormitory was named after Verna Pullen.

The first college classroom building, originally purchased in 1944 for Sunday school space for the church, was named the Buchanan Building. A confession of faith, based upon the orthodox literal interpretation of the Bible – the traditional Baptist view – was drawn up. The college was to be "evangelistic, missionary, fundamental, and pre-millennial" in doctrine and philosophy. The college creed was to "stand for the fundamentals of the faith. We believe and teach the Bible. We give emphasis to evangelism, missions, separated living, and the pre-millennial second coming of Christ."

From the beginning, Dr. Roberson was president of the new college. Dr. John Herrmann, a former teacher at Bob Jones College, then in Cleveland, Tennessee, was vice-president. Dr. Herbert Lockyer from Liverpool, England, was dean. Erna Werner was registrar, and banker Arnold Chambers was business manager. Initial tuition was listed at $50 per semester, but tuition was free for all students entering full-time Christian service, ministry, or missions – which constituted most of the Temple students in the early years. After the United States government's World War II Manhattan Project had been completed, partly at Oak Ridge, Tennessee, the fledgling college purchased from the government 25 or 30 mobile homes, where the project workers had been living, for $1 each. They were moved to a vacant lot at Willow and 23rd streets and quickly filled with married students.

In the first year immediately following World War II, Dr. Herrmann announced that Tennessee Temple College had been founded in the "greatest and gravest hour in human history," and Tennessee Congressman Estes Kefauver was invited to speak – but had to cancel out at the last minute. The first commencement in May of 1948 graduated 27 students – including 17 men and 10 women. By 1953 the graduating class numbered 77. From the beginning Roberson had strong support in the local community. At the time the college was started, Will Shepherd, editor of *The Hamilton County Herald* wrote, "For the past two or three years we have been watching the remarkable growth of the Highland Park Baptist Church, and no religious organization of local origin can boast of the rapid expansion, under the dynamic leadership of Dr. Lee Roberson." At the beginning, in addition to the 109 students enrolled in the day college, another 75 enrolled in night school – 50 of whom were licensed ministers in the area. While Congressman Kefauver (later a U.S. Senator and Democratic vice presidential nominee in 1956) wired his congratulations, the inaugural program of the college included short speeches by a county judge, a city commissioner, the local Southern Baptist association moderator, and Dr. J. Park McCallie of Chattanooga's private elite McCallie School.

The college opened at the corner of Orchard Knob and Bailey avenues on September 16, 1946, with 11 faculty members. Lee Roberson was hoping for 50 students. In fact, he said privately that he did not want any more than 50 students initially. Everyone was surprised when 109 full-time students showed up. "He was so scared he went home and went to bed," J.R. Faulkner recalled. "He went home not knowing what he was going to do with them." Roberson said years later that he was discouraged and told the Lord, "Take it away. I didn't mean to get into this." That first day he went home for lunch and told his wife he had made a mistake. "I got too many [students]," he said. "I can't handle this." But God confirmed the vision of what was to be done. Walter Wendelken estimated that in the early years 90 per cent of the college students came to Tennessee Temple through the personal promotion and direct invitation of Dr. Roberson as he traveled. Elgin Smith remembered those early days. "If Dr. Roberson was out preaching somewhere," he said, "and some students would come up to him and say, 'I just feel the Lord wants me to come to Temple, but I don't have any money,' he would say, 'Come on! Come on!' He'd put them on the payroll over there somehow. He'd get them started to school. It was amazing!"

Temple Baptist Seminary, a ministerial graduate school, was begun in 1953. Originally named Southeastern Baptist Theological Seminary, the name was subsequently changed when another seminary by the same name was established by the Southern Baptist Convention. At the time, Highland Park was still a Southern Baptist church, but its schools were never officially connected with the SBC. Dr. Roberson was the first president of the seminary, and for the first decade the vice-president was Dr. John R. Rice, the founder and editor of *The Sword of the Lord*, an independent fundamental Christian periodical.

Tennessee Temple College grew rapidly, as loyal alumni preachers kept sending more students from their churches. In the early years the ministry bought up the neighborhood property, as old houses in the area were purchased and used as classrooms before being torn down, so college buildings could go up. As always, Roberson ran a tight ship. The old houses could be hot in the late spring or early fall – with no air-conditioning. When Roberson saw a class take a break to buy ice cream from a street vendor, he sent Cliff Robinson to check it out. "Can't do that, can't do that! Keep them in the classroom," Cliff remembered Roberson telling him. By the 1970s Tennessee Temple's peak was about 4,100 students, with on-campus housing maxed out at 2,200 beds. The crowds for the commencement exercises were so large that the graduation programs had to be held at Chattanooga's Memorial Auditorium.

In the early years Temple's enrollment of young men mushroomed under the GI bill following World War II and the Korean War, and then later the Vietnam War. Throughout those years Temple received a heavy influx of married students – at one point with 1,400 married couples enrolled. J.R. Faulkner was in charge of finding all kinds of houses for the couples. It was a challenge. "I had the worst time, as business manager, trying to find housing," Faulkner recalled. "At one time we had a motel, Ridgeside Motel along Missionary Ridge – we had that motel rented! We had the Rancho Motel rented out in East Ridge. It was owned by one of our deacons. We had it full. And we had the motel in East Ridge, in town – we had that full. And we were busing the students in and out from the motels – single kids who didn't have cars, college students, all men. We didn't put girls out there. We were giving the dorms to the girls. We built houses down just below the soccer field – six houses. They were filled with girls. At one time I had a dozen older houses filled with girls. Some mothers [he chuckled] – we laugh now. They were hesitant to leave their daughters in some 'rat hole.' I recall telling Dr. Roberson we have 25 to 30 students, maybe 40 – we don't even have a bed for them. 'Go buy another house.' [Laughter] We were begging people to sell to us. At one time we had over 100 houses and buildings." Later many of the houses were torn down to provide sufficient parking space, as required by city code, when the new church auditorium was built. By then, dormitory buildings provided sufficient space for student housing.

In the 1940s, 50s, and 60s Tennessee Temple's growth was unsurpassed in independent fundamental Baptist circles. Faulkner said, "The GI bill was feeding the soldiers to us. We were unique. Where was the competition? Bob Jones had not come into the Baptist market at that time. Falwell hadn't started. Bob Gray in Texas hadn't started. Clearwater was dead. Hyles-Anderson had not started. Columbia Bible College was mid-trib. Bob Gray began back then in Jacksonville. Piedmont was not aggressive. There was no competition. Pensacola Christian College hadn't started. We had no competition out there."

The college became a mixture of 18-year-old freshmen, straight out of high school, and older war veterans, many of whom were married and were more mature service men – very serious about their work and about studying the Bible. The evening Bible school, composed primarily of working and married students, was thriving in the late 1950s and 1960s with men wanting to serve God. At its peak the evening Bible school had as many as 450 students. Roberson loved the Bible school. He was not concerned with matters such as accreditation, which did come to Tennessee Temple later. He wanted to see men trained for the ministry of the Word of God. "Students came with a vision to serve God and to do something for the Lord – get their Bible training," said Faulkner. "It was all built on that. The liberal arts came as a 'tag-along' because they were needed to build a well-rounded person. Every preacher boy needs speech and English. Dr. Bob [Jones] Sr. used to say, 'English is your gun. The gospel is your cartridge. If you've got a crooked gun, you're not going to hit anything.' I've often quoted him on that. Speech is the same way. So much needs to be based on grammar. Some of what is taught preachers today is appalling. What you are speaks so loud I can't hear what you're saying. What are you portraying? Dr. Bob Jones used to say, 'I want to teach you how to get in and out of a lady's parlor.' He required us all to take etiquette. They had demonstrations on the chapel platform – how to set a table, how to seat ladies, etc. Dr. Roberson had etiquette required in Bible school and the Bible majors in the early days of the school."

Many of the students – especially the married students in the early years – were working in on-campus or off-campus employment for 30 to 40 hours per week. A close-knit group of preacher boys, they would learn street preaching, jail ministry, hospital ministry, etc. A young man training for the ministry could "cut his teeth" on all types of ministries at Tennessee Temple. In his student days missionary Jerry Reece was president of the first organized missionary prayer band, a group of students committed to meeting regularly for prayer. During his four years as a college student Reece saw the enrollment of Tennessee Temple schools experience its fastest period of growth – more than tripling from 400 to 1,500 – between 1955 and 1959. Always Roberson had a strong emphasis on missions at the college. "It was the first thing you'd hear about when you came to Temple," said Reece.

Many faculty members who were hired stayed for years and became leaders in the Christian college movement. In February of 1957, after the death of Dr. Herrmann, Roberson asked Cliff Robinson to join the college board of directors. Robinson, a 1953 graduate of Tennessee Temple, taught Bible and New Testament Greek for 28 years. He served as dean of students and later as vice president for student affairs – and as an assistant pastor of the church. He taught the radio Bible class for 17 years and a men's Bible class for 11 years. Robinson possessed an uncanny ability to use alliteration in making outlines of his Bible teaching and preaching study materials. He published many of these outlines in book form. Once Wymal Porter arrived as a college professor, he never left. Porter, the main Bible teacher at the college for years, served as head of the

Bible department and dean of the college. A fine man, Porter had Dr. Roberson's complete confidence. It was Porter who wrote the school's confession of faith. Dr. John McCormick was considered a remarkable Bible teacher. Glenn Swygart came as a student in 1962 as the school mushroomed again in growth. Swygart graduated and left to earn his master's degree, returning to the faculty in 1969. He stayed for decades, as did Nat Phillips, whose mentor was Dr. Wendell Evans. Evans, who later became president of Hyles-Anderson College in Crown Point, Indiana, was on the faculty staff at Tennessee Temple from 1961 to 1972 – the last five years as dean of the college. Dr. Alfred Cierpke came from Germany after WWII, and later the library was named after him. Alice Scott was the bursar for many years at the college. Buddy Nichols, married to Roberson's eldest daughter, LeeAnne, taught at Temple and later became the college president. Lexy Wiggins was the college historian. Dr. Bruce Lackey was head of the Bible department and an accomplished musician. Firm but loving, attorney Glenn Copeland taught a business class at 7:00 AM. "I would close the door at 7," he said, and then he would tell the students, "I drove 12 miles to get here. What's your excuse?"

Nothing was hit-or-miss for the faculty. Their own attendance in their classes was mandatory, as were faculty meetings and church attendance – Sunday morning, Sunday evening, and Wednesday evening. If you were out-of-town, you were expected to attend another church on the road. Faculty members were permitted to supplement their income. A number of them were preachers. Nat Phillips stayed free from teaching Sunday school at Highland Park so he was available to go preach – or even serve as a pastor – in various churches. Roberson kept the teachers on their toes. It was not uncommon for him to walk past classrooms. If he saw a student asleep in the back of the room, he would go in and wake the student and instruct the teacher not to let that happen anymore. "Not in a mean way," said Phillips. "He started this university with an idea of something serious for the Lord."

The weekly faculty meeting on Thursdays at 10:00 AM followed a set pattern. The secretary would read the minutes, followed by reports from six different areas of campus – education, athletics, etc.

Dr. Roberson would make announcements, and then he would ask if anyone had anything to bring up. Rarely was a faculty member "called down" in front of others at the meetings. If Roberson had seen anyone release class early, he would remind them that class is to stay in session for 50 minutes. The faculty roll was checked, and each member turned in an activity report – listing their regular church attendance and church visitation.

Roberson was literally building a college from scratch. Some rules and traditions were simply practical. Early in the college years, in 1950, a winter storm made it difficult for students to travel home and back for the relatively short Thanksgiving holiday. Roberson considered the weather trouble a waste of time and money. From then on, he instituted a big Thanksgiving holiday weekend of activities on the campus. Moreover, as the college attracted international students, it was almost impossible for them to go home over the Thanksgiving weekend. So, Thanksgiving became a busy on-campus tradition.

Tennessee Temple students were an easy group of people to preach to in Roberson's day. They were energized and eager to learn. They paid attention. The atmosphere was exciting. "You did not want to leave," said missionary Roy Seals. "I knew people who stayed 10 years. God had called them [to go out and serve], but they would take extra Bible classes after graduation [just to stay]." Eventually, of course, they would leave – as that was Roberson's mission and the Lord's calling upon these young men and women.

The college atmosphere was exciting. It seemed that something was always going on. "Tennessee Temple was Dr. Roberson's child," said Bob Kelley. "He kept the best preachers in the world coming though there. He made sure the atmosphere stayed spiritual. You would come into chapel and be encouraged. Then, if needed, be rebuked. He was close to Tennessee Temple. That was his baby. He stayed right on top of it. The best church-building preachers and missionaries went out from Tennessee Temple in the 1950 to 1965 era. That was when the church got up to 10,000 in Sunday school. He kept everyone working – busy. There was an atmosphere of spirituality there. The emphasis on academics was good – but always it was heart before head. Keep your heart warm. Stay on fire for God. It was a well-rounded school, with sports and social activities."

Worshiping and serving at Highland Park Baptist Church was like a laboratory training experience for the preacher boys who enrolled at Tennessee Temple. Highland Park was a local Baptist church with the incomparable and unforgettable Lee Roberson touch. Fred Afman, who taught for 30 years at Bob Jones University, and then for more than 30 years at Tennessee Temple, saw a different style between the two schools. At Bob Jones, the choir wore robes and the chapel service was quiet and dignified. At Tennessee Temple, Roberson preached against robes (too formal), and the atmosphere was lively. As young men arrived, Roberson put them to work. When Tom Wallace arrived in 1950, the church was already huge – with thousands filling the old Chauncey-Goode auditorium, and the college enrollment at 600 students. Tom, who had been very active in his home church, figured such a large church would not need his service. But as he passed the church offices one day, J.R. Faulkner walked out and invited Tom to a workers' meeting for that Saturday morning. They were planning to start some new chapels. Tom Wallace has been serving God ever since.

The college students were involved in workers' meetings on Saturdays – for Sunday school, bus ministry, and chapel ministry. Church leaders such as Faulkner or M.J. Parker would oversee the meetings. Roberson would usually visit and give a short challenge to the young men – usually no more than 10 minutes.

The preacher boys, the heart of Tennessee Temple's mission, looked forward to the Thursday morning one-hour "Preacher Boys" class, taught by Roberson and Faulkner. Affectionately, the boys called the class "Robersonology." Officially called the "Enlistment and Developmental Leadership Class," it was a practical training class on pastoral leadership and ministry for preachers. It included the philosophy and methodology of the pastorate. The pastoral students were taught everything a young preacher would need to know in order to build a church – including preaching, soul winning, witnessing, how to set up church programs, such as visitation, etc. There was no text-book. It was practical training from the life and ministry of Lee Roberson. Roberson taught the preacher boys how to baptize – the Baptist way, of course, by immersion. As the students gathered around the baptistry, Roberson would choose a guinea pig and "baptize" the same student four or five times to demonstrate the procedure. Roberson taught the young men how to perform a wedding. They were instructed on personal hygiene – so important when praying physically up close with a hospital patient or enquirer at the altar, etc. The young preacher boys devoured Roberson's books, most of which contained his published sermons. It was not uncommon for Roberson to give freely a book to any student preacher, or visiting pastor or missionary, when they came to his office.

The ministry laboratory of Highland Park Baptist Church was immense. Tennessee Temple students taught Sunday school, worked with children in junior church, served in the bus ministry, went soul winning and visiting, etc. Preaching in the various chapels started by Highland Park served as another laboratory. David Copeland, Temple's very first student, served as pastor of several of Highland Park's area chapels. The chapel program provided ideal training for many preacher boys. Other students, like Bob Kelley and Ed Johnson, served as pastors of chapels. Lee Roberson told me he got the idea of the chapels from reading about Charles Spurgeon's 19th century ministry of training young preachers in London. Roberson wanted to plant chapels which would hold weekly church services in parts of the county where no genuine fundamental gospel work was going on. This would also provide a station where students could preach. The Tennessee Temple chapel program peaked at 76 chapels operating in four states.

Roberson rarely visited the chapels himself, because the chapel ministry services naturally coincided with the ministry schedule of Sunday services at Highland Park Baptist Church. The chapel ministry expanded from Hamilton County in Tennessee as far away as Alabama, Georgia, and even North Carolina. Several chapels became full-fledged churches on their own, independent of Highland Park Baptist Church – such as First Baptist Church of Lookout Mountain, First Baptist of Tiftonia, Park City Baptist, Sale Creek Baptist, Brainerd Hills Baptist, Stateline Baptist, Duncan Park Baptist, et al. In one year alone, 1973, the chapels reached 1,283 souls for Christ, with a combined average Sunday school attendance of 2,275 weekly. Whether it was a Sunday chapel service, or jail ministry, or nursing home ministry, the students submitted reports – attendance, salvation decisions, etc. – to Dr. Faulkner. Faulkner managed the chapel program and conducted the weekly meetings with the preacher boys.

To start a chapel with the support of Roberson, the chapel had to be under the auspices of Highland Park Baptist Church. When two Tennessee Temple preacher boys once approached Roberson with the idea of starting their own independent Baptist church in nearby Cleveland, Tennessee, they asked for Dr. Roberson's support. Roberson reminded them that the new church, like all the chapels, must be under Highland Park's authority. But one of the young men insisted that God had called them to start the church. With a smile, Roberson said, "You go do what God has led you. God bless you, my boy." He wished them well and offered to pray for them. But they were on their own. One of those boys was later to become a great missionary in Sao Paulo, Brazil, with Mount Abarim Baptist Missions – Dr. Thomas Gilmer.

College chapel services at Tennessee Temple were held at 10:00 AM every Monday, Wednesday, and Friday. Dr. Roberson would preach once or twice per week. Other speakers included Dr. Faulkner, faculty members, and visiting pastors and missionaries. Students loved to hear the great preachers who visited, but they also loved to learn from the pithy sayings of Lee Roberson. "'Be in your place, young people!' Things along that line really helped me to form some character," missionary Jerry Reece said years later.

Although incredibly busy, the disciplined Dr. Roberson gave the students the impression that he always had time for them – especially his preacher boys. "He would take time to pray with you about your concerns," Reece recalled. "I remember on several occasions he stopped and had a short word of prayer for God's guidance and leadership. That really impressed me. I feel like that was another one of the secrets to his success in the ministry. He was always ready to seek the Lord in prayer about decisions and about things that had to be done."

As Roberson traveled, he constantly promoted the college. Tennessee Temple would send out summer tour groups promoting the college – music trios or quartets, evangelism teams, etc. When Roberson was home he supported all the activities of the college. He and Faulkner would attend all of the ballgames of the Tennessee Temple Crusaders' sports teams and all of the recitals and concerts. "We felt the students needed that – to bring encouragement and to know that we were behind them," Faulkner recalled. "They worked years to get up to this point, and that was their time to shine and for us to listen. So, it was for me, and it was for Doctor. He'd be traveling all week. He'd come Friday night to a recital or a ballgame. He would attend those games." When Dr. and Mrs. Roberson would walk into the old McGilvray Gymnasium, filled with 2,000 to 3,000 people, everyone would stand to their feet and applaud. Temple had a great basketball program under Coach Bruce Foster and later Ron Bishop. Bishop led the Temple men's team to four national championships and 250 victories in 10 years. Bishop said of the standing ovations, "It embarrassed him [Roberson] a little bit. But when he and his wife walked in, that's what happened. I had coaches from secular colleges and universities say to me, 'Man, who's that guy? Man, students boo *our* president when he walks in.'"

Bishop appreciated the fact that Roberson made sure the coach had the resources to be successful. During Bishop's run of four national championships, Roberson was constantly in the dressing room. "Every game we won, he would come in the dressing room and pray with the guys," said Bishop. "He was always in that dressing room. He never came in when we lost. He loved winning. He did not have a mentality that 'winning was everything.' It's just – as a pastor, when you lose, best to just let the group be together. But he would come in and share the celebration when we won."

Roberson's discipline of college students at Tennessee Temple was very direct and strict. Everyone feared his wrath. He was known to call out students in the public chapel service and expel them on the spot. "One day in chapel," said Nat Phillips. "Dr. Roberson pointed to a boy on the front row of the balcony. I want 'John Doe' to stand up – called him by name. He stood. Dr. Roberson pointed at the clock. I want you to know at 10:11 AM, May 2, 1980 – or whatever date it was – you are expelled from Tennessee Temple University. I gave you a chance, and you have blown it. As soon as chapel's over, leave." Such stories were legendary. When Jerry Falwell was speaking at a banquet in the 1980s, a male student fell asleep. Dr. Roberson stood up, called him by name, and said, "Wake up! He'll be saying something that you need." The crowd came to attention and got so quiet you could have heard a pin drop. On one occasion Roberson interrupted an evening Bible school class to wake a student who had fallen asleep in the front row. The boy claimed he had been ill. Dr. Roberson instructed him that in order to stay awake he should raise one foot off the floor and hold it there. That was the same instruction he gave years earlier to Garland Cofield to stay awake when driving at night. Bob Kelley said, "Dr. Roberson used to teach that in preacher boys' class. Or, if you're traveling at night – eat apples while you're traveling [to stay awake]. He had an answer for everything. He made life a science."

In disciplinary matters, if a majority of faculty or administration saw the matter differently than Dr. Roberson, he would yield to their advice. The presence of standards and convictions, in some cases, and some of his methods were for the purpose of running a school – not necessarily to define Christian character and common practice. For example, Roberson might "read the riot act" in college chapel, but not in church. Sometimes preacher boys did not recognize the difference. They would graduate, become pastor of a church, and then unwittingly use Roberson's college tactics in a church. That would not set well with the people. The result would sometimes be unwarranted church trouble brought on by the young preachers themselves.

Roberson gave many students a second or third chance, if he believed they could be salvaged from misbehavior. He was slow to discipline the children of pastors because of the compassion and affinity he felt for the dad. Finally he would call a troublesome student in and say, "I've done all I can for you. You've disappointed your father. You've disappointed me. I've given you a second and a third opportunity." Ron Bishop said, "He gave my athletes a lot of leeway." Bishop said he also showed leeway for preacher's kids and missionaries' kids. "He may have hurt himself," Bishop said. "He just couldn't bring himself to dismiss [expel] one of his friend's kids. But there was a line – cross it, and it didn't matter who your daddy was. Cross that line, and you may as well stand at the foot of Mount Sinai because tablets are going to come down on you." But sometimes his compassionate heart as a pastor made it difficult for Roberson to discipline. E.C. Haskell Jr., college dean, sometimes thought Roberson would have been better off to stay out of the disciplinary end entirely. "I heard students come in and confess sins," Haskell recalled. "He would pray with them and dismiss them. When they walked out, I would say, 'Doc, do you understand what was going on there?' I would say, 'Those two students were involved in immorality.' He would say, 'No! No!' – as if that couldn't be. You could even use terms that he didn't recognize."

Dr. Roberson was even known to interrupt a speaker in chapel if he veered from what Highland Park Baptist Church and Tennessee Temple University believed. Stories are legendary of rare occasions where in the midst of a chapel sermon, Roberson – seated on the platform behind the pulpit – would stand to his feet, advance and place his hand on the shoulder of the guest speaker, as he said, "We don't believe that here, brother." The flustered guest would say something to the effect, "Well, okay, we'll leave that," and he would continue his sermon while avoiding further mention of the offending point or doctrine. Bob Kelley remembered when J. Oswald Smith gave his interpretation of Matthew 24:14 at a missions conference. The Scripture verse says, *"And this gospel of the kingdom shall be preached in all the world for a witness unto all nations; and then shall the end come."* Smith preached accordingly that the return of Christ could not occur until the entire world first heard the gospel. Roberson believed in the imminent return of Christ, that the Second Coming of Christ could occur at any time. Kelley said, "Dr. Roberson walked right up beside him while he was preaching and said, 'We don't believe that here, Brother Smith.'" The same thing happened with John R. Rice, who was preaching on the doctrine of storehouse tithing. Rice, an evangelist, did not share Roberson's view that the church member's tithe is to be brought to the storehouse, the local church. Both men were invited back again and again afterwards by Roberson, who loved and admired both and agreed with both on the vast majority of biblical issues. However, if a guest preacher used crude or distasteful humor, Dr. Roberson would literally turn red – and that man would not be invited back to Highland Park.

Roberson maintained standards and rules of personal conduct for the church members and especially for the college personnel. In his sermon, *Seventy-One Years of Fundamentalism*, he said, "In our activities, in our dress, in our appearance, in our alignment, we try to emphasize separation. The Word of God says, 'Come out from among them, and be ye separate, saith the Lord, and touch not the unclean thing, and I will receive you.' God says He will use us and bless us, if we stay separated. It has not been easy to hold to certain standards in the church and in the school. It has not been easy in our school to hold to separation when other Christian schools have strayed. The same is true of the church. Some churches do not have our standards. They have no objection to smoking. We say it is wrong. No Christian should smoke, and we stand against it."

In church he wanted all the ushers to wear ties and coats to receive the offering. At the college, the girls were not permitted to wear pants or slacks – always a dress or skirt. After graduation one year, a girl changed into pants to travel home with her parents. Dr. Roberson saw the girl with her family off campus at Shoney's Restaurant. He came back to the next faculty meeting and told the story of what he had seen. "We failed," he said. A rule against going to any movies was "a big thing here at Temple," said a faculty member. "You could get bounced out of here fast."

But even the complaints of the critics seemed to result in greater blessing for Tennessee Temple. Roberson recalled the story of a student who was so upset with the rules that he went to a newspaper, which published a story critical of Tennessee Temple. Roberson said the story was filled with falsehoods. Nevertheless, as people became acquainted with the old-fashioned rules of Tennessee Temple, the publicity of the newspaper article surprisingly resulted in more financial support and more student enrollments for the college. Some people, previously unfamiliar with Temple, were impressed with Roberson's old-fashioned rules and standards!

Roberson said publicly, "We make no apology for asking our young people at Tennessee Temple University to attend church Sunday morning, Sunday night and Wednesday night. That is what identifies our young people when they go out into churches and into homes where things are not as strict as we demand at TTU."

Roberson's disciplinary strictness was balanced by a desire to help students. He kept a fund in a desk drawer to help students who went through financial need. People would voluntarily contribute to the fund, and he would distribute the money as needed.

Constantly, Roberson challenged the students from the pulpit. In his sermon, *The Mad Race*, he proclaimed, "Young man, if God wants you in His ministry, be quick to say, 'Lord, I am ready to do Thy will.' Do not give excuses and seek to find a way out, but quickly agree with the Lord and enter into His work. Young lady, if God has called you into some service of our Christ, then, without hesitation, give yourself to the Lord and do His will. This mad racing humanity is so unconcerned about the will of God. But I hasten to say that there is nothing more important for you as a child of God than His will for your life."

Young preachers caught Lee Roberson's vision and led evangelistic, missions-minded churches. Some of the leading Baptist pastors of the last generation – especially in the independent, fundamental Baptist movement – were graduates of Tennessee Temple. Included were preachers such as Lou Davis, Ray Hancock, Jack Hudson, Ed Johnson, Bob Kennedy, Dolphus Price, Bradley Price, John Reynolds, brothers Clarence and Tom Sexton, Tom Wallace, Ray Young, et al. Paul Dixon, the extraordinarily successful president of Cedarville University in Ohio, was a graduate, as was Mike Loftis, the president of the Association of Baptists for World Evangelism (ABWE), and Mike Callahan, Joe Jordan, and Tom Phillips of Word of Life, plus missionaries Mike Patterson and Tom Gilmer of Mount Abarim International Missions. Many other preachers not as famous were graduates. "I'm so proud of my boys," said J.R. Faulkner. "They're like my own sons. They've been steady where they are." Jerry Matthiess worked under Bradley Price, when he was pastor of Central Baptist Church in Panama City, Florida. When Roberson was in the area for a speaking engagement, the church sent a music team for the service. Publicly Dr. Roberson put his arms around Jerry and Bradley and said, "Now, folks, these are my boys. This is what it's all about." Such opportunities became a showcase for Tennessee Temple University.

Highland Park Baptist Church became a "boot camp" of training for the Tennessee Temple preacher boys. "Every person who came to Temple had an opportunity to see the greatest church in the world, at that time, in operation and become involved," recalled Bob Kelley. "I became a student of that church. Always my goal was to employ the principles and pattern of Highland Park Baptist Church and Dr. Lee Roberson. What I learned from Dr. Roberson – those principles – worked."

And always Dr. Roberson kept these future potential pulpit giants in line. Missionary Tom Gilmer remembered the day when he and a friend thought they detected doctrinal heresy on the part of one of the Sunday school teachers – a "heresy" that later looked pretty minor to Gilmer in retrospect. But at the time the two preacher boys went in to see Dr. Roberson with their discovery. Roberson listened to their concern and then asked them, "Do you boys have confidence in the teaching of Dr. Cliff Robinson?" Robinson, an associate pastor, was teaching one of the large, main Sunday school classes at the time. "Oh, yes, sir, of course!" Gilmer and his friend responded. "Well, then," Dr. Roberson said, "why don't you two boys start attending his class this Sunday." That was the last they heard of the alleged heresy, Gilmer told me with a laugh years later.

At Temple the students – especially the young preacher boys – studied everything Roberson said or did. During chapel they would watch his facial expressions for approval or disapproval of musicians or speakers. Usually, after a special music number, he would arise and say something to the effect, "Thank you for that great song!" On other occasions, he might call for everyone to stand and sing a verse of a traditional hymn. Students wondered on such occasions if the special music had not met with his approval.

E.C. Haskell Jr. estimated that during Tennessee Temple's glory years under Lee Roberson that 30 to 35 per cent of the graduates of the college would go to the mission field. Scores of missionaries went out under Baptist International Missions, Inc., the Association of Baptists for World Evangelism, Word of Life, et al. Haskell, who later served with ABWE after 20 years as dean at Temple, remembered one year as late as the early 1990s when 17 of ABWE's 50 newly commissioned missionaries were Tennessee Temple graduates. On my first missions trip to Asia in 1998, I traveled with missionary Les Frazier and pastor Lou Davis to speak to the BIMI field conferences in Japan and the Philippine Islands. In both countries it impressively caught my attention how many of the veteran missionaries had come to the foreign field as graduates of Tennessee Temple during the Roberson years.

Many of the Temple graduates were ordained at Highland Park Baptist Church. Ordination services at Highland Park were a solemn time – held four or five times annually on Thursday evening after the visitation supper. Marriage ceremonies also were certainly not uncommon. Many young future pastors and missionaries were married in the chapel building after graduation. If graduation was on a Friday evening, there would be a procession of weddings on Saturday. The students would all share in the cost of the flowers, etc., as one wedding was held after another. Then it was off on a honeymoon – before leaving for their field of service. Roberson did not perform many of the college weddings. Usually the couples would choose one of the ordained faculty members.

Veteran Baptist preacher Jim Vineyard of Oklahoma City told me that he could see no individual on the horizon in the independent Baptist movement who could account for as many graduates serving as pastors, evangelists, and missionaries – as could Lee Roberson. The sheer number of years and number of graduates for an institution led by one man is unsurpassed in fundamental Baptist circles.

Through the years the training of Tennessee Temple went far beyond producing preachers and missionaries. It became a degree-granting institution offering majors in 11 fields – English, history, Bible, music, sacred music, elementary education, secondary education, psychology, speech, art, and business administration. Degrees and credits were recognized by leading universities and the Tennessee State Board of Education. Dallas Willard, acclaimed author and philosophy professor at the University of Southern California, graduated from Tennessee Temple. Victor Hazard, a dean at the University of Kentucky, is an African-American who played basketball for Coach Ron Bishop at Tennessee Temple. Jim Hammond, another Temple graduate, was sent to the Middle East to train Iraqi police officers during the war on terrorism.

Besides Tennessee Temple University, the Tennessee Temple Bible School held evening classes offering both three- and four-year diplomas. Temple Baptist Theological Seminary offered six graduate degrees, including the Master of Divinity.

After the struggle for housing in the early years, Tennessee Temple began to attract financial support from around the country. Churches, inspired by Roberson's ministry – and many of them led by Roberson's preacher boys – would put Tennessee Temple on their home missions support list. Millionaire businessmen such as Art DeMoss, whose life was spiritually impacted by Roberson, got behind the college financially. DeMoss was saved in a meeting with evangelist Hyman Appelman in Buffalo, New York. Appelman directed him to go to Tennessee Temple and see Roberson. Later DeMoss told Dr. Roberson that he did not feel called of God to be a preacher or a missionary but that God was directing him to be a Christian businessman. He moved to Philadelphia and made millions of dollars in the insurance business. Art DeMoss became a man of prayer – with a prayer list of more than 1,000 names. He was generous in his financial support of Tennessee Temple University. At his death in his 50s, DeMoss left $13-million to the college. Today one of the main dormitories on campus is named the DeMoss Building.

The example of Tennessee Temple became an inspiration to others. Dr. Arlin Horton talked casually with J.R. Faulkner about the college before starting Pensacola Christian College. Jack Hyles flew to meet with Faulkner and Roberson at length before starting Hyles-Anderson College. Jerry Falwell sat in Phillips Chapel and talked for two hours with Faulkner, discussing the operation of a college, before he started Liberty University. "How do you do this? That?" recalled Faulkner. "I told Dr. Roberson that Jerry Falwell is going to start a school." He did. Evangelist Ron Comfort said that no one was more helpful to him in his starting Ambassador Baptist College than was Dr. Roberson. Unlike some other college leaders, Lee Roberson spent hours with Comfort, giving him advice, ideas, and direction, and answering his questions on how to start and operate a Christian college.

CHAPTER 11

Crisis

Every individual, and certainly every preacher, faces periods of crisis in life – crises of faith, family, or ministry, which have a lasting impact and sometimes even threaten one's ability to continue in the ministry. Lee Roberson faced at least three such crises in his life.

The first crisis occurred in 1946, when Lee and Caroline Roberson's baby, Joy Caroline, died at nine weeks of age. Roberson was 35 years old and in his fourth year at Highland Park Baptist Church. That was the same year he started the college. In the summer of 1946 Roberson was preaching in revival meetings in a tent at Russellville, Alabama – sponsored by the First Baptist Church of Russellville, where Orman Norwood's mother was a member. The song evangelist was Homer Britton. The crowds were growing. During that revival week Roberson was sitting in the study of the pastor, Rev. Tom Bealle, on the morning of Saturday, August 10. He was preparing for the Saturday evening and Sunday services when the telephone rang. He recognized the voice of his secretary, Miss Louzelle Ware. She said, "Brother Roberson, I have sad news for you. Your baby Joy died a few minutes ago." Roberson said later he did not remember any reply he made. Joy was nine weeks old. Probably "crib death," it was totally unexpected. The shock was so sudden. Joy was their second child, born on June 6, 1946. LeeAnne, their first daughter, was born in 1941. Upon receiving the phone call, Roberson left the revival meeting, got in his car and started driving back to Chattanooga.

When Roberson arrived in Chattanooga, naturally his first question was in regard to what happened to Joy and why she had died. Caroline told him, "There was no illness. We don't know what happened. Suddenly she was gone." The funeral service was conducted the next day, Sunday, August 11, 1946. Joy was buried in Babyland at Greenwood Cemetery in Chattanooga. After the funeral, Caroline went with him as Lee Roberson drove back to Russellville, where he resumed the revival. God blessed mightily.

The loss of Joy caused tremendous grief for Lee and Caroline Roberson. But it did not shatter their faith in God nor deter them from their mission of serving Him. In 1946 Roberson had just started a summer camp for children, called "Children's Bible Camp," with an application fee of just one dollar. "The Holy Spirit impressed me to start a work for children," he said. "We had no money, no land, no organization; but I had the 'impression' from God – we had to respond!" Nine-week old Joy had died during the first session of the Children's Bible Camp.

When Roberson returned home for the funeral, he did not remember anything from his trip until he crossed the Tennessee River, about 30 miles from Chattanooga. He was brought to a stop by a large barricade, with a road sign reading, "Highway 41 Closed; Go to Highway 11, & Proceed to Chattanooga." As he was driving across the bridge spanning the Tennessee River at Jasper, Tennessee, the Lord seemed to speak to his heart and give him the idea of naming the newly begun children's camp after his baby daughter, Joy. Roberson purposed then to trust God to bring joy out of tragedy, and "Camp Joy" was born. It was then, after the death of baby Joy, that Dr. Roberson permanently changed his personal life's verse from I Peter 2:21 to Romans 8:28, *"And we know that all things work together for good to them that love God, to them who are the called according to his purpose."*

Roberson needed land for the new children's camp. Shortly thereafter he noticed in the daily newspaper the announcement of the sale of Tennessee Valley Authority property on Lake Chickamauga, outside Chattanooga. Roberson and one of his associate pastors,

Durward Williams, showed up for the auction with no money. "Neither could have bought the other lunch," J.R. Faulkner recalled. The auctioneer opened the bids on the property by announcing that the lowest bid acceptable would be $3,000, but that the property was worth much more. "He asked for bids," Roberson said. "I responded with an offer of $3,000. He called for other bids." No one bid against them. The beautiful property for Camp Joy was theirs for $3,000. Roberson asked the astounded auctioneer for time to raise the money. He walked out of the auction with 30 days to come up with the $3,000. He did not have the money, but he was operating on a motto he had preached for years, "Where God guides, He provides." And God provided. The money was raised within a month. Church members and friends donated quickly and generously. In addition, the TVA permitted him to use another 20 acres, and the new campgrounds was launched a short time later. Eventually the children's camp covered 114 acres of camp and recreational facilities. There was room for swimming, horseback riding – on one of the camp's 52 horses, and a host of other sports and activities. The campgrounds are located on Lake Chickamauga, 14 miles from Highland Park Baptist Church.

Camp Joy was built on the principle that the greatest need of boys and girls is Jesus Christ as Savior. Camp Joy has operated 10 or 11 weeks of the summer free to all children – boys and girls, ages nine to 14 – with the theme, "Where boys and girls begin to live." At its peak the camp averaged about 300 children per week, with its highest week's total of 365. The children would enjoy outdoor activities, hear Bible stories, learn memory verses from the Bible, and hear God's plan of salvation. The camp soon included a gymnasium, swimming pool, ball fields, canteen, large dining hall, horses, trails and stables, and an open-air tabernacle, plus housing for campers and counselors. Daily activities included Bible teaching, Scripture memorization, and special chapel services. Always Camp Joy's emphasis was on the spiritual – bringing children to the new birth through saving faith in Jesus Christ. The theme Scripture verse for the camp is Luke 15:10, *"Likewise, I say unto you, there is joy in the presence of the angels of God over one sinner that repenteth."*

As a child Lee Roberson had grown up poor, and he wanted to offer a week at Camp Joy to kids for free. The one-dollar application fee was dropped. "He wanted kids to have what he didn't have as a child," said attorney Glenn Copeland. The camp became an evangelistic center for children, with a full week of evangelistic preaching, Bible memorization, and personal counseling. Cliff Robinson told me of the days when he and J.R. Faulkner would go out to the camp at the end of the week. The director, David Bragg, had been dealing with the children all week. "Dr. Faulkner and I would go out at the end of the week – Friday afternoon," said Cliff. "We would hold a little service, with a message on salvation, and explain baptism. Many of those kids were baptized in the baptistry at the church out there. One week we had 112 boys coming forward. I baptized 112 one afternoon. It took me an hour and 20 minutes."

Children came to Camp Joy from well beyond the Tennessee Valley by the thousands. For example, in the summer of 1982 alone Camp Joy's impact was remarkable. The summer's attendance was 3,021, with 498 salvation decisions, 625 baptisms, 310 children rededicating their lives to Christ, 165 kids coming forward for the assurance of their salvation, and 16 committing themselves to full-time service for the Lord. In the summer of the year 2000 the 100,000th child attended Camp Joy. An 11-year-old, the child was honored in a Sunday morning service at Highland Park Baptist Church. The parents attended the service. Through the years more than 28,000 children made decisions for Jesus Christ at Camp Joy, with more than 1,700 young men announcing they were called by God to preach.

Financial support for Camp Joy was raised independently of Highland Park Baptist Church. Many church members supported the church, of course, as support came from individuals from all over America. Dr. Roberson would join David Bragg, the director for 30 years, for lunch each Friday during the summer camp season. "He was the boss," Bragg told *The Chattanooga Times Free Press*, "but he was humble about it. He would not micro-manage it, as long as I was getting success." During the camp season, as Roberson would visit Bragg for lunch, he would offer his suggestions but not interfere with the running of the camp. When Roberson visited, the children would flock over to see him. "It was his favorite place outside the church," said Bragg. "He loved the kids."

Do you really ever get over the death of your own child? As a preacher, Dr. Roberson often spoke of Joy and used the story of Camp Joy through the years as an illustration of how to deal with grief – how to turn tragedy into triumph. In his sermon, *Have You Forgotten?*, Roberson said, "To me there is nothing so sad as the death of a baby or a small child." To the end of their lives, it seemed that Lee and Caroline Roberson personally spoke more and more often about the loss of their baby daughter, Joy. "He's always kept her in mind," said J.R. Faulkner. In a sermon, Roberson once said, "In a time of darkness, when our baby died, and I felt I couldn't go on, God said, 'Here is a verse for you for the rest of your life,' and He gave me Romans 8:28. I held on to it then, and I am holding onto it now."

Camp Joy gave the Robersons solace. "He loves Camp Joy," Jerry Mattheiss said. "That's his baby." Dr. Roberson would get excited when a child – maybe a little five-year-old boy – would get saved at Camp Joy. He cared about children. He would tell pastors, "Thank God for children! Thank God you're still reaching children. Don't ever quit reaching children." In 1971 Caroline Roberson told a newspaper reporter, "Once, at the hospital in Birmingham, a minister asked a young man, [who was] not expected to live, if he were a Christian. 'Yes, I accepted Christ years ago in Chattanooga at Camp Joy,' he said." The reporter wrote, "And this story has happened over and over again."

Throughout his ministry, Lee Roberson emphasized reaching children. He felt it was the way of Christ, who said, *"Suffer the little children to come unto Me, and forbid them not: for of such is the kingdom of God." (Matthew 10:14)* In his sermon, *The Day of the Bulldozer*, Roberson said, "When a little boy or girl comes forward, do not look at that one and say, 'He is so young.' Have a great concern for your children and seek to bring them early to the Savior." In his book, *Diamonds in the Rough*, Roberson wrote, "Some years ago when we first began this work, the bus children came rushing into the church. Some were not so clean. One usher straightened himself up big and tall and said, 'If you're going to have a church for the riffraff, count me out. I'm leaving.' He left, and no one asked him to return. He showed us that he had not the Spirit of the Lord Jesus Christ about children."

In 1990, Dr. Lee Roberson, then 80 years old, preached at First Baptist Church of Hammond, Indiana, and at its school chapel at Hyles-Anderson College. Marlene Evans, wife of the college president, asked Roberson, "Why do you keep on going?" Dr. Roberson's answer was simply, "I just want to reach one more kid."

* * *

The second crisis of Roberson's life and ministry involved Highland Park Baptist Church and Dr. Lee Roberson leaving the Southern Baptist Convention in 1955. Although Highland Park was to become a leading church in the independent, fundamental Baptist movement in America, it was not originally Roberson's design to leave the SBC. A half-century later details and reasons for the separation were sketchy, and most of those who remembered the events of those days were decidedly in support of Roberson in this matter. The congregation of Highland Park Baptist Church clearly stood behind Roberson, and Roberson always insisted that any outward, public trouble in the church over this issue was almost non-existent. Nevertheless, the personal crisis for the then 46-year-old preacher, who had spent his entire adult life as a Southern Baptist, was traumatic. Some Roberson intimates believe it led him to suffer a very short-lived nervous breakdown at the time.

As a young man, Lee Roberson attended a Southern Baptist college and a Southern Baptist seminary. From 1931 to 1955 he served on the pastoral staffs of Southern Baptist churches. Prior to his accepting the call to Highland Park, the Southern Baptist state convention of Alabama had asked him to become the state evangelist. After the explosive growth in Roberson's early years as pastor of the church, Highland Park Baptist Church actually led the entire 26,000-plus churches of the Southern Baptist Convention in baptisms annually from 1945 to 1955. Orman Norwood later remembered taking associational letters to Tennessee Temple's Dr. Alfred Cierpke, who would represent Highland Park Baptist Church at the Hamilton

County Baptist Association meetings. In those days Roberson required all faculty members at Tennessee Temple to be members of Southern Baptist churches. Roberson counted many of the leading Southern Baptist preachers among his friends. In his early years he was influenced by older Southern Baptist preachers like B.B. Crimm. There was talk of nominating Roberson to become president of the entire Southern Baptist Convention. "In those days I knew the pastor of a huge [SBC] church in Birmingham," said missionary Garland Cofield. "He told me if Dr. Roberson had 'played his cards right,' undoubtedly he would have been president of the Southern Baptist Convention." Orman Norwood said, "Among Southern Baptists, none were so widely respected as Dr. Lee Roberson." Roberson had several honorary doctorates from Southern Baptist schools and was widely respected. Renowned Southern Baptist Dr. Herbert Lockyer wrote the introduction to Roberson's first book and served as the first vice president of Tennessee Temple College.

So, what happened?

It would be easy to say that Roberson left the convention because of the increasing influence of theological liberalism in the Southern Baptist Convention and his conviction to remain true to Scripture in all of his associations. However, that does not seem to be the case. Although one of Roberson's mentors, J. Frank Norris, claimed he could detect the early trends of liberalism among Southern Baptists years earlier, theological liberalism was not yet a significant issue among Southern Baptists in the 1940s and 1950s. Prior to Roberson's arrival in Chattanooga, Highland Park Baptist Church leader Arnold Chambers had expressed dissatisfaction over one case of SBC Sunday school literature and how it was handled. However, it was not until years later that theological liberalism crystallized as an issue in the convention before such Southern Baptist leaders as Adrian Rogers in the 1980s turned the convention's theological direction back toward its conservative foundation.

But back in 1954, the Hamilton County Baptist Association took action to censure Highland Park Baptist Church. The association issued a letter on December 13, which was published in the *Chattanooga News Free Press* on December 23, claiming that Highland Park's sympathies were not with the Southern Baptist

Convention. One of the key association leaders was even a Tennessee Temple graduate. Specifically, the Hamilton County association protested two aspects of Roberson's ministry: first, that Tennessee Temple College was not approved by the Education Commission of the Tennessee Baptist Convention; and, second, that Highland Park Baptist Church was giving more money to independent "faith" missions than to the SBC's Cooperative Program. The association's letter charged that Tennessee Temple "does not cooperate with our Southern Baptist program, and does not promote our cause and program, and has shown a non-cooperative attitude."

The action was taken without prior notice or contact with Roberson or his staff. Arnold Chambers ushered a group of Highland Park deacons, including R.R. Shedd, Dr. E.C. Haskell Sr., and R.O. Stone to the associational meeting. Chambers complained to the Hamilton County Baptist Association that this action against Highland Park Baptist Church was wrong and that it was not brotherly. He defended the standards and principles of Tennessee Temple College, and he demanded an apology. The association moderator flatly said there would be no apology.

Roberson responded publicly in a Sunday evening church service on December 26, 1954. Tennessee Temple's Dr. Fred Brown, a respected teacher and preacher, wrote a published rebuttal to the association's charges on behalf of the church. Highland Park Baptist Church asked the association to publish a correction of so-called illegalities and inaccuracies. Failure to do so would be interpreted as withdrawal of Highland Park Baptist Church from the Southern Baptist Convention. J.R. Faulkner said it was the only time Lee Roberson ever answered critics. "The local Baptist association had released some information that was not true – just plain falsehood," said Faulkner. "So, our men drew up a response to the letter – dealing with the things mentioned. We made a full-page statement. I drew that up. It appeared in the newspaper."

A joint meeting on March 14, 1955, between committees representing both sides failed to resolve the conflict. Highland Park Baptist Church subsequently stopped sending in denominational reports, stopped sending messengers to the state convention, and stopped sending the SBC Cooperative Program money. Highland

Park Baptist Church's deacons passed a resolution to repudiate the executive committee of the Hamilton County Baptist Association and to withdraw from its activities "until an appropriate retraction or apology" by the committee has been made. The resolution noted that the association had violated its own constitution in "that it allegedly represents and has undertaken to establish itself as an ecclesiastical tribunal." Terming the association's action "illegal," the church stated that failure to take the requested action would be construed as an "action on the part of the Hamilton County Baptist Association to withdraw fellowship of the Hamilton County Baptist Association from the Highland Park Baptist Church." There is no record of any formal response from the association.

A public statement by the church was issued – effectively severing the relationship with the association and the entire Southern Baptist Convention. "We just started ignoring them," said Faulkner. "There was no official withdrawal or anything." Roberson said later in a sermon, "A committee from the [SBC] Sunday School Board in Nashville was sent to see me. These men begged me to stay in. I said, 'No, I cannot do anything else but this.' I lost every friend, as far as I knew, in almost one week's time. I had nowhere to turn. My friends were in the Convention." Tennessee Temple was no longer recommended by the SBC. Highland Park no longer encouraged its branch chapels to become autonomous Southern Baptist churches. Many friendships continued, but the official relationship between the church and the Southern Baptist Convention came to an end. These events changed the course of Baptist history in the South. By 1956 the independent Southwide Baptist Fellowship, a fellowship of pastors, was founded at Highland Park Baptist Church. It would grow to more than 3,000 members in the years to come.

J.R. Faulkner believed two factors motivated the association to take action against Roberson – money and buses. Under Roberson's leadership, Highland Park Baptist Church was directing its massive missionary giving independently of the Southern Baptist Convention. And Highland Park was sending its fleet of church buses all over Hamilton County picking up children for Sunday school right under the noses of the other Baptist churches in the association – not to mention the aggressive home visitation program and the Sunday chapel services being established all over the area by Highland Park. One of Roberson's associates remembered, "It disturbed pastors. His buses were running into their communities picking up people." Roberson himself told me years later, "I'm sure they maybe disliked some part of it – like the buses going out all over the city and bringing people. I'm sure it bothered some of them, but not much was said about it." With the support of Roberson and Highland Park, a number of the church's chapels had become Southern Baptist churches, independent of Highland Park – including Lookout Mountain, Brainerd Hills, Duncan Park, First Baptist of Sale Creek, and South Cleveland. Later, following the break with the SBC, Highland Park stopped releasing its chapels to become independent but instead kept control of them. Through the years some of the chapels severed and became autonomous – such as Grace Baptist and Lakewood. Other churches and pastors may have felt threatened by such evangelistic outreach. In addition, Faulkner said, "They were fighting our schools – saying we don't need a school. We've got Carson-Newman in Tennessee. That is denominationalism – dictating to a church what it can do. This is a local, autonomous body, free to do what it wants to do with its money – build a school, whatever. They ought to be rejoicing at what's happened."

Lee Roberson was a maverick. He never took the active step of choosing to leave the Southern Baptist Convention, even though he operated independently, as he believed the Lord was leading him. "We kept waiting for Doc to pull out," recalled Baptist pastor Tom Wallace (a student at the time), "but he didn't do it. They pushed him out." And Roberson's church stood fully behind him. At one time Highland Park Baptist Church had been contributing substantially to the Southern Baptist Cooperative Program, but Roberson initiated a "World-Wide Faith Missions" program which supported missionaries independent of the SBC. Highland Park began to designate its giving as it chose, rather than to turn the money over to the SBC Cooperative Program. And Tennessee Temple College was independent – not affiliated with the SBC. "Highland Park was not associated with Southern Baptist causes," recalled Wallace. "It was just an independent Southern Baptist church. In name Southern Baptist, but that was it."

The SBC action caused very little stir in the church. The action of the association seemed to make the church stronger and more united behind Roberson. Many church members felt the censure had been unfair. "Really the Southern Baptists pulled away from us," recalled church member Jean Smith. "It wasn't all done the way they wanted – as far as the Cooperative Program is concerned." Jean, along with her husband, Elgin, moved to an SBC church years later, after Roberson retired. While there was little church-wide controversy at the time Highland Park left the SBC, Jean did remember the church losing some pretty strong leaders who wanted to stay with the SBC. In addition, Faulkner said, "We had two or three deacons who were strong Southern Baptists back then. They would have loved to stay [in the SBC]. But they didn't make an issue of it. They were aware that what Dr. Roberson was saying was true. He'd preach missions so strong – one of his passions was to get the gospel out to the ends of the earth. We couldn't feed that through the Cooperative Program. He just didn't have a heart for anything like that. Faith missions came along. It was built up across the nation – Sudan Interior Mission, China Inland Mission, Far East Gospel, old Indian missions, South African missions – a number of African missions. This fascinated Dr. Roberson, so we started a strong missions program. He started these Sunday night and Wednesday night offerings – even to this day all go to missions. He never saw the need [for the Cooperative Program]. He was for 'Faith Promise.' He was not against [the Cooperative Program]. But you didn't tamper with 'faith missions.'"

In a magazine interview years later, Arnold Chambers said, "You've always got a group that say, 'If we had stayed in [the SBC], we could have done more good than if we'd stayed out.' I'm not sure of that. I haven't had any regrets about it." Chambers had already been concerned with some of the Southern Baptist Sunday school literature in those days, and he was not satisfied with the way the SBC responded to his complaint.

Elgin Smith remembered the Southern Baptist controversy this way. "I was a deacon when the association removed our church from the Southern Baptist Convention," Smith recalled years later. "Dr. Roberson told the deacons – kind of an ultimatum – that he would let them [the association] do it, but he would stay there [at Highland Park]. And he walked out of the deacons' meeting and left it up to the deacons – whether to become an independent church or to remain in the Southern Baptist Convention. Of course, the deacons did decide that whatever Dr. Roberson wanted, which was to accept the resignation request the convention had issued to our church. I remember the cause was 'World-Wide Faith Missions,' which Dr. Roberson had established in our church – and Dr. Roberson funding through our church to support and send out missionaries rather than through the Cooperative Program. That was a big issue. So, the deacons agreed to withdraw from the Southern Baptist Convention, and Dr. Roberson stayed on." Roberson said years later, "We just withdrew from the convention altogether. I carried it out quietly. Nothing much was said about it [publicly]." The local newspapers published a little news on the issue. Tom Wallace said, "Around the church we didn't hear anything about it." Walter Wendelken felt that behind the scenes some of the opposition to Roberson was strong, but he said it made the church stronger because the membership thought the whole matter had been unfair to Roberson.

"Dr. Roberson was hurt when the association took action," said Orman Norwood. "He lost good friends." Always a private man, Roberson kept his disappointment quiet. "If he were suffering, you did not know it," said Bill Mattheiss. "He did not talk about it." Roberson recalled, "I had some letters from Southern Baptist men – not many, but a few. Some of them predicted we'd fail – get out of the convention, lose power and prestige, and so forth. It didn't affect a thing in the world. It helped us, really. Just go ahead with the Lord and keep on building."

Nat Phillips grew up in Chattanooga and came to Christ at Highland Park Baptist Church. Later he left town to attend Southern Baptist schools before returning to spend a career teaching at Tennessee Temple under Dr. Roberson. "I was always a Southern Baptist – nominally," Phillips told me. "I went independent, smoothly – just where the Lord led. I believed the same things both times. When I knew Highland Park, it was Southern Baptist. When I was gone, it stopped. They pushed him out the door. In the Southern Baptist Convention, he was baptizing thousands of people per year.

No one could touch him – some wanted him out. Evidently God's hand was on Dr. Roberson. I don't see how anybody with any spiritual discernment could deny that."

Attorney Glenn Copeland was young during Roberson's early years at Highland Park Baptist Church. He remembers missions support being an issue with the SBC. "They wanted it all through them," Copeland recalled. Copeland's view was that when the local association objected to Roberson's missions program, Dr. Roberson "felt led to drop out." Copeland does not remember any outward crisis in the church, with only minimal mention of the issue from the pulpit. "I don't recall losing any [church members] – hardly any," he said. Jean Smith remembered losing a few key leaders who wanted to stay with the SBC. Bill Mattheiss said it was "just a few – probably less than six, with ties pretty strong [to the SBC]."

Over time some of the few church members who left decided Roberson was right and returned to Highland Park Baptist Church. Some left and began attending Woodland Baptist Church in Chattanooga, where J. Harold Smith, a prominent Southern Baptist preacher, served as pastor. Smith, a friend of Roberson, had preached at Highland Park a number of times. Smith, like Roberson, had a huge main auditorium Bible class in Sunday school. Later, after Smith left Chattanooga, his former church broke up the auditorium class and followed a new plan of smaller Sunday school classes. Tom Wallace, on his bus route, would run into people who complained about the change, quit going to Woodland, and were not attending church anywhere. "That's not right not," Wallace would tell them, "why don't you ride our bus and come with us?" Wallace said, "We got a whole bus-load who transferred membership to Highland Park."

Lee Roberson clearly aligned himself with the independent, fundamental Baptist movement – including such independent Baptist leaders as John R. Rice, editor of the decidedly independent and fundamental *Sword of the Lord* tabloid magazine. Rice, who had deliberately left the Southern Baptist Convention, editorialized against the SBC repeatedly – criticizing what he saw as growing theological liberalism in SBC schools and compromising methodology. Originally a Southern Baptist pastor, Clarence Sexton said it was the example of Highland Park Baptist Church which led him to become an independent Baptist. He liked Highland Park's emphasis on the inerrancy of Scripture and the local church headship of Christ. Lee Roberson's differences with Southern Baptists did not begin in Chattanooga. In his sermon, *"The Imminent Return of Christ,"* he told how an SBC official had differed with his emphasis on the imminence of Christ's return during his previous pastorate in Fairfield, Alabama. However, such differences are not uncommon among evangelicals and Baptists and are not tied to SBC beliefs.

Nevertheless, Roberson never fought against Southern Baptists, nor did he openly criticize them. "They actually made Highland Park the independent church it is," said Dr. Fred Afman, for many years a Tennessee Temple professor. "I don't think he wanted to pull out. He had a lot of friends there. He had been one of them for a long time, but he wasn't going to let them control his church. He would support the missionaries he wanted to support. They left him." Through the years Roberson continued to welcome conservative Southern Baptist preachers to his pulpit – men such as his mentor, R.G. Lee. The greatest revival anyone remembers at Highland Park occurred under the preaching of a Southern Baptist guest preacher, J. Harold Smith. To the end of his life, Roberson would on occasion preach for a Southern Baptist church or in a conference on the same platform with Southern Baptist preachers. A number of Tennessee Temple graduates became Southern Baptist preachers. Roberson always treated them with love and respect. And many conservative Southern Baptist churches continued to send students to Tennessee Temple University. In 2002, Baptist pastor Randy Ray told me, "To this day, Dr. Roberson has never [totally] broken with Southern Baptists. To this day, Southern Baptist churches still contact him for pastors and references."

Dr. Fred Afman taught the Bible for Dr. Roberson both at Tennessee Temple and on the radio. When Afman was invited to fill the pulpit of a Presbyterian church, he went to J.R. Faulkner for advice. Would that be a problem? "No, no – they're friends of ours. You go," Afman recalled Faulkner telling him. "I helped them from time to time. It was the same at a Southern Baptist church – the same answer. They [Roberson and Faulkner] had a lot of friends among

Southern Baptists. He didn't spend his time fighting. He would say, 'They left us. Stay the course.'"

With Roberson's fellowship with the Southern Baptist Convention abandoned, the Southwide Baptist Fellowship was founded in 1956. Lee Roberson was the key founder. Baptist leaders such as Harold Sightler and John Waters in South Carolina had already approached Roberson with the idea of starting a fellowship of churches. "It would not have got off the ground without him," Wendell Evans said of Roberson. "Southwide started over in the corner of the dining room," Faulkner told me. "There were five or six of us. We had a summer pastors' school here – before [Jack] Hyles picked it up, which was fine. We started as a Southern Baptist pre-millennial fellowship. We decided then the idea of the Southern Baptist title was tying us with the denomination – that we ought to drop that and start using Southwide Baptist pre-mill. Then we dropped the pre-mill term. We decided that was not essential to salvation and chose a less divisive name. I was in it all. I've been moderator three times." That early meeting included Roberson, Faulkner, Sightler, and John R. Rice. "It just happened," said Faulkner. "We were having lunch together. It was not a 'called meeting.' It just happened to be at the head table in the dining hall where Dr. Roberson and I ate each day. That particular day these men were available to have lunch with us, and we filled up the table. The conversation went in that direction, and they decided we'd have a meeting. So we tied into it and started promoting it. It developed."

Southwide Baptist Fellowship's first meeting was held at Highland Park Baptist Church. Then, to accommodate pastors coming great distances, the meeting was moved around to various cities – including Jacksonville, Charlotte, Winston-Salem, and Louisville. One year Southwide met at Jerry Falwell's Thomas Road Baptist Church in Lynchburg, Virginia. "I was the moderator there," Faulkner recalled with a laugh. "That was a joke. Jerry's such a strong personality he took that out of my hands. Jerry knew what to do. He just ran with it!" The size of the crowd necessitated bringing the annual conference back to Highland Park, as not even Thomas Road was large enough in those days. "Southwide was to be in the hands of a floating committee – no leadership at all," Faulker said with a laugh. Lee Roberson was clearly the leader.

A pre-organizational meeting was held during Highland Park Baptist Church's annual missions conference in November of 1955. The following March, 147 preachers and laymen registered as charter members and adopted a fundamental statement of faith. The new fellowship was launched in a meeting at Highland Park's Phillips Chapel on March 20, 1956, with 147 charter members. Originally called the Southern Baptist Fellowship, an organizational meeting at Highland Park Baptist Church in November of 1956 attracted about 450 pastors – almost all Southern Baptists. The charter membership had reached 423. The speakers for the first conference included Warren Wiersbe and Southern Baptists R.G. Lee and J. Harold Smith. Besides Roberson, key leaders included Harold Sightler and John Waters, both of whom had been receiving pressure in South Carolina for their increasing independence from the Southern Baptist Convention. The new organization was to be a fellowship of pastors – not churches. The pastors and their churches started pulling out of the SBC one by one. The fellowship's name was officially changed to Southwide Baptist Fellowship at the eighth annual meeting in 1963, because the members were no longer Southern Baptists. "They were comfortable with this," recalled Tom Wallace. "They were all independent-minded Southern Baptists." The SBF was to grow to more than 3,000 members in the years to come.

John R. Rice, who had pulled out of the Southern Baptist Convention, began editorializing about the issue in his *Sword of the Lord*, then a prominent voice among independent-minded pastors. Some prominent preachers were pulling out of the SBC. The independent Baptist movement gained momentum across America. Some Southern Baptists, who felt they could no longer associate with Roberson, began to criticize him. And Southwide Baptist Fellowship in turn followed suit in criticizing the SBC. "Later on some of the men began to blast the SBC at the Southwide meetings," said Wallace. "I was bothered about that. I think a lot of the people were, too. We would have 700 to 800 preachers there – with 150 of them Southern Baptists. They were coming out one by one. Give them a chance to see the difference. Politics was not the issue. They would come over and catch 'the fever.'"

Conversely, Roberson was also criticized by some independent, fundamental Baptists for not being a "militant" enough of a fundamentalist – by not openly separating from and criticizing those with whom he disagreed, such as Southern Baptists. He was criticized for not being a "fighting fundamentalist" and for not being strong enough on ecclesiastical separation. One trendy book on fundamentalism called Roberson a compromiser for cooperating with anyone who did not fit the independent, fundamental Baptist mold. Bob Kelley said, "Those who criticized him for not being a militant enough fundamentalist – that didn't bother him. It didn't matter what anyone said. He just didn't worry about opinions. He never answered them. He wouldn't bother with it – no way, shape or form. He had one goal, and that was to please the Son of God. He was a great man. I remember a certain book written – classified him as a moderate fundamentalist. It bothered me a great deal. He was a father of modern fundamentalism."

Roberson, always fiercely independent, charted his own course as he saw it – true to the Word of God and to his own conscience. He was not afraid to welcome a guest speaker who was true to the same Lord and to the same Word of God, even if the speaker had some secondary differences. Early in the first decade of the 21st century David Bouler, then the pastor of Highland Park Baptist Church, was criticized by some independent Baptists for including a Southern Baptist preacher among the guest speakers at the independent Southwide Baptist Fellowship, founded by Roberson. In his own defense, Bouler claimed publicly at a Southwide preachers' luncheon that Southwide had always had a history of including conservative Southern Baptist speakers. I had an appointment that same afternoon to interview J.R. Faulkner for this biography. Trained as a journalist, I immediately asked Faulkner if Bouler's explanation was historically accurate. With a smile, Faulkner pulled from his file lists of past years' Southwide speakers. Besides the independent Baptist speakers listed, just as Bouler had claimed, there were scattered among the names numerous Southern Baptists – plus guest preachers who were from the Christian & Missionary Alliance, at least one Methodist, and a Presbyterian or two – not to mention other Evangelicals. Such cooperation had always been Lee Roberson's pattern.

Guided by Roberson's heart for world-wide evangelism, some Tennessee Temple graduates launched missionary enterprises which reached across all denominational lines. The late Max Helton, a Tennessee Temple graduate, established a nationally famous non-denominational ministry, of which Lee Roberson was proud. After serving as a pastor of independent Baptist churches and teaching at Hyles-Anderson College, Helton founded Motor Racing Outreach, a nondenominational chapel ministry for the NASCAR stock car drivers, their crews, and families. Preaching to as many as 500 people each week before the televised race, Helton saw dozens of race car drivers come to Christ – including famous race car drivers such as Darrell Waltrip, Jeff Gordon, Dale Jarrett, Bobby Labonte, Ken Schrader, et al. Dr. Roberson openly approved of what Helton had accomplished, and Helton remained close to Roberson to the end of Roberson's life. Helton's roots ran deep in Roberson's ministry. As an infant, Helton was dedicated to the Lord by Roberson during the first annual missions conference at Highland Park Baptist Church in 1946. Shortly before his death, Roberson encouraged Helton to take a position on the Tennessee Temple University board of directors. Roberson gave Helton the distinct impression that he longed to see the old days when a solid evangelical Presbyterian like Donald Grey Barnhouse could be invited to preach in chapel without arousing criticism from separatist-minded independent Baptist pastors.

Nevertheless, the personal crisis of leaving – voluntarily or involuntarily – his life-long association with the Southern Baptist Convention took a toll on Lee Roberson. One close family intimate, a preacher who asked not to be named as the source, told me, "It was at age 46 when he had a nervous break-down – over the Southern Baptist crisis. The doctors said he wouldn't preach again for six months. He preached in two weeks. To me, it was 'death to self.'" At the time it was rumored among the church members and college students that Roberson had suffered a stroke, nervous breakdown, or perhaps a temporary memory loss. Some remember that Roberson suffered a breakdown of some sort at the time. Orman Norwood was a student in those days. He remembered that Roberson's dark hair turned white at the time. After a period of absence for Roberson, J.R. Faulkner introduced Roberson in chapel. Norwood remembered the day. "Students, look who's here," Norwood remembered hearing Faulkner say. "Everyone stood and applauded. Doc [Roberson] stood and weakly waved. He really shut down for awhile. Somebody else preached every service." It resulted in a temporary loss of memory. Roberson did not know people for awhile. Faulkner had to re-introduce him to such people as Dr. E.C. Haskell, Sr., chairman of the deacons and Roberson's close personal friend, as if he were a stranger. Roberson's wife, Caroline, never talked about it. J.R. Faulkner never mentioned this episode in Lee Roberson's life.

Biographies of England's legendary Baptist preacher, Charles H. Spurgeon, report a similar crisis in his early years. He appeared to suffer a temporary nervous break-down after the seating stands at London's Royal Surrey Gardens Music Hall collapsed under the weight of the crowd – killing seven worshippers while Spurgeon was preaching. Spurgeon was out of the pulpit for a few weeks and testified to a "death to self" personal spiritual experience that brought him through the crisis. Similarly, the famed George W. Truett, for 47 years the pastor of First Baptist Church of Dallas, Texas, felt he could never preach again after a hunting accident took the life of his close friend, J.C. Arnold, the Dallas chief of police. It was Truett's gun which discharged, killing Arnold. The accident plunged Truett into a period of indescribable grief. After Truett said Christ spoke to him in a dream, he returned to the pulpit and preached on "the unsearchable riches of Christ." One of Lee Roberson's favorite verses – he preached frequently on it through the years – was John 12:24, *"Verily, verily, I say unto you, Except a corn of wheat fall into the ground and die, it abideth alone: but if it die, it bringeth forth much fruit."*

In 1996, Lee Roberson preached for Pastor Tom Messer at Trinity Baptist Church in Jacksonville, Florida. Like Highland Park Baptist Church, Trinity had left the Southern Baptist Convention years before Messer became pastor. Roberson publicly offered the younger Messer advice. Roberson publicly said that in retrospect he thought it had been a mistake to leave the SBC. It would have been better, he said, to reorganize it. He was fascinated by the effectiveness of a synergistic effort such as the Cooperative Program. Yet he never looked at missionaries as "denominational employees," and he felt that one of the flaws of the SBC was that so few churches really knew their missionaries. Roberson publicly challenged Messer to consider beginning an independent Baptist convention or start a cooperative program among independent Baptists – but with some of the strengths of the independent system.

Within a year after Roberson's death in 2007, Highland Park Baptist Church re-affiliated with the Southern Baptist Convention – more than half a century since the church had left the SBC. Prior to Roberson's death, Nat Phillips told me that he did not believe the separation from the SBC would even have happened – were it today. The SBC has turned its direction back toward its conservative theological roots. After Lee Roberson retired from the Highland Park pastorate, and with the inevitable change that followed, many church members and leaders – who fully supported Roberson – left Highland Park Baptist Church. Including early church leaders, a number of them joined Southern Baptist churches. The SBC today is also probably more tolerant of "mavericks." There is more leeway for churches to operate in an independent manner and less pressure to conform. Strong Southern Baptist churches, such as Johnny Hunt's First Baptist of Woodstock, Georgia, Charlie Martin's First Baptist of Indian Rocks, Florida, and Ken Whitten's Idlewild Baptist Church in Tampa, Florida, contribute generously to the SBC Cooperative Program and also maintain strong "faith" missions programs at the same time. And on the other hand, some Southern Baptist churches give only nominally to the Cooperative Program. Today there is wide latitude.

Roberson was an icon in the independent, fundamental Baptist movement. But he was strangely silent on some of the classical issues of the independent movement – such as insisting on the King James "only" position (in Bible versions) and opposing Southern Baptists. He was a maverick. He moved forward serving God with whomever would move forward with him. Yet, he was not unaware of who he was and where he stood. He was not a puppet. He clearly felt comfortable in the independent, fundamental Baptist movement but never "wrote off" like-minded, conservative Southern Baptists.

Leaving a denomination was not without controversy. Nevertheless, many of history's past heroes were maligned in their own day. After all, like Lee Roberson, Charles Spurgeon himself was censured almost unanimously by the large Baptist association of London during the famous "Downgrade" controversy late in Spurgeon's life. Spurgeon's biographers say he never completely got over it.

* * *

The third major crisis in Lee Roberson's life occurred in 1973 – one decade before he retired from his Highland Park Baptist Church pastorate. An inveterate speaker, Roberson had difficulties with his throat in the early 1950s which resulted in surgery. By 1973, after preaching an average of at least 10 times per week for more than three decades, at age 64, Roberson lost his voice. He had lost it once briefly as a young man when he was an opera singer, but in 1973 doctors were initially baffled. After preaching in a big, open-air tabernacle near Chicago one night, he found the next morning that his voice was gone. He had to leave the meeting and go home. He returned to Chattanooga and began to visit doctors. The problem appeared to be with his vocal chords, but no one could give a precise diagnosis at first. Roberson traveled all over the country to see doctors who specialized in voice. He was out of the pulpit and unable to speak above a whisper for a year. Late in life, Roberson told me that he had feared then that he would never be able to preach again. At the time no one seemed to be sure whether his throat was inflamed, irritated, or injured. J.R. Faulkner said, "We were afraid it was cancer. He went to the best clinics in Houston, Mayo – three or four places. A famous doctor in New Orleans told him, 'You've got to face it. You've just ruined your throat. You're never going to preach again.'"

Unable to preach at the time, Roberson told Arnold Chambers privately, "Arnold, I think I'm going to resign." Chambers responded, "Resign what?" Roberson said, "Well, I don't feel like I'm able to preach – and earn my salary." Chambers was adamant in his response to Roberson. "Dr. Roberson," he said, "if you can walk or crawl up on that platform and sit down Sunday morning, Sunday night, and Wednesday night, you have earned your salary way over. Let Dr. Faulkner come in to preach. As long as you're sitting on that platform, everything will go on just exactly like it always has, because of all that you've accomplished here – the Lord working through you. Please, for heaven's sake, don't do anything like that."

Security director Bill Long was in the deacons' meeting the night Roberson informed them of his voice problem. Long recalled the events. Lee Roberson stood up and said, "Gentlemen, I've been to a clinic. I've been having trouble with my voice. It's not likely that I'll ever preach again." Roberson said he would continue to seek treatment and see if his throat problem could be corrected. The deacon chairman, Bill Morton, spoke up, "Dr. Roberson, one thing we have plenty of around here is preachers. I recommend you take the time off needed and have whoever you want to preach. It would be nice if you could sit on the platform and give announcements and the invitation when you are able – and do that at an increase in salary!" Roberson was perturbed about the suggestion of a pay increase. "I don't want any increase in salary," Long remembered him saying. "He was very hard-nosed about it, when that was suggested."

For one year J.R. Faulkner led the church, sharing the pulpit with Cliff Robinson. A few guest preachers were invited to Highland Park. Lee Roberson sat silently on the platform during the church services. "Doc would sit on the platform and not preach," Faulkner recalled. The staff and deacons wanted him on the platform. They considered his presence an inspiration for the entire ministry. Caroline Roberson worried that if Lee could not preach, he would be like a fish out of water. Dorothy McCormick was among the ladies of the church who helped look after the Robersons' youngest daughter, June, at home – as the Robersons traveled seeking medical help for his throat. They did not talk about it a lot. "He had some low points, but I never observed them," Faulkner said. Church members worried. It simply was not the same without Dr. Roberson in the pulpit.

Roberson was hospitalized for a full month's time over a six-week period. Afterward, he would sit on the platform during the church services. Toward the end of the year, he would lead in prayer and give announcements during the services. "The place was packed to the rafters," Faulkner said. "There was no faltering. We just kept it on, and God blessed mightily." Roberson avoided people because he could not talk, and he was on medication. "I would stand by him and refresh his memory – call their names," said Faulkner.

But for one full year Roberson could not preach at all. He continued with all his other work – able to speak only between a whisper and a rasp. He could not take any preaching meetings. Co-workers said he acted the same through out the year – showing no signs of worry. But it was hard on him. "He wouldn't talk about it," said Cliff Robinson. "But you could tell it bothered him. A man who studied opera couldn't project." Privately, Roberson confided some of his fears to Walter Wendelken. "It was very hard on him," Wendelken recalled. "It was hard for him to endure. He feared he might lose his voice. He talked about it a lot, but not complaining – just facing reality." During that year Roberson was very supportive of those filling in for him. Faulkner said, "I'd find a letter pushed under my door. 'Thank you for the message yesterday.' He'd pick up some thought and make a comment on something he liked [in the sermon] – always short, one-page letter, written. He was a gracious man."

It seemed no doctor could help him. Roberson told Faulkner he was probably going to resign. But first, he said, "We'll wait on the Lord." Finally, after nearly a year's search a physician in Chattanooga said he could help. He performed a surgical procedure on Roberson's throat. It failed. Roberson waited weeks – with no talking at all. The doctor said, "Let me try it one more time." This time it worked. Lee Roberson's voice problem was cured. He was back in business – preaching. On his first out-of-town preaching meeting after the year's voice problem, Roberson was invited to preach at Grace Baptist Church in Middletown, Ohio. The pastor, Ron Schaffer, would never forget the service. Roberson had to hold the microphone close to his mouth, but he could be heard. At the end of his message the gospel invitation was given, and the altar was full – with 25 people coming forward to receive Christ as their Savior.

In his sermon, *The Verse That Jumped from the Page*, Roberson recounted how the Lord had blessed Highland Park Baptist Church during the year when he could not preach due to his voice problem. "And in the strangest kind of way," he said, "God kept blessing this work more and more. The offerings were up to the top. Praise God! Every single portion of our missions – Camp Joy, Union Mission, World-Wide Faith Missions, everything – up on the very top! Tennessee Temple schools – the very finest and best. The best enrollment in the summer school we had ever had. The largest number of new students coming to Tennessee Temple we had ever had in the school's history. Everything was moving! That just showed this little preacher something. It didn't depend so much on what I was doing. It depended on the working of the power of God through our lives."

After the throat problem Roberson permanently changed his procedure in the pulpit. Instead of standing back 20 inches from the microphone, he would stand with the mic close to his mouth when preaching – to keep from straining his throat. When he preached on the road, he would request a microphone right in front of his mouth. Inevitably some church sound technicians would turn the sound volume down, which would result in some strain on his voice. At home in the Highland Park pulpit he would not hesitate to give instructions from the pulpit. "Don't touch that mic," he would direct. His desire was not to be loud but to alleviate the strain on his voice. Trained in voice and music, Roberson regarded voice quality as important for a public communicator. After the successful surgery, his voice would crack some, but over time his voice returned completely. "He would preach a message probably the same length of time – almost to the minute," said Bill Long.

Some of Roberson's associates saw another change after the voice problem. Through the years, Faulkner said, "He'd be sick and never tell you. He'd never talk about illness or weakness on his part. That was the thing about him all these years. He'd be preaching with a temperature and never say a word about it – if his throat was bothering him and hurting." E.C. Haskell Jr. recalled, "He had a hard time understanding anyone with illness – for years – until he went for that year and didn't preach. It changed him. It gave him more compassion. I used to tell him he has a V-8 engine and doesn't understand others who have a V-6 or V-4. 'We're going to get there, but not as fast as you. Everyone can't operate the same as you do. It doesn't mean they're weak. It's the way they're built.' That [crisis] helped him." The year of uncertainty about his health seemed to increase Dr. Roberson's tenderness and sympathy. Clarence Sexton recalled, "One seminary professor said he changed after that. He was more compassionate – cried in the pulpit."

After the episode with his voice, Lee Roberson was to serve Highland Park Baptist Church as pastor for another 10 years. "But I think that's when the church first realized he was getting old," said Sexton.

*   *   *

Lee Roberson humbly believed that God used difficulties in his life to teach him lessons. In his sermon, *What Makes People Great?*, he said of baby Joy's death, "I did not understand it. And maybe, in a way, I did not want to understand it. I was trying to run from the thing God was trying to say. Why the baby died, we did not know. We examined our hearts. We willingly accepted any chastening that God might give us. But it might have been – I believe it was – that God wanted something done about Camp Joy. Now, for all these years we've run a camp every summer where we've taken [thousands] of boys and girls free. Literally thousands have been saved." He went on to say in the same sermon regarding his throat problem, "God was teaching me a lesson. I learned some things in that single year that changed my life."

Despite the fact that Lee Roberson and the great Highland Park Baptist Church departed from the Southern Baptist Convention, his career was remarkably free of trouble within the local church, and he avoided almost all national controversies in the world of Christian evangelicalism and fundamentalism. The harmony in his life and ministry can largely be attributed to the way he handled such matters.

At Highland Park he faced very little challenge to his leadership. There was almost no open opposition. "There never has been here," said J.R. Faulkner. "They accepted Dr. Roberson's leadership."

Nevertheless, like any church, there were problems. Some of the members did not like the poorer, shabbily dressed "bus people" coming into the church, and some complained about how crowded the church had become. Some felt that the church membership was neglected in favor of Roberson's attention to the college students. Some complained of his tight leadership control.

When there were complaints or criticisms, usually they revolved around the accusation that Roberson's leadership was too strong – that he was a dictator. Walter Wendelken said critics like that were always around but would rarely express themselves openly. The support for Roberson was always too strong for any opposition to gain a foothold. But Wendelken remembered one occasion in the late 1950s or early 1960s. "I was invited to a meeting once," he said. "I didn't know what it was about. They wanted me to be critical of Dr. Roberson. I said, no, he's my pastor, and that was that. But it was there. I knew how they felt – that he was a dictator." With Highland Park running 5,000 in attendance, a group of 200 people once wanted to pull out. They approached J.R. Faulkner. Dr. Roberson was out of town. Faulkner's advice to the group was simple. "You'll have to talk to Dr. Roberson," he said.

Some church members claimed there was an occasion when Roberson resigned in the late 1960s. A number of church leaders, some of whom were political leaders in the community, wanted him to quit emphasizing doctrinal issues such as separation. Rather than fight, Roberson turned in his resignation. But the church wouldn't hear of it. Dr. E.C. Haskell Sr. led a quick response which succeeded in getting Roberson to reconsider. "He actually resigned," recalled Tom Wallace. "It was in the newspaper." Thereafter, when Roberson stayed, a few of the unhappy political leaders left the church.

In the late 1950s and 1960s many fundamental churches quit participating in Billy Graham's crusades because of the ecumenical involvement of theologically liberal pastors and churches. But in 1951, when Billy Graham held a crusade in Chattanooga, Highland Park Baptist Church cooperated. Tennessee Temple students helped build the downtown field house at Warner Park for the crusade. Orman and Betty Norwood were among a number of Highland Park members who sang in the crusade choir each night. Highland Park

Baptist Church sent buses of people to the crusade. Billy Graham spoke in chapel at Tennessee Temple from I Corinthians, chapter 13. "Cliff Barrows will be here. Don't miss it!" announced Lee Roberson. At the crusade, Dr. Roberson assisted the elderly Ernest "Pappy" Reveal to the platform to lead in prayer. Dr. and Mrs. Lee Roberson and Dr. and Mrs. J.R. Faulkner joined Billy and Ruth Graham for dinner at a restaurant. The restaurant owner, always calling Roberson, "Dr. Roberson," came out and gave a country ham to Billy Graham as a gift. Lee and Caroline Roberson also hosted the Grahams in their home for a meal.

Later when Billy Graham's ecumenical cooperation became a controversial issue among fundamentalists, Lee Roberson quietly backed out of such cooperation. "Dr. Roberson never said a critical word about it," said Faulkner. "If he had anything to say, it was always positive. That was his position on all issues. He just never had a critical word about anything. Consequently, George Dollar in his book called Lee Roberson a compromiser. That grieved me. He's anything but a compromiser. George Dollar wrote me and asked me for information. He was re-issuing his book. I ignored the letter. I didn't want to rebuke or argue, so I ignored it. But that whole group was critical of us because we didn't come out against Billy Graham. Doctor just would not do it." In such matters, said Faulkner, "Dr. Roberson never answered back in writing. He won't talk about the brethren. You never heard him in the pulpit here call anyone names."

Roberson rarely referred to such matters in the pulpit. In his sermon, *The Fine Art of Criticizing*, Roberson said, "I am a fundamentalist! I believe the Bible from cover to cover. I have critics who call me a 'liberal.' If I were weaker, it would turn me away from fundamentalism. I am not weaker. I ignore the criticism!" In his sermon, *Seventy One Years of Fundamentalism*, he said, "Anyone who casts doubts upon our fundamentalism is perhaps one of three things – or all of them. He is ignorant of our work; he dislikes some of us personally; [or], he is jealous of Highland Park Baptist Church and Tennessee Temple University. There have always been critics... Now, I don't mind critics on the outside. If some rank modernist or liberal criticizes me, that doesn't bother me. But it does trouble me when the inside family of fundamentalists begin criticizing one another. This is contrary to the Spirit of our Lord. I believe all the Bible. I preach all the Bible. I won't change."

Ed Johnson, always loyal to Dr. Roberson, said, "He avoided controversy. We were not exposed to the rise of the neo-evangelicalism in my days at Temple. Doc stayed away from that controversy." Johnson pointed out that Dr. Roberson would also have a wide array of evangelical mission boards represented at the missions conferences – some, such as the Sudan Interior Mission, were outside the independent, fundamental movement. Some fundamentalists would criticize Tennessee Temple and Roberson for such associations. Roberson never understood that. He was always loyal and spoke highly of his friends. Nat Phillips, who remained close to Roberson, said, "Dr. Roberson was extremely loyal to his friends. I think maybe he probably defended some people when they shouldn't have been defended. He's extremely loyal to his friends." One family friend suggested that as with great men, a strength can become a weakness – such as being loyal to someone who no longer deserves it.

Roberson did not hesitate to stand behind those whom he felt were criticized unjustly. When it became common for some independent Baptists to criticize independent Baptist leaders such as Jerry Falwell or evangelist Tim Lee for preaching for Southern Baptists or other non-independent Baptist ministries, Roberson never wavered in his support of such men as Falwell or Lee. He felt that men like Falwell and Lee had a heart for the Lord and for souls, and that was all that mattered to him.

It was Lee Roberson's way. Mention a preacher around him and he would say, "Good brother! Good brother! Does a good job!" He refused to be boxed into anyone's theological or ecclesiastical boundaries. After leaving the Southern Baptist Convention, he was not about to let a new independent movement define him. Tennessee Temple students remember hearing the famed Southern Baptist, R.G. Lee, preach his sermon, *Payday Someday*, at Highland Park Baptist Church. They remembered hearing Bill Bright of Campus Crusade speak in chapel. Bright's interdenominational ministry was considered too cooperative and not "separatist" enough by some independent fundamental ministries. "That defined some lives," said Ron Bishop. "Bob Jones really reacted to that." It was said that Fred Brown of Tennessee Temple had a tremendous effect on Billy Graham's life. Some of the great preachers of the Southern Baptist Convention, such as Jerry Vines and Junior Hill, publicly gave great credit to Roberson's influence in their lives. Two years before he died Lee Roberson accepted an invitation from Bailey Smith to preach at a Southern Baptist meeting.

When Jack Hyles' ministry became embroiled in controversy and suffered widespread attack, Dr. Roberson continued to preach for him annually. "He never let that controversy affect him at all," said Faulkner. "Inwardly, he may have had reservations, but you never heard a word – never heard it at lunch, never heard it at the table where the conversation would come up. You know he didn't like that kind of stuff about anybody – any controversial subject. He'd change the subject." Roberson said privately, "I don't believe a bit of it," and he encouraged Hyles not to answer his critics. "They had a fabulous relationship," said Wendell Evans. He called Dr. Roberson one of Hyles' heroes.

Lee Roberson did not spend his time criticizing. He always emphasized the positive. If a ministry with which he previously cooperated changed and became "liberal," he would quietly back away. He would not invite that ministry to Highland Park again, but he would not openly criticize it. As far as the periodic issues of controversy in fundamentalism, he avoided many of them. If he did not agree with another preacher, he continued to treat that preacher with respect. When a famous Presbyterian preacher was in Chattanooga to speak as a guest at First Presbyterian Church, Dr. Roberson invited him to speak in his college chapel. But when that same preacher criticized the way Baptists give the gospel invitation – by inviting people to come forward and be "interrogated," Dr. Roberson never invited him to speak again.

"Dr. Roberson was very careful," said J.R. Faulkner. "He wasn't very tolerant with people on the great fundamental doctrines of truth." He would permit wider latitude on secondary matters of preference but not on matters which affected the gospel of salvation. "He could discern those things," said Faulkner.

Negativism and criticism simply were not a part of Lee Roberson's life. In his sermon, *Seven Words to Live By*, he said, "I get sick and tired of all these whimpering, whining Christians. I meet them everywhere – complaining, complaining. They act like God is dead. They are always finding fault."

CHAPTER 12

World-Wide Faith Missions

Within three years after Lee Roberson became pastor of Highland Park Baptist Church, in 1945, Annie Catherine Phillips, daughter of Lee Roberson's predecessor at Highland Park, left Chattanooga as a "home missionary" to teach the Bible in Kentucky. Her dedication electrified the church. Later she went to the foreign mission field. Roberson and his church set a goal of helping to finance 100 missionaries, home and foreign, with monthly support – a goal that was reached in 1954.

In the 1950s the family of brothers Fred and Elwood Anderson were missionaries in Africa under the old Congo Gospel Mission, with home headquarters in Indianapolis, Indiana. The two brothers were students at Tennessee Temple College. Their parents had gone up the Congo River, 300 miles north of the Congo city of Leopoldville, to establish a mission station and had remained there for nine years without relief. Fred, the younger of the two brothers, came into Dr. Lee Roberson's office crying. He begged Dr. Roberson to send missionaries to the Congo in relief of his parents – just so they could come home for a break. While evangelical missionaries normally receive a furlough every four years, Fred's parents were approaching one decade in Africa with no furlough yet in sight. As pioneer missionaries in a new territory, they were exhausted and, of course, missed their family.

The Andersons were frustrated with the operation of the Congo Gospel Mission. They felt it was not aggressive enough in sending out new missionaries and was simply relying on continuing support for the aging missionaries already on the field. At Roberson's direction, Fred Anderson asked several of the Congo mission board members to visit Chattanooga to see Roberson. J.R. Faulkner sat in on the meeting. They agreed that Roberson would organize a new southern division of the Congo mission. He would send out new missionaries and raise financial support for them, while the CGM board continued to provide support for the existing missionaries. "We'll take responsibility for the ones we're sending there," Faulkner recalled, "and we'll see if we can help. You carry on, and we'll help. It was logical. So, we sent 14 missionaries into the Congo to relieve the Andersons." On November 9, 1955, the southern branch of the Congo Gospel Mission was formed at Highland Park. Along with Roberson, preachers such as Monroe Parker and Harold Sightler were involved. The Congo missionary work began to expand. A school to train national pastors was started in the Congo, along with a couple of more churches and a medical clinic.

But in 1959 the Marxist revolution drove all foreign missionaries from the Congo – later named Zaire, and then in modern times re-named the Congo. At that time the Communist rebels burned the CGM mission station to the ground and permanently expelled all foreign missionaries. Mercifully, all 14 of Highland Park's missionaries were rescued, although one family, the Brownings, was held captive for three days before British helicopters rescued them. All the missionaries were taken to Paris and eventually brought back to the United States. The CGM southern branch went in debt some $8,000 to fly the missionaries home. Dolphus Price was the treasurer. J.R. Faulkner was the secretary. "We got them out," said Faulkner. "But we had to borrow to get them home. Now we had 14 missionaries and no field. The idea then was to send them into the Caribbean – Nicaragua, Guatemala, and so forth. So, we did."

In those days Roberson operated a short-lived "Pastors' School" during the annual Summer Bible Conference. Preachers came from all over the South to attend the school. One night of the conference, Roberson announced, "I want to meet about 100 of you preachers over in Phillips Chapel, because I have something on my heart I want to talk to you about." The meeting was held after lunch the next day. Roberson announced his burden to organize a new missions sending agency and support the 14 missionaries already on the field. But his goal was to go beyond the 14 – he wanted a missions outreach that would embrace the whole world. The pastors quickly adopted his proposal and voted to begin a new missions board – later known as Baptist International Missions, Inc. BIMI's missionary purpose was to be three-fold: a) Evangelism; b) Church-planting; and, c) Training of national leadership in the foreign countries. The BIMI board organized and chartered in the state of Tennessee. The first president of BIMI was missionary Tom Freeney, at one time a member of Highland Park. When age and health forced Freeney to retire to Central Florida, Don Sisk, a veteran missionary to Japan, became president and did "an amazing job," according to Faulkner.

The goal of Lee Roberson's life was to see as many souls as possible gathered into the kingdom of God through faith in Jesus Christ. Whether at home or abroad, he believed with all of his heart that every soul on earth is in need of personal salvation, and that such salvation is only available to mankind through faith in the redemptive work of Jesus Christ on the cross of Calvary. He believed that the gospel must be proclaimed to every individual, and that every individual must embrace that gospel. Lee Roberson would not approve of becoming a theologian at the expense of evangelism. Everything to which he committed his time was evangelistic. Roberson loved music, but he wanted music to result in evangelism. Lloyd Smith, a musician, used to write cantatas for churches, visit churches and put on the production, inviting Dr. Roberson to come in and give a short, evangelistic message. Roberson loved it.

No visitor to Highland Park Baptist Church could miss Roberson's emphasis on missions. This focus was visible behind the choir loft at the front of the main sanctuary where national flags of various foreign countries were displayed, with a map of the world, and the Scriptural command printed, "Go ye into all the world and preach the gospel to every creature."

Roberson carried a burden for souls and the urgent message of the gospel through out his life. Evangelist Joe Shadowens remembered a church service at Highland Park in the early 1970s in the Chauncey-Goode auditorium. During the invitation Dr. Roberson came down from the pulpit. Ignoring the aisles, he walked over the top of seven church pews right down the middle of the auditorium and touched a man on the shoulder. He led the man down to the front of the church and prayed with him, as the man opened his heart to receive Christ.

At different times various people would volunteer to me different ministries which they claimed were Lee Roberson's real "baby" in his ministry, or the thing to which he was most committed. I heard this said by different people – regarding his local church, the college, Camp Joy, Sunday school, the bus ministry, or missions. The truth probably is that all these evangelistic or soul winning ministries entwined to reveal the heart of what Lee Roberson was all about. Evangelism was his "baby."

Accordingly, he committed his life to spreading the gospel. He guided Highland Park Baptist Church into every kind of ministry possible to reach lost souls – Sunday school, soul winning visitation, street preaching, rescue mission, foreign missions, church planting, children's camp, vacation Bible school, radio broadcast, jail ministry, etc. Roberson created an evangelistic atmosphere at Highland Park. He preached with a sense of urgency – calling people to "walk the aisle" or "come forward" during the gospel invitation at the end of the service to receive Christ as Savior. Often it seemed that the invitation lasted longer than the sermon. And Roberson's evangelism was not limited to his local church. In his early years he was a full-time Southern Baptist evangelist. Throughout his ministry he preached weekly around the nation and the world. It was not uncommon for him to see dozens of people saved in evangelistic services. For example, when he conducted a revival campaign in High Point, North Carolina, no less than 240 people publicly professed faith in Christ for salvation in the services.

Jesus has a heart for souls. He said of Himself, *"The Son of Man is come to seek and to save that which was lost."* (Luke 19:10) The Apostle Paul said of Christ, *"Christ Jesus came into the world to save sinners..."* (I Timothy 1:15) Gloria Shadowens, Roberson's secretary for more than 25 years in the latter part of his life, said of Roberson, "If you loved souls, you could be close to him. If not – he didn't have time for you." Everything at Highland Park Baptist Church was pointed toward winning souls to Christ and building up the church. All Tennessee Temple students were required to be in some kind of church ministry, and most of those various ministries – such as Bible clubs, jail ministry, or, nursing home ministry – included soul winning or personal witness as part of their mission.

In 1948 at Highland Park Baptist Church, Roberson launched "World Wide Faith Missions," a program to raise financial support for missionaries around the world through faith-supported mission agencies. Beginning with four or five missionaries, World Wide Faith Missions expanded to help support hundreds of missionaries. World Wide Faith Missions was not a mission board, but simply the church fund set up to support missionaries through the offerings of the people. Roberson began his life-long practice of receiving two church offerings for missions each week – both Sunday evening and Wednesday evening. All of the "loose" offerings, or undesignated contributions, in those services were added to money designated for missions. The concept caught hold and took off. "It gave me a chance to emphasize missions twice a week," Roberson said. "I did it to keep missions before the people – to keep missions before their minds. It became a big, big offering. People started giving to foreign missions. They would mark their offerings. I began bringing in missionaries to speak. They liked that. They kept on giving." For many years, half of Highland Park's weekly giving went to missions. In addition, a special love offering would be received for a visiting missionary speaker. The church reached its goal of helping to support 100 missionaries around the world in less than a decade. Later that total reached more than 560 missionaries supported through approximately 80 independent "faith" missions boards. Typically the church would make a monthly commitment of $25 to $75 to a missionary couple. By the last years of Roberson's pastorate, Highland Park Baptist Church was committing nearly $1-million annually to missions through the World Wide Faith Missions offerings, plus other designated missions offerings.

In 2001 J.R. Faulkner told me he sent out 252 Christmas cards to missionary families the church was supporting – families "we're contributing to," he said. "We 'contribute to,' instead of saying 'support.' Support has a broader meaning – meaning you've got the whole thing. We contribute to the support of 252 families." It was Highland Park's practice that if the Sunday and Wednesday evening missions offerings did not cover the complete missionary support commitments, then the difference would come out of the church's General Fund.

To stir the cause of missions, Roberson had missionaries speak at the church frequently. "I kept missionaries before them all the time," he told me. Roberson himself would meet visiting missionaries at the airport and would take a personal interest in their families back home. And always there was the annual missions conference, organized by Cliff Robinson and held the first week of November. Typically between 75 and 100 missionaries representing around 30 independent "faith" mission boards would come to Highland Park each year for the week-long conference. Cliff Robinson would alternately choose from nearly 80 such faith missions boards from which to invite the missionaries each year. During the conference week the missionaries were constant guests in the homes of church members. At the conference missionaries would speak every day – three missionaries in the morning, and two in the evening. Dr. Roberson made the annual missions conference a major undertaking – one of the highlights on the church calendar. "He had an outstanding impact on preachers all over the world," said Les Frazier, a veteran BIMI missionary to Japan. "Every year he had a long, good, well-planned missions conference. Many pastors I've been with patterned their missions program after what they learned at Tennessee Temple."

During the annual missions conference, each missionary would set up a display booth representing his or her ministry. Students would visit the booths and learn more about worldwide missions. The entire church and college campus would be decorated with the year's missions theme. Cliff Robinson would write letters in advance to the principals of the local public schools, offering to bring a missionary into the school. The idea of a missionary representing the culture of a foreign land would interest the school leaders, and Robinson succeeded in having many of the missionaries speak and show visual slide projections in public schools. Always the missionaries would include the gospel in their presentations.

Roberson constantly challenged the young preacher boys at Tennessee Temple University to answer God's call to missions. Seeing young people respond publicly to the call to missions at the annual conference was a highlight of the church year. It was only natural that Roberson's priority of supporting missionaries and his training of young missionary candidates at the college should be joined together in a missionary enterprise such as Baptist International Missions, Inc. Through the years more than 500 missionaries with BIMI were Tennessee Temple graduates, and many became among the most effective missionaries in the world – and always among the most evangelistic missionaries in the world.

Among the early missionaries sent out from Tennessee Temple was Frank Rosser. After graduating from Temple in 1955, Rosser went to Nicaragua in 1956 and later helped Tom Freeney start Baptist International Missions, Inc. Rosser was the first missionary to join the initial group rescued from the Congo in becoming BIMI missionaries. Rosser did not want an administrative position that would keep him serving in headquarters instead of on the mission field. He accepted a position as assistant director of BIMI, to facilitate his return to Nicaragua. On occasion he traveled the world as the assistant director, but he spent most of the next 50 years in Nicaragua establishing more than 150 churches – three of them larger than 1,000 in membership, nine more churches of 500-plus members, and BIMI schools with more than 5,000 students. All the churches were later served by national pastors and became self-supporting and debt-free. Rosser had a remarkable missionary career. While he was in Nicaragua, he faced some unusual persecution. At one time his house had been taken from him on false charges brought by opposition Roman Catholics. Also, he had been stoned and persecuted with tacks to flatten his automobile tires and threatened by enemies who used a dangerous snake to frighten his family. But Rosser continued faithfully and in time saw many people come to faith in Christ – including a witchdoctor and his family. When I met Rosser, he was nearly 80 years old. He had just returned from a special celebration at his first Nicaraguan church, with 3,300 in Sunday school that day. He told me he had been planning to retire but had changed his mind! He returned once again to Nicaragua.

As BIMI's worldwide outreach expanded, missionary Ray Thompson was sent to St. Thomas in the Virgin Islands of the Caribbean, where he established the Bluewater Bible College. When Thompson arrived, there were practically no Baptists in the Virgin Islands. Furthermore, a person needed a Roman Catholic baptismal certificate to do almost anything in that society. However, a half-century later the Virgin Islands were 42 per cent Baptist. "We just did what Dr. Roberson taught," said Thompson.

After graduating from Tennessee Temple, Jerry Reece began initially as a missionary supported entirely by one Tennessee church. Later he joined BIMI. Reece took only nine months' furlough in his first 15 years on the mission field. He served in Nicaragua and El Salvador, and later he became a Caribbean director for BIMI.

And, of course, some of the Highland Park missionaries served through missions boards other than BIMI. Missionary Garland Cofield was growing up at Highland Park Baptist Church even before Roberson arrived, and Cofield launched into missionary service before BIMI was even formed. "Dr. Roberson was my champion, my hero," said Cofield. "When I bought a travel trailer to do evangelistic work, he came out and dedicated that." Cofield and his wife, Reba, went to Canada, built a Bible camp in the north woods, and began missionary work among the North American Indians. The first church he started in the north woods later was supporting 14 missionaries itself – sending out people to plant new churches as far as 200 miles away. Roberson visited and preached at that church. Cofield started another dozen churches himself. He would see 800 visitors per week at his evangelistic summer camp in Canada and then spend the winter months visiting the Indian reservations. In later years, after Cofield's first wife, Reba, died, he continued his missionary work with his second wife, Helen.

Roberson was proud of Solomon Owolabi, the son of a tribal chief in Nigeria, Africa, who came to Tennessee Temple for his Bible training. Owolabi, who had an amazing testimony of faith in Christ, returned to Africa and built three large churches where thousands of people came to Christ. Owolabi's son, James, was also trained at Tennessee Temple and became a youth pastor and an evangelist. James, who had an overflowing love for the Lord, later served on my pastoral staff in Florida.

Roberson himself traveled to the mission field to preach – "not as much as I would have liked to," he said. He visited such places as the West Indies, Mexico, Japan, Israel, and Canada. His commitment to the local church and the demands of the huge Highland Park Baptist Church ministry kept him at home most of the time. "I didn't go a whole lot to the mission field," he said. When he preached on one occasion in Jamaica, Roberson faced unusual spiritual darkness and resistance to the gospel message. Nat Phillips remembered, "He came back from Jamaica and said it was the only place I've been that I couldn't preach." Phillips added, "He was not a great traveler. For years he used to say he'd go to the 'Holy Land' during the millennium. But he did finally go."

One of Lee Roberson's rare missionary trips was a memorable week-long trip to Japan in 1970. Roberson loved the dignified Japanese people – the respectful way they bowed, honored their elders, etc. He told the missionaries that Japan was the only mission field he ever visited to which he would like to return. When he first arrived, Roberson worried that the interpreter would have difficulty with his rapid style of speaking. But God blessed his preaching in Japan. The first night Roberson preached in Japan a passer-by on his way to commit suicide overheard Roberson preaching, walked into the service, and received Christ as his Savior. That same night a professor from the University of Osaka came to Christ. Such conversions are particularly unusual in a predominantly Buddhist country like Japan, where the gospel is largely unfamiliar.

Roberson preached in the largest Baptist church in Japan in Osaka, a church of about 350 in attendance at Senri Newtown, for Pastor Sogora Ogawa, who was saved under the ministry of BIMI missionary Don Sisk. Ogawa's son, Isaiah, later graduated from Tennessee Temple and returned to Japan to serve with his father at the church. When Roberson visited Osaka, a group of missionaries and pastors, including missionaries Ron White of BIMI and Sisk, plus Pastor Ogawa, took Roberson to the top of a tall tower overseeing the city of Osaka. The population of the greater Osaka-Kobe area was then about 10-million people. Lee Roberson stood there with tears of compassion streaming down his cheeks as he saw the lights of Japan's third largest city – and the millions of unsaved, mostly Buddhist, souls those lights represented. Afterward, Roberson was very challenging as he spoke to the missionaries in their summer field conference. A missionary asked Roberson, "How can we build big churches in Japan like in America?" Roberson's response was poignant. "Has anyone done it?" he asked. He was told the answer was, no. "When someone does it," he said, "then they can tell us how to do it."

In Japan a young missionary named Janet Burchell, with limited education and training, asked Roberson for advice. When he suggested she come to Tennessee Temple to complete her education, she told him she had no money. Roberson instructed her to come anyway – that the Lord would take care of her. He told her to look him up when she arrived. As instructed, she made the trip back to America and went to Roberson's office to see him. He saw to it that she was given a missionary scholarship. "Well," he said, "you're a missionary. I guess we could give you a missionary scholarship!" Later in his office, he told her, "Every time I have seen you go by [the big window in his office], I have prayed for you and for Japan." When the time came for her to return to Japan, Roberson helped Janet and her husband, Ralph Burchell, raise support to go back as missionaries. The Burchells raised their financial support in an unusually quick period of nine months and left for Japan in 1976. I met them on a missions trip in Kobe, Japan, in 2003. In 2010 they were still serving there.

It was on Roberson's trip to the Holy Land in Jerusalem that he picked up a large picture entitled, "The Weeping Boy of Jerusalem." He saw the picture in a little shop window. It caught his attention because of the tears streaming down the face of the little boy. It reminded him of all the boys and girls in the world who are lost without Jesus, and it reminded him of the ministry focus to children of Camp Joy. So, he brought the picture home and had it reproduced in poster-size to help promote Camp Joy. He used that picture as a symbol of compassion and evangelism.

Roberson always remained on the board of directors of BIMI. By the end of his life, BIMI was supporting more than 1,000 missionaries in 90 countries – with annual support of nearly $22-million coming from some 8,500 churches. Originally located at East Ridge, Tennessee – just outside Chattanooga, BIMI later established beautiful, permanent headquarters near Harrison Bay, just north of Chattanooga. Late in Roberson's life, BIMI named its newly built main auditorium after Lee Roberson. The entrance to BIMI headquarters is on "Compassion Lane," a street name chosen by Roberson. At Roberson's funeral, BIMI President Dr. James Ray said, "We just did everything he ever said!" As a student years earlier Ray had been known all over the Tennessee Temple campus as "Jimmy" Ray. As was the custom among the preacher boys, Ray went in to visit Dr. Roberson at his office and seek his advice as Ray was preparing to graduate and take his first pastorate. Roberson was direct in telling Jimmy Ray, "Billy Graham gets away with it, but you are not going to get away with it. From now on, it's James." Ray related the story years later at Dr. Roberson's funeral. "I went in there 'Jimmy' – and I came out 'James'," he said. "You just did it."

Late in his life, I asked Roberson if he were ever tempted to go himself as a missionary. "No," he said. But he loved missionaries. Missionaries in Japan fondly remembered Dr. Roberson's visit. At the conference in Japan evangelist John R. Rice publicly chastised the missionaries for not bringing more souls to Christ. Of course, the largely Buddhist nation of Japan is a very challenging mission field for the gospel. In the same meeting when Dr. Roberson's turn to speak came, he publicly asked Roland Simeonsson to stand. Roland and his wife, Sandra, were Tennessee Temple graduates and among the first missionaries sent to Japan by BIMI. The Simeonssons spent their lives in Japan. Dr. Roberson publicly told the conference how proud he was of Roland Simeonsson. Lee Roberson was always a champion of any student who graduated from Tennessee Temple. And he was a champion of any missionary.

Lee Roberson's life was committed to reaching souls for Jesus Christ – through evangelism, witness, soul winning, missions, rescue mission, radio – in whatever way possible. In his sermon, *God's Abundant Blessings*, Roberson told about the day when he watched a bulldozer demolish the church-owned house on Bailey Avenue, where he and his family had lived for years. His memory went back to the night when a deacon named W.I. Powell knocked on the door of the pastorium and introduced to Roberson a lost man named Bill Morgan. Roberson led the man to a saving knowledge of Christ. Morgan became a faithful Christian. Then Roberson said he recalled a man named Jowers who came down Market Street in Chattanooga and stopped in front of the Union Gospel Mission. Jowers took a knife and slashed his own throat from ear to ear, then dropped over in the gutter right in front of the rescue mission. Jowers was rushed to a hospital emergency room, and his life was saved. Roberson visited him in the hospital, and his soul was saved. A month later as Roberson gave the gospel invitation on a Sunday morning a well-dressed man walked the aisle and said to Roberson, "I have accepted Christ. I want to join the church." Then he asked Roberson, "Do you know me?" Roberson said, "I don't believe I do." The gentleman said, "Oh, yes, you do." His name was Jowers.

When missionary Mike Patterson's growing ministry expanded in Cuernavaca, Mexico, he invited Dr. Lee Roberson to preach for the dedication of their second building. The crowd packed the building out, with chairs brought in, and standing room only. Roberson preached in English, as Patterson translated into Spanish. When the gospel invitation was given, the altar was flooded with dozens of people who came forward to receive Christ. Patterson, who later would become president of Mount Abarim Baptist Mission International, was thrilled. Later that day, Dr. Roberson asked to see Patterson alone in his office. Mike was worried. Like all Tennessee Temple preacher boys, he wanted Roberson's approval. He invited Dr. Roberson into his office and closed the door, all the time wondering – what have I done wrong? Have I done something to offend my hero? But Roberson's approval of Patterson's ministry was overwhelming. With tears streaming down his face, Dr. Roberson said to Mike Patterson, "If someone had told me you could see results like this, I would have begged God to let me be a missionary."

CHAPTER 13

The Spurgeon of His Generation

Lee Roberson was 18 years old when he preached his first sermon at a little Baptist mission church located in Jeffersontown, Kentucky, just outside Louisville. His Scripture text for that first sermon was from Mark 4:1-12 on the "Parable of the Sower." Lee, who had learned to type in high school, typed out his first sermon on green typing paper – double-spaced. As he spoke, he followed his manuscript closely. When he lifted his hand momentarily, a gust of wind from a little window at the side of the pulpit blew all the sheets of his sermon notes to the floor. A bit humiliated, he bent over and picked up the sheets, arranged the pages, and resumed his sermon. He later reminisced, "The message was exceedingly short, much to the relief of both preacher and audience."

It was at age 18 that Lee Roberson answered God's call to preach the gospel. The call to preach "hit me pretty solidly," he recalled years later. Sensing that divine call as a teenager, Lee was quickly licensed to preach by his home church, Cedar Creek Baptist Church, outside Louisville, Kentucky. A few weeks later Lee went away to college to study for the ministry. His first opportunities to preach were in little churches in the neighborhood of Russellville, Kentucky, at that time the home of a small Southern Baptist school named Bethel College. From such humble beginnings, he was to spend the next four score years – eight decades – preaching untold thousands of sermons to crowds of all sizes.

Roberson was a great preacher. He was not the type of spellbinding orator that his mentor, R.G. Lee, was. Nor was he a detailed, verse-by-verse expositor like radio minister J. Vernon McGee. Although his simple style of speaking contrasted with the flowery eloquence of the 19th century British preacher, Charles Spurgeon, Roberson was sometimes called "the Spurgeon of his generation" because of the impact of his preaching and the size of the crowds to whom he preached. From the pulpit he held the attention of some 5,000 listeners three times per week for decades. Roberson preached with a simplicity that was profound in a direct, straight forward style. He spoke with confidence and authority. His sermons were almost always topical in style – with a simple outline emphasizing plain themes of salvation, soul winning, godly living, and faithfulness to church. His focus in preaching was on the Bible and its Scriptural principles. Lee Roberson unapologetically preached the Bible as the literal Word of God.

Roberson's technique for preaching was rapid and fervent in delivery. There was a motivational pressure – do it now! Roberson would preach topically from the Bible in order to persuade the listener to a decision. He preached primarily to motivate people to make decisions to serve and obey God. An invitation for response from the congregation was given in every service, and each sermon was delivered to elicit a type of spiritual commitment on the part of the listener – to repent, to trust, or to obey. As he preached, he verbalized a strong emphasis on the first words of his sentences, such as, "Let's go!" or "Stand up!" or "Now, wait a minute!" Thus, his style was very commanding and riveting.

Roberson's heart-beat was always for evangelism. As a preacher, he did not feel that being a Bible expositor would fit his personal approach to proclaiming the Word of God. Almost all of his sermons had a strong evangelistic appeal. If Roberson preached on the home, or on prayer, there would still be a strong evangelistic appeal. "There never was a message I can ever remember without the gospel being presented somewhere in that message," said veteran Tennessee Temple University teacher Glenn Swygart. Presbyterian preacher Ben Haden said, "The highest compliment I heard, from a man in his church – 'Ben, he never speaks to the giraffe.' I don't think there's a seminary in America which teaches preachers to preach like Jesus. They all make it elitist. They all want to complicate the gospel. He's kept it simple. Lee Roberson has never forgotten the 'guts' of the gospel – which is to be saved."

In a *Chattanooga News-Free Press* article published in 1971, reporter Helen McDonald Exum described Roberson's speaking style. "He speaks rapidly," she wrote. "Lee Roberson speaks so rapidly that you wonder when he takes a breath. It is not at the end of every sentence. He is enthusiastic, zealous, so filled with the many things that must be said that he hurries through." This, she wrote, was true in his giving church announcements – not just in preaching. He missed no detail, she wrote.

"His messages were simple – yet preached with such authority and power in the pulpit," said veteran BIMI missionary Les Frazier. "God the Holy Spirit was controlling him. There was an impact on the people – so convicting. There were two aspects so common to his preaching – salvation and service." Frazier compared Roberson's simple preaching style with that of one of history's greatest evangelists, D.L. Moody. Attorney and Highland Park member Glenn Copeland remembered Roberson's preaching as, "Straight down the line on salvation. You need to be Christian. He would cover the entire Bible with his sermons and topics." Texas preacher Clyde Box marveled at how Roberson would give a "simple invitation" with the power of God – as people came forward. Indeed, Roberson preached with God's hand upon him. Several years afterward, college educator Wendell Evans, still vividly remembered the power of one illustration in a sermon on prayer by Dr. Roberson in May of 1995 – an illustration which changed Evans' life.

Roberson's focus on preaching was deliberately topical, whereby a sermon is built around a biblical topic drawn from various passages of the Bible. "It always appealed to me – I don't know why," Roberson told me. He heard a number of outstanding Bible expositors at seminary in Louisville, but "try as they could, it didn't appeal to me." He chose the topical style. "I tried to work on the idea of reaching the hearts of the people more than anything else to say things that would open their eyes, so they could think and get the message," he said. "I took lots of general ideas of homiletics, and so forth, and made my own outlines myself."

Roberson's choice of sermon topics was guided by "the need of the hour." He said, "I was usually impressed by some need we had. It might be something that had maybe come to me during visitation – a need among the people we were going to visit, or maybe a need of the church. I would observe things in the church – what needed to be done. I stayed on certain lines a lot – soul winning, a whole lot on soul wining. Later I began to deal with the work of the fullness of the Holy Spirit, dying to self – things that were important."

Each week Roberson always tried to select his sermon topic by Wednesday evening, so that he could announce at the midweek service his sermon title for the following Sunday – hopefully promoting interest. J.R. Faulkner would put a paid advertisement in the Saturday newspaper by Thursday's deadline, also announcing the sermon for the coming Sunday.

Dr. Fred Afman, a preacher and Bible scholar who taught at Tennessee Temple for more than 30 years, said of Roberson's preaching, "He never attempted to be spectacular or appeasing the audience. The message was always the most important part of his presentation. Get that message across – simple outline. Never be detracted by excessive explanation or excessive illustration. The point had to be driven home – usually with his right hand. 'This is the point I want you to get!' As far as being a brilliant 'exegeter' of Scripture – no, but it was always a simple, plain exegesis of that passage. Understandable. So you were fed by it. You were nourished by it. And you weren't sidetracked by it. Dr. Roberson by his very demeanor commanded your attention. You knew he was giving you something that was valuable, personal, applicable, and in a sense, well outlined."

Evangelist Ron Bishop's view of Roberson's preaching style was similar. "He was not a great expository preacher," said Bishop. "He was not a great teacher." Florida preacher Randy Ray explained it this way, "If you gave me a choice to go hear great preachers – he may be four or five on the list. But if you ask me who do you want to be influenced by – he'd be No. 1 on the list because of his leadership." Highland Park secretary Dorothy McCormick said, "He was a preacher – not a teacher. He taught with his life."

"His preaching was very simple," said Oklahoma City pastor Jim Vineyard. "He did not try to be cute. He did not try to alliterate everything. He just put it out there."

Roberson tried to give a simple truth which the listener could "take home with him." He preached with a deliberate, definite style, as if he always knew where he was going. In the forward to a book of sermons entitled, *This Crisis Hour*, Roberson wrote, "At the beginning of my preaching I endeavored to be plain and straight forward. I wanted the glorious truth of Christ and His saving power to be evident to every person, whether young or old. I did not want to conceal the magnificent truth of His saving power and the glorious secrets of victorious living." Missionary Garland Cofield said, "He never brought a poor message." Cofield recalled that Roberson's deacon chairman for some 30 years, Dr. E.C. Haskell Sr., once said, "I never heard him preach a bad sermon."

Tennessee Temple teacher Nat Phillips saw Roberson's topical style as valuable. "I suspect part of his success was the fact he was simple," said Phillips. "He gives you the text. He gives you the points. He gives you illustrations that go with the points. I've heard preachers say they preach to a 5th grade or 6th grade level. I think he preached simple sermons that people could understand."

Roberson tried in the pulpit to focus on the positive side of life – not negatives. "Keep your mind on the positive," he said. "Get away from the negative. Be strong on the positive. I never tried to preach negative sermons. Give people a definite thought every time. Give them a thought – dying to self, evangelism, soul winning, missions. I didn't deal with the negative side. It was there. To me, appeal to the mind." He never got side-tracked on tangents. Everywhere he traveled it was the same – preaching the Word of God and teaching preachers how to build soul winning Sunday schools.

If Lee Roberson himself was discouraged, he would try to correct it before preaching. "Yes," he said, "I'd sometimes feel like I was failing. I'd talk it over with my wife. We'd pray about it. Not very often. But once in awhile we did. Most of the time, I came on out of it. I could get myself in line to be ready for Wednesday and then the next Sunday from there. The big thing is not to reveal your feelings. It is better not to reveal how you feel. Be the same way every time – always positive every time, no matter how I felt inside, positive announcing the sermon and message and so forth. Keep their minds on the positive side. If you're negative or failing, you're not doing good. They get the idea the whole thing is going to pieces. People grab a negative idea. They love to get a hold of it. So, I kept on the positive side."

Although he typed the first sermon he ever preached, through the years Dr. Roberson wrote out his sermon manuscripts in long-hand. Late in life he preached from those longhand manuscripts – written in cursive. His handwriting was excellent – large and easily readable. But for most of the years of his ministry his secretary would type the sermon outline which he carried to the pulpit. "I did a lot of dictating of sermons on tape at home," he said. "When I preached, I could have the whole thing in front of me, if I wanted to – or if I didn't. I'd take some notes and cover what I was going to do. I did a lot of sermons with just the outline before me."

Lee Roberson would privately rehearse his sermons in his office before preaching them in public. "Not always out loud," he told me, "but I would take my notes – put them on my desk here, and walk around the office and go through my entire message. I did a lot of reviewing."

In his early 90s, Dr. Roberson showed me boxes of files in his office containing volumes of hundreds and hundreds of sermon outlines – all categorized and dated. The shelves of his office walls appeared to be full of 40 years of sermons from his Highland Park ministry – all kinds of sermons. For example, there were complete sets of sermons from entire books of the Bible such as the Gospel of Luke and the book of Acts. Lots of Sunday night series of sermons were filed – usually seven in a series. The sermons were neatly typed in small, five by eight inch, three-ring binder notebooks. The notebook covers appeared to be vinyl or imitation leather. All neatly typed out by his secretary, the outlines contained a fair amount of black underlining, exclamation points, and various other notes which Roberson had added through out – but nothing extensive was added as the sermons appeared to be pretty thoroughly typed out.

"Most of the time," he said, "I carried this notebook with me – one notebook. I would open up to the sermon I was going to preach that day. It was already typed out. I'd carry the Bible. Then I had my notes in front of me. Then I would underscore certain things that I wanted to emphasize." He would also make corrections or add further thoughts.

In his early years of preaching, Roberson carried the notebook to the pulpit. In later years, he would fold a page of typed notes in half and secure the page in his Bible so that a rubber band held it in place. He showed me an example. "Every one of them – same way for 40 years," he said. "All in book form. I'd have them marked. I'd do the marking of them for my benefit, so I could see them better. For years I preached with a notebook like this open all the time." He showed me how he would pull the outline from the notebook and tuck it in his Bible. Folded over once, the sheet of paper sideways gave him four sides of notes. He would have two or three pages sometimes – each with four sides of written notes. "I would put them in my Bible, with a rubber band on them," he said. Dr. Roberson did not ever carry a full manuscript into the pulpit. He did not read his sermons. He wanted notes which gave him the sense of the message in order to remind him where he was going in the sermon.

Through his ministry at Highland Park Baptist Church, Dr. Roberson said, "I never repeated a sermon that I can recall – in 40 years. A lot of them were the same [i.e., similar], but there was no repetition. I never did take the same one in the pulpit – never, never." He did, of course, preach the same outline at different places. For example, a sermon outline in his file might have several hand-written dates in the upper right corner of the first page, denoting when and where it had been preached – first at Highland Park Baptist Church, then years later a shortened version on radio, and perhaps again on the road as a guest speaker at another church. He showed me one sermon outline dated when it was first preached at First Baptist Church of Fairfield, Alabama, in 1940 – his pastorate before moving to Chattanooga. The sermon outline was dated then as being repeated three different times on WDYN radio – but never at Highland Park Baptist Church.

Roberson was legendary for preaching punctual sermons. "I never preached over 30 minutes – never," Roberson said, "sometimes less than 30 – but not over. They [the church members] knew that. They knew that when they came to church. I didn't say anything about it. They just knew that automatically. I did the same way all the time. So, I did the same three times a week – Sunday morning, Sunday evening, and Wednesday. I preached three messages – all about the same length in time." As a rule, he preached sermons about 25 minutes long – maybe 28 minutes, but never over 30 minutes. Some church members claim he often preached only 22 or 23 minutes. Bob Kelley said, "He preached three times a week. That's 150 sermons a year. He did not try to preach it all at once. I believe he felt you could preach too long." It was a pattern Lee Roberson learned from his college pastor, Finley Gibson, at Walnut Creek Baptist Church in Louisville in the early 1930s. "Dr. Roberson's sermons were always short here," said Walter Wendelken, his associate at Highland Park. "That was wise. It takes an awful good speaker to hold your attention more than 30 minutes." Speaking away from Highland Park Baptist Church at conferences, Roberson would speak longer – closer to a full 30 minutes. But always he was concerned with the listener's attention span. "He could say more in a few minutes than most people can," said Wendelken.

Roberson carefully followed his deliberate practice of preaching no more than 30 minutes. He explained, "I feel that you will tax the people in their listening after you go beyond 25 to 30 minutes. They'll listen the first 15 minutes very carefully. After the first 15 minutes, a few of them fade away a little bit. But if you stay too long, you'll lose half the audience. They'll begin looking at their watch – wonder what time it is, and look around. So, I avoid it. In my early days I heard some good men – but too long!"

And Roberson's invitations after the sermons usually took 10 to 15 minutes – sometimes as long as 30 or 40 minutes, as people continued to respond by coming forward publicly. This added to the length of the service – not to mention the baptisms which always followed the invitation. Always there was his appeal to the sinner to come to Christ. Typically, he would publicly say, "Do you know Him as your Savior? Can you say, 'He is mine'? Have you accepted

Him but turned away from following Him? Would you come back this morning and confess to Him, 'I want to follow Thee and do Thy will for the rest of my days?'" For example, he concluded his sermon, *The Bible Secret of Success*, with his typical gospel invitation: "But I must make an appeal to those who are lost! My friend without the Savior, you have one great pre-eminent need, and that need is Christ. How we should thank God that the door is open and that He invites you to come. How precious are the words, '...him that cometh to me I will in no wise cast out.' Come to the Lord Jesus Christ, and come now. Come as a sinner lost and undone. Come to receive all that Christ has for you – life and peace and joy forever." Although Roberson would also give an invitation for new members to join Highland Park Baptist Church, his invitation for salvation clearly was focused upon the individual listener's personal relationship with the Lord and not upon a decision to join the church. "Salvation is found only in Jesus – not in churches, not in denominations, not in works, not in reformation," he would say. "But salvation is found in Jesus Christ, the Son of God. Therefore, repent of sin and believe in Him!"

Following the invitation, J.R. Faulkner would usually need to lead the congregation in only one verse of one song before Roberson was ready to baptize. Roberson would immediately leave the platform, go "back-stage," change into waders and an alternate jacket, and re-appear in the baptistry behind the choir loft. At Highland Park, Roberson said, "We have given an invitation in this church since 1942, and we have had responses all through these years. In 1942, when I first came as your pastor, we started out on Wednesday night inviting people to be saved. I have had people say to me, 'Why do you give these invitations? Why not give them just once a week? That is enough.' Some have even criticized our baptizing on Sunday morning, Sunday night, and Wednesday night. 'Why not baptize only one time a week?' they ask. I am trying to emphasize that our business, our desire, is getting people saved. And this is the record that I want to leave: Lee Roberson believed in getting people to the Lord Jesus Christ, and he believed that Christ is able to save to the uttermost all who will repent and will come to Him."

Roberson's preaching and entire ministry was based upon his belief that the Bible is the verbally inspired Word of God. In his sermon, *The Toughest Words Ever Given to Man*, he said, "God is the author of this Book. We do not say that the Bible contains the Word of God. The Bible *is* the Word of God. This is the Book! There are 66 books in the Bible – 39 in the Old Testament, and 27 in the New Testament. But the Bible is one Book, and God is the author." In his sermon, *Inspection Day for Highland Park Baptist Church*, he said, "I believe the Bible from the first word of Genesis to the last word of Revelation! Not a single line, not a verse, not a chapter, not a story, not a miracle, not a parable would I omit from the Word! This is God's Book, and I believe it. Now, it is my business to preach the Word of God. I am to declare the message that God has given."

Always there was an emphasis upon personal faith in Christ for salvation and a review of how to receive Christ as Savior in every sermon. In his sermon, *The New Birth*, Roberson told about a revival he preached where many people were saved. "I repeated every night the message of salvation," he said. The host pastor expressed surprise that so many were saved and why he had not seen more salvation results in his own preaching. Roberson asked the pastor if he preached often on the theme, "Ye must be born again." (John 3:3-7) The pastor said, "I make it my business to preach on that theme at least once per year." Roberson said, "I quickly told him that I try to bring this theme before people in every sermon. The new birth is God's one way of salvation." Roberson had no patience with any minister who tampered with the biblical plan of salvation. In his sermon, *The Big Work of an Ordinary Man*, he preached, "Still others make salvation so easy as to be meaningless. They teach that salvation is by joining a church or being baptized or going through some ritual. My Bible declares that salvation is by believing on the Lord Jesus Christ."

In the pulpit, Roberson did not hesitate to preach hard against sin. In his sermon, *Paul, the Fundamentalist*, he addressed the "wretchedness of sin" with the words, "Why is this wrath of God revealed? Because of the wretchedness and the evil and awfulness of sin. Sin brings the wrath of God. God hates all sin. He hates the sin of commission. He hates the sin of omission. God hates all sin! It matters not what the sin may be. If it is sin – if it is wrong, then God hates it!" He thundered against the liberalism and humanism in theology and education. In his sermon, *Christ and Salvation*, Roberson analyzed a recently published theologically liberal article. "Such gross ignorance of the Scriptures is sickening!" he preached. "I believe the inerrant, inspired Word of God! This article ridicules the teaching of the Word, the teachings of our Lord, and the Holy Spirit, on judgment and hell. This is what we find in many places in this hour. Colleges, universities that once were sound and fundamental are now turning to light, insipid, foolish declarations regarding God, Christ, heaven, and hell."

At times Roberson could be pointed and direct with his listeners. In his sermon, *Paul, the Fundamentalist*, he goes on to say, "Here is the picture, and God reveals the awfulness of sin. Are you listening to me? I know you get put out with me sometimes. You say, 'Brother Roberson, you ride too heavily upon certain ideas.' A little while ago I saw two or three people shake their heads as if to say, 'We don't believe what you are saying.' I was saying, 'You must put Jesus first!' If you are covetous and stingy in your giving, you are evil and wrong!"

In preaching, Roberson was very proper – always cautious and tasteful with humor. Lee Roberson's words in the pulpit – or in private – always had a sense of propriety and dignity. His sermons contained nothing resembling crude or questionable language. Nor did Roberson focus attention on himself. There was very little use of the personal pronouns "I" or "me" in his preaching. He would tell very few sermon illustrations and stories about his family. "I don't bring them in too much," Roberson told me. "No. It was by design. I tried to avoid involving them in the pulpit part – the public part of it. I never wanted to embarrass my children by saying things. I know some men do, but I didn't do that. Some pastors do it too much – what the wife said, what she did, and so forth. I didn't do that much – no." There was no syrupy praise of others in his preaching. Lee Roberson did not deter from his main focus. He stood up and preached the Word of God without apology. He was not flashy or showy. People respected him.

In private or in the pulpit, Lee Roberson's speech was always edifying. "He just had a class that was all its own," said Jim Vineyard. "I've never heard him tell a joke. Lee Roberson is never in a state of levity. You never see levity in his preaching. Classiness. He reminds me of R.G. Lee."

The listeners, especially the college students, were encouraged to take notes during Roberson's preaching. Many of the students at Tennessee Temple would keep a notebook of his sermon outlines. The preacher boys would analyze his sermons. They recognized that his sermons were simple – not flowery nor complex like Charles Spurgeon's sermons.

To be an effective preacher requires reading. Roberson told me that he studied the "usual" Bible commentaries, such as Matthew Henry. Roberson read books all the time. "I read everything I can find," Roberson said. "I take notes. I read all the time – mostly at night. I had people getting books for me constantly – sending them to me. I'd read them and mark them. I'd use some. Some I wouldn't use. I like to read sermons, books of sermons. R.G. Lee – I guess I read everything he ever wrote – men like that. I have most of [George W.] Truett's sermons at home. You kind of build on that. You can see how they think. I liked that. I like Truett's method more than Lee. Lee's a little flowery for me. You know how R.G. Lee was. But Truett was more of a practical type that I could get a hold of."

From the time he began preaching at age 18 Roberson read numerous sermons – books of sermons, such as the sermons of T.D. Talmadge and many sermons by Charles H. Spurgeon. Some of those sermons he felt were too dry. His goal was to build interesting messages on simple outlines. Roberson read books from the libraries during both his college and seminary days. He never quit reading books. He read books at home. He took books on vacation with his family. He carried books when he traveled. On two occasions J.R. Faulkner traveled with Roberson for special mission services in Puerto Rico and other Caribbean islands, where Roberson would preach, and J.R. would lead the singing. "He had these books – a satchel bag full of books – just the right width to fit between his legs on the plane," Faulkner said with a laugh. "I carried his books for him – through the islands of the Caribbean."

Roberson had a life-long habit of marking every book he read. He would underscore items of interest and make notes, so he could refer to them later. "I don't lose anything," he said. "I kept notebooks my whole life – every thought. I guess I've used hundreds of them. I keep them before me and keep writing down things that may appeal to me. I may never use them. I have outlines of sermons by the scores that I just put aside. I may use them. I may not. I've done that my whole life. I have notebooks. I write things."

Although Roberson would use some sermon studies, such as books of sermon illustrations, most of his illustrations were drawn from the notes he made during his constant reading week by week. He would make a note of a certain illustration on a piece of paper and include that with the week's sermon preparation. "I'm looking for illustrations all the time," he said, "out visiting, in people's homes, etc. I try to get things that will help. A typical Sunday illustration would come from the previous week." Roberson also often used sermon illustrations from the current events of the day, gleaned from his daily reading. In the preface to his book of sermon notes and illustrations, *The Gold Mine*, Roberson wrote, "I look constantly for illustrations! I read for them; I listen for them; I search for them. I try to wedge my way into the thinking of a man through a story or a daily happening that will help me drive home some great, important, vital Bible truth. Illustrations are attention-getters! I read, listen, and watch for stories and anecdotes that will gain the attention of the audience and will enable me to plant in their hearts some lasting lessons. Illustrations come from everywhere – books, newspapers, magazines, and plain, everyday living. Illustrations should be used carefully – not for filling up a sermon or stirring foolish laughter, but to point men and women to Christ."

Did Lee Roberson try to emulate any particular preachers in the pulpit? "I can't recall," he told me. "I knew a lot of men. I watched all of them, but I don't recall trying to imitate one of them. No."

Roberson authored more than 40 books which were published through the years – mostly books of his recorded sermons or compilations of sermon illustrations. Sitting in his office, he leafed through books of sermons he had preached. He gave me several books. I already owned others. Some, he said, were written in shorthand by a secretary as he preached from the pulpit. Most of them were recorded from his written sermons. "I'd write out my sermons – what I was going to preach," he said. "I'd have them typed out. Then I might add something to it when I got through preaching. We put it in book form. I had no thought of doing anything – just that the Word might be known better." Possibly his first book published was a book of sermons entitled, *Are You Tired of Living?* It came out in 1945.

Cassette tapes of his sermons were sold by the thousands both at Highland Park Baptist Church and around the world. "He realized the importance of having his messages recorded," said Walter Wendelken, who helped with the sound and recording systems. "But I could not get him interested in having real fine equipment. The equipment I had was not radio quality – not as good as it should be. I sent tapes to the missionaries. They loved them. We got good reports. They appreciated them." Roberson never used a lapel microphone, but when they became popular late in his pastorate, he had a man demonstrate one for him. Occasionally, a guest speaker would use one at Highland Park. But by the end of Roberson's life, Tommy Sneed, the general manager of radio station WDYN-FM, told *The Chattanooga Times Free Press*, "He was always excited about new technology. He didn't understand computers. [He was very interested in] the fact we were streamlining audio over the Internet. He didn't understand it, but he said, 'Thank God for it. You use it.'"

For years Roberson's sermons at Highland Park were broadcast live over radio – Sunday morning, Sunday evening, and Wednesday evening. In 1968 Tennessee Temple University launched its own full-time radio station in WDYN-FM. Originally a 10-watt station, it was to grow to 50,000 watts. It could nearly be heard as far away as Atlanta.

Roberson's preaching carried an emphasis on the salvation of souls in every sermon. "He put much emphasis on winning souls to Christ – the salvation of people," said Wendelken. "This was constantly coming out in all his messages and his speaking to people. 'This is our goal.'" Bob Kelley recalled, "He preached death to self, selflessness, faithfulness, priorities – first things first. His sermons always incorporated these. There would be a different title,

Scripture, introduction, icing and appeal, but when it was all through they were the same themes. Prayer. Emphasis on prayer. Pray all the time. Series on prayer. Prophecy." He preached frequently on "death to self." Tom Wallace recalled, "He hammered on it all the time."

Following his sermons, Roberson expected the visible results of people coming forward during the public altar call at the end of the service. Long-time church members like Tennessee Temple instructor Glenn Swygart could only recall one service where no one came forward. "Dr. Roberson was very upset about it – very upset that no one had come forward," Swygart recalled. "He made it clear that he wanted people coming down the aisle every service. I remember that one case. He was upset."

Dr. Roberson preached annually for me in the churches I served as pastor. More than once I accepted the call to a troubled church which had previously experienced considerable difficulty. As I faced rebuilding ministries, Dr. Roberson taught me that one sign of a "wounded" church was the absence of anyone coming forward at the invitation. He said it would take time for a church to heal and begin to respond publicly. I found his words to be true. When I was pastor of Temple Heights Baptist Church in Tampa, Dr. Roberson preached for us in a service where no one came forward. Despite the "troubled" situation I had inherited as the new pastor, he was quite upset and chastised me privately. The next time we had Dr. Roberson at our church, I warned our pastoral staff in advance to be sure to have people ready to come down the aisle to make public commitments to Christ! Thankfully, they did.

Roberson would follow very few "rabbit trails" in his preaching – getting off the subject onto side issues. His sermons were focused – straight forward. He went straight to the point and said what he wanted to say. "Straight down the line," he would say. "Never vary." Roberson told me, "Some preachers make the pulpit kind of a center for expressing themselves about so-and-so and this-and-that. I didn't do that. I stayed with the gospel. I left everything else outside." In his sermon, *Some Deacons Excel*, he said, "We're to give the gospel and lay upon people the need for salvation. I'm a little disturbed that in many places churches delay giving the gospel and pressing for decisions."

Lee Roberson believed in the sacredness of the pulpit. "I do," he said. "Yes, sir! I feel like I have an obligation when I'm there. I've got something I've got to do. I make it two-fold. I want to get people saved. I want to show saved people how to live. Two big things. We worked here 40 years. Gave an invitation every hour. Had people come forward every hour – salvation and rededication over things that came up in their lives." When it came to the pulpit, Roberson did not talk about sports or other distractions. He preached – right down the line.

Roberson always preached from the King James Version of the Bible, but he did not make an issue of it. Early in his ministry, he even spoke favorably from the pulpit of the New American Standard Version of the Bible, as did John R. Rice and other fundamentalists at the time. Although Roberson clearly aligned himself with many men who did endorse the King James as the only legitimate Bible translation, he never took that stand himself. "He's not a 'KJV only' man," said Temple instructor Nat Phillips. "But he does publicly say things sympathetic to them." When the KJV issue gained traction among fundamentalists in the early 1970s, it created some controversy at Tennessee Temple, especially among the preacher boys. At the time Roberson announced that he was going to make a public statement on the issue. Members of the Bible faculty feared that Roberson would come out for the "KJV only" position. Dr. Fred Afman went to see him to discuss the issue before Roberson was to make his public statement. "I said, 'I appreciate the predicament you're in,'" said Afman. "'But you can't just automatically wipe out all the tools we use.' He said, 'No, that's not what I'm going to do.' So, he began his [public] presentation. The King James fellows – we had a large student body – thought they were 'God-called' and those of us who had degrees were 'man-called.' He had their attention. They thought he would come down on their side. But he announced, 'Now, our professors are going to be able to use all their tools to teach you. That's why they're here. So they will use different versions, the Greek and the Hebrew. You pay attention!' I appreciated that. The [evening] Bible school was ready to explode over the 'KJV only' issue. No one here was anti-King James, but it could be interpreted that way. I appreciated the balance he used in dealing with a delicate subject."

Tom Wallace said that Roberson was sometimes accused of being "soft" on issues like the King James Version. "People who said that didn't know him," said Wallace. On one occasion a KJV-only student attended a staff meeting and charged that Dr. Roberson was a heretic. When the college staff told the student that he was expelled from the school, the student ran from the meeting. Cliff Robinson chased him down, physically tackled him, brought him back to the meeting, and insisted that he apologize to Dr. Lee Roberson. He did apologize.

Roberson preached what he believed the Bible taught – boldly, confidently, and without apology. It was not uncommon for him to make blunt, bold assertions on biblical issues such as tithing. For example, in his sermon, *Does Jesus Live at Your House?*, he exclaimed, "I make no apology for saying that every child of God should be a 'tither.'" In his sermon, *Is He Lord of All?*, he said, "The tithe is not yours but God's. The blessings of God are promised to those who honor the Lord with the tithe."

Because of his prominence, some of Roberson's sermons became famous. Some of his well-known sermon titles included, *Have Faith in God*, *A Mother's Faith*, *Be Ye Therefore Steadfast*, and, *Does Jesus Live at Your House?*

In his sermon, *Do We Need A New Gospel?*, Dr. Roberson stated that he did not enjoy preaching about hell – that he would rather preach about God's love and about heaven. "But one day I shall give an account of myself and of my ministry to God," he said. "In that day I do not want my hands to be stained with the blood of others. Therefore, I must faithfully proclaim the truth of God's wrath upon all who reject the Savior." Roberson recalled the day when he preached strongly on hell in a week-long series of revival meetings at Woodlawn Baptist Church in Birmingham, Alabama. Many people were saved in the meetings. The church was the second largest church in Birmingham at that time, and Roberson described the pastor as a wonderful man. Roberson related the story in his sermon, *Seventy-One Years of Fundamentalism*. "[The pastor] called me back in his office one night toward the end of the week,"

Roberson remembered. "He said, 'I promised the deacons when I came to this church that I would not preach on hell. So, I have not preached on hell one single time in these five years! Now, I regret it so much when I see what God has done here in just a week's time. My church has been dying because I have been holding back from them the Word of God!'" Roberson concluded, "I have these many years preached the truth of heaven and hell. I have emphasized it for 71 years."

And always Roberson preached with a sense of urgency. "Every sermon should stress the danger of delay!" he preached. "What we do for God, we must do now. Don't wait another day. If you are unsaved, come to Christ today."

Roberson had a creative and poignant way of proclaiming the truth from the pulpit. For example, in preaching on the trials and suffering that people must walk through in life, he would say that "many great Christians go to heaven by night."

The Temple students, especially the preacher boys, picked up constant themes and principles of life from the oft repeated words of Dr. Roberson. "Be steady, be steady," he would say. He challenged them – always be looking forward, always going ahead, always positive. He would challenge the college students with, "Young people, have faith in God! Have faith in God!" Or he might say, "Quitters are a dime a dozen! Anybody can quit. Finish! Finish! Finish!" Students remember him preaching, "Critics are a dime a dozen. Anybody can criticize!" He repeated the same themes: "Never get side-tracked. Stay right on it. Don't get side-tracked – right down the line."

The college students loved to hear from the pulpit Dr. Roberson's descriptive phrases like, "pusillanimous pussy-footers" or "some little pygmy of a compromiser." He would criticize whiners, gripers, and nit-pickers. "Don't be negative," he would repeat. "Don't be negative. We don't need that. Always be positive. Be steady. Submission. Surrender to God. Do the will of God."

Many of Roberson's sermon titles were clever and intriguing. One of his more famous sermon titles was, *Punching Holes in the Darkness*. In that sermon he declared the mission of Christians is to shine the light of truth in a spiritually dark world. In his early years in Chattanooga, he preached a sermon entitled, *Who Killed Dallas*

Case? The entire sermon was built around the death of a boy named Dallas Case.

Normally Lee Roberson's preaching format was pretty straight forward and traditional. But on occasion he would plan something very creative. For a series of Sunday evening messages on the Second Coming of Christ, Roberson set up J.R. Faulkner to illustrate each message in the series with a chalk drawing. The series lasted seven Sunday nights. Wooden planks were placed at water level over the baptistry behind the pulpit, so J.R. could stand and move around as he drew a picture on the back wall of the baptistery behind the preacher. J.R. would draw in the background early, and then cover up the picture with a curtain. At some point in the sermon Roberson would summon J.R. to finish the illustration for the main point of the sermon – taking about five to eight minutes to chalk in the complete picture – as Roberson continued to preach. For the series, Faulkner researched for ideas that related to the second coming. These sermons were later published in the book, *Some Golden Daybreak*.

Roberson preached with the same fervent passion whether the crowd was large or small, whether he was preaching at a nationwide conference or in the rescue mission downtown. He traveled to preach at other churches and at church conferences almost every Monday and Tuesday of the year. Through the years Lee Roberson preached regularly in the largest independent Baptist church services and conferences in the world, such as the annual Pastors' School hosted by Jack Hyles at First Baptist Church of Hammond, Indiana – not to mention the Southwide Baptist Fellowship conferences which Roberson frequently hosted.

Preaching sermons was Lee Roberson's life. He loved a crowd. He loved the church services. He loved to preach. The always undaunted Garland Cofield grew up at Highland Park Baptist Church. He once asked Dr. Roberson, "Dr. Lee, you have a huge crowd waiting out there. What's the last thing you do before going out?" Roberson's answer was simple: "Check my fly."

Once when Cofield was singing in a quartet traveling with him, Roberson forgot his Bible. He asked Garland if he could borrow his Bible. He took Garland's Bible, turned to the Scripture, and preached from it. "He never skipped a beat – no notes, of course," Cofield remembered. In his own Bible, as Roberson heard other preachers from time to time, he would write down the sermon title or topic, date, and name of the preacher.

Roberson's sermons were published all over America in such publications as *The Sword of the Lord* and later on various evangelical and fundamental Christian websites. Hundreds of Lee Roberson's sermons were published in more than 45 books. Always at the end of the written sermon a clear gospel invitation was printed. And sometimes at the end of the book, clear instructions on how to receive Christ and how to write to Dr. Roberson were included.

Lee Roberson's preaching was true to the Word of God as he understood it. In his sermon, *Seventy-One Years of Fundamentalism*, he said, "I must preach so that lost men will hear and know that in Christ there is salvation. I must preach His death, burial and resurrection. I must preach the simple way of salvation: 'Except ye repent, ye shall all likewise perish'; 'He that believeth on the Son hath everlasting life'." In his sermon, *Coming to Chattanooga – Soon*, he appealed to both saint and sinner: "Christian, is there something in your life that is not right? Is there something that needs correcting? Then, get it right now. Correct it now. Child of God, be ready for His coming. Sinner friend, without Jesus Christ you are not ready. But you can be ready, if you will repent of your sins. Will you now take Christ as your personal Savior?"

CHAPTER 14

The Pastor's Touch

To serve as the senior pastor of a mega church is a remarkable challenge. Lee Roberson's early pastorates certainly experienced growth, but Highland Park Baptist Church mushroomed in extraordinary growth in the 1940s and 1950s. No sooner would the church build a new auditorium than it would be filled with people. And the growth never stopped throughout his 40-year-and-six-month pastorate. With the addition of a college, national opportunities, and worldwide travel, the demands of Roberson's schedule only increased. Nevertheless, Roberson never relinquished his commitment to his responsibilities as the pastor of a local Baptist church, and he retained an uncanny ability to remember people's names – regardless of how many thousands of people were added to his church membership.

No matter how large the ministry grew, Roberson retained a warm, personal, pastoral touch. "You never left his office without praying," said Glenn Swygart. "He'd get down on one knee and pray before you left – everyone, always. The first time I went to his office as a student right before I graduated, I had a reverential fear. He was busy – there were people waiting to see him all the time. He gave me a warm handshake – it completely disarms you. You wish you would have gone other times. He would always take time for anybody that came in."

Office visits to see Dr. Roberson were always short – no more than 10 minutes. Visits by phone were short. Like many of Dr. Roberson's preacher boys, Ed Johnson would call for advice in regard to his ministry. "From Minnesota I would call his home phone," Johnson said. "He would answer. Finally, 'Now, this is costing you money. We had better hang up. Let's have a word of prayer.'" In his office, Johnson recalled, "He would stand up. He would kneel and pray. You were done."

J.R. Faulkner said that Lee Roberson was one of the kindest and most generous men one could ever meet. "But he was not for long conversations," said Faulkner. When students would come in for counseling, Roberson could tell quickly how important or complex the issue was. If it were something serious, he would spend a longer period of time with the student. Otherwise, his visits were usually five to eight minutes long. "He'll get to the point where he has an answer for you," said Faulkner. "'Now, let's have a word of prayer about it.' He gets on his knees beside you. Takes you by the hand and prays with you. Then he walks you to the door while he's talking. He knew how to wind one up without wasting long periods of time." Praying with people before they left his office was a habit of Roberson's from the beginning of his ministry.

Roberson always maintained the practice of making pastoral visits to the hospitals nearly every afternoon he was in town. His practice was to visit all the area hospitals and see all hospitalized church members each week. "I'd cover all the hospitals – three or four a week," he told me. "I'd go to see them and pray with them – all the people, the sick. Call on every one. Visit all the time. Lots of visiting. Kept it up. Did that for years. Hospitals every day, every day." Roberson told me that in the South, in his day, people expected pastors to make hospital visits. "I made them all – every hospital," he said. "In my day it was a serious thing." Roberson went each week to the hospitals in the Chattanooga area – Erlanger, Memorial, Parkridge, Campbell's, Newell's, Red Bank, East Ridge, Diagnostic, Tepper's, Children's, etc. He would check regularly at a nurses' station to see if it was okay to visit a particular patient.

J.R. Faulkner said, "I try to teach preacher boys here you can build your church visiting the hospitals and funeral homes – not just for members of your church, but for people of your community. Go by the funeral home. Sign the register. Look in. 'We're praying for you. Anything we can do?' Build a reputation. Dr. Roberson did that from the day I met him."

At hospitals, Roberson visited primarily church members, but also some friends of church members. His hospital calls were short – no more than five minutes. He would never sit down in a hospital room. He would stand at the foot of the bed, quote a verse of Scripture, pray with the patient, and then maybe say, "Well, I have to get on my way. Glad you're doing well. If I can do anything for you, let me know about it." He would pray, shake hands, and leave. While he might quote Scripture during the visit, he did not carry a Bible with him at the hospitals. His hospital visitation style was to be positive, be brief, and be gone. He would wash his hands before visiting another hospital room – something Faulkner taught the preacher boys in the college.

Roberson tried always to be available when needed. Because of the size of the church ministry and Roberson's absence during his traveling ministry, much of the church visitation was turned over to Walter Wendelken. "If I felt his presence there would be meaningful or helpful," said Wendelken, "he would always go. If they wanted him for the funeral service, he was always there." Although not ordained, Wendelken was full-time as one of Roberson's assistants and conducted many a funeral. He was an effective lay speaker.

J.R. Faulkner said of Roberson, "He would not shuck off anything on me that he felt required the pastor's attention. Many times he made a comment about making sure we followed up on someone in the hospital – just to remind me that we need to visit if he can't make it, if he were out of town or whatever. The person was on his mind. By the time he would get into town, freshen up, get the cigarette smoke off – [from other passengers] from the old plane days, it was afternoon. He just has to make contact. If he can't go, he'll pick up the phone and call the hospital."

To the end of his life as pastor emeritus of Highland Park Baptist Church, Roberson would check the list of hospitalized church members and make hospital calls. If a church member's name was on the Wednesday night prayer list, that member was likely to receive a written note from Dr. Roberson informing the individual that he was praying for him or her. When missionary Garland Cofield suffered a brain hemorrhage around 1990, it was not known if he would survive. The prayer need was announced in the Highland Park Baptist Church midweek prayer service. "Dr. Roberson was the first person there at that hospital," recalled Cofield. Years after that when a physician gave Cofield and his first wife, Reba, the diagnosis of her terminal cancer, Roberson was the first person at the hospital. "How did he even know?" asked Cofield. "How does he do that? It was just like he was wired some way – to find out these things. He's there." Years earlier Garland and Reba had lost a son. The body was transported from Pensacola to the Chattanooga Funeral Home. "When we got there," said Garland, "Dr. Roberson and Mrs. Roberson were the first people that came. It's incredible. You can't describe him. As far as I'm concerned, he can do no wrong."

Roberson would spend his mornings in his office and make pastoral visits in the afternoons. Most of his studying was done at home at night. In his church office he kept a notebook at his desk where he wrote the name of everyone who came in, and he would write down something about the visit. "You couldn't go in there and waste time talking," said security chief Bill Long. "If you continued, he would stand. If you carried on much longer, he would walk to the door, and you would walk to the door. 'Let's have a word of prayer.' He would pray with you, open the door, and you were out of there. He was time conscious." As the ministry expanded in size, fewer of the church members would approach him for counseling, but students in the growing college would come more frequently. If Roberson counseled a couple with a marriage problem, he tried never to "blame" either party. His goal was for both to deal with the problem. He would listen to the aggrieved party, and then he would ask the same person, "Now, where did *you* go wrong?"

Roberson's red-carpeted office reflected his heart – missions and preaching. One wall of his office was covered with a map of the world which reflected his passion for foreign missions. The book cases were covered with missionary curios and memorabilia which constantly spoke of getting the gospel to every part of the world. The remaining material in his office included the notebooks filled with sermons. Roberson was first and foremost a preacher of the Word of God. In later years his office was primarily lined with shelves full of theology and ministry books and files of sermon outlines. There were pictures of people everywhere – family, friends (especially preachers), and memorable church events. The wall behind his desk and chair was covered with pictures. Under the pictures were cardboard boxes full of more sermons.

The ministry of Highland Park Baptist Church, with its area chapels, was so large that Roberson had frequent funerals. It was not uncommon for him to conduct three to five funerals in a week. Some calls to preside at funerals also came from the radio audience. If a key church member died, Roberson did not hesitate to cancel out-of-town speaking engagements – an arrangement which the host pastor understood in advance. As always, even when it came to a funeral, Lee Roberson hated to waste time. Although he would show up at the funeral only one minute before the appointed time, the funeral directors always knew he would be there. And Roberson was always trying to help the down-and-out, even when it came to funerals. He personally paid for many funerals he conducted for the needy. If he conducted a funeral where a very small gathering of mourners was anticipated, he would engage people from the church to come so as to fill out a crowd of respectable size and provide comfort for the bereaved family.

True to form, the funerals Roberson conducted were always short and very much to the point. His funeral services were very dignified. Roberson did not like lengthy eulogies, but he would personalize each funeral and publicly give condolences to the family. He always presented the gospel in his funeral message. He followed the same format — song, Scripture, prayer, another song, the funeral sermon, and it was over. The first song might be a solo or a congregational number, depending on the family's request. If the family wanted a third song, it would be at the end. Otherwise, the organ postlude followed. A few men and women from the church were called upon repeatedly to assist in conducting funerals. Jean Smith was the primary soloist, and Roberson's secretary, Dorothy McCormick, frequently sang at funerals, as did bass singer Neil Queen, a member of the church.

A typical funeral would last 30 minutes, with Roberson preaching for 10 to 15 – maybe 18 – minutes. His pastoral demeanor was gentle and loving. Roberson would bring a consoling message – always with the gospel. He would find a way to work the gospel in gently. He did not normally give a public gospel invitation at a funeral, although on occasion he would have everyone bow their heads and pray before he asked for raised hands for anyone to indicate that they prayed to receive Christ. "Not too much of that with him," said Faulkner. "He knew his audience so well." Roberson would personalize a funeral. He would point out the good things about the deceased – never anything negative or sad. If he knew the deceased were a Christian, he would share that truth publicly and focus on the benefits of the gospel. If he did not know the deceased or did not believe the deceased were saved, he would by-pass any such comment and focus on what the gospel says to the listener.

Roberson always wanted Faulkner to assist him at funerals. In the early years many church members wanted funerals at the church. But through the years Roberson and Faulkner gently encouraged people to use the funeral home, due to the convenience it offered. Roberson worked most frequently with the Chattanooga Funeral Home or the Turner Funeral Home. The two cemeteries most used for the funerals Roberson conducted were Hamilton Memorial Gardens and Chattanooga Memorial Park. Roberson wanted everything done punctually and properly. At the church the ministry staff would instruct the funeral director on where to park the hearse and how to conduct the parking and procession. Roberson did not hesitate to instruct or correct a funeral attendant or service participant. For a church member, Dr. Roberson always went from the funeral home to the cemetery. At the graveside he would give a brief comment about heaven, read a Scripture, and close with prayer. If Roberson were out of town, Walter Wendelken would handle the funeral, but Roberson did not hesitate to come when he could. "We ministered to our members and friends," said Wendkelken. "He would never say no. He would not let us say no. When people needed him, he was there. That was what made his ministry so great."

With such a large ministry entailing so many people, Roberson also performed many weddings. The main auditorium was too large for most weddings, so many ceremonies were held in a wedding chapel across the street – equipped with dressing rooms for the bridal party. Many out-of-town students chose to hold their weddings back at their home churches, but every year there were a few who wanted to be married at Highland Park. "The weddings would be brief, short, abrupt – and off they'd go," said J.R. Faulkner. "He'd say now be sure to be in Sunday school tomorrow at 9:45." Roberson had a short format all his own. If a couple wanted a more extensive wedding, he would direct them to get a different preacher. "He would tell them, 'This is the way I run a wedding,'" said Faulkner. "He gives his outline. That's it. I guess that helped me get a lot of weddings that I didn't want along the way. But he was quite precise about it – it being a spiritual service, not a show or entertainment. And I tried to keep mine that way as much as I could." But Faulkner would give the couple some leeway as he considered the wedding a one-time important event for life. If they requested him, Roberson would preside at the wedding. Sometimes couples were intimidated by Dr. Roberson's image and schedule, so they would request Dr. Faulkner for a wedding. J.R. would insist they get Roberson's permission first. Roberson always graciously acquiesced.

Roberson performed some weddings for faculty members, such as Glenn Swygart, or Jim Jorgenson. Swygart remembered that Dr. Roberson was at his wedding rehearsal, which was unusual. Roberson's wedding demeanor was kind and gentle. When the Swygarts were standing too far apart, Roberson pushed them gently together. When Elgin Smith and Jean Cofield's wedding was planned for the old Phillips Chapel, Roberson said there would be too many people for the facility to hold and instructed them to move the wedding to the newer and larger Chauncey-Goode auditorium. He was correct. Generally, Roberson's weddings were considered as being average in length. His wedding comments were focused on God creating the family and the church as institutions. The couple could choose their wedding's musicians, but Roberson was strict on the traditional, conservative music he would permit at a wedding.

Swygart told me, "I had unsaved family members coming to my wedding. We talked about giving an invitation. I asked him. He told me he had never had anyone saved at a wedding or a funeral. Of course, he always made the gospel clear."

Roberson regarded his calling as pastor of the church as his foremost responsibility. In his early years at Highland Park he would miss Sundays occasionally to preach revivals at other churches. But J.R. Faulkner remembered the day when Roberson came home from a revival meeting and decided to make a change. "He came home and made up his mind that he wasn't going to take any more meetings that took him away on Sundays or Wednesday nights," said Faulkner. From then on, he continued to travel every week – but not on Sundays or Wednesdays. He would travel Mondays and Tuesdays and return home for college chapel on Wednesday morning, church prayer meeting on Wednesday evening, and his pastoral class at the college on Thursday morning. At times he would make hospital calls on Monday morning before leaving town. If it was possible, he would travel all night on Tuesday in order to be home by Wednesday morning chapel. He was very careful to be at home – even if it meant canceling a scheduled out-of-town meeting, if he felt his presence as senior pastor was required in the minds of his people.

There were duties and responsibilities which Roberson felt applied to the pastor, and he retained those duties as long as he served as pastor. During the height of Roberson's ministry Highland Park Baptist Church was baptizing more people annually than any other church in America. Dr. Roberson personally baptized every one of them. "As far back as I can remember when I came here, he always did the baptizing – through 1983 when he retired," said J.R. Faulkner. After the sermon Roberson would publicly announce the baptismal candidates' names at the altar at the close of the invitation. A deacon or counselor would then direct the baptismal candidate back to the changing rooms – men on one side, ladies on the other – to dress for baptism. At the conclusion of the public invitation, Roberson would turn and say, "Brother Faulkner, let's have a song. We'll be baptizing in 90 seconds." One attendant stood ready with Roberson's waders, and another man held Roberson's coat. And 90 seconds later Roberson would be dressed for baptism and standing in the baptistry pool. Faulkner said, "I would always be ready to lead a song. I'd cut it off when he was ready." Three or four men were backstage to assist.

Roberson had three colored lights – red, blue, and white – set to glow alternately during the baptizing. He would mention each light. "Red speaks of the blood of Christ shed on the cross for our sins. Blue speaks of the death and burial of Christ, [while the candidate was momentarily under the water]. White speaks of the resurrection [when the candidate came up out of the water]. We're raised to walk in newness of life." He would call them "the lights that teach" and would often say a word about each light. Three light switches were located on the wall at the head of the steps going up to the baptistry. A deacon would stand there and operate the lights as Roberson spoke. As each light shined, the entire baptistry would be flooded with light – red, blue, or white. The idea of having three colored lights to represent baptism came from Roberson himself.

At one time Highland Park Baptist Church was baptizing more than a thousand people annually. As Roberson baptized a convert, he would go through the questions like a machine gun: "Do you believe Jesus Christ died on the cross for your sins? Have you received Him as your personal Savior? And now do you want to follow Him in believer's baptism?" Upon the candidate's affirmative response to the questions, Roberson would say, "Amen! In obedience to the divine commandment of our Lord and Savior Jesus Christ, and upon your profession of faith in Him, I baptize you, my brother [or sister], in the name of the Father, Son, and Holy Spirit. Amen." It was then as the convert came up out of the water that the white light would come on. The ladies would leave the baptistry in one direction for their changing room; the men in the other direction. Meanwhile, the next candidate would come from the opposite side – to keep things moving – alternating male and female, as possible. If a husband and wife were baptized together, the wife would go first while her husband came into the water and stood there observing. Then, the husband would be baptized as the wife watched the ceremony.

"He baptized my daddy right over there in that baptistry," said J.R. Faulkner, who was on the church platform as the song leader at the time. "My dad was a Methodist all his life – he and my stepmother. He sat in the second or third row. He got up and came on the invitation. He was already paralyzed and came with a crutch. Dr. Roberson looked at me and motioned. I knew he was there. I turned and went down and talked to Dad. He said, 'I want to be baptized.' My dad had been a song leader in the church and active in a Methodist church as far back as I could remember. Back in my teen years I could see my dad leading singing in the Methodist church. He told Dr. Roberson, 'I've been wanting to do this for years. I have not been satisfied with my baptism.' He had been sprinkled. My step-mother was baptized at the same service."

Missionary Jerry Reece said of Roberson, "He kept the waters of baptism moving. I think that inspired every student to be a soul winner." Reece, like many students, came out of a small Baptist church that would typically see as many people baptized in one full year as Roberson was baptizing each Sunday.

Like baptism, when Roberson conducted the Lord's Supper, the ceremony was well coordinated. The deacons and the church organist would know what to expect from Roberson in the order and flow of the service. The Lord's Supper was always treated with dignity as a solemn observance. Because of the large size of the church and deacon board, it was very impressive to see all the deacons lined up all the way across the front of the auditorium. Several communion tables were used to hold the traditional Baptist elements of the Lord's Supper – unfermented grape juice and unleavened bread. Dr. Roberson administered the service himself. When the serving of the communion elements to the congregation was completed, the deacons sat down at the front of the auditorium, and Roberson served them. The Lord's Supper was normally observed one Sunday per quarter – four times a year.

Roberson believed his role and image as a pastor should be conducted beyond reproach. He wanted to be true to the biblical admonition of being blameless and above reproach. He always stated publicly that no one would ever catch him in a compromising position. Temple students remember him publicly claiming that if he saw the car of his daughter, LeeAnne, broken down on Shallowford Road that he would call someone to go pick her up, because if he were to stop, passers-by might see him – he was well known – and not know that the woman getting into his car was his daughter. He told the church that if his secretary were walking home three blocks from the church in the pouring rain without an umbrella, that he would not stop and pick her up – for the same reason. "She'll have to walk," he announced publicly. Friends might smile at his personal rules, but they respected the image he was portraying.

As a pastor, Roberson permitted no sales at the church on Sundays. Even during special church conferences, Roberson would not permit guest ministries to sell books, records or tapes on a Sunday. A common practice in many churches, it had been traditionally considered contrary to the Lord's Day in the past. Some people did not understand his standards – especially the dress code for college. Boys had to have haircuts. Girls had to wear skirts. "Lots of students didn't understand the rules and regulations," said Dorothy McCormick. But when she approached him about permitting the teen girls to wear pants on a horse-back riding activity, he permitted it. "Just dress modestly," he said.

As a pastor, Lee Roberson understood the polity and structural makeup of a Baptist church. He always taught his preacher boys that when you resign as pastor from a church, you should leave it. Ron Bishop remembered his words, "Don't give notice. Leave. You pack your bags, walk out, and leave." When Tom Wallace resigned his pastorate at Bible Baptist Church in Elkton, Maryland, he sought Roberson's advice. Wallace, who had been at the Elkton church a long time, explained that he was going to resign and then stay at the church for about three months to help the church find a new pastor – before he moved on to another pastorate himself. Wallace recalled Roberson's reaction. "No, no, no," he said. "As soon as you resign, get on out of there." Wallace argued that he had won most of his church members to the Lord, that they loved him, and that he wanted to guide them in the selection of their next pastor. "No," Roberson said, "that church is going to change. The very minute you give your resignation, that's going to be a different church." Wallace recalled, "He said you won't recognize it." Wallace told Dr. Roberson that he respected his wisdom, but that such an immediate change would not happen at the Elkton church. Wallace proceeded to resign on a Sunday morning. He knew there would be tears and emotion after his announcement, so he slipped out while one of the church leaders closed the service in prayer. "That night we went back," Wallace said. "He was totally right about it. Folks who had been leaders sat down. Others who had not been leaders rose up and became vocal and almost took over. He knew what would happen, and I didn't. He really, really has wisdom."

Late in Roberson's life, Jerry Mattheiss told me he knew people at Highland Park Baptist Church who would not make a decision until they asked Dr. Roberson to pray about the matter at hand. "They'll tell you right up front, 'I'm going to wait to see what Dr. Roberson says about it,'" said Mattheiss.

Lee Roberson always conducted himself in a proper manner. Never was there even the hint of a scandal or impropriety in the life of Dr. Roberson. "The way he conducted himself, it was impossible," said Walter Wendelken. "He didn't hug [women]. No one could doubt where he stood." Garland Cofield said, "He never would be alone in his office with a woman. He always had a secretary. She was all business – just like him. His office had a glass window, and she was always right there. He was so careful about things like that." Roberson himself told me, "Never allowed any question or doubt. Never a problem – stayed completely away from it." Years later Randy Ray saw Dr. Roberson come into Northside Baptist Church in Charlotte, North Carolina, for a Southwide Baptist Fellowship meeting. "A lady who knew him came up and hugged him and kissed him on the cheek," Randy said with a laugh. "Dr. Roberson was so embarrassed he turned beet red. I thought he was going to die!"

His ministry ethics, as well as his personal conduct, were above reproach. Neither Roberson nor Faulkner wanted access to the financial funds of the church. Neither man even carried a key to the finance office. "I never wanted to go near the money," said Faulkner. Nor did either man ever want it to appear that they were taking financial advantage of any other ministry. Once when Roberson traveled to speak for Tom Wallace, Wallace's assistant pastor, John Russell, took Roberson to the airport and prepared to purchase his airline ticket – as a favor. But Dr. Roberson insisted on paying for his own airline ticket. Russell insisted that his church pay for it, and Roberson finally took the ticket from Russell, but he never used it.

And as Lee Roberson traveled, he was in demand all over America as a speaker. But he would not cancel a small church in order to take a big one.

Roberson was a humble and modest man. "He never wanted to be first," said J.R. Faulkner. "He was very gracious about special days – honoring him on his birthday, or anniversary. He never wanted to make anything of it. I saw him refuse the keys to a brand new Chrysler shortly after I came here. The deacons bought the car, parked it up here and were presenting the keys to him in some kind of a meeting they were having. He wouldn't take it. He wouldn't go near it. He was very proper about receiving gifts. It may be that early on he wanted to send a message, 'You can't buy me.' I don't know."

When wealthy Christian businessman Art DeMoss died in 1979 at age 54, DeMoss's will was probated. Roberson and Faulkner were surprised to learn that DeMoss had left $5-million for Tennessee Temple University, along with $5-million for each ministry of Jerry Falwell (Liberty University) and Bill Bright (Campus Crusade for Christ). Roberson said, "We had some people back of us who gave, but I never changed my program or mention of them – didn't say anything about it publicly. But I have had some big gifts to come from different ones. I never did approach them much. I talked to someone about gifts, but not much – maybe two or three times, maybe. Always they came to me – who wanted to give something. I wouldn't let them tie strings to it. It had to be a gift free – that we could put in our budget and use it and go ahead. But I never made a promise. We had some pretty big gifts. Art DeMoss – I led him to the Lord and baptized him here. He went back to New York City and became a multi-millionaire. Through the years he gave us millions of dollars. But he never asked one favor one time – not of me or anyone. He gave a lot of money. Art was a big help in the early days – built buildings and getting things going. He got started with nothing at all – didn't have a penny when he got saved here in Chattanooga. He went back up north and started making money hand over fist day and night. He stayed the same – never did change a bit. Humble man. Very discreet man. Very helpful to us. Never did ask any favor. Never asked for any honor. He gave millions of dollars." And of course, DeMoss was only one of many people who generously supported the vast ministry of Highland Park Baptist Church. For example, another such person was Bill Morton, who donated 100 pianos to the ministry – including five grand pianos.

Roberson himself lived frugally. He simply said he did not need much money to live on. However, some preachers did feel that this put an unrealistic expectation on others. A veteran missionary told me that this concept unintentionally hurt other preachers by setting the financial standard of paying pastors unreasonably low. And obviously Roberson's modest salary kept the salaries of his own church staff low as well – as they naturally were paid less than Roberson, the head of the ministry. When Dr. Roberson resigned, his successor was unfairly criticized when the salaries for the new pastor and assistant pastors were set higher – closer then to the prevailing national averages for large churches. In addition, Roberson's work ethic may have set an unreachable standard for others. Randy Ray, always loyal to Roberson, said, "He never took time off. That caused him to be revered. But it also caused others to struggle – who couldn't keep up."

Lee Roberson was generous with the money he personally possessed. He constantly gave money out of his own pocket to help other preachers, needy college students, or the down-and-out. And he donated many books to the Tennessee Temple University library.

"People used to give him money for the school," said Clyde Box. "They'd give him money and say, 'Help the students.'" In 1974 when Box's mother died, Box instructed his own granddaughter, then a student at Tennessee Temple, to notify Dr. Roberson that she needed to come home to Texas for the funeral. When she went in to see Dr. Roberson, he informed her that he had heard about the death, and he handed her a round-trip airline ticket – already paid for! Such was his generous heart.

Neal Thompson, a very successful businessman and a long-time church leader at Delaney Street Baptist Church, in Orlando, Florida, attended Tennessee Temple in the 1950s and remained a close friend of Roberson's throughout the years. Dr. Roberson gave Thompson the number to the direct telephone line into Roberson's office. From time to time, Roberson would call Thompson and tell him about a financially needy but worthy college student. Thompson would say, "How much do you need?" And then he would send the money to Roberson, who would disperse the funds to the student's expenses to enable the student to remain in college. A number of businessmen never forgot their loyalty to Dr. Roberson. They believed in what he was doing, and they completely trusted him with the expenditure of God's money.

One of Roberson's greatest abilities as a pastor and leader was his ability to encourage people. "He didn't be-little people," said Dorothy McCormick. "He made you feel like you're the most important person in that room, and that's the honest truth!" BIMI missionary Steve Nutt said, "He never forgot a name or where you were from." As a pastor, Roberson doled out compliments. Dorothy said he learned early in his ministry how to compliment a new baby – even if it were not the most handsome. "What a baby!" he would say. She added, "He loved children."

Many lives were touched by a thoughtful, written note of thanks or encouragement from Dr. Roberson. "You can't do anything but what you'll get a thank-you letter," said Fred Afman. "Or maybe you don't do anything, he just thought about you – the good job you're doing or maybe he heard something you'd done. A thank-you note. Amazing." Lee Roberson always wrote encouraging notes to people. "It was a matter of policy for him – always to write encouraging notes," said Faulkner. "If you put anything in writing, make it positive. If you can't say anything positive – good about anyone in writing, then don't say anything at all. If you have something negative to say – if you can't face a person eyeball-to-eyeball, then forget about it. Do not put anything critical or negative in writing. It was a principle of life for Dr. Roberson – a philosophy."

Missionary Mike Patterson said, "He answered my prayer letters – literally!"

Dorothy McCormick said that with Dr. Roberson, everything was big – whether it was the church auditorium, the size of the crowd, or a new program or goal, and anything could be accomplished. "He has encouraged me five or six times to be something that I don't think I can be and to do something that I don't think I can do," said Nat Phillips. "He told me once, 'I wish you would just quit going out to preach and take a Sunday school class here at Highland Park and build the biggest Sunday school class in Chattanooga.' When Dr. Roberson's son-in-law [Bill Ormsheier] came out to East Ridge, Bill said Dr. Roberson told him to go out there and build the biggest Sunday school class in Chattanooga." Another person challenged by Roberson's vision was Jean (nee Cofield) Smith. She was a teenager when Dr. Roberson started encouraging her to sing. She sang publicly in church and on radio for a half-century. "I would never have gone as far in music if it hadn't been for him," she said. "He really did encourage me and use me."

CHAPTER 15

Chattanooga

Coca Cola and Krystal hamburgers both originated in Chattanooga, Tennessee. But it is doubtful that either had as much direct impact on the city of Chattanooga as did the ministry of Highland Park Baptist Church, which burgeoned under the leadership of Lee Roberson's 40½ -year pastorate. During Roberson's ministry, Chattanooga became an unofficial, international capital of the independent, fundamental Baptist movement. Para-church ministries were born in the city out of the fruit of Highland Park's evangelistic outreach. Other inter-church ministries moved to Chattanooga to make the city their headquarters. The financial impact for the city of Chattanooga was remarkable. Such ministries revolved around the Highland Park mega-church, along with Tennessee Temple University – at one time the largest independent Baptist college in America, not to mention the great nationwide conferences which were hosted at the church.

This remarkable financial impact caught the attention of the city during the 1970s when the mayor of Chattanooga proclaimed a "Tennessee Temple Week" in the city. E.C. Haskell Jr., then dean of students at Temple, conducted an eye-opening four-day promotion of the college to the community. "I got Tennessee Temple to pay faculty and student employees in $2-bills," E.C. said. "We cashed the pay-checks from the banks. We set up an exhibit at one of the big malls. We gave cards out to hand out when they paid the bills.

At the mall we had booths for every department and every division at Tennessee Temple – just to promote Temple and let people know the financial blessing Temple was to the community. It just woke people up! Customers coming in and paying with $2-bills gets your attention. We were running around 3,500 to 4,000 students – probably $40-million a year – with that many people paying rent, car payments, and so forth – groceries, doctor bills."

Roberson maintained good relationships with city leaders. Of course, some city officials were members of Highland Park Baptist Church. At one time Chattanooga Mayor Robert Kirk Walker was president of the Men's Bible Class at Highland Park. Nevertheless, Roberson did not court city officials – they courted him. He was faithful in following the biblical injunction to honor and pray for our political leaders. They in turn were glad to attend Highland Park Baptist Church on special occasions, as they surely realized the political impact of being seen by so many people in a favorable circumstance with Dr. Roberson. The politicians knew that they had an influential leader on their hands, and they would seek his pulse on various community issues. If a social issue with spiritual implications arose in the city of Chattanooga – such as alcohol or pornography, city leaders would often wait to hear Lee Roberson's position. But Roberson had no serious battles with the city. "I tried to keep friends with the mayor and the commissioners," Roberson said. "Once a year we would have 'Chattanooga Day' (at church) – have them come. We did a lot of things to keep their mind on the church, so they would not be against it. They wouldn't join, but they were for us. We would recognize them. People like to be recognized – the leaders, the principals from the city and county high schools – good people, dignified. Shocked a little by the way we were doing things, but they'd accept most of it."

Nat Phillips once said, "The city's politicians treat Dr. Roberson like he's a big shot. Anytime Dr. Roberson wants someone, they're right here. When someone comes through town running for governor, they see Dr. Roberson."

Because of the size of Roberson's ministry, his influence in the city was respected and carried clout. Early in his ministry in Chattanooga, when an effort was made to overturn the city's conservative and traditional Sunday blue laws, Roberson joined the Chattanooga Retail Merchants Association in opposing the change.

"Dr. Roberson always had a good relationship with the city fathers," said J.R. Faulkner. "But he never participated in anything political. You didn't see him in any of the clubs downtown – Rotary, Civitan, etc. He didn't oppose them, but he just didn't participate – 'I'm too busy. I've got my job to do.' Maybe go to speak to one of these on occasion – very seldom. They named a fire-truck for him – still driving around here." They also named a street after him – Lee Roberson Street, running right past Highland Park Baptist Church.

Lee Roberson was widely respected in Chattanooga because of the far-reaching ministry of Highland Park Baptist Church. Roberson had an amicable association with the headmasters of the McCallie School – co-founder Dr. Spencer J. McCallie, and later his son, Dr. Spencer J. McCallie Jr. The co-founder's father had been Rev. T.H. McCallie, a well known and respected Presbyterian minister in Chattanooga in the late 19th and early 20th centuries. The school was founded in 1905 on what was then a rural area on the western slope of Missionary Ridge – later on, not far from Tennessee Temple. Through the years the McCallie School developed into an exclusive prep school, where such luminaries as NBC's Tom Brokaw and media mogul Ted Turner attended as boys. Tennessee Temple students were often employed at McCallie School. The school cooperated with Highland Park in sponsoring Billy Graham's crusade in the early 1950s. "They worked together to build the Billy Graham field house at Warner Park," said J.R. Faulkner. "It's still down there. McCallie boys worked with our boys putting the seats together. We had good rapport." The McCallies helped keep the Bible in the public schools for many years, and the McCallie School would hire Temple students to teach the Bible.

Roberson's independent ministry philosophy did not lend itself to interdenominational fellowship or ecumenical associations. He maintained a courteous relationship with other evangelical preachers in the city – men like Ben Haden of First Presbyterian Church. They would see each other coming and going at the airport. Roberson said he made little mention of other pastors publicly and did not criticize or praise them. His relationships with them were largely superficial, he said – "because they were of a different denomination entirely, with a different idea what was going on from us, and separate from us." J.R. Faulkner remembered a citywide evangelistic outreach held at a large theater in Chattanooga. There was J.R. on his knees leading an enquirer to a saving knowledge of Jesus Christ. And there was Ben Haden sitting on a bench a few feet away doing the same thing. "We ate out of the same trough," said Faulkner. "We sat at the same table together." St. Andrew's United Methodist Church sits on Bailey Avenue literally in the middle of the Highland Park and Tennessee Temple campus. Committees from the two churches met years ago to consider a purchase by Highland Park, but the deal never materialized.

Ben Haden and Lee Roberson were not particularly close friends, as both were busy with their individual ministries. Neither sought the other out. "I guess I just admired him from afar," Haden told me, "because the Lord's hand was so obviously on him. It fascinated me that he drew people from all over the United States because their pastors said, 'This is where you want to go.'" While Haden did not concur with Roberson's independent and somewhat separatist philosophy of ministry, he said, "I think he's probably been more used (of God) than any pastor in the city." Haden appreciated the friendliness of J.R. Faulkner and the opportunity to work with Highland Park Baptist Church from time to time. "I have no animus toward Tennessee Temple," Haden said early in the 21st century. "I am putting a man through seminary there now. I have hired from Temple. I have done nothing but encourage them."

Highland Park Baptist Church's aggressive evangelism helped fill up other churches in the Chattanooga area – mostly Baptist churches. Not every one who responded to the gospel message through Highland Park's outreach chose then to attend Highland Park. "We put people in nearly every decent Baptist church in town," Faulkner said. Independent and Southern Baptist churches alike all over the tri-state area enlisted pastoral staff members who were trained at Tennessee Temple.

Nat Phillips said that Lee Roberson received some criticism in Chattanooga, but not much. "One pastor of a Southern Baptist church was always negative," said Phillips. "But the people were always sympathetic to Highland Park. The situation is better now with Southern Baptists. There was a time before Highland Park when there was not one independent church in town. Now there are scores. Most don't do much fighting."

Lee Roberson was not unaware of the impact Highland Park Baptist Church was having on the city of Chattanooga. Always the promoter, in his sermon entitled, *The Conscience of a Great City*, he reminded his people, "The largest crowds of any church in the city or the state attend our church week after week. Larger crowds come to Highland Park every week than attend the concerts, plays, or even the wrestling matches of our city. Only God can measure the impact of our church on our great city."

Highland Park Baptist Church even became a tourist attraction in the sphere of fundamentalism, and the local newspaper, *The Chattanooga Times Free Press*, treated major events at the church as newsworthy matters. The newspaper had a strong Christian influence. Its long-time publisher was the son of a preacher. The newspaper was one of two major dailies in America which did not accept whiskey, beer or cigarette advertising. It committed five pages every Saturday to free church news, and Highland Park Baptist Church always ran a quarter-page advertisement, which would publish how many visitors had come the previous Sunday – and from what states of the union. Once on a special anniversary, the newspaper surprised Dr. Roberson by featuring Highland Park Baptist Church and running 10,000 extra copies for distribution. The newspaper published that Lee Roberson was a Christian statesman – "a treasure of Hamilton County."

Largely because of Highland Park Baptist Church, Chattanooga grew as a hub of evangelical activity. After Highland Park Baptist Church left the Southern Baptist Convention, the Southwide Baptist Fellowship was founded on March 20, 1956, in Phillips Chapel. There were 147 charter members, predominantly pastors, who united to provide fellowship for fundamental Baptist pastors. Initially, a number of the members were Southern Baptists, but it eventually evolved into a nationwide, independent Baptist fellowship. A statement of faith was adopted at a large public rally at Highland Park Baptist Church on November 28, 1956. Within years the membership grew to 3,000 pastors, many of whom would bring family members, staff members, and church members with them to attend the annual Southwide conference. The conference rotated its annual meeting among churches in different cities, such as Charlotte and Jacksonville, but Highland Park hosted it more often than any other church. The impact of Southwide alone on the Chattanooga economy was significant, as the annual meeting would fill motels and restaurants for several days.

In the 1950s Roberson brought hundreds of preachers into Chattanooga by hosting a summertime one-week "pastors' school." It was a ministry refresher course and a time of fellowship – much like Southwide later became. Although it was not as large as Southwide would later become, it filled Phillips Chapel and had to be moved to the Chauncey-Goode auditorium. The place was full. Pastors loved it.

"I'll tell you one thing," said Bob Kelley, "the city of Chattanooga knew Lee Roberson, Highland Park Baptist Church, and Tennessee Temple were there! They couldn't get around it. There were as many people coming to visit Chattanooga, as tourists, as for any other institution there. Put 'em all in there – Ruby Falls, Fort Oglethorpe. Highland Park Baptist Church helped put Chattanooga on the map." Years ago the church displayed a huge map of the United States inside the doors just outside the main auditorium. On the map were red thumb tacks designating cities from where church visitors had come. The map was covered with red thumb tacks.

Other ministries, spawned by Highland Park Baptist Church, regularly brought in visitors to Chattanooga. Baptist International Missions, Inc., which was founded at Highland Park Baptist Church, became an international missions board headquartered outside Chattanooga. The International Board of Jewish Missions, originally founded in Atlanta as a Southern Baptist mission to Jewish people, moved to Chattanooga. Its director and founder was Dr. Jacob Gartenhaus. His successor, Orman Norwood, told me, "Dr. Gartenhaus said Dr. Roberson was the main reason he brought IBJM to Chattanooga. That's why we came."

Evangelists and Christian musicians chose to make Chattanooga their home and Highland Park their home base of operation.

Evangelist and gospel song writer Charles F. Weigle authored more than 1,000 songs and was acclaimed for his song, *"No One Ever Cared for Me Like Jesus."* In 1951 an aging Weigle walked into the Highland Park Baptist Church office one day. "I was there," said J.R. Faulkner. "He came in. He said, 'I'd like to speak to Dr. Lee Roberson.' I knew him, but I didn't recognize him at first. 'Dr. Roberson, there's a gentleman to see you.' Doc was surprised. He talked to him about how much he enjoyed his music. 'What are you doing here?'" Weigle, then 80 years of age, explained to Roberson that he would like to spend his remaining years near a college campus, like Tennessee Temple, to help train and inspire young people in the Lord's work. Roberson volunteered to provide housing for Weigle. "That conversation resulted in Dr. Weigle coming here," Faulkner recalled. "We put him in the only missionary room we had – over in that old building across the street. We fixed it up for him nicely and called it the 'Weigle Room' – until we built the music center. We named the music center for him and put an apartment in the back. He lived there until he was 95 – the last 15 years of his life right here on this campus. He was still writing songs. *'A Garden of Roses'* was written right here – written and sang for the first time publicly in the Chauncey-Goode Auditorium. 'Got a new song.' He'd sing it in chapel or church. He'd say, 'I kind of like it, don't you?' That basically was what he'd say when he'd turn around after singing."

Roberson was impressed with how Charles Weigle continued to grow spiritually even at age 95. Ever ready to sing without notice, Weigle always carried a song-sheet in his pocket. In his sermon, *The Key to Spiritual Growth*, Roberson said, "I never saw such a man in my life. The last time I saw Dr. Weigle in his room in the Weigle apartment, he was sitting in his chair reading the Word of God and putting little notations by the side of verses – at 95 years of age! Shortly before that he had said to me, 'I think I will just go home now, if you don't mind – if you'll just pray and release me from my promise.' I had prayed a few months before for God to let him live to be 100 years old. That's what he wanted, so I prayed for it. But when he was 95, he said, 'If you don't mind, just change that prayer. I think I'll go home now.' And in a few days he was gone. That's what he wanted."

On Weigle's 95th birthday – November 20, 1966 – Highland Park Baptist Church hosted a big birthday party for him at the City Auditorium in downtown Chattanooga. The auditorium was packed out with people. The mayor was there. Dr. Weigle sang his signature song, *"No One Ever Cared for Me Like Jesus."* A few days after the 95th birthday celebration, Weigle became ill and eventually was hospitalized across the river at Currey's Clinic. A nurse called Dr. Roberson and said, "Dr. Roberson you're going to have to come and talk to Dr. Weigle. He keeps wanting to go home, but he's not able to go home." Dr. Roberson said, "Ma'am, I don't think you understand him. He's not talking about coming back to his apartment. He's talking about going home to heaven. But I'll come see him." Roberson visited Weigle and prayed with him. The nurse shed tears when she realized which "home" Weigle was talking about. A day or two later Charles F. Weigle was called "home" on December 3, 1966. He was buried next to his wife near Kissimmee, Florida. He still owned a little cottage on a lake near Kissimmee. In his will, Weigle left the cottage to Tennessee Temple. The college sold it and put the money into the Charles F. Weigle Music Center.

CBMC, the Christian businessmen's ministry, originally started in Chicago but located its national headquarters in Chattanooga, just a couple of blocks from Highland Park Baptist Church. After businessman Art DeMoss came to Christ under Hyman Appelman's ministry in 1951, Appelman sent Art to Tennessee Temple. When Art's brother, Ted DeMoss, came to Christ at about the same time, Ted also came to Chattanooga, joined Highland Park, and started his insurance business. Ted was actively involved in CBMC and financially supported Tennessee Temple. To this day there is a building on campus named after him. Ted always loved and supported Dr. Roberson, even though he personally moved to First Presbyterian Church under Dr. Ben Haden's ministry there. Ted DeMoss came to believe that his goal of reaching professional men and businessmen with the gospel was not best suited for Highland Park's aggressive approach to reaching the masses. Ted wanted to start a Sunday school class specifically for such men. In earlier years Dr. Roberson had a practice of giving the gospel invitation by asking everyone who was saved to stand up. "If you're not a Christian," he would say, "remain seated." Ted brought to church an unsaved businessman with whom he was dealing spiritually. When Dr. Roberson gave that invitation, Ted remained seated with his unsaved friend. But Ted felt uncomfortable with the approach, and after that he moved to First Presbyterian, where he continued to lead a number of wealthy businessmen in Chattanooga to the Lord. Most of them became members of First Presbyterian Church or Lookout Mountain Presbyterian Church. At one time Ted had been a deacon and trustee at Highland Park. Despite his switch to First Presbyterian, Ted DeMoss never forgot Lee Roberson's ministry. When he died, Ted DeMoss left money to Camp Joy, Tennessee Temple University, and the TTU seminary.

Included among other ministries headquartered in Chattanooga was the Christian Police Officers Fellowship, with offices right down Bailey Street, a short distance from Highland Park Baptist Church – across from Tennessee Temple University. The Fellowship of Christian Peace Officers was headquartered one-half block from the church. The Joyful Christian Ministries, founded by the family of the late Dr. John R. Rice and originally known as the Joyful Woman ministry, was also headquartered in Chattanooga.

Ron Bishop, one of Roberson's protégés, launched his own sports evangelism ministry. Called *Score International*, the ministry makes its headquarters in Chattanooga. Reggie White, the National Football League star of the Green Bay Packers, had a strong testimony for the Jesus Christ before his untimely death. Reggie came to Christ in Chattanooga through a Word of Life basketball program, sponsored by Highland Park Baptist Church.

Lee Roberson set a standard in Chattanooga that was followed by an informal network of Baptist preachers all over the world. He had tried to make the principles of his ministry "simple" and "copy-able," and he had far-reaching influence in fundamental circles. "God raised him up," said Clarence Sexton. "What was done at Highland Park was done everywhere. When they started singing *Golden Daybreak* at Highland Park, it was done everywhere. God gave him visibility. He exalted the Lord." A number of Roberson's preacher boys went out from Chattanooga and started evangelistic, soul winning ministries. Some became more interdenominational than Roberson. Some served in the Southern Baptist Convention. And always there was an evangelistic focus, born and nurtured in their hearts by Dr. Roberson.

Inspired by Roberson's innovative efforts to reach souls for Christ, the late Max Helton launched the fabulously successful Motor Racing Outreach ministry to the NASCAR stock car racing community. A life-long close friend to Roberson, Helton was a Tennessee Temple graduate. After serving for years as a Baptist pastor and missionary, Helton worked with such renowned drivers as Darrell Waltrip and Lake Speed to begin MRO, with headquarters in Charlotte, NC, near the hub of NASCAR. Helton became known as the chaplain of NASCAR. All of the dozens of auto racing team members and family members attached to each race car travel from city to city some 38 weeks of the year. Helton would preach to a chapel of 500 people before each race. At one time more than 30 of the drivers had made a public profession of faith. Helton led drivers like Jeff Gordon and Ken Schrader to the Lord and performed the weddings for many of the young drivers. During the three to four hours of the race itself, the MRO ministry team would conduct a combined program similar to Sunday school and daily vacation Bible school for hundreds of children in the racing community. MRO's Ron Pegram told me that before Max Helton started the MRO ministry the only women in the garage area were girlfriends of the drivers. Now, wives and entire families are there every week. Max Helton's connection with Highland Park dated back to the 1940s, and Dr. Roberson was always proud of what Max was doing with NASCAR.

It was in the balcony at the Chauncey-Goode auditorium that Jim Tatum, the Jacksonville clothier and a Southern Baptist, was called into his unique ministry of serving God as a businessman. For years he would travel to church conferences and sell suits to preachers at a discount – as his ministry for the Lord.

When Paul Freed, the founder of Trans World Radio, wrote his memoirs describing the ministry of TWR, he sent a copy of the book to Lee Roberson. Inside the cover of the book, *Towers to Eternity*, Freed had hand-written a note to Roberson which read, "Only eternity will reveal how much you and your wonderful people have meant to this work and to me personally down through the years."

Then he signed his name, and designated beside it, Galatians 2:20, his favorite Scripture verse.

While the college and the national ministries associated with Highland Park have brought a constant flow of visitors to Chattanooga for years, the city of Chattanooga did draw the line on one issue. "We tried to get the city to let us build a special building for guests with rooms," J.R. Faulkner recalled. "The city refused, due to code. They feared it would draw the ire of the motels and hotels." At the time, Faulkner suggested to Roberson that in the next building constructed on campus guest rooms be included in each corner of the building. That was exactly what they did. To this day the DeMoss Building has four guest rooms – one in each corner of the ground-level floor.

Chattanooga was to remain home for Lee Roberson until the end of his life. When the famous Moody Church in Chicago tried to call him as pastor, Roberson recommended George Sweeting. When a pulpit committee from Fort Smith, Arkansas, showed up at Highland Park, Roberson sent them to hear J. Harold Smith at Woodland Park.

The impact of Lee Roberson on Chattanooga was remarkable. When my son, Dan Wigton, attended Tennessee Temple in the late 1990s to train for the ministry, he said that it seemed like everywhere he went on door-to-door church visitation, people in Chattanooga had been touched by the ministry of Highland Park Baptist Church. Someone they knew – perhaps a family member – had been saved or baptized at Highland Park or Camp Joy.

While Roberson's impact was overwhelmingly positive, there were drawbacks and differences at times. Dr. Ben Haden, the pastor of First Presbyterian Church in Chattanooga for three decades, was highly complimentary of Lee Roberson. But he did express basically two criticisms in looking back over Roberson's long ministry. "I have never criticized Lee Roberson to anyone," he told me. "But when you tell me you're going to write a balanced report, I'm going to give you a couple of negatives." His first complaint was about the separatist philosophy of Roberson's independent Baptist ministry. "He has a tendency to think that he, and he alone, in this town is preaching the gospel," said Haden. "Some of the independent

Baptists are violently anti-Billy Graham – the idea being unbelievers sitting on the platform and cooperation of unbelieving churches. Well, I've worked with Billy Graham. To me, to have evangelism, you have to have cooperation of other churches. I could never vouch for the faith of all the pastors in any cooperative effort. I never vouch for the members of the choir. I feel at home in any believing church – not denominational structures. I also welcome anything for Christ." Haden said he did not view Tennessee Temple as extreme in separation as some independent Baptists, but he believed cooperation with unbelieving church leaders was valuable in that it gave their people exposure to the gospel. He said he feared the day will come when most ministers will not preach the gospel and will make Christ inclusive.

Of Lee Roberson, Haden said, "We have never had cross words. We did a funeral together in his church. I speak well of and support Lee Roberson. I have nothing but admiration for him personally."

Haden's second criticism of Highland Park's ministry was regarding the aggressive nature of its evangelism. "I stopped going downtown on Saturdays because of Temple [ministerial] students street preaching," he said. "Their approach bothered me." Haden described Temple preacher-boys street preaching in the open air, not looking the listener in the eye, and not listening to the response of the listener. Haden recalled, "'Are you saved?' 'Yes.' 'How?' 'By the blood of Jesus Christ alone.' They would proceed to give the plan of salvation – not listening to a thing said. I was offended by the way the gospel was thrown to the air and people were ignored, because I believe our business is people."

Haden viewed Roberson's ministry as far more than local or regional – it was national. "I think he's had terrific vision," said Haden. "I think he's been blessed anywhere's he's gone. I think if he had gone to Alaska, he would have been blessed there. I think he's a gifted, gifted man. I can't think of a greater gift than leading people to Christ."

Through the years the Highland Park area of Chattanooga deteriorated. A fashionable, up-scale area of the city when Lee Roberson arrived in 1942, by the time he retired it had digressed into a typical ghetto-type area – with drugs, prostitution, and crime. "It never seemed to stop us," said Roberson. "We just kept on building up in this one area all around us. Being on a main street was a help to us." Roberson never considered moving Highland Park to the suburbs, he told me, because he wanted to reach the city. He had more than one chance to move Tennessee Temple University – when Fort Oglethorpe, an army base, closed its doors after World War II, and later when the beautiful Calvin College campus on Lookout Mountain became available in 1960 for $250,000. "We could have bought it for $225,000 – twice they tried to sell it to us," said J.R. Faulkner, "but Doctor said, 'No, we're not going to separate the church and the school [geographically]. And the church is here to minister to the city.' That is why there was no serious consideration of moving to the suburbs, because he wanted an inner city impact on the town." Roberson did not want the college physically separated from the church. "He was building a church No. 1," said Faulkner. "The college was just an appendage – a tag-on ministry, just like Camp Joy, the Union Gospel Mission, the chapels, the school. These were just drag-alongs. The church was No. 1, and it's always been."

The decision not to relocate the college surely limited Tennessee Temple. It hindered J.R. Faulkner's efforts of recruiting new students. "Now, that means we can't have a campus like most colleges have," said Faulkner. "When I visit a church, someone has a daughter – they have a vision of ivy-covered, colonial, grass lawns, especially in the South. I try to acquaint them ahead of time. But you feel it once you get into it. We do not have buildings as others, because we had to build our buildings on property as they became available to us, according to the need at the time."

Lee Roberson viewed every individual soul – regardless of race or ethnicity – as created in the image of God. However, he was limited in his day by the prevalent practice of segregation in society and even in the church. When Roberson began his ministry at Highland Park Baptist Church in the Chattanooga of 1942, black people were not normally welcomed into white churches in the deep South. Roberson embraced integration when it came later, and in the early years he wasted no time in reaching out to the African-American community. Through out his ministry he tried to open the door to African-Americans.

In the segregation era of 1947 Roberson was instrumental in the founding of a Bible college specifically for African-American ministerial students. Roberson met with several members of the black community of Chattanooga and started a school initially named New Monumental Bible School, under the auspices of Tennessee Temple. It opened its doors on October 10, 1947 at the New Monumental Baptist Church, whose pastor was Rev. J.B. Outlaw. In the beginning, 77 students enrolled, and 24 received certificates for completing the program. In 1948 Highland Park gave $500 toward the down payment on a property for the college located at 1005 E. 9th Street (later named Martin Luther King Jr. Boulevard). On September 14, 1949, the college received its charter under the new name, Zion Bible College and Seminary – with 10 students in the college, eight in the seminary, and 75 in the Bible school. Tennessee Temple's instructors taught at Zion. Later the college was turned over entirely to African-American leadership. Located next to the University of Tennessee at Chattanooga, Zion was renamed City College in 1964 and eventually merged with the UTC in 1969. Dr. Horace Traylor was president of Chattanooga City College when the merger took place.

Looking back on the days of segregation, J.R. Faulkner recalled, "We had a lot of black preachers and students who wanted to come to Temple. They would ask me, 'Why can't we come and get the Bible training?' I would just melt inside. I could personally find no reason. I loved these men. There was nothing we could do – at the time – because of the feeling of people. Now, blacks have been baptized [at Highland Park] and into the membership for years."

Like most predominantly white churches in America, Highland Park Baptist Church did not have many blacks. But Roberson welcomed black choirs, such as the very popular Eureka Jubilee Singers to minister at the church. Roberson preached as a guest at a number of predominantly black churches and was well received. "I preached for them all the time back in those days," he said.

On one occasion when Dr. Martin Luther King Jr. came up from Atlanta to visit Chattanooga, Dr. Roberson met with him. "A couple of preachers brought him out here to our office," said Faulkner. "We had prayer together." Roberson said later that King sat across his desk and gave a clear testimony of being a born-again Christian – something Roberson believed in deeply. Roberson later told black evangelist Ed Carter that Roberson was one of the few fundamental Baptists who would give King "the time of day." The focus of King's ministry differed from that of Roberson. While Roberson spent his life on the evangelism of souls, King's passion was to see black people treated with dignity and equality in American society.

In trying to reach African-Americans with the gospel, Roberson said, "It was not a matter of opening doors. They were open already. So, we didn't have any change. We made no speeches or declarations or anything at all. We just received them when they came. If blacks came, or were saved, and wanted to be baptized, I baptized them, and they came right in. By keeping it open, it brought to us those who wanted to come."

By the 1970s in the South, blacks still were very limited in being permitted to associate with whites. But Highland Park Baptist Church was then bringing in blacks on its Sunday school buses from the downtown public housing. One of the youths reached with the gospel was Reggie White, an African-American who later became a star pro football player in the National Football League and later became a preacher. Highland Park ministry workers discipled Reggie White.

During the segregation era Highland Park's Union Gospel Rescue Mission did not originally cater to black people. But when some members and friends of the church were burdened to start a new mission directed toward minorities, Lee Roberson gave them their first donation with which to get started. "He was for reaching minorities but fearful people wouldn't accept that," Walter Wendelken recalled of the time.

In 1976 Ed Carter, who later became a Baptist evangelist, was the first black American student to enroll for graduate work in Temple Baptist Seminary. "When I went to Temple, there had been black Africans – from the Solomon Islands, West Indies, Jamaica," said Carter. "There were some [black Americans] in the college [undergraduate]." Carter had met Lee Roberson, when Dr. Roberson was preaching in his area. "We shook hands. 'How are you doing, son? Are you called to preach?' 'Yes.' 'If you need any help, call me.'"

After graduation, as an evangelist, Carter stayed as a member of Highland Park Baptist Church and made it the home base of his ministry. He said, "I've gotten flack from my friends, especially from black preachers. 'What are you doing in a church that's pastored by a white preacher?' That's what they say. 'That don't look too good.' That's where God led me. I'm staying until God moves me. God led me to Highland Park. I don't operate to please men. I'm doing it for the glory of God. There are blacks there – other nationalities. Yes, it is predominantly white, but that is where God has put me. That is a New Testament church – composed of people of all walks of life. We're not starting black churches. We're starting New Testament churches. They will be mostly black, but we're trying to reach every nationality. To reach just one nationality of people – that is not a New Testament church. Look at the day of Pentecost!"

Ed Carter was impressed with Roberson's effort to start Zion College. "Dr. Roberson said his greatest mistake was turning the school over to others," said Carter. "He said, 'I wish I had never done that.'" Carter was also impressed with Roberson's effort to treat blacks equally. Carter was honored to become chaplain of the student body at Tennessee Temple. "I remember standing in line at registration," said Carter. "I overheard two white guys. 'Psst, he's going to be chaplain.' 'A black chaplain?' They were pointing to me. I never looked around to see who it was." Carter was the first American black nominated for student president. Solomon Owolabi, who was from Nigeria, had been student president – "but he was African," said Carter. "I would have been the first black American, but I didn't get it. (He lost the election.) That was okay. Then I became chaplain of the seminary. When I graduated in 1981, I got a standing ovation. Dr. Roberson said, 'They love you. They love you, son.' He kept saying that." Regarding Lee Roberson, Carter concluded, "Blacks, black preachers – those that know him – have the highest regard for him. They all respect him."

Lee Roberson's concentric impact for the gospel of Jesus Christ stretched from Chattanooga to the far mission fields of the world – reaching black and white, rich and poor. "He's in a class all by himself, as far as I'm concerned," said missionary Garland Cofield. "I'm so glad I got to see it all. I'm really so thankful."

CHAPTER 16

'Til Death Do Us Part

As Lee Roberson became an icon in fundamental Baptist circles, he personally remained a rather reticent man who treasured privacy for himself and for his wife and family. The result was a life-long mystique and aura surrounding his personal life, his personal habits, and his family life. The growing legion of church members, Tennessee Temple graduates, and other followers of his ministry around the world were intrigued by the mystery of Lee Roberson. Everything he did or said became a topic of interest among his many admirers.

Lee and Caroline Roberson's life-long marriage was truly a love story. When they met, he was strikingly handsome – and she was a beautiful brunette. They were devoted to each other. They were married 68 years – "til death do us part." Throughout their marriage, Lee wrote Caroline love notes, which she carried in her purse and would show friends.

Caroline was dedicated to her husband and to his ministry. In line with his lifestyle of propriety, she was known around his vast ministry and through out the fundamental Christian world as "Mrs. Roberson." At Highland Park Baptist Church she sat through every church service. In the old Chauncey-Goode auditorium she would always sit down front in the second row – and the same in the new building. "She was there for everything," said Jean Smith. "She was right with him all the time." Lee Roberson's only sister, Darlene

Munafo, said, "She's been a wonderful, devoted wife – I'll tell you that!"

Caroline Roberson depicted a genteel type of southern belle – with grace and dignity. A godly woman, as she directed a ministry, such as the church nursery, she was a leader and could be authoritative. She walked with God and was a help-meet to a great preacher. She was a woman of prayer. Caroline once spoke to a ladies' meeting and described how when she would go downtown shopping she would pray for God to give her a parking space. And He would. Caroline was content to stay in the background of her husband's immense ministry, but she would speak at ladies' meetings. Caroline always taught Sunday school. She was at her husband's side for banquets, special programs and activities at the church or college. She also managed his travel schedule and kept records of every sermon he preached. Dr. Roberson said, "I never made a decision about this church or school that I didn't talk to my wife."

Caroline Roberson was well-known for directing the nursery, which was emulated by many of the current and future pastors' wives who came through Tennessee Temple University. The nursery was her ministry. She was the overseer of a nursery which often held 300 babies – more souls in one church nursery than many pastors have in their entire church. The nursery was a very large nursery – not only because of the size of the church but also the great number of young couples in the college. Lee Roberson recalled that when he first visited Highland Park Baptist Church as a prospective pastor, the chairman of the Board of Deacons, Bob Shedd, took him on a tour of the church facilities. When Shedd showed Roberson the "Cradle Roll and Nursery Room," it had one baby bed, a box of toys, a rocking chair, and two or three pictures on the wall. "This room is well equipped and adequate for our needs," Shedd told him at the time. Years later, before his death, Shedd saw the nursery mushroom in size. Roberson instituted an annual "Baby Day," each year on the Sunday after Mother's Day, with a parade of babies presented publicly in the morning church service. The nursery attendance on those days was typically between 275 and 320.

Anyone who knew the Robersons knew that they were extremely close to one another. "Dr. Roberson has many friends

– only one 'dear' friend, his wife," said Clarence Sexton. He was totally devoted to her, and she to him. But she could tease with an air of feistiness. Their son, John, said she was the boss. That was clear on one occasion in Tampa when we took the Robersons to the Colonnade Restaurant, on the waterfront of Tampa Bay. A member of our dinner party ordered honey-crusted jumbo shrimp and offered one to Dr. Roberson. He said that yes, he would like one. As he raised the shrimp almost to his mouth, Mrs. Roberson said, "You can't have that," and she took it out of his hand and ate it on the spot. Dr. Roberson went on as if nothing had happened. We all laughed together.

As devoted as she was to her husband, Caroline Roberson did not hesitate to decide some issues for herself. When Dr. and Mrs. Roberson were traveling in the Holy Land, their group had stopped for a shopping trip on a Sunday. Dr. Roberson refused to go shopping – presumably because it was the Lord's day. Mrs. Roberson said, "I know, but I'm going." And she went shopping. He did not. When they arrived in London, England, Mrs. Roberson asked Orman Norwood to keep Dr. Roberson busy at a British museum, while she took her heels off, put on flats, and went sight-seeing.

Many of the books of Dr. Roberson's sermons, which were published, were compiled by Mrs. Roberson. She helped build his ministry – working behind the scenes. "They didn't want anyone to know," said Bob Kelley.

Every pastor is criticized. A man in such a high profile position as Lee Roberson was going to get his share of criticism. However, if criticism of him reached Caroline's ears, he would never hear about it. Caroline Roberson would never tell her husband anything negative – always seeking to protect him from criticism. "She wanted people to like him," said Dorothy McCormick, Dr. Roberson's secretary. "She loved him. Mrs. Roberson was very strong. She knew what was going on. She was very close to him in the work. She was in the middle of everything – the nursery. She was on top of what's going on – visitation. She was in the homes of new babies."

While theirs was a model marriage, they were also human. Dorothy McCormick remembered rare occasions when Mrs. Roberson would call the church office and ask with a laugh, "Was

Lee quiet when he came in?" Dorothy mentioned he could lose his temper, but it would never last. Caroline Roberson explained that Lee only had a temper in the pulpit – and that even then, he only appeared to be angry – especially when the college students were around. Out of the pulpit, he could be the opposite of his strong public persona. Orman Norwood recalled Mrs. Roberson's words. "A lot of people are scared of my husband," she said. "So, they will go to Dr. Faulkner instead. Sometimes they are surprised because *he* will jump all over them!" Missionary Garland Cofield remembered a show of temper in Roberson's early years. Cofield, who was already a member of Highland Park when Roberson first arrived, traveled with him frequently to meetings in those days. "I remember one day," he said. "Somebody had said something about Mrs. Roberson. He was so mad. He was shaking his fist, and his neck was popped out. He says, 'If that ever happens again, I'm going to ram this right down his throat.' He sat there shaking."

As Lee and Caroline Roberson spent their lives together serving God, how fitting it was that their lifelong Chattanooga home would be at a place called *Missionary* Ridge. During the Robersons' early years at Highland Park, they had lived in the church parsonage, or pastorium, right next to the Chauncey-Goode church auditorium on Bailey Avenue. On occasion in the early years Roberson conducted weddings in the parlor. Later it was named Herndon Hall and was turned into a guest house and church nursery. At that time the church built a new home for their pastor, and later the Robersons built their Missionary Ridge home, designed by Caroline, at 28 Shallowford Road, where they lived for many years. When the Robersons made the one-mile move to the Missionary Ridge home, Dr. Roberson called Dr. E.C. Haskell Sr., his close friend and chairman of the deacons, and told him that he was in need of $100 to make the move. Dr. Haskell gave it to him.

A winding road near the McCallie School would take them to their home, which set up high on Missionary Ridge – famous during the Civil War fighting – overlooking Chattanooga. The Roberson house set high above Shallowford Road on the hillside. The Robersons entered their house from the driveway in the back. The white and yellow, two-story house was designed with the view of

Chattanooga. Large picture windows in a front living room, almost as wide as the house itself, presented not only a view of the city but the historic Lookout Mountain as well. The Robersons loved it there. Dr. Roberson enjoyed looking over the city from his home and standing at the large picture windows in the long living room at the front of the home with binoculars in hand as he examined the view toward Lookout Mountain. A long hall-way led to smaller rooms extending from the front living room. The Robersons' bedroom was enlarged and expanded in later years. Dr. Roberson's study went off the bedroom. An addition was made to the other end of the house in later years, making a nice dining room area and a little larger kitchen area. A small upstairs room was added – where sometimes grandkids would stay.

Members of Roberson's vast ministry only on rare occasions visited the Roberson home. It was surprisingly modest. The Robersons were quite content with a simple setting.

Sheila Wharram, who served as the secretary at the International Board of Jewish Missions for Dr. Jacob Gartenhaus and later for Dr. Orman Norwood, became perhaps Caroline Roberson's closest friend and a frequent visitor to the Roberson home. Sheila, born in England, loved Highland Park Baptist Church. When God spoke to her heart about full-time ministry in 1973, she made a public commitment during the closing invitation at a church service. Mrs. Roberson, still the nursery director, counseled with Sheila at the altar and then put her to work serving in the nursery. She and Mrs. Roberson became very good friends, and later Sheila would become director of the Highland Park nursery. "The way I became her friend was by working in the cradle roll," Sheila said. "We would go on visitation together. That is how I got to know them. Then she started inviting me to their house for Christmas and Thanksgiving."

Lee Roberson said publicly that he did not socialize much, because he felt that if he went out with one family of the church that others would be upset – and it certainly was not possible to socialize with everyone in such a large ministry. Caroline Roberson had followed her husband's conviction that a pastor and his wife could not have close friends within the church for fear of showing favoritism. She would have the ladies over to her house only on rare occasions for women's missionary meetings. In the early years, before the church grew so large, Garland Cofield remembers the Robersons coming to eat at his home more than once. In those days, said Jean Smith (Garland's sister), "They were in our house. My mother and dad had them over for several meals. Basically he would come at the time of the meal, eat, thank you for a wonderful meal, and he'd go. He had something to do. It was just him and his wife, very gracious – gotta be going." Jean remembered one time when he stayed an hour. "We were so surprised!" Often when they hosted the Robersons, it was along with a guest speaker like John R. Rice or Hyman Appelman.

Dr. Roberson always had to be on the go at home, as well. An impatient man, he hated to be late. His children remembered him at the back door of the house hollering to Mrs. Roberson, "Let's go! Let's go!" He never wasted time. Nevertheless, Mrs. Roberson was not intimidated. "My mom was in charge," said Johnny, their only son.

The Roberson home included three children, plus an adopted fourth child. In a biographical sketch on Roberson published in the 1980s, Ed Reese wrote, "The Roberson children are all a credit to the godly heritage of their parents."

Their first child, LeeAnne, was born on May 2, 1941. "LeeAnne is like her father – strong willed, and so forth," said Nat Phillips. "She was very close to her father." LeeAnne, who spent her student days at Tennessee Temple, was always well liked. "Everyone knew she was his daughter," said Bob Kelley. "She was very popular and well-liked – very proud to be Dr. Roberson's daughter." LeeAnne later taught English at Tennessee Temple. Her husband, L.W. "Buddy" Nichols, taught psychology and later became president of Tennessee Temple – spending his life in ministry. (Buddy was also close to Dr. Roberson – like a second son.)

The Robersons' only son, John Charles Roberson, a gifted businessman, originally served in several church pastoral positions before entering the business world. He was involved in a variety of successful business ventures, which included managing radio, TV and tape ministries for churches. He assisted Lester Roloff in the broadcasting of his ministry for years. He helped Tennessee Temple start its WDYN-FM radio station when it began broadcasting in 1968. John also sold radio time for Highland Park Baptist Church. A family friend said, "He knows how to make money." Nat Phillips knew the Roberson family for many years. "Johnny's a good boy – a good man," he said. "He's a genius as far as being a business man." Family friends suggested that John worked behind the scenes to ensure the financial security of his father and mother, and he became increasingly close to his parents in later years. Like his dad, John enjoyed cars. He liked to restore old cars, and he always kept his dad in a new car. And John supported the Lord's work. He visited ministries such as Garland Cofield's mission in Canada.

As often occurs in a family, the youngest daughter, June, was always close to her parents – literally living next door for a number of years. June was Lee Roberson's baby daughter. Phillips recalled, "June went on a choir trip overseas. Dr. Roberson was waiting on her when they returned. He hugged her and said, 'Well, you've gone on a trip like this once. No more.' He missed her so much." June married Bill Ormsheier. An outstanding singer, Bill served as minister of music in Baptist churches in Lakeland, Florida, and Dallas, Texas. June, who inherited her father's penchant for music, was an asset to Bill's ministry, as a pianist. During her Highland Park days, June would often sing or play the piano for the radio broadcasts. At one time during Bill's college days at Temple, Nat Phillips gave Bill the opportunity to work with Nat in a Chattanooga area church. "He's a good man," said Phillips. "You can't imagine how much the family appreciated that. Mrs. Roberson thanked me time and again."

An adopted daughter, Patty, joined the family when she was very young, after her natural parents died. She married and moved away, returning home for special family events such as Dr. Roberson's birthday.

Lee Roberson's relationship with his children was not like a typical family. "We were pretty close," he said. "They were very faithful – no problem there." But the demands of a huge, multi-faceted ministry, plus his constant travels, took him away from home much of the time. There were times when Dr. Roberson would come in from travel late and gather everyone in a circle for prayer before he would go to bed. Yet he was strictly devoted to the ministry to which God had called him. He always put his calling first and foremost. Hardly anyone was surprised at the conclusion of LeeAnne and Buddy's marriage ceremony on a Saturday evening when Dr. Roberson announced to the crowd, "Don't forget to be in Sunday school Sunday morning." At Lee Roberson's funeral, his son addressed a huge crowd representing ministries from around the world. "As a family," John said, "we endured a lot for the sake of others. We gave our dad to you." One long-time family friend told me, "I think there were times growing up when Johnny needed his dad around. I think most of his kids probably suffered some." Ron Bishop suggested that if Dr. Roberson had it to do over he might focus more time on his family – as the awareness for such a priority for preachers' families is much greater now than it was in Roberson's day. "In the 1940s and 50s," Bishop explained, "you just sold out to God."

Absent or not, "his kids idolized him," asserted Randy Ray. "He was always bigger than life – even to his kids." John Roberson revealed publicly at his father's funeral, "We didn't care if he was famous. We knew he would love us and take care of us. We all wanted his approval."

Dr. Roberson's love for his family was unquestioned, but perhaps because of his upbringing he sometimes had difficulty demonstrating his love. Walter Wendelken surmised, "I think he had a rough childhood. He told me about it. At weddings, receptions, and the like, he was uneasy. He never learned to be with people. It went back to his childhood days. I don't think he was shown any love by his parents. It made it hard for him to express love." And what preacher's family has not at times felt like part of the congregation or felt like they had to get an appointment to see dad? One family friend said of the Robersons, "It was almost like they were his congregation. He was the type of person who can't get really close to anyone. It's almost like I've heard them say they would have to schedule a time to see him – like they were part of his congregation. I know he loves his kids. But he doesn't show it. She does. She's more loving – as far as hugging, and so forth. That's just the way he is. His family understood his role as a great man. I think they realized it."

One close family friend believed that Lee Roberson did not have a great capacity to show love. The family intimate remembered when one of Roberson's married daughters was in the hospital for major surgery. Dr. Roberson came into the hospital room prior to surgery. "We're praying for you," he said to his daughter. "God's going to take care of you. Let's pray." The family friend, a preacher, added, "He had given himself so completely to the Lord that he didn't have much left. But he loved his family dearly." When their adopted daughter would come to town, it was not unlike Lee Roberson to tell his wife, "Give her some money. Tell her we love her." The depth of love no doubt was there, but the expression of love was often brief and somewhat limited.

At the end of Dr. Roberson's life, his son recounted, "He never talked a lot. The last few years he started telling us he loved us." With his grandchildren, Roberson showed his love and fondness – but, like many men, not necessarily on their level. Caroline, however, was more openly affectionate, and both of them were proud of their grandchildren.

Every family faces problems. When divorce would touch the Roberson family – as it does many families, it was hard on Dr. Roberson. "When you've preached against it all your life," a family friend said, "it's hard when it hits your own family."

After Dr. Roberson's resignation from the pastorate of Highland Park Baptist Church, his family had a big adjustment to make, as the Roberson family faced an unsettling displacement from a way of life they had known for decades. Some friends saw it as being traumatic. "They had a hard time adjusting to his leaving (the pastorate)," one family intimate claimed. Dr. Roberson was no longer their pastor. And their defined role at Highland Park immediately changed as well. Facing an understandably difficult situation, Buddy eventually left his position at Tennessee Temple, and LeeAnne feared the entire ministry was changing and not honoring her father's legacy. A family friend expressed to me, "Her whole world fell apart. Her identity, with his prominence, and her position were gone." Consequently, Buddy and LeeAnne left Highland Park Baptist Church to attend another Baptist church in Chattanooga before he took a position with a different ministry. Over time the entire family – except for Dr. and Mrs. Roberson – left Highland Park, but all remained faithful to the Lord and active in various churches.

Lee Roberson was famous for always wearing a dark, navy blue, double-breasted suit. He never dressed casually. He kept several identical suits – all ordered from a Chattanooga tailor. He never went shopping or to a mall. He wore a white dress shirt, some variation of a red tie, and the same kind of black shoes – size 11-B – and socks. It simplified his life. He never wanted to look flashy. "Everything about him was thought through," said Bob Kelley. "Nothing was spur-of-the-moment – not even his clothes." E.C. Haskell Jr. said, "He told me he did that because he tried to eliminate a lot of what he called non-essential decisions early in his ministry. So, he didn't have to make a decision about what suit he's going to wear or what tie." Wearing the same suit also helped him avoid the appearance of ostentation. He said privately that no one knew when he had a new suit. J.R. Faulkner explained to the preacher boys that the day came when Highland Park was so busy – so much was happening – that Roberson also decided to wear a dark suit in order always to be ready for a funeral or other formal functions which could occur without notice.

Roberson's double-breasted suit became a trademark for him. He even published a book of sermons entitled, *Double-Breasted*. But in the early days of his Chattanooga ministry he still wore a variety of clothes – including lighter colored suits. His wife bought his shirts, ties, and suits. Caroline knew his tastes. For a time he liked rather expensive pure cotton shirts, which she ordered from London. Then for many years his shirts were a wrinkle-free, cotton and polyester mix from J.C. Penney. "He knows nothing about what things cost – personally," said Clarence Sexton. "He would think it sinful that I paid $200 for a pair of shoes for him. He doesn't know what they cost. He doesn't know what his suits cost." In his early years, Roberson wore a hat – as did other men in society.

Personally Roberson was always neat and well groomed. He always went to the same barber. "He is so prim and proper – even in his home," pointed out Sheila Wharram. "He never takes his jacket off. The only time I've seen him take his jacket off was to go feed the dog. Everyone else is casually dressed on Christmas Day. He has on a double-breasted suit, shirt and tie." As a teacher at Temple, LeeAnne once shared with her class that her father would wear a double-breasted suit even on vacation. If the family stopped to play put-put golf, he would take off his jacket and play in his shirt sleeves. Afterward he would put the jacket back on.

Roberson's dress style was so well known in his vast ministry that it became folklore as to when anyone had ever seen him dressed in other than his unvarying dark navy blue double-breasted suits. The joke among students was that Dr. Roberson must sleep in that suit. Church members and college students would never see Dr. Lee Roberson without his dark blue, double-breasted suit coat – even when it was hot outside. But J.R. Faulkner remembered seeing him at a wedding in the 1940s. Roberson was driving a 1942 or '43 Pontiac and was wearing a wide-brimmed gray felt hat, with brown shoes, and a gray suit. "I can still see that!" Faulkner told me in 2002. Faulkner recalled that in the old days Roberson wore a watch with a chain – it dropped into his pocket with a little loop and came back up and hooked in the eye of his lapel. "He would take his watch out and look at it. Pretty soon preacher boys all started showing up the same. Dr. Roberson stopped it. That's when he started using a handkerchief (in his front pocket). He didn't want little 'Lee Robersons' running everywhere – human nature being what it is." Sure enough, missionary Jerry Reece said with a laugh, "Most of the students all felt like that was what you had to wear in order to be a preacher."

Some people remembered seeing Roberson in a gray single-breasted suit in his early years in Chattanooga. Garland Cofield said of those early years, "I knew where he got those suits, because I would ask him. So, I had to have me a suit like his. I remember he wore Kuppenheimer suits. It was a top brand suit back then. I got me a double-breasted dark blue suit!" Nat Phillips remembered as a high schooler seeing Roberson wear a single-breasted suit, with a vest, and the watch and chain in his pocket. Cofield remembered only one occasion seeing Roberson in his shirt sleeves. "It was sweltering hot – like 100 degrees at Camp Joy one time," he said. "I saw him take his jacket off and speak in his shirt sleeves." It was the talk of the place – "Dr. Roberson doesn't have his coat on!"

When I was the pastor of Faith Baptist Church of Avon in Indianapolis, Indiana, we invited Dr. Roberson for meetings. He was to arrive in town on a Saturday and preach for us on Sunday. Early Saturday afternoon I visited the motel to leave a welcome package with a letter outlining the Sunday schedule for the Robersons upon their arrival. To my surprise, they had already arrived on Friday – a day early. Dr. Roberson was walking and praying in his shirt sleeves – tie on, but no jacket – in a tree-shaded corner of the motel parking lot. Ed Johnson said, "I remember the first time I saw him without his coat on. I almost went into cardiac arrest. It was at a motel door in Rosemont where he was staying. He came to the door without his coat on." One year, as a joke, at Christmas someone gave him a bright red jacket. He took off his double-breasted coat and tried on the jacket in public. Someone took a picture which later appeared in the college yearbook.

Occasionally when it was cold, Roberson would wear gloves. On a trip to the Holy Land, the Robersons were at the Acropolis in Athens, Greece, with the Orman Norwoods and the Jack Van Impes. It was too cold to stay for the out-door lecture. Orman offered Roberson a hat. "No," he said, "I never wear a hat." Norwood was with Dr. Roberson in the 1980s when they stopped in Louisville, Kentucky, to visit Roberson's father and step-mother. Roberson wore his dark blue double-breasted suit. In later years when Dr. Roberson had minor eye surgery, Jerry Mattheiss and David Snow went up to visit him in the hospital. "He was in pajamas," Mattheiss said. "I said, 'Doc, you're out of uniform.' He said, 'They won't let me wear my suit in here!'"

When Clyde and Betty Box traveled with the Robersons on an overseas preaching trip, they all stayed in a "bed and breakfast" type of a rooming house in London, England. Each couple had their own bedroom, but all guests had to walk down the hallway for bathroom facilities. Betty encountered the dignified Dr. Roberson in his bathrobe in the hallway. "Horrors!" Clyde Box recalled with a laugh. Dr. Roberson was embarrassed. Betty relieved the situation by saying simply, "Dr. Roberson, I've seen that before!" Everyone laughed about it later.

Disciplined and devoted, Roberson almost never took a day off. To the end of his life, he would go in to his office on Thanksgiving Day and on Christmas Day. He would be home by noon, and with his family he would unwrap Christmas presents after lunch. June and Bill, who lived next door for a time, did not want to wait. They opened presents after breakfast, and then joined the family after lunch for the rest of the gifts. Family gifts were opened, as well as gifts from church members. Sheila Wharram would take pictures. "The most down-to-earth I ever saw him was on Christmas – still in a suit," she said, "but he enjoys it." John Roberson said his dad loved Christmas. He loved Christmas lights – the more the merrier! He would open presents with a knife – "Man, what is this? Who's this from? Well, I don't know what that is. What am I supposed to do with that?" Understandably, he was a hard one for which to shop. One year a bow-and-arrow set fascinated him – only for about 10 minutes. One recent year the family had a star named after him. After gift opening, Roberson would take a nap, and then get up and watch a ballgame on TV.

Clyde and Betty Box often exchanged Christmas gifts with Lee and Caroline Roberson. One year Box sent Dr. Roberson a small, round trampoline. "He won't lie," Box said with a laugh. "He wrote me, 'I think it's a wonderful gift. I stood on it once. I plan to stand on it again.'" Evangelist Jim Lyons told Box that Dr. Roberson sent him Christmas lights one year – after Christmas!

Lee Roberson's idea of a vacation usually meant meeting the family in Gatlinburg, Tennessee, after Thanksgiving and staying in a chalet for a day or two. Two days seemed to be the most he would ever take away from the Lord's work. His daughter, June, said he would take two bags of books on vacation. He was reading all the time, it seemed. He did not waste time. He would stay in the motel room and read while the family went shopping. Yet he would also play miniature golf or cruise on a moped around Gatlinburg with his grandchildren.

When Caroline would persuade her husband to take a longer vacation, he would always line up an itinerary to preach somewhere

– usually for pastors who were Tennessee Temple graduates. He told me that part of his thinking was that he hesitated to take vacations after being out-of-town so often to preach. "I took one or two," he said. "Maybe one Sunday out, but that was all. Not over two – I don't think, in all the time. I was gone so much on Mondays and Tuesdays with outside meetings, I'd have been embarrassed to do much more. I was gone every Monday and Tuesday." But no one at the church ever complained. It was simply his choice. Lee Roberson just did not believe very much in taking time off from work. In his early years he preached against vacations. When he would go to his office on holidays and Saturdays he never understood why other people were not there at work. He was from another era. Sheila Wharram saw the same pattern in Dr. Jacob Gartenhaus of IBJM. Like Roberson, he also worked seven days per week and did not take vacations. These were great men of another age. In Roberson's early years, whenever he did take a vacation, church members remembered that he would preach almost every night somewhere. "Wherever he was going," said Jean Smith, "he would let people know he was coming. They'd want him to preach!"

On one occasion when Temple faculty member Glenn Swygart and his wife took a weekend off to spend in Gatlinburg, they were pleasantly surprised to see the Robersons there. Dr. Roberson was walking with his wife in the heart of the town. He was wearing a double-breasted suit, while his wife was still shopping. He was carrying a sack, as they headed back to the Holiday Inn, where they were all staying. Caroline loved to shop in Gatlinburg.

E.C. Haskell Jr. would sometimes tease Mrs. Roberson. Once when the Robersons had traveled to Florida, E.C. asked her if they ever went to the beach. Mrs. Roberson said to him, "Are you kidding? I'd be so embarrassed walking on the beach with a man in a double-breasted suit." E.C. told me, "I don't know how he relaxed. My dad said he only remembered twice seeing him with his coat off in 37 years. He never saw him go in a restroom. He worked that close, even after deacons' meetings – very unusual man."

Lee Roberson's work ethic was focused on ministry. At home he did not cut the grass. A college student – or perhaps someone from the church – would mow the lawn. He was not very adept around the house. "He's not a bit mechanical," affirmed Gloria Shadowens. "I think Mrs. Roberson took care of the oil in the car," suggested Dorothy McCormick. Each lady worked closely with him for years as his secretary. When his dictaphone would not work, Gloria recalled, "He brought it to me. 'I can't get this to work.' I changed the batteries. 'Oh?!' he said. I fixed it another time. Something was loose." He did not help his wife with the dishes, or the coffee, or cooking or anything like that. His family would joke that he never really fixed anything – he left that to mother. He did not go shopping. He would never go into a store. He was always engrossed in ministry. Even at restaurants countless times he would make notes on a napkin – usually planning something work-related. "His hobby was his ministry," observed David Wingate, a long-time Temple faculty member.

Nevertheless, Roberson taught his son how to kick a football. But he did so dressed for ministry. John Roberson told the story at his father's funeral. Wearing a tie and dress shoes, Dr. Roberson had told his son, "You want to kick it high." And then he kicked the football – through a window of the church annex building. "All right, Johnny," he said. "Go up and get the ball. We're done."

Lee Roberson and J.R. Faulkner never ate a meal in each other's homes. Faulkner, who worked at Roberson's side for some 40 years, was in his home only on three occasions. "This is going to shock you," Faulkner told me with a chuckle. "I was in his study at his home twice in all those years. He was out of town. His secretary was asked to do some work in his office – to make room for some books. While they were gone, she asked me to come with her to get some ideas about the shelving. I was there then. Then at a later date they had an open-house for some reception of some kind. And I went – along with many others." Later, as Johnny was growing up, the Robersons added a room over the garage of the old parsonage to give him his own bedroom. Faulkner was in the house during the construction. "Apart from that, that was it!" he said. "There was no reason. He was always so close to the church, and so much of his time was spent in his office. There was no need for me to have to be over. He worked all the time." It was a way of life for Roberson, who never would eat in a church member's home, so as to avoid the appearance of showing favoritism. The church was so large he could not possibly eat in every member's home.

Roberson was a very private man outside the pulpit and a man of few words. He had very few social contacts. "He wasn't one that you could get real close to," said Walter Wendelken. In his work Roberson was closest to J.R. Faulkner – and at different times to Dr. E.C. Haskell Sr. or Bill Morton. "He was close to Dr. Fred Brown," said Wendelken. "He always enjoyed Fred Brown. Dr. Roberson took him into his confidence. When he was in town he had lunch with him – the only man I knew he went to lunch with."

When Roberson traveled to preach, Mrs. Roberson would take him to the airport – in earlier years June would go with them. Mother and daughter would wait for a moment. He would turn and wave. On the rare occasions he was hospitalized, he would rather not have visitors – except family. It would be announced in church – no visitors. Although he made frequent ministry calls and visits, he was in very few homes socially through the years – maybe the homes of a half dozen deacons. Most of his socializing revolved around church events. "He would shake hands with a lot of people," Bob Kelley said. "When it was time to go, he would give Mrs. Roberson a signal – and they were gone." When a church service was over, he was not one to stand around. He would leave. But he was always accessible. Church members and college students alike would stand in line daily to see him in his office.

Lee and Caroline Roberson always stayed in touch with Lee's only sister, Darlene Munafo. She told me in 2002, "The last time I talked with him on the phone, he didn't have much to say. He never does. His wife has been his mouthpiece all these years. I talked with her for a long time. She says, 'Just a minute, I'll put your brother on the phone.' It took awhile. 'Hi, Sis, how are you?' A man of very few words. 'You're not doing so well, are you?' I'm just fine. I'm just fine. 'Well, God bless you!' He's done."

Caroline Roberson was equally private. Although she ministered to the ladies of the church, she was not very close to them. "She was not a real social person," said Jean Smith. "She was just always by his side. She always was in every service." Rarely was anyone other than family members invited to their home. Sunday nights after church were for the family at home. Children and grandchildren would visit – everyone sitting at the table, eating and talking. Finally, Dr. Roberson would rise and say, "You all can stay as long as you want. I'm going to bed." And off he would go to get his pajamas, housecoat and slippers.

Once when Dr. Roberson was hospitalized for minor surgery, no one but the family knew about it. J.R. Faulkner did not even know at the time. In later years when Mrs. Roberson was hospitalized, Jerry Mattheiss would jump at the chance to drive Dr. Roberson back and forth to the hospital. "That's when I really got to know him," said Jerry. "He doesn't offer anything, but if you ask him, he'll tell you."

Darlene Munafo, like her brother, grew up shy. Because she was a talented singer, Dr. Roberson would always put his sister on the spot to sing at the huge Highland Park Baptist Church when she visited him. "I got to the point where I didn't even want to visit him," she said with a laugh. "I didn't, because I never knew what to expect in Chattanooga. I was church soloist for years and years – a worrier. I would be sick for a week before I had to sing. But I'd always do fine. The solos would come out beautiful, and people would say it was so beautiful and all that. But it would just do something to me. I was shy when I was a little girl. I remember my first solo at church. I was five years old, singing, *Jesus Loves Me*. My brother was good to me." When the Robersons traveled for his speaking engagements in Florida, they would visit Darlene, who lived in St. Petersburg. "The last time they were here," she said, "he preached in a little church down here in Pinellas Park." On that occasion Dr. and Mrs. Roberson stayed in a motel, planning to leave at 5:30 AM – driving, as always.

When Lee Roberson was 92 years old, I asked him if he ever had any hobbies. "No," he said. "I didn't do much. I just did two things all my life – the church, being a pastor; the meetings outside – usually Monday and Tuesday I'd be gone. I did it every year." He reportedly golfed in his younger years, but no one could remember with whom or when. He simply did not have the time or the interest for hobbies.

Lee and Caroline Roberson always had breakfast at home together every morning at 6:30. She would fix him bacon, sausage and eggs. He liked Tabasco sauce on scrambled eggs. The Robersons set up a buzzer connected to their bedroom, so she could signal him from the kitchen when breakfast was ready. She would simply press the buzzer in the kitchen, and he would know that breakfast was ready. He would set a newspaper at the side of his plate, read the Bible, and pray. When Dr. Roberson finished breakfast, he would put a portion of his eggs and sausage out for the dog. At his father's funeral John Roberson told the crowd that in later years he found breakfast a good time to visit his dad.

Often Dr. and Mrs. Roberson would go out to restaurants together to eat. Dr. Roberson would try to avoid a restaurant which served liquor – if he could help it. If he were a guest of someone else, as he traveled, he would not make an issue of it. However, rumor had it that he knocked a beer bottle off a table once when someone tried to serve it to him. On a missions trip in Cuernavaca, Mexico, he was not happy when a fancy restaurant tried to serve him a gratuitous drink at the end of the meal. Lee and Caroline Roberson were quite content at Shoney's in Chattanooga – "That's the best place to eat," he would say. During the years she was his secretary, Dorothy McCormick enjoyed the frequent opportunities of eating out with Dr. and Mrs. Roberson – usually at Shoney's. Later the Robersons enjoyed Ryan's or the Cracker Barrel. For years he was seen most often at Wally's Restaurant. As he traveled, he often preferred to eat at McDonald's. Late in life the Robersons would not wait in line at a cafeteria after church. They were happy to pick up their food at McDonald's or Hardee's and take it home.

"You could not take Dr. Roberson to a fancy restaurant," said E.C. Haskell, Jr. "He just would be so uncomfortable. Take him to Friday's or Shoney's. Dr. (John R.) Rice was the same way. We had a *Sword of the Lord* Conference, and a group of preachers – I was there – were invited to a really nice, swanky restaurant. Dr. Rice sat there, ordered a (soft) drink – but not from the menu. He could not bring himself to spend that much money, even though he wasn't speaking. Dr. Roberson was the same way." Missionary Frank Rosser saw the same side of Roberson. No matter what steakhouse you took him to – he never wanted to go anywhere fancy, and he always ordered something simple like a hamburger. Rosser believed that he wanted to avoid any criticism of extravagance as a preacher. When Dr. Roberson preached for me in Bay City, Michigan, in the early 1990s, I asked him if I could take him out after the Sunday evening service. I would have taken him to the finest restaurant in town, but he asked to go to the little McDonald's right next to his motel. As we talked, he ordered a hamburger and coffee.

Roberson's favorite meals were fried chicken or roast beef or cornbread casserole – always with coffee. He liked coffee with cream for every meal – never soda pop or water. At home he liked to tease. He would take the hot spoon from the coffee and touch the back of someone's hand – either one of the kids or their mother. At Christmas, Sheila Wharram made an English trifle dessert, which he loved. And always he loved Caroline's pumpkin pie – later made by daughter LeeAnne from her mother's same recipe. He liked Russell Stover candy – often sticking his finger in a couple of pieces until he found one he liked!

On one occasion Dr. Roberson enjoyed it when a church in Richmond, Virginia, surprised him with a birthday celebration. After speaking on a weekday morning, he was invited to a luncheon with 60 pastors. On a pre-arranged signal, Orman Norwood brought Roberson in, and the preachers sang, *Happy Birthday*. Roberson conducted a 30-minute question-and-answer session for the pastors and then sat down to lunch. The church had prepared a huge birthday cake in the shape of a Bible with Roberson's life verse, Romans 8:28, inscribed with frosting. In his 90s, Dr. Roberson was scheduled to preach for me in Tampa on his birthday. Clarence Sexton called me and asked if we could trade dates. I acquiesced, as Clarence wanted to plan a huge birthday celebration for Dr. Roberson in Knoxville, Tennessee.

College students used to marvel at how trim Dr. Roberson stayed – never putting on weight no matter how much he traveled or how many banquets he attended. "He was strictly disciplined in his eating," said Dorothy McCormick. "The night he would come back into town (from traveling), he would go to his study with an apple." Lee Roberson rarely ate between meals. He would carry apples for a snack when traveling. He did not eat before preaching. But always he was gracious as a guest. Late in the 1990s when Dr. Roberson preached at my church in Tampa, after the Sunday evening service I planned a fellowship meal for all our Tennessee Temple students, graduates, and parents. He briefly addressed about 30 of us, and then he and Mrs. Roberson sat down with us and enjoyed the meal and the fellowship.

When Dr. Roberson traveled, Caroline would pack his suitcase. She would pack little snacks, such as chocolate kisses, along with little personal notes. He liked Hershey's kisses. When the Robersons traveled together, Dorothy McCormick would stay with June, when she was young. When she was older, June would look after the house. June would also leave for her dad Hershey's chocolate kisses. On the road, Dr. and Mrs. Roberson would leave their motel in the morning for a walk – she in casual walking clothes, and he in a navy blue double-breasted suit.

At home Lee Roberson sometimes liked to relax by reading a book or watching TV – or even studying or dictating letters. "He doesn't really know how to relax as such," said Sheila Wharram. He did not watch a lot of TV or listen to the radio very much. "I rarely turned on the radio except to listen to a church program," Roberson told me. "We never watched TV very much – never did have much time." He loved to read, and at times he liked to watch television at home. He would lie in bed at night, with a book in hand, a yellow legal pad at his side, and the TV turned on – with his glasses down his nose, so he could see the TV as he read. He would sometimes watch ballgames – primarily basketball or football. His favorite teams were major league baseball's Atlanta Braves and college basketball's Indiana Hoosiers and Louisville Cardinals. And Lee Roberson liked TV westerns – especially *Gunsmoke*. He was a fan of John Wayne. Caroline Roberson loved to read mysteries and would watch her favorite TV shows – *Murder She Wrote* and *Columbo*. They would also watch *Larry King Live* together. And Dr. Roberson always enjoyed music and was pleased when people would sometimes bring him a CD or a tape.

Lee Roberson liked books and read constantly. Normally he did not sit in the living room or the kitchen to read. He kept his books in the bedroom or in his study, where they would be setting around everywhere – even on the floor. Mrs. Roberson once told a ladies' group that her husband had nine books open in their house at one time – in the bathroom, bedroom, kitchen, etc. Everywhere he would go, he would be reading. Besides his constant reading of theological and spiritual books, Roberson enjoyed reading about such historical figures as England's Winston Churchill and Margaret Thatcher. He admired the courageous stands that Mrs. Thatcher took. He loved the English and Scottish writers and enjoyed reading works of the preacher Charles Spurgeon. He was pleased when Sheila Wharram returned from England with a book for him about Spurgeon's Metropolitan Tabernacle.

Caroline Roberson enjoyed sewing and loved to make kids' clothes for her children and later for her grandchildren. She would sew apron gifts for the church nursery workers at Christmas. She also liked flowers – especially roses.

Dr. Lee Roberson had a surprising affinity for firecrackers. On the July 4th holiday Mrs. Roberson would have to endure his setting off firecrackers in a dish in the house. And he also loved big cakes – whether for a church celebration or at home.

Roberson had a life-long interest in cars. "He always had a big, beautiful car," said his sister. He was not a mechanic, nor would he spend very much money on cars. And he did not know anything about auto racing. But he liked the looks of cars – especially red cars – and the speed. "I never came to town but he didn't ask me, 'What are you driving?'" said John Roberson. "We would pull the hood and look at the motor." He liked to drive fast. He would crawl in town, but on the open freeway he would drive fast on his way to preaching meetings. He did not care if he had to pay a few dollars in speeding tickets in order to get to where he was going. "For years he carried a deputy sheriff's badge," said Orman Norwood. "It was given to him by a policeman in school. He deputized him." In Roberson's later years as pastor emeritus of Highland Park, his office was right next door to Jerry Mattheiss, then the music director at the church. "He loves cars," Mattheiss told me in 2003. "We'll talk cars. He likes pretty cars. He likes fast cars. He likes hot-rods. I purchased a car this summer. His wife was in the hospital. I went to pick him up and take him to the hospital. 'Man, this is a hot-rod,' he said. It was an older Cadillac. 'This will go! Let's go!' That's a side of him no one knows. He would get catalogues and calendars with pictures of cars on them. 'Hey, I got something I want you to see.' We'll look through the catalogues. 'See right there!'" He liked convertibles. The church tried to give him one once, but he took it back. And someone gave him a red model car – not the kind he really liked. "You can have it when I'm gone," he told Jerry.

His son, John, always wanted to give him a Cadillac. But Dr. Roberson wanted to avoid any image of ostentation on the part of a pastor. In earlier years he drove a "fast-back" maroon Pontiac. Later he drove a Buick Park Avenue for many years. When he got a new car, he always wanted an identical maroon Park Avenue, so that no one could tell he had a new car. After he resigned the pastorate at Highland Park, John persuaded him to own a Cadillac, which he drove to meetings. However, eventually he got rid of it, as he simply felt uneasy about his image as a man of God.

Late in his life Roberson received a Lincoln Continental as a gift from First Baptist Church of Hammond, Indiana. To put the car in Dr. Roberson's name, John Stancil told him, "I need you to sign three papers for me here. I'm not at liberty to tell you what it's about. You'll just have to trust me." Roberson replied, "I've never done this in all these years, and this is not a good time to start." But Stancil insisted, "I promise you that you won't have to worry. I promise." Roberson said, "If you're not going to get me into trouble, okay." And he signed. "Now, what have I signed?" he asked. "Am I in trouble?" Stancil said again, "I'm not at liberty to tell you." Shortly thereafter the brand new Lincoln was delivered. At first Dr. Roberson did not want to drive it because it was different from his Buick Park Avenue, and he was not sure he wanted to be seen in a Lincoln – too extravagant. So, when his family finally sold his Buick anyway, he started driving Mrs. Roberson's car. Caroline called his secretary. "He stole my car!" she said with a laugh. Finally, he adjusted to the new car and enjoyed the Lincoln. In his older years, church leaders offered to provide a chauffeur for Dr. and Mrs. Roberson as he traveled to preach in meetings. He would decline. He liked to drive and resisted any effort to keep him from driving.

For awhile Roberson kept homing pigeons at his home. They were gray – the kind with short fluffy feathers growing around their heads and feet. He would feed them corn and talk to them, and friends and church members would feed them when he traveled. Caroline did not like the pigeons, as she considered them too much trouble, but Lee liked them and would smile when he talked about them. He would take his jacket off to feed them. He would give one away on occasion, and once he gave one to a Temple graduate who had a gospel magic ministry. On occasion a pigeon would escape. Finally, he gave up keeping pigeons.

From childhood Roberson always loved dogs and kept a dog. His sister, Darlene, showed me a picture of her as a little girl standing on one side of the family's large German Shepherd, and Lee Roberson as a young man standing on the other side. "He always loved dogs," said Randy Ray. "If he had a dog, he wanted you to know about it." Over the years he had a large Great Dane and later a German Shepherd – a German Shepherd named "Doc" was the family's favorite. Roberson would feed his dog in a stainless steel bowl. "It sleeps outside, Caroline says," said Darlene. As Dr. Roberson aged, he told me he found himself spoiling the dog by feeding it scraps off the table. "I don't know if I should," he said.

Lee Roberson never owned a computer or a cell phone. In fact, he did not like to talk on the telephone. He always carried a pocket knife. Bob Kelley said, "Dr. Roberson never fully got the country out of him. He loved to come to Franklin Road and sit out in the country – see the horses, the farm. He loved the Bill Rice Ranch."

Often Roberson would jingle loose change or keys in his pockets. And always he loved to work. He loved to get something done! His sister, Darlene, described him as a perfectionist.

CHAPTER 17

"Don't Limp"

The legacy of Lee Roberson's life was his unparalleled ministry at Highland Park Baptist Church and Tennessee Temple University. He served Highland Park as pastor for 40 years and six months from 1942 to 1983 – setting off a tidal wave of evangelism with an eternal impact through out the world. During those years he baptized more than 60,000 people. Tennessee Temple became the largest Bible college in America at one time. The Lee Roberson Center was built on campus in the 1970s to honor the founder. The new mammoth main auditorium of Highland Park Baptist Church, built to seat 5,850 people, was opened on Sunday, September 6, 1981. On September 14 when a chapel service was held in the new auditorium it was the first time that all the students and faculty from the kindergarten, elementary school, high school, and university met together in one building. Lee Roberson was then 71 years old. The new auditorium cost $4-million and was completely paid for shortly after its completion.

As Lee Roberson aged during his 40-and-one-half-year pastorate at Highland Park, on occasion he would tell Caroline that he was going to resign – that he felt he could not do the job anymore. Each time, he would change his mind, as he waited on the Lord. "I'd think of resigning," Roberson told me. "I'd get discouraged sometimes, but I didn't indicate it publicly. Never said a word about it – not a word about it. Kept on going – until finally it was time. I resigned

– retired at [nearly] 74. I felt like I'd done my best work here – 40 years and six months. I was a little weary of so much of the necessary things you have to do if you're a pastor. I felt led of the Lord to resign and retire fully, completely from the activity of the church altogether. I worked with the school quite actively for awhile – tried to ease my way out of it, so it wouldn't be disturbed too much."

Earlier, at age 72, Dr. Roberson was planning to resign as pastor of Highland Park Baptist Church when Dr. E.C. Haskell Sr. died. Haskell had joined Highland Park Baptist Church in 1941, the year before Roberson arrived. Shortly after Roberson's arrival, E.C. became a deacon and then later served for more than 30 years under Dr. Roberson as chairman of the Board of Deacons. A close friend of Roberson, Haskell had his pastor's complete confidence. Dr. Haskell was still practicing dentistry at age 81 when he died. More than 4,000 people went through the funeral home – with more than 100 persons telling the family that Dr. Haskell had led them to Christ. With the loss of Haskell, Dr. Roberson changed his mind about resigning, as he did not feel the timing was right to step down. He had worked very closely with Dr. Haskell. Roberson stayed on for another three years in order to help develop new lay leadership. Later he wondered if he had made a mistake by staying on.

When the time to resign finally came, Lee Roberson simply felt it was God's will. "Dr. Roberson could have stayed as long as he wanted," said Bob Kelley. "He felt his time was up. It was God's will." In his sermon, *The Right Medicine for America*, Roberson said, "I felt led of God to retire. I simply knew it was God's will. I offered my resignation at almost 75 years of age. I told my people that God had led me." He informed his deacons in advance. They were nearly finished with the building of the new auditorium and were preparing for the building dedication service when Dr. Roberson told them his plan was to see through the completion of the new building, then resign the church, and stay on with the school. Bill Mattheiss, then a deacon, recalled his words, "I think God's telling me it's time to move on." At the same meeting Roberson anointed J.R. Faulkner to take over as pastor.

The day when Roberson chose to announce his resignation after 40 years and six months at Highland Park Baptist Church, he permitted no celebration or festivities. Just as he had begun his ministry in Chattanooga on a Wednesday night in November of 1942, he chose the midweek service on Wednesday, April 27, 1983, to announce his resignation. Near the end of the church service he simply announced publicly that he was resigning and that in just a few minutes he was going to walk out as J.R. Faulkner would lead the church in a song. He said publicly that he would take his wife by the hand, get in the car and drive away. He wanted no talking or shaking of hands with him and his wife. He made the announcement at the end of the Wednesday evening service and walked out. He did not stay around to talk with anyone. Lee Roberson took his wife of 50 years by the hand, and the two walked out of the church together as the crowd watched. Caroline Roberson had a slight limp. Her husband leaned over and gently whispered, "Don't limp." He wanted to leave with dignity. In the silent crowd, security chief Bill Long's 10-year-old daughter started crying. She whispered to her father, "This is like losing someone in the family."

Soon thereafter Dr. Roberson was named "pastor emeritus" by Highland Park Baptist Church – a title he retained to the end of his life. He always maintained an office at the church. He also held the title "chancellor" and later "chancellor emeritus" of Tennessee Temple until the day he died.

Roberson was 73 years old when he resigned Highland Park. By the end of his life nearly one-quarter century later, he had 10 grandchildren and 13 great-grandchildren. His grandchildren recognized that they did not have the type of grandfather who was going to retire to a front porch rocking chair. Roberson's sermon, *Caleb's Old-Age Pension*, was published in 1999 in a book entitled, *The Big 90* (Roberson's age then). In the sermon, Roberson exclaimed, "It is good to see our mountains and determine to conquer them. As a man of 85, Caleb moved forward. He found no time to stop. What is the thing that God wants you to do? Have you ceased in your activity because of age or perhaps because of infirmity? Caleb might have taken his old-age pension and sat down to do nothing, but he did not. He said, 'I want to press forward, conquer the enemy, and secure this land.'"

Roberson marveled at the ministry God gave him traveling weekly to preach all over America after the resignation. When he resigned at Highland Park, he did not know what the future held for him – but the invitations to preach around the country just kept coming. These unsolicited invitations charted his future. With his wife's assistance, he would handle the booking and scheduling of his meetings himself. He was in demand in conservative Baptist circles – preaching more than 100 meetings per year in his 70s, 80s, and 90s. Most of the meetings were two-day meetings; some were three days; and, some were longer. Roberson's book of sermons, *Preaching to America*, was published in 1999. The back of the book lists 15 pages of more than 1,800 cities in America where Dr. Roberson preached between 1983 and 1998 in the 15 years following his retirement from the pastorate. That was an average of 118 sermons per year for a man who was then between 75 and 90 years of age. It was estimated that he preached some 3,000 sermons between his retirement from Highland Park Baptist Church in 1983 and his death in 2007. "I do it because I like it," Roberson told me in his early 90s. "I enjoy what I'm doing very, very much. I think I can still help some people maybe by going to churches – help the pastor and his people. Not trying to get a name – not trying to get money. If they pay my expenses, fine. If not, I don't say a thing and go on my way. When I retired at 75, I thought perhaps I was right near the close of my life. The Lord has kept me here. I keep on going."

On occasion Ben Haden would cross paths with Lee Roberson at the airport. Haden, who retired from First Presbyterian in 1998 and continued to operate his TV ministry out of Chattanooga, marveled at Roberson's energy. When Roberson was in his 90s, Haden said, with a chuckle, "I laugh every time I see him in an airport. He has the energy of a man in his 20s. Just keeps on keeping on!" Evangelist Ed Carter would run into Roberson at the airport. "I never did see him pick up his luggage," noted Carter. "They must have had someone from the college run out and get it. Immediately he was gone."

For many years, as he preached around the nation, Roberson traveled by air. He quit flying in the late 1990s when he was in his late 80s. "I didn't like to fly," Roberson said. "So, I began driving." His secretary, Gloria Shadowens, remembered his decision. At his age, he missed a connection and spent a night sitting in an airport. "When he finally got home," she recalled, "he said, 'I'm not flying anymore.' It was just too hard on him. And he hasn't. He never flies." His decision curtailed traveling to preach in some meetings – such as the West Coast. But he would still drive as far as Florida, Oklahoma or Texas. Before he would leave for a meeting, Gloria would fill the trunk of his car with books of his sermons to sell.

After years of traveling to preach, Roberson was a member of the million-mile flying club and could have flown for free. "He doesn't like to fly," said Faulkner. "He wouldn't ride first class." He enjoyed the change to driving. He loved to see the countryside.

Mrs. Roberson would travel with him. Gloria Shadowens would map the trip. Dr. Roberson would drive, following his wife's directions. Caroline was his co-pilot and navigator. On one occasion, Dr. Roberson asked Jerry Mattheiss for directions. "I started to tell him," Jerry remembered with a laugh, "and he said, 'No, you tell her,' and pointed at his wife. She's the navigator, he said. So, I started telling her. She said, 'Why are you telling me? He won't listen to me.' So, I followed them to make sure they got it right." They all laughed about it.

When Mrs. Roberson was hospitalized, Jerry visited the Robersons in the hospital room. It was evident that Dr. Roberson was tired, but he would not leave Caroline's side. Mrs. Roberson insisted that Dr. Roberson go with Jerry and take a break from her bedside. Jerry recalled, "He said, 'I don't have a thing to do.' I said, 'Yes, Gloria has some papers for you to sign.' Mrs. Roberson said, 'You need to go.' He got ready to go. I said, 'Dr. Roberson, I've known you 50 years. I've never seen anyone tell you what to do until now.' He said, 'She tells me all the time.' They just laughed!"

Besides preaching in the regular church services wherever he traveled, Roberson would typically give a lecture to all the church's Sunday school staff one hour prior to the Sunday evening service. If he were sharing the pulpit in a conference, he was always gracious and deferential to the other speakers. Les Frazier of BIMI preached a missions conference for Pastor Max Barton in Greenville, North Carolina, with Dr. Roberson. Frazier developed and explained the "Faith Promise" missions program for the church, and Roberson was the main speaker. Frazier found Roberson, then over 90 years of age, completely engaged and involved in the entire conference – panel discussions, questions from students, etc. "I was challenged," said Frazier. "He was gracious and humble. He would defer to me on the time and opportunity. He would step back. He was a great man."

In later years as Roberson continued to age, he seemed to lose some of the projection – his booming voice – from the pulpit. But his sermons remained clear and understandable – with very little repetition even into his mid-90s. Always there continued to be a straight, clear presentation of the gospel. "The message is still the same," Cliff Robinson said then. "It doesn't change – not chasing any rabbits." But eventually, on occasion he would be more forgetful. For example, one ministry anniversary celebration, he was asked to lead in public prayer, and he proceeded to pray for the building – as if it were a building dedication. No one cared. Everyone was just glad he was there!

Late in his life, Roberson also shortened his sermons – often preaching just 10 or 12 minutes. In his early 90s when Dr. Roberson preached for me at Temple Heights Baptist Church in Tampa, we were broadcasting our Sunday morning services live on the radio. Our morning worship hour would start with an informal song service at 10:50 AM, and then we would go on the air live from 11:00 AM to 12:00 noon. During the service, Dr. Roberson was introduced to preach by 11:30 AM, giving him approximately a half-hour before we went off the air. To my surprise, he preached less than 15 minutes and was finished by 11:45. Our radio attendant had to scramble to telephone the station to inform them that we were going off the air early! Thereafter, when Dr. Roberson returned to our church, I would plan the service accordingly.

In the Sunday evening service, Dr. Roberson asked me to hand out 3x5 index cards to the congregation for the people to write prayer requests on the cards. During the invitation at the end of the service, people were invited to come forward and place the cards with their written prayer requests on the communion table in front of the pulpit. Dr. and Mrs. Roberson then collected the cards of prayer requests and took them back to their room at the Holiday

Inn on Fowler Avenue, where they prayed over each written prayer request.

Roberson preached the last quarter century of his life each Christmas for Pastor David Bragg at Lakewood Baptist Church in Harrison, Tennessee, just outside Chattanooga. Bragg was the director of Camp Joy for 30 years. While Dr. Roberson slowed down physically, Bragg said, "In the pulpit, he was a different person. He came alive. That was his domain."

The older Dr. Roberson got, the more his family and friends worried about his driving. After flying for years, he turned entirely to driving – partly so his wife could accompany him. As he aged, people would offer to drive for him, but he would not hear of it. And he did not like delays. On one occasion he left Oklahoma City in the middle of a blizzard. It concerned the host pastor, Jim Vineyard. "Mrs. Roberson was visibly shook," said Vineyard. "I tried to talk him out of it." Temple alumni would offer to drive for him, but Roberson knew what he wanted to do – he wanted to keep driving himself. And he would not slow down. When Roberson was in his 90s, he passed Jerry Mattheiss on the freeway. Mattheiss was driving the speed limit of 70 mph. "I had to speed up to catch him," said Jerry. "It was him!"

As his short term memory slipped with age, Dr. Roberson would depend on Caroline for directions. But he continued to do all the driving. In his 90s, on one occasion when they arrived in Tampa for services at my church, the Robersons got lost. I received a phone call from a gas station attendant and went quickly to guide them to the motel. But his preaching was always sharp and clear.

While he was in Illinois to preach at a Baptist church, a thief broke into his car and took his books and Bible from the motel parking lot. Mrs. Roberson said she had never seen him so upset. He wanted to turn around and go home. But he didn't.

Gloria Shadowens, his secretary for the last quarter century of his life, was amazed that his work schedule was just like it was when he was still pastor of the church. He would come to the office daily – bringing dictation with him. He would study, make calls, meet people, and continually write new sermons. "Today he came in," she once told me. "He said, 'Last night I thought of this – Yes or No.

I might call it the Yes or No sermon. When you say Yes to Christ, you say No to the devil. When you say No to the devil, you say Yes to God.'"

Before God called him into the ministry, Jim Vineyard was a green beret in the U.S. Special Forces. One time in later years Dr. Roberson decided to get his wife a handgun, to help ensure her safety at home while he was traveling. He asked Vineyard to teach her how to shoot it – a .22 pistol. Roberson recounted the story with hilarity from the pulpit how Mrs. Roberson accidentally shot out the overhead lights at the indoor shooting range. Jim Vineyard and Lee Roberson decided it was probably best for Mrs. Roberson *not* to have a gun.

To the end of his life, Lee Roberson maintained an extraordinary respect from those who knew him. "I don't think there is anyone in fundamentalism who doesn't respect him," said Bob Kelley. A number of preachers told me they kept every letter he ever sent them. Many a preacher has a file folder of such letters.

"Dr. Roberson will always be my hero," stated Ron Bishop. "At the time I came to Temple he was like 'God.' I don't say that in a way to worship him. I knew when I was in his presence I was in the presence of the Lord because God's hand was upon him." Bishop always treasured his relationship with Dr. Roberson. Late in Roberson's life, Bishop was honored to receive a $500 check from Roberson for a Score International mission project.

Roberson's followers were not used to hearing anyone call him anything but "Dr. Roberson." It sounded strange – and made people laugh about it – to hear his wife or someone from his past refer to him as "Lee." Even J.R. Faulkner would refer to him in the third person as "Doctor." The generation of preachers the ages of Jerry Falwell and Jack Hyles looked up to Dr. Roberson. As Lee Roberson out-lived most of his generation, finally, in the minds of many, he had no peer remaining but John Rawlings. One preacher told me that Rawlings was the only man he had ever heard call Dr. Roberson by his first name, Lee. Ron Bishop heard Claude Martin give a testimony late in Martin's life. As a young man, Claude was the boy who brought Lee Roberson to Sunday school for the first time. "Claude Martin was the only man I ever heard call him 'Lee,'" said Bishop.

From the early years, Garland Cofield also remembered a Southern Baptist song evangelist named Homer Britt. "He was about the same age as Dr. Roberson," said Garland. "He really liked him. Homer's the only man I ever heard call him 'Lee.'" Clyde Box said he personally called other preachers by their first name, as they did him – men like Jack Hyles, Bob Gray, or Curtis Hutson – but never Lee Roberson. Out of respect, it was always "Dr. Roberson," Box said.

Like every great leader, Lee Roberson was to some extent a child of his times – influenced and affected by the cultural events of his day. He assured me that he always stayed focused on the Lord's work – no matter what happened in the world around him – including World War II, the cultural and social upheavals of the 1960s, the Vietnam War, etc.

Looking back over his ministry, Roberson told me that he had no regrets. In one interview, Roberson indicated that if he were starting his ministry over again, he would give more emphasis "to the individual." He said, "I might have encouraged more young people if I had dealt with them personally or in small groups."

A gifted musician, Roberson never permitted the music in his ministry to change from the traditional style. J.R. Faulkner pointed out, "When he left, this contemporary stuff we're getting so much of now had not started then – you know, the Nashville sound. We didn't have that, but we had great congregational singing." Roberson did not embrace modern, contemporary Christian music – even in later years. Musician Jerry Mattheiss said, "I talked to him a lot about music. He won't fuss about different styles of music. I know he has his own tastes. If he were (still) a pastor, it would be a certain style. But he's not going to throw bricks at someone because they're doing something else. He has told me, 'Jerry, I've preached behind some stuff you wouldn't believe. But you just do your best and go on.'"

Lee Roberson remained old-fashioned and unchanging in his beliefs and the way in which he practiced his ministry. He never wavered from his view of separation – that a Christian should not smoke or drink, attend movies, or play cards; that women should not wear pants and certainly not be ordained; that men should have short hair; that the King James Bible should be used. One preacher told me, "Dr. Roberson was an innovator and a pioneer. But as he got older, he didn't want to change. I heard him preach against 6:00 (starting time) Sunday evening services. He feared people wanted to get home early just to watch TV." Roberson would complain about the effect society's changing dress habits was having on the church. During the later years of his pastorate, if he saw a lady wearing slacks in church, he would complain, "I saw a girl dressed like a man." Jean Smith said affectionately, "He didn't like anything that was change. He did not like change. He wanted everything exactly the way it was when he came there in 1942. He didn't want anything to change." Nat Phillips added, "I really don't believe the way he operated here from the 1940s to the 1980s would work as well now." One close family friend told me late in Dr. Roberson's life, "In some sense, he's a lonely person. I see that more now later in his life. He expects everything to be like it was 20 or 30 years ago – the same at Highland Park Baptist Church."

But a number of his friends said Roberson mellowed some through the years – with the changing culture. Max Helton taught at Hyles-Anderson College years before launching the nondenominational Motor Racing Outreach ministry. Helton, who always remained close to Lee Roberson, was convinced that the strict separatist position of other fundamental colleges had pushed Dr. Roberson and Tennessee Temple further to the right than Roberson actually wanted to go. Before launching MRO, Helton started a new church in upscale White Plains, outside New York City. One of Max's neighbors, who was one of the wealthiest lawyers in New York, invited Max and his wife to a neighborhood cocktail party at their house. Everything Max had ever known gravitated against going to a cocktail party, but he wanted to befriend and reach his neighbors with the gospel. He wanted to meet them and not make them feel rejected by his Christian standards. So, he called Dr. Roberson and asked him what he should do. Max never forgot Roberson's advice. Dr. Roberson instructed Helton that Jesus went among "winebibbers" and that Max should go. So, he went. My first 20 years in the pastorate were in the Midwest. When I accepted the call to a Florida church in 1997, Dr. Roberson told me point-blank that I could not maintain in Florida the same kind of personal standards of separation that I had preached in the Midwest as a pastor. He did not elaborate on what he meant, but I never forgot it.

Dr. Roberson was opposed to the widely adopted modern concept of pageants, dramas, and cantatas in church. In his day, on Easter Sunday he just preached. In later years he did not change his philosophy on how to build a Sunday school. He did not think biblical methodology changed with the times. He told me he believed the philosophy he used in the 1940s and 1950s would work today. Jerry Mattheiss was with Dr. Roberson late in Roberson's life when he preached in Panama City, Florida. The crowd was large, and a number of people were saved. On the drive with Dr. and Mrs. Roberson back to the motel, Jerry noticed tears and asked Roberson what was wrong. "It works," he said. "It works. If you get lost people there – under the preaching of the gospel, they will get saved. It still works."

In May of 2002, Dr. Roberson reiterated to me, "I think people are about the same. They'll respond. They're hungering for something. They're looking for it. They're looking for reality. Any man can do the job – who will go at it with his whole heart, plan, pray, and keep on doing things, anywhere you put him, if he wants to. But most preachers I meet are not quite willing to do the things that should be done – three big services a week. They don't quite see that. I tell them, you're making a mistake. Make Wednesday night a big thing. Have the choir sing on Wednesday night. Take an offering. Preach a sermon. Give an invitation on Wednesday night. I did it for 40 years – every Wednesday. Build the Sunday night big – just like Sunday morning. Use the choir. Three times a week. They make Sunday morning big. Sunday night is second. Wednesday night is not important. They don't see the importance of building a big Wednesday night prayer hour. They don't do much of that. My people got to visiting a lot, and we kept on going – 30 to 40 people a week coming down the aisle saved. It'll work the same way today."

Dr. Roberson's approach to church building never changed. In 2002 he told me that for someone starting out in ministry today, "I'd build my church. I'd make it whatever you want – evangelism, or Bible-teaching, or whatever. Give yourself to it. I'd try to stay on that one track – the thing you want to get done. Me? I'd try evangelism – Sunday morning, Sunday night, Wednesday night – the same way all the time. I'd baptize at the end of every service."

When Dr. Roberson preached for Pastor Tony Hutson in Murfreesboro, Tennessee, Tony asked him why churches were no longer seeing as many people saved like in days of the past. "He dropped his fork – with a clang," recalled Hutson. "He looked at me eyeball-to-eyeball. He said, 'One of two things is wrong.' Up until now he had been talking softly and light-heartedly. Now he was talking with authority. 'No. 1, the gospel has lost its power, or, No. 2, you're not putting the gospel out like you ought to.'"

Roberson preached for Hutson on a special Sunday promoting the bus ministry. The service included a large, energetic choir of 9- to-10 year olds singing on the platform, a big expectant crowd in the main auditorium, and an exciting atmosphere of anticipation. At age 92, Dr. Roberson was sitting on the front row with Mrs. Roberson. Tony worried that the excitement and events of the day would be too strenuous for the Robersons and that perhaps they would not relate to all the kids. He need not have worried. Hutson said, "Dr. Roberson got up. 'Man,' he said, 'this is exciting. This place is alive.' He preached for 30 minutes, then he went to the invitation and gave an altar call for 45 minutes. People would start to leave the altar. He would call them down. 'You can't do business with God in two minutes.' Then he went down the row at the altar. 'Give a testimony and tell what God has done for you.' Even Mrs. Roberson was at the altar. He pointed at her, 'What have you come for? What are you praying for?' She said, 'I'm praying for an unsaved nephew, a doctor.' It was exhilarating, exciting. He would help them out – not trying to embarrass anyone. He was very much in charge. He was very vigorous."

"Dr. Roberson did not worry about what people thought," recounted Bob Kelley. "He did it his way in his time in his era. He did have the fortune to pastor during the years a man could build a church. It was not unusual to see 20 to 25 adults saved and down the aisle. I saw them. It's a different day and age now. His was not the day of comfort and convenience like it is today."

Lee Roberson just never changed. Roberson was in his 90s when Glen Swygart attended a birthday celebration for Roberson. "I was standing by the door," Glenn said. "I saw Dr. Roberson go outside in the rain. There stood a man from the mission – just recently saved. I saw Dr. Roberson standing there with his arm on his shoulder praying with him."

After Lee Roberson's resignation at Highland Park in 1983, J.R. Faulkner, who was aging himself, became the pastor and served for two years while the church looked for a permanent successor. The church continued strong under Faulkner's leadership – with the building packed out with people. In the fall revival meetings of 1984 the ushers had to put out 1,200 chairs to hold the crowd.

A number of Dr. Roberson's protégés were considered as the next pastor, but some of the church leaders felt there should be a change. J. Don Jennings, a friend of the ministry, but not one of Roberson's preacher boys, was called as pastor. Jennings served five years. After Roberson resigned, change at Highland Park was inevitable. Lee Roberson never liked change. During Jennings' five years, he changed the Sunday school system. When Jennings resigned, J.R. Faulkner became the interim pastor. "Dr. Roberson wanted me to change it back the very first week Dr. Jennings left," Faulkner remembered with a laugh. "'Now, Brother Faulkner, let's straighten out the Sunday school.' I got a note from him. But I didn't touch it. You're in the process of calling a pastor. If I change now, then the new pastor comes – he may jerk the people around again. That would not be good. The best thing for us to do is pour oil on the water and win souls between now and the time you call a new pastor."

Again, as when Dr. Roberson resigned, various names of some of his preacher boys were floated around – men like Paul Dixon, Bob Kelley, Bradley Price, Randy Ray, or Clarence Sexton. Some Roberson intimates surmised that he personally wanted Clarence Sexton, but Sexton did not believe it was God's will for him. And one long-time church member pointed out to me, "That would not have worked – too strict!" Bob Kelley was scheduled to preach "in view of a call," but he canceled out due to his struggling personal health. Randy Ray was invited by the deacons to come as a candidate but did not feel it was God's will for him. Finally, the chairman of the pulpit committee, Dr. Barkev Trachian, guided the selection committee to David Bouler, who became the pastor of Highland Park Baptist Church on August 18, 1991.

To the end of his life, Dr. Roberson kept an office at Highland Park Baptist Church as pastor emeritus of the church and chancellor of Tennessee Temple University. He would speak occasionally in the college chapel, raise money for the school and participate regularly in such university activities as commencement. As Roberson continued to travel and preach, he never seemed to change one iota. He remained the same as he had always been – straight down the line. When he was in Chattanooga, he would check the church hospital list daily and call on the older church members whom he knew. He would send out letters and notes of encouragement by the hundreds. Bill Long saved 17 such letters. And Roberson stayed involved in the lives of the older church members. Dr. and Mrs. Roberson showed up on the 96th birthday of Jean Smith's mother, who was a long-time member of Highland Park.

When E.C. Haskell Jr.'s mother died at age 90, E.C. asked Dr. Roberson to conduct the funeral. When Haskell informed the funeral home that Dr. Roberson was going to preach the service, there was silence on the phone. Then the funeral director gently enquired, "You do realize he's 94 years old, don't you?" Haskell answered, "Yes." Roberson was actually preaching a meeting in Florida at the time and had to drive back to Chattanooga to preside at the funeral. At age 94, he did just fine – much to the relief of the funeral director.

Roberson's presence surely continued to cast a long shadow over Highland Park Baptist Church. "He stayed out of the way," observed Faulkner. "He stayed on the road. He started doing what he wanted to do. He would drive in, change his clothes, and he was gone again – always promoting the college, always positive. I don't think he ever gave Dr. Jennings a bad day when he was here. If he did, nobody ever knew about it. He never opened his mouth."

Lee Roberson had served Highland Park a period of 40 years from 1942 to 1983. With the ministry transition following the retirement of a legendary leader, complaints about change were inevitable. David Bouler recalled that when people would complain to Roberson about changes which Bouler had brought into the church, Roberson would point at Bouler and tell them that Bouler is the man who is in charge now. Bouler, a great admirer of Roberson, went early in his new pastorate to Roberson's office and asked Roberson to lay hands on him and pray for him. Later at Roberson's funeral, Bouler celebrated the fact publicly that Highland Park Baptist Church was still standing for and proclaiming the same gospel truth that Roberson had always championed.

Throughout his later years Lee Roberson continued to minister to his friends around the country. When Marlene Evans died, her husband, Dr. Wendell Evans, received five letters from Dr. Roberson over the month following her death. "I have every letter he's written me," said Evans. "He's a tremendous letter writer."

In his sermon, *Have Faith in God*, Roberson reflected, "In a recent meeting an audience member asked me, 'What is the one thing that has kept you going for over 70 years?' Without a moment's hesitation, I answered, 'Faith in God.' If I keep my eyes on the Lord, I can keep going."

In 2001, J.R. Faulkner received a short letter from Lee Roberson. It read, "I wish we could do it all again."

CHAPTER 18

I Promise

Lee Roberson never lost his focus on serving God. In his sermon, *Seven Words to Live By*, published in 1994, he said, "I made a promise to God when I got saved at age 14. Nobody asked me to. I just decided that was what I wanted. 'I'll never miss a service in church for the rest of my life unless I'm ill.' I am now almost 85, and I have not missed a service since I was 14, except when I was in the hospital – not Sunday morning, Sunday night, nor Wednesday night. I have been overseas, and I have been around the world, but I have not missed a service. I promised God, 'I'll give a tithe all my life,' and I have. God has kept His Word to me, and I have kept my promise to Him. I promised God to read the Bible every day, and I have done it for all these years. And I have prayed every day."

And Lee Roberson never lost his burden for souls. In 2004, when he was 95 years of age, he was asked to give the closing prayer at a meeting with the International Board of Jewish Missions in Chattanooga. He walked to the pulpit and declared, "I want to say one word – hell. Men are dying and going to hell. We must reach them." And then with tears streaming down the cheeks of his face, he offered the closing prayer.

And he never quit serving God. He once proposed, "Let your goal be big enough to challenge you all the days of your life." Within days of his death, he was still making plans for what he could yet do for the cause of Christ. When Lee Roberson was in his 90s, his sister, Darlene, told me on a Saturday, "He doesn't think he's slowing down. He doesn't want to be. Buddy [Nichols] says his preaching's fine. The sermons are all good – but he's a little on the forgetful side. She [Mrs. Roberson] says to me he's a little depressed because they hadn't gotten him a church to preach tomorrow. He doesn't want to sit back. So, I guess he'll die with his boots on."

Because of his advancing age, the day came when his family wanted him to cancel his meetings and to stop driving. "He wouldn't hear it," one friend said. "He just dies if he's not preaching." When Roberson preached for me in Tampa at age 91, Mrs. Roberson said to me then, "If Lee were to quit traveling and preaching, he would die."

During Roberson's last years, missionary Ray Thompson would often take him to the barber shop. The barber told Thompson that he felt like he was cutting the hair of Moses. Thompson had wondered if Dr. Roberson would take off his double-breasted suit coat at the barber shop – to get a hair-cut. He did.

Like Roberson, J.R. Faulkner was also slowing down. Faulkner was no longer preaching much due to failing eyesight. Occasionally he would be invited to an independent Baptist or Southern Baptist church in the Chattanooga area, and he would go and share a new poem he had written. As he sat with me in his office, he laughed at his frustration with the computer. "I joked with Dr. Roberson," he smiled. "I wish we could do it all over again – but still without computers."

Lee Roberson and J.R. Faulkner continued to keep regular office hours in their 80s and 90s. Faulkner was 88 when he told me in his office, "Brother Wigton, I can't turn loose. It's the hardest thing in the world! To think that I could be in here as long as I have – I come over here and sit with not one thing in the world to do but dream or think of a poem. Nobody cracking the whip or nobody looking for me. I think, why don't you stay at home and do something. I sit home a day, and I feel like I've spent it. I'll tell you – put in 50 years to this place, seven days a week."

And neither Roberson nor Faulkner missed an opportunity to minister in a church. When I visited J.R. Faulkner in his office in 2004, he had just returned from the 50th anniversary of Community

Baptist Church up on Signal Mountain outside Chattanooga. The church had been started in March of 1954 in a renovated chicken coop. The pastor, then a young man named Morgan, was a student at Tennessee Temple. He began the church as a chapel out of Highland Park Baptist Church. In 1954 Faulkner had helped him open the new church. They painted the chicken coop, put in pews, refurbished the building, and started the church. A lady owned the property and deeded it to Highland Park Baptist Church. Years later, Pastor Morgan and the church asked Dr. Roberson to deed the property permanently to Community Baptist Church. At Dr. Roberson's direction, Highland Park did so. Community Baptist was averaging 100 in attendance on its 50th anniversary, and Pastor Morgan was completing 50 years at the same church. And J.R. Faulkner, who had been there at the beginning, was there to commemorate the golden anniversary of the church.

In one of our last interviews, I asked Dr. Roberson if he had any regrets. He replied simply, "Not on the church here. No. I don't have regrets over what I did. I gave three invitations every week. I baptized every week I was here for years. I have some personally – maybe some things I could have done personally. They're not too important to other people. But I've enjoyed it." He knelt by his desk, took my hand and asked me to pray. Then, as I walked to the door, he said, "God bless you, brother. Keep going! Hammer away!"

In 2005, Caroline Roberson became seriously ill and was hospitalized. During the days when she was in the hospital, Lee Roberson was at her side constantly. He would not leave without kissing her good-bye. He did not want to go to the house without her. When everyone insisted that he take a break, he would go home, take a nap, and then call her. Caroline did not want Lee to know how badly she was doing physically. She would say, "I feel terrible, but don't tell my husband."

Caroline Allen Roberson died on Sunday morning, June 26, 2005, at age 89. As always, she had laid everything out on the Saturday night before to prepare breakfast for her husband on Sunday morning. Early in the morning Dr. Roberson knew something was wrong. He dialed 9-1-1, and an ambulance was dispatched to take her to the hospital. Then he called his son-in-law, Buddy Nichols, who took him to join her at the hospital. Shortly thereafter the doctors told him that she was gone.

Dr. Roberson planned the memorial service for his wife. A close friend and one of Dr. Roberson's preacher boys, Clarence Sexton, pastor of Temple Baptist Church in the Knoxville suburb of Powell, Tennessee, conducted the funeral service at Highland Park Baptist Church in Chattanooga on the following Wednesday, June 29. Sexton preached a marvelous funeral message regarding Mrs. Roberson's life, from Psalm 90:17, entitled, *The Lady with the Beauty of the Lord*. Sexton pointed out, "She never lost interest in the work of the Lord and in the life of her husband." David Bouler, J.R. Faulkner and Cliff Robinson each spoke briefly, and Jean Smith sang Caroline Roberson's favorite hymn, *Blessed Assurance*. After Dr. Roberson gave a short testimony, Walter Wendelken closed in prayer. Memorial contributions were designated for Camp Joy.

At the close of the hour-long funeral, Lee Roberson spoke for about six minutes as he offered "testimony" about his wife. At age 95, his words were remarkably sharp. He stood behind a microphone beside her casket on the main floor in front of the church platform, where he had preached so many times. Warm and positive, he spoke with dignity and clarity. He told how the Lord "led me to the one I should marry." He said that all he had ever done through Highland Park Baptist Church had been accomplished after he had first consulted his wife and prayed with her before proceeding. He sought her advice and suggestions – "most of which were followed completely," he said. "I listened. I owe everything to my wife from the human side for her blessings, her help, and her grace." Her advice, he said, was "invaluable." Roberson described his wife as a "remarkable woman – quiet, genteel, gracious, wise." Roberson said that while his wife did not like to speak in public, she had a hand in everything which happened in his ministry. Lee and Caroline Roberson were married for 68 years.

During the two years following Caroline's home-going, Lee Roberson's preaching opportunities became fewer and fewer. Advancing age and declining health slowed him down. Years earlier in his sermon, *America – Where Are Thy Gods?*, Dr. Roberson had said, "I have only one life. Maybe I'm not doing what I ought to do.

But, oh, I pray every day, 'O God, let me use this one day in the best way.' I've got eternity! I've got heaven awaiting me! But, I've got just this one life in which to serve Him." In his sermon, *If I Should Die Before He Comes*, published in 1994, Roberson revealed that he kept a long, white envelope on his desk at home with instructions for his own funeral. The envelope was marked, "If I should die before He comes." Included, he explained, was the name of the funeral home, the participants in the funeral service, the length of the service, the music, the place of burial, etc. Later, at Roberson's funeral, his son-in-law, Buddy Nichols, pointed out that Roberson had directed and approved every part of his own funeral service.

The last sermon Lee Roberson preached in the auditorium of Highland Park Baptist Church was in the fall of 2006, from Romans 8:28, *"And we know that all things work together for good to them that love God, to them who are the called according to his purpose."* This was his life verse, adopted after the death of baby Joy.

As Lee Roberson's final days approached, he was still planning things to do and writing new sermon outlines. For several years he had warned preachers when confirming a meeting where he was to preach, "Remember my age." In other words, he was saying that by the time the date arrives for the meeting, he might not still be alive. Dr. Roberson seemed to sense when he was reaching his final days on earth. Just weeks before Dr. Roberson's death, Ray Thompson had to surprise him in order to take him to the barber, so that he would not fuss about going. Thompson picked him up for lunch one day and told him that afterward he would take him to get a haircut. Roberson replied, "Oh, I thought I'd just let the undertaker take care of that." In those final days, he had a tendency to live in the past. When they would drive past the late Fred Brown's old house, Dr. Roberson would say, "Hi, Fred!"

In Roberson's closing days, his son later described, he still had ideas and plans for what he wanted to do for the Lord. By then he was no longer able to write, so he dictated sermons he would never preach. Desiring to honor their father and continue the legacy of his ministry, Dr. Roberson's children proposed a foundation in his name a year before he died. When he read the proposal, he wrote on it, "Perfect," and signed his name. The Lee Roberson Foundation was set up "to provide financial scholarships to Christian men and women who are in college, graduate school or seminary." All board members would serve without compensation. Every dollar was to go directly to student scholarships. It was dear to Roberson's heart. Three weeks before he died, Lee Roberson shared with his son, John, "I want to be remembered not with bricks and mortar but for helping young people."

His last sermon outline was dictated on April 14, 2007 – just 15 days before he died. It was entitled, *Heaven: Man's Greatest Experience*. His outline read:

> Heaven is full of peace, joy and fulfillment.
> Heaven is full of believing men.
> Heaven is full of assured men.
> Heaven is full of resting men.
> Heaven is a promised place.
> Heaven is an assured place.
> Heaven is a place beyond the dreams of men.
> Heaven is beyond all human understanding.
> Heaven is eternity.
> Heaven is loving.
> Heaven is real.
> Heaven is God Himself.

His sermon notes included, "I have preached about Heaven for almost 80 years. The promises of God have never lost their precious appeal. The promises of God are revealed in His Word. Jesus said, '*I go to prepare a place for you.*'" It was the last sermon outline – one that he never preached – for a man who spent 79 years preaching the Word of God. On April 29, 2007, Lee Roberson went to Heaven.

Like his wife, Lee Roberson died on a Sunday morning – at 4:45 AM on April 29, 2007. A Sunday morning seemed appropriate. Word of the death of Dr. Lee Roberson quickly circled the globe. Highland Park's WDYN-FM radio station's online website was overloaded with 68,000 hits from as far away as China and India. An online "Google" of Lee Roberson's name would bring more than 950,000 queries in 1.4 seconds.

The funeral was scheduled for Thursday, May 3, at 1:00 PM. Visitation was held in the East Chapel of the Chattanooga Funeral Home at 404 S. Moore Road on Wednesday from 2:00 to 4:00 PM and 6:00 to 9:00 PM. A steady stream of hundreds of visitors came through the funeral home to pay their respects and to greet the Roberson children, and their families. Memorable family and ministry pictures graced the funeral home rooms where the long line of people passed through.

On Wednesday afternoon at 3:30 Roy Ackerle brought J.R. Faulkner to the funeral home to pay his respects. Faulkner, growing increasingly feeble at age 92, was nearly blind. He carried a cane. Ackerle assisted him. The visitation room where Lee Roberson's body lay was crowded and noisy. A long line of people were expressing condolences to the family members and were alternately crying and rejoicing over memories. As Dr. Faulkner approached the casket, the room quickly grew silent. J.R. Faulkner leaned over and placed a kiss on the face of Lee Roberson. You could have heard a pin drop.

Several years earlier, when Dr. Roberson was preaching in a church service with Bob Kelley present, Roberson stopped in the middle of his message, pointed at Kelley and said, "Bob, I want you to preach my funeral." Mrs. Roberson was present. But by the time Dr. Roberson died at 97 in April of 2007, Bob Kelley was already gone. He died at age 65 on October 28, 2006. More than once Dr. Roberson had also said he wanted his dear friend, Clyde Box, to participate in the funeral, but Box deferred when the time came. Paul Dixon, a Tennessee Temple graduate, family friend and the fabulously successful president of Cedarville University, preached the funeral message entitled, *The Man Who Walked with God*, from Genesis 5:22. He preached from Lee Roberson's Bible. His three sermon points were: 1) It was a difficult walk; 2) It was a faith walk; and, 3) It was a long walk.

The day of the funeral was warm and overcast in Chattanooga. The crowd began arriving early, with small clusters of preachers forming – from a generation influenced by Lee Roberson – and friends gathering in the parking lot and around the main auditorium of the great Highland Park Baptist Church as early as 9:00 AM, for the 1:00 PM funeral. The church was scheduled to be opened at 11:00 AM but was opened 45 minutes early due to the gathering crowd. By 1:00 Highland Park Baptist Church was packed out with more than 5,000 people present. Included in the crowd was a "Who's Who" of preachers, missionaries, and Christian leaders – primarily from the independent Baptist movement but also including Southern Baptists and others. Due to the size of the crowd, it was impossible to tell who was there in person and who was not. It was said that Jerry Falwell and Jerry Vines planned to be there. A statement by Falwell was read in public. "Lee Roberson was the founding father of today's Baptist movement," Jerry asserted. Falwell called Roberson a noble statesman and an "old war horse of the faith [who] never wavered in his bold proclamation that the crucified Christ is the only way to heaven and the only way to discover true spiritual peace." Falwell added, "No one else can touch the hem of his garment. A mighty oak has fallen." Less than two weeks later, Jerry Falwell himself was to join Lee Roberson in glory. Falwell died on May 15, 2007, at age 73.

After serving together with Lee Roberson for 58 years, J.R. Faulkner was physically unable to speak at the funeral. He walked with assistance to the side of the pulpit and stood with a cane, as Roy Ackerle read Faulkner's majestic written statement. "Never has any person been so blessed of God in being allowed to serve at the side of Dr. Lee Roberson – my dear friend and pastor," Faulkner's words declared. J.R. Faulkner received a standing ovation. As he stood weeping, before the huge crowd, he placed his hand on his heart. When Roberson and Faulkner were both in their 90s, Faulkner had made his own personal funeral arrangements. But Lee Roberson would have none of it. "No – no time for that!" he had said.

The funeral lasted three full hours – from 1:00 PM to 4:00 PM. Greetings were brought from civic officials and dignitaries. A number of preachers – including Cliff Robinson, Clarence Sexton, James Ray, and Orman Norwood – spoke briefly, as well as a number of family members. Jean Smith, Dr. Roberson's favorite soloist, sang two songs – *The Loveliness of Christ* and *O That Will Be Glory*.

Immediately following the funeral at Highland Park Baptist Church, Lee Roberson's body was taken to Greenwood Cemetery in Chattanooga where it was laid to rest – alongside the body of Caroline Roberson, and just across from Babyland, where their baby, Joy, was buried. David Bouler, Roberson's pastor at Highland Park, and Danny Lovett, president of Tennessee Temple, each spoke at the graveside. Five doves were released – three by the Robersons' three surviving children (LeeAnne, John, and June), representing the Trinity, plus two doves released by Bouler and Lovett, representing Lee and Caroline Roberson. The graveside service was short. The sky was cloudy. It started to sprinkle rain a little bit but then stopped almost as soon as it started.

When he was in his 90s, I listened to Lee Roberson preach a sermon in which he testified, "I am burdened for souls. I want to hear Him say, 'Well done, thou good and faithful servant.' I want God to be pleased with my life and receive commendation at the judgment seat of Jesus Christ."

On August 1, 2006, at age 96 – about nine months before his death – Lee Roberson published a letter which he called his farewell letter and final testimony. "I believe the Bible!" he wrote. "I believe in the promises of God regarding our future life! I believe 'to be absent from the body is to be present with the Lord.' I believe the future will hold some of the most glorious blessings that one could ever conceive. We will be present 'with the Lord.' The Apostle Paul said 'this is far better.' The future is bright! I know the Lord may come at any moment. He has promised, 'I will come again.' Continue in His great work! Give attention to the winning of souls and exhort yourself to a close walk with God."

Timeline of the Life of Dr. Lee Roberson

November 24, 1909	Born in English, Indiana
1924	Led to Christ by Mrs. Daisy Hawes
1927	Graduated from Fern Creek High School, Louisville, KY
1929-31	Attended University of Louisville & Southern Baptist Theological Seminary, Louisville, KY
1931	Ordained at Virginia Avenue Baptist Church, Louisville, KY
1931	Pastor, Prescott Memorial Baptist Church, Germantown, TN
1932	Called to Greenbrier Baptist Church, Greenbrier, TN
1935	Evangelist, Birmingham Baptist Association
October 9, 1937	Married Miss Caroline Allen in Birmingham, AL
November, 1937	Called to First Baptist Church, Fairfield, AL
May 2, 1941	Daughter LeeAnne born
November 18, 1942	Called to Highland Park Baptist Church, Chattanooga, TN
December 13, 1942	Began radio broadcast, later named *Gospel Dynamite*

January 19, 1944	Began publishing *The Evangelist*
June 6, 1946	Daughter Joy born
July 3, 1946	Established Tennessee Temple College
August 10, 1946	Nine-week old Joy died
1946	Camp Joy established
1947	Chauncey-Goode auditorium completed – seating 3,500
July 10, 1947	Son John Charles born
1948	Worldwide Faith Missions launched
1948	Sunday school bus ministry begun
May 22, 1949	Daughter Patty born
1950	Union Gospel Rescue Mission established
1951	Tennessee Temple Elementary School established
March 21, 1954	Daughter June born
March 20, 1956	Co-founded Southwide Baptist Fellowship
May 26, 1968	WDYN Radio began broadcasting
September 6, 1981	Dedicated new 5,850-seat church auditorium on Bailey Avenue
April 27, 1983	Resigned as pastor of Highland Park Baptist Church
1983 to 2007	Full-time evangelist
June 26, 2005	Caroline Allen Roberson died
April 29, 2007	Dr. Lee Roberson died

List of Principal Sources

Interviews

The following people, listed alphabetically, were interviewed by the author between the years 2002 and 2008:

Fred Afman, Ron Bishop, David Bouler, Clyde Box, Ed Carter, Garland Cofield, Glenn Copeland, Wendell Evans, J.R. Faulkner, Les Frazier, Tom Gilmer, Ben Haden, E.C. Haskell Jr., Max Helton, Tony Hutson, Ed Johnson, Bill Long, Bill Mattheiss, Jerry Mattheiss, Darlene Munafo, Bob Kelley, Dorothy McCormick, Orman Norwood, Mike Patterson, Nat Phillips, Wymal Porter, Randy Ray, Jerry Reece, John Reynolds, Lee Roberson, Cliff Robinson, Clarence Sexton, Gloria Shadowens, Joe Shadowens, Don Sisk, Elgin Smith, Jean Smith, Glenn Swygart, Jim Vineyard, Tom Wallace, Sheila Wharram, Walter Wendelken, David Winget, et al

Books by Lee Roberson
"A Winner Never Quits & A Quitter Never Wins!" *(Sword of the Lord Publishers, Murfreesboro, TN, 1994)*
"Be Filled With the Spirit" *(Published by Lee Roberson)*
"Coming to Chattanooga – Soon" *(Sword of the Lord Publishers, Murfreesboro, TN, 1980)*
"Compassion Unlimited..." *(Johnson Printing Company, Birmingham, AL)*
"Death...and After?" *(Published by Lee Roberson, 1954)*

"Diamonds in the Rough" *(Sword of the Lord Publishers, Murfreesboro, TN, 1997)*
"Double-Breasted" *(Sword of the Lord, 1977)*
"Fireworks Don't Last" *(University Publishers, Chattanooga, TN, 1982)*
"For Preachers Only..." *(Sword of the Lord Publishers, Murfreesboro, TN, 1973)*
"It's Dynamite" *(Sword of the Lord Publishers, Wheaton, IL, 1953)*
"Kings on Parade & 5 Ancient Sins" *(Published by Lee Roberson, 1956)*
"Lee Roberson Classics" *(Faith Baptist Church Publications, Fort Pierce, FL, 1996)*
"Mr. Saint and Mr. Sinner" *(Published by Lee Roberson, 1963)*
"Preaching to America" *(Sword of the Lord Publishers, Murfreesboro, TN, 1999)*
"Some Golden Daybreak" *(Christ for the World Publishers, Orlando, FL, 1957)*
"The Big 90" *(Sword of the Lord Publishers, Murfreesboro, TN, 1999)*
"The Faith That Moves Mountains" *(Sword of the Lord, 1984)*
"The Gold Mine" *(Sword of the Lord Publishers, Murfreesboro, TN, 1996)*
"The Hallelujah Chorus" *(John the Baptist Publishers, Milford, OH, 1996)*
"The Key to...Victorious Living" *(Published by Lee Roberson, 1978)*
"The King's Water Boy" *(Published by Lee Roberson)*
"The Man in Cell No. 1" *(Sword of the Lord Publishers, Murfreesboro, TN, 1993)*
"This Crisis Hour" *(University Publishers, Chattanooga, TN, 1991)*
"Two Dogs and Peace of Mind" *(Sword of the Lord Publishers, Murfreesboro, TN, 1974)*

<u>Other Books</u>
"Get A Glimpse of the World's Largest Church" *(Johnson Printing Company, 1973)*

"Great Soul-Winning Churches" by Elmer Towns *(Sword of the Lord, 1973)*

"The Ten Largest Sunday Schools" by Elmer Towns *(Baker Book House, 1969)*

"Vision to Victory – A Fifty Year History of Tennessee Temple University" *(Published by Tennessee Temple University, 1996)*

<u>*Other Sources*</u>

"A Century of Ministry for Christ – A History of the Highland Park Baptist Church" by Ray Staszewski (Originally written for *Realife* Magazine, reprinted in "This Crisis Hour," a book by Dr. Lee Roberson)

"A Lasting Legacy" by Clint Cooper, May 5, 2007, *Chattanooga Times Free Press*

Funeral of Lee Roberson – Bulletin & Public Comments, May 3, 2007

Highland Park Baptist Church "Centennial Sunday" brochure, October 28, 1990

"The Lee Roberson Story" by Helen McDonald Exum, August 29, 1971, *Chattanooga News Free Press*

"The Life & Ministry of Lee Roberson" by Ed Reese, *Fundamental Publishers, Glenwood, IL*

Various issues of *The Evangelist*, published by Highland Park Baptist Church

Various historical and publicity materials of Highland Park Baptist Church

Various Internet websites dealing with the life & ministry of Dr. Lee Roberson

Author

JAMES H. WIGTON has served as Senior Pastor of Delaney Street Baptist Church in Orlando, Florida, since 2007. He serves in leadership offices with the Greater Orlando Baptist Association, the Florida Baptist Convention, and the Florida Association of Christian Colleges & Schools.

A pastor for more than 30 years, he has served churches in the Midwest and Florida. He has preached in nearly a dozen foreign countries and weekly on radio for nearly 20 years.

A graduate of Ohio State University in journalism, he is a former newspaper editor and reporter and has contributed to numerous Christian magazines. He earned a Ph.D. in Pastoral Theology from Indiana Baptist College.

He and his wife, Jackie, have three married children and six grandchildren.

CPSIA information can be obtained at www.ICGtesting.com
Printed in the USA
LVOW08s1927301114

416323LV00001B/75/P